PAST

PRESENT

and FUTURE

The Archaeology of Northern England

PAST
PRESENT
and FUTURE

The Archaeology of Northern England

Proceedings of a Conference
held in Durham in 1996

*Edited by Catherine Brooks, Robin Daniels
and Anthony Harding*

Architectural and Archaeological Society of Durham and Northumberland
Research Report 5

In association with
English Heritage
CBA North

Durham
2002

Published by Roger Booth Associates.

Architectural and Archaeological Society of Durham and Northumberland
c/o Department of Archaeology
University of Durham
South Road
Durham
DH1 3LE

Typeset and Printed by:

Roger Booth Associates
46 Keymer Road
Hassocks
West Sussex
BN6 8AR

ISBN 0 9510388 4 2

Contents

Preface

The papers in this volume were, with a couple of exceptions, presented at a conference held in Durham from 12-14 April 1996, entitled "Past, Present and Future: the Archaeology of Northern England". This was held under the umbrella of the local group of the Council for British Archaeology (CBA North), with assistance from the Department of Archaeology of Durham University, and was attended by 172 people. The organising committee consisted of Robin Daniels, then of Cleveland Archaeology Section (now reborn as Tees Archaeology), with Mike McCarthy, Lindsay Allason-Jones, Chris Tolan-Smith, Barbara Harbottle, Stafford Linsley and Anthony Harding. We were fortunate that almost all the leaders in the field, in terms of creating our modern understanding of the archaeology of the northern counties of England, accepted invitations to speak, and most have allowed their contributions to go forward to publication here. This is not to say that coverage of all periods is equal – there are some notable gaps, systematic reviews of the Neolithic and earlier Bronze Age in the north, of the Viking period, and of monasteries and castles, being merely the most obvious. Nevertheless, we hope that the papers now published here can serve as a useful *tour d'horizon* for professional archaeologists and interested amateurs alike, both inside and outside the region.

As well as the papers included here, papers were given by Richard Bailey on "The Scandinavian impact", by Mark Macklin on "Sedimentary investigations in the Tyne valley", and by David Cranstone on "The lead industry". The material from these papers has been published elsewhere. Conversely, there is a paper by Robin Daniels on medieval boroughs that was not given at the conference, and session chairpersons have provided brief introductions to the written versions of their session papers.

The papers were initially collected in and edited by Catherine Brooks of Carlisle Archaeological Unit, which had offered to publish the volume. Some delays in the submission of articles and commentaries meant that by the time the volume was nearly complete, that Unit was in an advanced stage of negotiations to move elsewhere, and the present enterprise necessarily became a low priority. In the spring of 2001, regional officers of English Heritage enquired whether the volume might be taken forward by another organisation, as part of their Regional Research Frameworks initiative. Accordingly, the editing and production was handed over to Robin Daniels and Anthony Harding, who offered to see the volume through to completion; the Architectural and Archaeological Society of Durham and Northumberland agreed to publish it in their Research Report Series if financial guarantees were forthcoming. Thanks to the generosity of English Heritage, and the kind assistance of Kate Wilson, this funding has been made available.

Most of the initial editorial work was done by Brooks, but Daniels and Harding are responsible for errors that remain. They owe her a great debt of gratitude. Thanks are due to the original sponsors of the conference for financial help and organisational assistance; to the session chairpersons; to Roger Mercer who opened the conference and John Barrett who closed it; and to English Heritage for finally allowing publication to go ahead. Graphics work has been done by Margaret Finch.

RD/AFH
Hartlepool/Durham
February 2002

List of Figures

Chapter 1: Introduction

Anthony Harding[*]

The conference that gave rise to this volume started life as a review of the archaeology of the north, defined as the CBA Northern Region or the counties of Cumbria, Northumberland, Tyne and Wear, Durham and Cleveland, twenty years on from the ground-breaking publication that set the agenda for the modern archaeology of the region: *Archaeology in the North. Report of the Northern Archaeological Survey* (Clack and Gosling 1976). Almost all the contributors here refer back to that volume, and rightly so, because it was in many ways seminal. It was also in some ways far ahead of its time, since many of its recommendations now seem obvious, so familiar have they become in terms of modern practice. Indeed, it is hard to think of another volume that encompassed so thoroughly and systematically both the current situation in a region period by period, and a clear-sighted review of what was needed in terms of practice and legislation.

This is not to say that *Archaeology in the North* was perfect. The period reviews are rather uneven, which reflects the identity, interests and expertise of those writing them. The choice of detailed surveys, which form the Appendices, was largely automatic since these were the subjects of recent detailed work. But they gave a bias to the volume: largely urban; mainly eastern (in the west only Carlisle was given detailed treatment); and heavily weighted to Medieval and Post-medieval. But in spite of this, there is much to admire in the volume and much that is still of great value. The section on the Iron Age, for example, owed much to the presence in the north-east of two Iron Age scholars of major national significance (George Jobey and Dennis Harding) and remains a *tour de force*.

Archaeology in the North was the result of the work of the Northern Archaeological Survey, set up in Durham in 1974 with funding from the Department of the Environment and the University of Durham. It completed its main work in a single year, with two archaeologists, a draughtsman, and two secretaries, though the process of publication took much of another year to complete. Individual sections were written by specialist contributors, and the whole volume was edited by Dennis Harding. The accompanying Gazetteer, which actually appeared before the main report in 1975, was largely the work of a group of dedicated friends and colleagues of Rosemary Cramp, many of whom had been students of hers in Extra-Mural classes.

Of course there were critics. Typically, Andrew Selkirk (*Current Archaeology* 54, 1976, 219) was one; he described it in a short review as "rather a mess", comparing it unfavourably to a volume on the small towns of Hampshire. While even its admirers knew it had shortcomings, messiness was not obviously one of them – the graphics by Brian Gill, for instance, are among the most excellent archaeological productions of the 1970s. In *Current Archaeology* 55, 253, a letter from Dennis Harding attempted to set the record straight, but also pointed out the prejudice, superficiality and ignorance that underlay the original review. Selkirk merely reiterated his own prejudices, and failed completely to notice the real sting in the tail of Harding's letter.

Of the Committee that oversaw the production of *Archaeology in the North*, and the contributors, sadly four members are no longer with us: Dorothy Charlesworth, Barri Jones, Charles Daniels, and George Jobey. Several others have retired, though (like Brian Roberts and Rosemary Cramp) they remain highly active; three others, Dennis Harding, Martin Carver and Chris Morris, all then in Durham, have succeeded to chairs elsewhere and are still in post. Peter Clack has left archaeology; Paul Gosling was until recently an English Heritage Inspector; Brian Gill worked freelance as an editor and illustrator within archaeology, but unfortunately died in 2001.

Much has changed in the institutional framework as well. In 1976, state archaeology was in the hands of the Department of the Environment; English Heritage did not exist; the Royal Commission on Historical Monuments (England) did (and still did at the time of the 1996 conference). Archaeological Units were just beginning to exist, but there have been many new ones in the north, and some closures, since then. There was at the time only one county archaeologist in the region (Tom Clare in Cumbria, who was on the Survey Committee); now all counties have at least a County Archaeologist and a Sites and

[*]Address: Department of Archaeology, University of Durham, South Road, Durham, DH1 3LE

Monuments Record Officer, while the National Parks of Northumberland and the Lake District also have an archaeologist, as does the National Trust in the Lake District. Sites and Monuments Records (SMRs) did not exist as such in 1976, though the OS record cards held in the Department of Archaeology of Durham University formed the basis of the SMR subsequently formed by Durham County Council. There was no statutory protection for sites other than the very modest degree provided by the Ancient Monuments Acts. One of the biggest changes of the early 1990s, the advent of PPG16, was undreamt of.

Yet *Archaeology in the North* foreshadowed many of these events. It specifically recommended that archaeology figured in "Structure and Local Plans"; that the investigation and recording of sites should be a statutory requirement before development could proceed, and that legislation should be presented to Parliament to ensure this. It recommended that a "more flexible funding system" be established, by which the DoE could respond more effectively to unexpected threats to sites. It recommended that Durham and Northumberland "should give urgent consideration to the appointment of County Archaeologists in their planning departments", and that increased funding should be made available to museums so that the standard of services could be maintained and improved, and that conservation facilities should be extended and rationalised on a regional basis. One thing it did not mention was developer funding; but at the time the assumption was that the State would pick up the bill for rescue archaeology, and that sites would be excavated (and destroyed), rather than have threats to them mitigated or removed altogether.

An intriguing postscript lies in Appendix B(vi), "Information retrieval, Planning and the Computer", by P A G Clack. A programme was written in the Durham University Computer Unit to facilitate the production of site lists, but Clack indicates that the Survey team had not found it particularly helpful; indeed, he stated that it had "severe limitations", and most of the work was done using paper records. It goes without saying that nowadays no one would even consider starting such a project without full use of computer technology. Indeed, had the Northern Archaeological Survey begun work even a few years later, it would have been able to benefit from cheap and (relatively) user-friendly desk-top computers and software, of a

sort that is taken for granted nowadays. The amount of time that could have been saved, in creating lists of sites, or producing digital maps, can only be guessed at. This is most evident from the part of *Archaeology in the North* that most people still do not see, the Gazetteer, which was kept restricted because of sensitivities about site information and locations; and indeed, one may criticise the whole enterprise for not integrating this production into the main report (which, indeed, barely refers to it).

The political landscape of Britain has changed dramatically since 1976, and even since 1996, when the present conference took place. As the publicity for it stated: "Just as *Rescue* galvanized archaeological endeavour in the early 1970s, we are now at a crossroads and the aim of the 1996 conference is to provide a new stimulus. The conference will review our knowledge within each of the major chronological periods, and thus provide a broad basis for determining future research directions." In 1976, a Labour government was in power, though it lasted only until the "winter of discontent" in 1978-79. In spring 1979 the Conservatives came to power under Margaret Thatcher, and – with the one change of leadership, to John Major – remained there until 1997. It is interesting to reflect, therefore, that the major changes in archaeological administration came about during their stewardship. Much of this was because of their ideological commitment to reducing the power of the centralised state and public spending, which meant that it was politically desirable to remove functions that did not have to be under political, or Whitehall, control from government and to place them under the responsibility of "quasi-non-governmental organisations" (quangos), English Heritage being a prime example. Although its core funding comes from the state, it is an organisation that is independent of government, though its actions are overseen by a government department (formerly the Department of the Environment, now the Department for Culture, Media and Sport, created by the incoming Labour government of 1997). The other aspect of Thatcherite Britain that left a big mark on archaeology was the rise of private archaeological contractors in the 1980s. From a situation where a few big, mostly urban, units, such as those in Canterbury, York or Lincoln, held the field, and derived most of their funding from grant aid from the Department of the Environment, the situation changed radically to one where large numbers of units, small and large, were found all over the country, deriving most if not all of their income from developers. Most fieldwork is now conducted by such units, and most of it is small-scale. English Heritage retains a modest capacity to undertake excavation, usually where no other solution is possible. Since 1999, it has also acquired major facilities to undertake survey since the amalgamation of RCHM(E) into English Heritage. It continues to have a major role in science-based archaeology, including conservation, geophysics, analysis, archaeobotany and archaeozoology, through its Ancient Monuments Laboratory and its regional contractors (a situation that is currently under review).

The other major change has occurred since the conference of 1996, following the election of the Labour government in 1997: the creation of a Scottish Parliament and a Welsh Assembly, and of regional Assemblies in England (developments in northern Ireland are not relevant to our present theme). Following the passage of the Regional Development Agencies Act 1998, the eight Regional Assemblies (more correctly "Chambers") started their life in April 1999. That for the North-East (Northumberland, Durham, Tyne and Wear, and Tees Valley) is based in Newcastle and has 72 members, of whom two-thirds are from local government and the remainder from a variety of "social partners".[1] That for the North-West (Cumbria, Lancashire and the conurbations of Merseyside and Greater Manchester) is based in Wigan and is similarly constituted; its main role at the moment seems to be to deal with Regional Planning Guidance, something that the north-eastern Assembly will also soon take over. At present, the role of these bodies is poorly defined and most people are unaware of their existence – probably because their members are appointed rather than elected, with a majority coming straight from local councils. But they could become important for archaeology, if the Scottish model is anything to go by, not least because regions are now expected to have a regional cultural strategy and regional development plans. Other organisations have also regionalised, notably English Heritage, whose Newcastle office deals with the bulk of the work in the northern region.

Seen from Westminster, there might appear to be no great desire to embark on regional government in England; most English people probably think that the devolution to Scotland and Wales was merely political necessity rather than the outcome of rational planning, and do not (yet) take it very seriously. As measures such as the abolition of tuition fees for higher education students, or the principle of state provision of nursing care in old age take root, however, they may think again, even though these will eventually require the raising of additional tax revenue. In archaeological terms, Scotland has already gone a different way from England, since it has decided for the present not to merge the Scottish Royal Commission (RCAHMS) with Historic Scotland, but to preserve it as a separate organisation, albeit not a Royal Commission. And Historic Scotland itself has shown itself perfectly capable of going down different paths from English Heritage – frequently, it must be said, more enlightened ones. All this has implications for archaeology and archaeologists in Scotland.

What does this imply for the North of England? At present, not much, one might think; but that situation could change. If regionalisation is taken further (i.e., if the Regional Assemblies acquire real power), then certain English regions will demand greater freedom from London control. People in the South-East of England, where so much political and commercial control is centred, and where population development pressures are greatest, certainly underestimate the extent to which the regions see themselves as separate. This is particularly true of two regions: the South-West, and the North-East, though it can be argued too for the North-West and for the Yorkshire conurbations. Not only are they geographically furthest from London (and even if train journeys to the capital are fast they are not cheap), but they are psychologically and culturally very different places from the Home Counties. It is already true that in widely differing spheres such as the arts, transport, and planning, regional policies are being developed that could create major differences in public provision between regions.

There remain many uncertainties about the future archaeological map of England. There is a move to make the provision of SMRs a statutory duty for counties, but no agreement on how

1. At present the web sites for the two northern assemblies provide minimal information (http://www.northeastassembly.org.uk and http://nwra.gov.uk/rpg/). Thanks are due to Stephen Barber from the NE Assembly offices for providing the information given here.

this might be achieved, what exactly the SMR would have to consist of, and who would maintain it. Some counties – and Durham and Northumberland are blazing a trail here with their "Keys to the Past" project – are embarking on projects to make their SMRs more accessible, while at the same time facing financial stringencies that could endanger the whole basis for the SMR in the first place. The Treasure Act 1996 has greatly improved the situation with regard to the reporting of "Treasure", and the Portable Antiquities Scheme, by which finders of artefacts are encouraged to report their finds to Portable Antiquities Officers, has been a huge success (even though most archaeologists would have preferred a scheme based on compulsory rather than voluntary reporting). The prospective extension of the Treasure Act to encompass prehistoric objects of base metal as well as any prehistoric object any part of which is precious metal should increase the volume of finds reported. So far, however, there is no Portable Antiquities Officer for the northern region, and finds continue to be made without full – or any – reporting. A bid has recently been submitted to the Heritage Lottery Fund for an extension of the scheme, which would then cover the northern region along with most of the rest of England and Wales, but at the time of writing the outcome is not known. Most worrying, rumour has it that the Department for Culture, Media and Sport wants to shed the entire burden of running the scheme. Archaeologists in the North must lose no opportunity of making clear to the DCMS that the Portable Antiquities Scheme must continue, and in enhanced form.

Now the North, as defined in this volume, is not homogeneous; most obviously, the area west of the Pennines is different from the area east of them. Nevertheless, in archaeological terms there is frequent interaction and interchange, brought about not least by the CBA's regional remit.

Is there, then, an "archaeology of the North", different from an archaeology of Scotland or the English Midlands? Contributors to this volume, while mainly restricting themselves to consideration of sites and monuments in the five northern counties, are national experts who set their material in the context of wider developments. For archaeologists in Durham and Cleveland, one

cannot operate in isolation from Yorkshire; for those in Cumbria and Northumberland, the same is true as regards Scotland (and Lancashire in the case of Cumbria). But the North does have certain characteristics which make its archaeology different. In the earliest periods (Young), the Palaeolithic is all but absent, while there is a rich but understudied Mesolithic. In the Neolithic, the region contains the most important axe factory in the entire British Isles at Great Langdale (Quartermaine), and a concentration of ritual monuments of national significance in north Northumberland (Bradley), though other sites are few and far between – curious, when one considers how abundant the evidence in Scotland is in this period. At least part of the reason for this must be invisibility, as Clive Waddington's work in the Milfield Basin (1999) has shown. In the Bronze Age, survey work has shown how rich both Cumbria and Northumberland are in agricultural settlements (Quartermaine, Welfare), though this richness is still relatively untapped as far as excavation is concerned.

The Neolithic and Bronze Age also saw the appearance of rock art and the North is the richest area of England for this resource. The initiation by English Heritage of a project to study the art and make recommendations for its conservation is to be welcomed. A preliminary report has been circulated to selected individuals and institutions, though there seem to be no plans to make the work – or indeed the art – known to a wider circle of people, or the public at large. The fact that the project is based in Bournemouth does not assist in this respect.

Finally for prehistory, the Iron Age is exceedingly well represented and increasingly well studied. George Jobey laid the foundations; Colin Haselgrove and his research students over the years have built up the structures – though not merely within a regional framework. It might also be said that while parts of the lowlands are now well studied, much remains to be done in the uplands, especially in the Cheviots.[2] The results of the work by Topping and McOmish at Wether Hill, and by Archaeological Services University of Durham at Ingram, will be crucial in this respect.

When we move on to matters Roman, the North is of course different in one very major respect: it has the Wall. Naturally this has a big

---

2. George Jobey once wrote a short guide to the Iron Age in the Cheviots, his *Field Guide to Prehistoric Northumberland Part 2* (Frank Graham, Newcastle, 1974), long out of print and seemingly impossible to find even in second-hand bookshops; but an invaluable little book that deserves to be revived. Jobey used to maintain, when asked why Part 1 never appeared, that he had never had a second spare weekend!

influence on what is done, archaeologically speaking, in the region – and beyond it. Some archaeologists appear to feel that the influence of the Wall is entirely negative, or to think that Roman archaeologists are some kind of intellectual pigmy, unable to conceive of a world beyond their own narrow horizons (eg Frodsham's ill-judged and choleric remarks: 2000, 15, 26f.). Wiser and more widely read scholars realise that what people write is a product of the age and the intellectual and investigative climate that surrounds them. Naturally the principal modern scholars of the Wall, David Breeze and Brian Dobson, have changed their views over the years as new discoveries have emerged, and one can hardly criticise them for not knowing in 1978 of air photographs that were taken in the 1980s. What is fascinating is to see how we can now expand our understanding of both the Wall and the military sites that lie near it in the light of our knowledge of both civil and military activity in the first and second centuries AD, and later (Crow). Who would have thought ten years ago that the fort at South Shields would be underlain by Iron Age round houses? Yet this can now be see to be part and parcel of what the imposition of a Roman presence on a "native" landscape involved.

Not all Roman activity was military, and our understanding of the development of Roman towns and *vici* has been advanced enormously by work in Carlisle and elsewhere (McCarthy). At the same time, investigation of biological materials from prehistoric and Roman sites has completely changed the way we look at the centuries both before and after the birth of Christ, and nowhere in Britain is this information more complete or more fully studied. The groundbreaking synthesis by Jacqui Huntley and Sue Stallibrass (1995) was not only the first such account in the country, setting the standards for other areas; it is also in a constant process of updating as more information becomes available (Huntley). In other respects, the Roman North can be seen to fit within a pattern of study that is country-wide, though finds such as the Vindolanda writing-tablets have an unusual importance, and not just for Britain; while other material consolidates our knowledge about such matters as gender, industry, religion and domestic life (Allason-Jones).

Moving on in time, we find that questions of the Roman-Early Medieval transition are no easier to understand in the North than they are in the South, though recent work at Birdoswald,

Norton and Easington provides some important clues (Loveluck), and the material from Milfield (discovered just too late to figure in *Archaeology in the North*) is interesting for a slightly later period. Anglo-Saxon monastic archaeology has been the subject of long-term study by Rosemary Cramp, and the recent work at Whitby will supplement the major discoveries at Jarrow, Monkwearmouth, Whithorn and elsewhere (Newman), while the study of secular settlement has benefited greatly from the excavations at Thirlings and elsewhere (Loveluck). In 1976, Hope-Taylor's report on Yeavering had not yet appeared; as arguably the single most important site publication from the Early Medieval period for our region in the last 30 years, subsequent workers have had the task of assimilating its extraordinary results, and comparing them with those of other sites in the North-East.

The early stone churches at sites like Jarrow and Escomb, however, disguise the fact that the North in subsequent periods (until the Norman Conquest) was relatively impoverished in architectural terms. And other silences, or gaps, are the almost complete absence of datable pottery in the North until the eleventh century, the lack of a mint in the area, and the late development of urban centres, which mean that scholars working in this period still struggle to understand both the chronology and other aspects of social, economic and cultural development. The absence of evidence for widespread Scandinavian settlement in the North-East also contrasts strikingly with Cumbria and Yorkshire, and aligns it culturally with Scotland rather than with those areas; the Tees acting as some kind of boundary, as it did at other periods of history and prehistory.

The other major Early Medieval publication which demands mention, but which no article in this volume covers, is the *Corpus of Anglo-Saxon Stone Sculpture in England* (vol. 1, *Durham and Northumberland* by Rosemary Cramp, 1984; vol. 2, *Cumberland, Westmorland and Lancashire North-of-the-Sands*, by Richard Bailey and Rosemary Cramp, 1988). Suffice it to say that this monumental work will not be replaced in several lifetimes and represents a major triumph of scholarship. The North is fortunate indeed that its holdings are completely covered in these two volumes; some other, less fortunate regions, will need to wait a little longer before they can enjoy the feast.

The North is rich in medieval monuments of all kinds, and some of them are considered in detail here. The more obviously medieval towns, such as Hexham, Barnard Castle or Durham, are just the tip of the iceberg when it comes to considering the origins of urban settlement in the region, and Darlington, Newcastle, Carlisle, Berwick, Hartlepool and a number of smaller towns have all provided important material in recent years (Graves, Daniels). Even with the contraction in archaeological funding of late, it has been possible to undertake fairly substantial work in town and city centres (eg Durham, Darlington, Carlisle), which has come up with important new information to supplement that highlighted in the Appendices to *Archaeology in the North*.

Finally, the post-medieval period has seen perhaps the biggest change in approach of all, encapsulated by an approach which attempts to see castles in their social context rather than as pieces of military architecture (Johnson). In this, questions of the homogeneity of "the North" come to the fore. Were Northumbrian peasant-farmers really more akin to lowland Scots than to Kentish yeomen? Or were they *sui generis*, some kind of proto-Tynesider, as separated by culture and custom from their Scots neighbours as they were from the landed aristocrats of England whose land they worked? These questions of geography and identity keep recurring, which might suggest they are insoluble. At least when we reach the Industrial Revolution, when communications became much faster and more efficient, we can speculate that developments in our area were rapidly transmitted to other areas (and *vice versa*) (Linsley). The North-East is exceptionally well-provided with industrial monuments – not only railways, but lead mines (Killhope), blast furnaces (Allensford), forges (Derwentcote), bridges (Causey Arch) and many others. One could equally have devoted space to vernacular buildings of the post-medieval period, which Norman Emery, Martin Roberts and others have shown to be so rich and varied; and one could have speculated on the extent to which there was a north-eastern and a north-western tradition in this field and what it might have signified.

Archaeology in the North is different from *Archaeology in the North* in many ways. Much more is known about many periods and areas than was the case in 1976; the political and legislative framework has changed out of all recognition; there are many more archaeologists working in the region than there were, though most work outside the framework of regional research objectives that the regional committees of 1976 attempted to promulgate. It is encouraging, therefore, that English Heritage is attempting to revive the establishment of regional research frameworks, not least by assisting the publication of this volume. Some of these developments, such as those relating to Portable Antiquities and Treasure, are mainly positive; others, such as the lack of major excavations, are (or soon will be) largely negative in implication. The enormous rise in public interest in archaeology, built upon the success of television programmes such as Time Team or Meet the Ancestors (there have been several programmes based on northern sites), means that archaeology is largely a welcome visitor on the leisure scene, even if at times inconvenient to planners and developers. Regional policies being developed in the Regional Assemblies and elsewhere must be seen to take archaeological considerations into account, which they have not done so far, and English Heritage has a key role to play in this. It will be the task of the archaeologists of the North to ensure that the progress in making archaeological concerns known to the world at large is as effective in the next twenty-five years as it has been over the last twenty-five.

Chapter 2: Archaeology in the North

R J Mercer[*]

'The North' is a term used throughout England with widely varying connotations. From 'anything north of the Thames' (remember the Northern Line), to 'anything north of Hatfield' (and the North) to 'anything north of the Trent' (where accents are said to change), 'north of the Humber', or as I think this volume would have it, 'north of the Tees'. Of course, in a former era, 'North Britain' was a politically correct term for Scotland, where 'the North' is a term reserved for the region north of Inverness – unless, of course, you live in Inverness, when the term is reserved for Caithness and the Northern Islands.

Within this geographical kaleidoscope we encounter an extraordinary effect, as viewed from the south, that may be termed a 'concertina' effect. As one looks north so the concertina is compressed, even in the minds of those who would regard themselves as geographically aware, so that distances contract as an inversely proportional effect establishes itself. As a consequence 'The North' becomes a unity, conceptually relatively small, as one quarter of the land mass of England is diminished by perception.

The North (*sensu* the north of England) has always had its own identity. The Neolithic, while fostering a degree of uniformity that survives only until the middle of the Bronze Age, nevertheless does show clear distinctions, that are not just environmentally determined, between north and south. By the Later Bronze Age the distinctions are clear, and they continue and intensify through change and adaptation into the first millennium BC. The nature of the Roman occupation illustrates the difference that Roman commanders saw, initially, in both the land and the people as they moved north beyond the Humber, and they perpetuated that perceived distinction in their organization of the Province in the third century, to create *Britannia Inferior* with its capital at York. Undoubtedly the tempo of life in that northern province ran to a military tune until the very end of the Roman hegemony, and even then it is likely that military and quasi-military components may have had some role in the emergence of independent states in the north of England, eventually subsumed within the expansion of the Anglian kingdom of Northumbria. By the seventh or eighth century the north represented the apogee of British cul-

tural achievement with its own archbishop at York – a scintillation dulled by, among other things, the Norse incursions which, if anything, added in their own way to northern individuality. This individuality was fast producing a quite distinctive series of dialects that were causing difficulty to the southern ear of William of Malmesbury by the 1130s, and were the subject of Chaucer's southern wit in *The Reeve's Tale*, written in the late fourteenth century (Honey 1991, 17).

It is clear that William I went to work in northern England with a different will and perception, and it is the recalcitrance and conservatism (as he would have seen it), as well as the violent rivalry between neighbouring families, encountered there that led to the creation of the Council of the North in 1483 by Richard III. This body had primarily judicial, but also governmental functions, and was to last for two centuries.

Since the middle of the seventeenth century, the north has assumed another mantle of individuality as its fast-flowing rivers, its geological foundation and its native skills in textiles and metallurgy led it to become the cradle of the industrial revolution – a land of fast-growing towns and mass-produced and mass-consumed energy that lent colour to the contrast drawn so expertly by Elizabeth Gaskell in her novel *North and South*. My first point is this, then: the individuality of the North, however that is delineated, is a long-standing tradition.

If this individuality is of long standing as a divider of North and South, it should not be allowed to distract attention from the fissile nature of the North itself, whether interpreted as Northern England or seen to include Scotland. It is the writer's contention that far more, and far greater, cultural variety exists north of the Trent than south of it. I chose, when introducing this conference, to illustrate this point by reference to modern processes of market research in which I quoted from a number of sources (notably Elliston-Allen 1968). What is clear from all these sources is that vastly more variety exists (or existed in the 1970s) in the way people choose and use food and other products in the north of England and in Scotland than in the south of the country, and this variety of cultural

*Address: Royal Commission on the Ancient and Historical Monuments of Scotland, John Sinclair House, 16 Bernard Terrace, Edinburgh, EH8 9NX

identity (for that is what it is) is micro-regional-
ized intricately, with dramatic differences occurring to either side of the Pennine divide, as well
as from Tyne-Tees to Tees-Humber, and from
Eden-Lune to Lune-Ribble, and Ribble-Mersey.
It is probable that this accentuated micro-region-
alisation has diminished in profile sharply with
the levelling effect of 'supermarketing', but it
was still very much alive a quarter of a century
ago and serves to illustrate (I hope amusingly, in
the instance of some of the details furnished during the opening session of the conference) the
cultural diversity and unevenness that has, it
seems, always characterized 'the north' in con-
tradistinction to the south. Indeed, I would go as
far as to suggest that in this synchronic and
diachronic diversity lies another reason why the
archaeology of southern England has formed the
dominant text for Britain, as scholars have consistently found that the broader, more even and
more consistent pattern of development that can
be perceived there lends itself more readily to
the provision of a working model (as well as the
provision of a teaching model!).

With these issues in view, I suggest that, for
some time to come, micro-regional studies will
remain an important way forward in northern
England for archaeological research. The consequent dangers will lie in fragmentation of study
and isolation through introspection. The consequent need for overview has, however, been satisfied in the last decade or so in a series of works
(Higham 1986; Annable 1987; important components in Chapman and Mytum 1983; and
Miket and Burgess 1984), and this conference,
of course, harks back to the publication twenty
years ago of *Archaeology in the North* (Clack
and Gosling 1976) – the first attempt to survey
Northern English archaeology and to place it
and its requirements in a national setting. It is an
absolute requirement that this latter process
should continue, and that the individuality of
northern archaeology should be expressed at a
national level at every available opportunity by
publication, by example and by active representation on national bodies.

Archaeology in the North introduces the
theme of this conference. In that volume, three
basic recommendations were made: first, that
the appointment of County Archaeologists be
encouraged (with the development of their cog-
nate and consequent SMRs); secondly, that
increased resources be made available for fieldwork and excavation in advance of development; and thirdly, that a small regional

secretariat be established to act as coordinating
agency for all aspects of archaeological fieldwork in the region.

This writer will not attempt, at any length, to
make a judgment upon the degree to which these
three recommendations have been successfully
met – that was, to some extent, the purpose of
the conference and will emerge from the following papers. In brief, the impressionistic sense is
that we do now have adequate county representation with appropriate, if surely under-
resourced, SMRs. There is a sense that
something has gone seriously wrong with
resourcing which, now wholly focused as it is
upon developer-funding, is failing to deliver
energy to the point of archaeological (as
opposed to developmental) need. The third recommendation has never really been acted upon,
and may be over-ambitious. Groups of period-
and topic-interested workers operating as 'clear-
ing-houses' for their own areas of interest may,
however, be an inexpensive and viable way forward here, which may help to bring order to the
disparate and incomplete record that is the
inevitable product of the kind of resourcing
upon which we are now brought to depend.
Whether developer-funding works well in areas
where there is a buyers' (developers') market as
opposed to a sellers' (planners') market is a
problem which may emerge as a *leitmotif* of the
contributions that will follow.

Acknowledgements
My thanks are due to my daughter for her assistance
in the typing of this essay, and also for her advice on
matters of history.

Section 1: Earlier Prehistory

Introduction

*Anthony Harding**

Prehistoric studies in the North of England (as defined geographically in this book) are alive and well, as the three contributors to this section make clear. Indeed, the overall impression emerging from the 1996 conference was that archaeology as a whole in the North is in a vibrant and exciting state, in prehistoric as well as historic periods. The up-beat note that this conference struck contrasted strangely with the pessimistic tone adopted by some speakers at a 1998 conference on northern prehistory in Newcastle (subsequently published as *Northern Pasts*: Harding and Johnston 2000). Admittedly the North was defined there as meaning north of the Trent rather than north of the Tees; and the list of speakers was quite different, many being new to the area and not able or willing to take wider perspectives into view. Certainly the lack of participants from English Heritage was bemoaned at both conferences, but gripes about lack of public funding for northern projects seem misplaced. The present volume indicates many instances of fieldwork, often large in scale, undertaken by one or more of the major public bodies active in archaeology in the North. It is hard to avoid the conclusion that it is often easier to say negative than positive things, especially when one's knowledge base is limited.

This is not to say that everything about northern prehistory is in a rosy state. Robert Young especially makes clear that there are large gaps in our knowledge about the earlier periods – the Palaeolithic obviously, the Mesolithic to a significant extent. It is nevertheless exciting to see that a significant number of Palaeolithic finds are now coming to light. Indeed, the area around Morecambe Bay has long been known as a source of early prehistoric cave sites, though their precise date and status remain a matter of some debate. Cumulatively, the total body of material makes it pretty certain that there was human occupation of much of the North during the late Devensian – though not, as far as we know, any earlier than this, or at least not in any form that can currently be recognised.

With the Mesolithic we are on firmer ground, though it remains true that the vast majority of known Mesolithic sites consist of nothing more than flint scatters. A major exception is, of course, the Eskmeals group of sites in west

Cumbria, for which the final publication is long overdue. It is likely too that Hartlepool Bay has, or had, the potential to give information comparable to that recovered from the Star Carr/ Seamer Carr area of North Yorkshire. Recent work has greatly expanded knowledge of what Trechmann long ago realised was a crucial area, though inevitably in an inter-tidal area that has seen many modern disturbances the results are going to be hard to understand. But the very fact that the foreshore produced a wooden hurdle only a few years ago, the date of which lies on the Mesolithic-Neolithic interface, shows that much more must remain to be discovered. If further major sand movement takes place in and around the Bay, we may predict that these important and exciting finds will be added to, and, let us hope, set in fuller context – particularly that relating to the transition to the Neolithic.

Young concentrates on areas other than Northumberland in the Mesolithic (Low Hauxley apart), but there are clear signs that knowledge of that county in the Mesolithic is about to change. The late Joan Weyman did more than anyone else to put the study of early lithics in Northumberland on the map, and her work is now being strikingly complemented by that of Clive Waddington, whose doctoral study of the Milfield Basin will soon show not only that there was a substantial Mesolithic presence in that area, but also that it was strongly concentrated on certain ecozones. The Northumberland Coastal Survey can also, when published, be expected to give some indication of where detailed work on the Mesolithic might profitably be concentrated. It is inconceivable that so long and (on the face of it) so favourable an environment for Mesolithic occupation should not host other major sites, or more accurately, activity zones.

Even the Neolithic is known only patchily in the northern counties, as Richard Bradley intimates. It is an interesting point whether this patchiness arises from the lack of work and funds, or from the record itself. Bradley implies that the answers to the questions he poses at the end of his paper are achievable, once we admit that we know less than we once seemed to know about earlier prehistoric communities in this

*Address: Department of Archaeology, University of Durham, South Road, Durham, DH1 3LE

area, and start to rebuild our ideas from the foundations up. Since Bradley has undertaken fieldwork in Northumberland and Cumbria, and in other areas outside the soft underbelly of British prehistory (I refer to Wessex), he is in a position to speak with authority. That does not mean that his solution is the best one, or that we must accept the agenda he suggests.

Let us imagine a scenario based on an attempt to answer such questions as: Who visited and used these sites? Were they an entirely local population? The answer will depend, one assumes, on study of the artefacts – flintwork, for instance – found on the sites and in the surrounding area. That means that a project similar to the Stonehenge Environs Project, might be applied to a set of major monuments in the North. The problem of working with prehistoric sites in the North of England is the lack of artefactual material on them. Not only dating but also analysis of subtle inter- and intra-site variations are thereby rendered infinitely more difficult. In any case a number of fieldwalking surveys have taken place in the North, though they have admittedly not been very extensive. The Durham Survey took a random sample of the area between Tees and Tyne; a number of parts of Northumberland have been fieldwalked, most recently a transect of the Milfield Basin by Clive Waddington. Bradley himself refers to the work of the Cherry family in Cumbria. Jan Harding's work in the Vale of Mowbray (admittedly outside the area under present consideration) also deserves mention. Valiant and valuable though these efforts have been, only the most sanguine of observers could begin to maintain that the volume of material which is thrown up is comparable to what surveys in Wessex produce. In other words, it is doubtful that Bradley's questions can be answered by archaeological techniques currently used in southern England; I look forward to being proved wrong.

Instead, the North needs a research agenda for prehistory allied to a technology that can achieve the goals set for it. Bradley touches on this though he does not make it explicit. Though surface survey in the northern counties is generally unrewarding in terms of artefacts produced, there is a lot to be gained from integration of the artefactual record with that of the natural environment. I have already referred to the work of Clive Waddington (1999), which will be extremely influential. Similarly, the work of Kathryn Pratt on the analysis of pollen diagrams

for later prehistory in the whole area between Tees and Tweed will bring a major advance in knowledge. One crucially important source of information is air photography, allied to geophysical survey. I have no doubt that the work I undertook on henges in the Milfield Basin in the 1970s could now be greatly enhanced in subtlety and sophistication by the use of geophysics. Likewise, as knowledge of site morphologies is improved through excavation and fieldwalking, it will become possible to identify much more closely those sites that really do belong to the Neolithic and Early Bronze Age, and those that do not. The work of Alan Biggins in south Northumberland is a case in point, making use as it does of all three technologies. This is not to say that problems of identification do not continue to exist. Gordon Barclay has recently extended the number of known henge sites in Tayside, but he would be the first to admit that since these remain untested by excavation an attribution to the henge class is a matter of presumption rather than proof. But the very fact that Tayside, like north Northumberland, has become an area of intense archaeological interest indicates how rich the archaeological record really is in certain nodal areas, and what possibilities there are for fruitful study.

When we turn to the question of upland landscapes, presented by Jamie Quartermaine, the potential is clear to see – if hitherto underestimated. The uplands of northern England, like those of many parts of Scotland, Ireland and Wales, are an enormous archaeological resource, without known parallel in Europe (one must be cautious in this regard, as it is unlikely to be the case that the British Isles are really so unusual). One could go so far as to say that any hitherto unsurveyed area of moorland in the northern hills will produce evidence of prehistoric exploitation. Certainly that was the case with the Lake District surveys carried out by the Lancaster University Archaeological Unit, though less so in the Howgill Fells. By far the commonest monument type is the field system, which usually means groups of small clearance cairns with irregular stone banks running through them. Quartermaine mentions the spectacularly well-preserved Barnscar site in west Cumbria, but there are many others. Straying southwards for a moment, it is worth recalling that Yorkshire and Derbyshire are also rich in such sites, as my survey of Danby Rigg and John Barnatt's of sites in the Peak District confirm. Northumberland also has plenty of field systems of presumed prehistoric date, and unlike those elsewhere they really do seem to include all the elements of a prehistoric (Bronze Age?) living system – houses, burial cairns, and fields as defined by clearance cairns and walls. The aerial surveys of Tim Gates, and the ground surveys of the Royal Commission, provide an extraordinarily detailed picture. Though dating is often no more than presumptive, exciting work by Max Adams and Peter Carne in the Ingram valley is revealing something of the potential time-depth involved. The Cheviots are another enormous archaeological resource that has barely been touched, in spite of the pioneering work of George Jobey. What elements of this resource belong to the Bronze Age, what to the Iron Age and later periods, remains to be seen.

One of the excitements of working with northern prehistory is that the sites and landscapes are only now unfolding. To make progress in Wessex prehistory you have to work on the level of the minute analysis of lithic distributions or minute differences between one group of artefacts and another – a methodology which has come to be accepted *faute de mieux*. In the North we still have the pleasurable task of locating and familiarising ourselves with the major sites, and setting them within their local, regional and national context. Because in many areas the level of preservation is so good, and because the extent is so great in relation to centres of population or learning, the scope is vast. To say we know little is to exaggerate. To say we could know much more is absolutely true. To work to the agenda defined by the contributors to the prehistoric section of this volume is to embark on an exacting, but ultimately rewarding, journey that will in time come to play its full part in the writing of British prehistory.

Chapter 3: The Palaeolithic and Mesolithic Periods in Northern England: An Overview

*Robert Young**

'Twixt the optimist and the pessimist
The difference is droll:
The optimist sees the doughnut
The pessimist sees the hole.'
(M Wilson – *Optimist and Pessimist*)

This quotation may seem a strange beginning to a review of the Palaeolithic and Mesolithic archaeology of northern England, but it does serve, in a flippant way, to indicate that there may be *at least* two opinions about the present state of our knowledge of the early prehistory of the region. Continuing with the doughnut analogy, pessimists might suggest that they have nothing really new to get their teeth into and that, for the Mesolithic, little has changed since *Archaeology in the North* was published in 1976 (Clack and Gosling 1976). Optimists, of whom I am one, would certainly argue that twenty-five years on the picture makes better sense than it did in 1976 and that there *are* now trends and developments afoot which will make the future study of the northern Palaeolithic and Mesolithic a very tasty subject indeed.

But this is to get ahead of ourselves, because if works of regional synthesis published since 1976 were examined, eg Higham's *Northern Counties to AD 1000* (1986), then pessimists might be forgiven for thinking that things were broadly the same as they had been in the late seventies. Indeed, if one looked for published articles which mention Palaeolithic and Mesolithic archaeology in the North's three leading archaeological journals, then the situation of research stagnation would seem to be confirmed. In the *Transactions of the Architectural and Archaeological Society of Durham and Northumberland/Durham Archaeological Journal* for 1973-99, some 125 archaeological articles and substantial notes were published. Of these only four dealt with aspects of the period under study here. In *Archaeologia Aeliana* from 1976-2000, of the 266 archaeological articles and Museum Notes, only seven dealt with, or mentioned, earlier prehistory. Similarly, over the same period, 242 archaeology-related articles appeared in the *Transactions of the Cumberland and Westmorland Antiquarian and Archaeological*

Society, but only twelve discussed aspects of Palaeolithic and Mesolithic archaeology.

Material published in other sources and current ongoing work give me cause for my optimism, however, and allow me to suggest that interest in the earlier periods is still alive and definitely kicking in the region. My first aim is to outline developments in early prehistoric studies in the north from Clack and Gosling's benchmark publication in 1976, by considering three interlinked themes, based on the writing of the late Sir Grahame Clark (1972), with my own modifications:

1) '**Typology**': the recognition, definition and broad dating of artefactual assemblages; distributional studies; raw material studies; formation process studies.
2) '**Stratigraphy**': the enlisting of quaternary research as a means of establishing the age and environmental contexts of Palaeolithic and Mesolithic assemblages and material.
3) **Function/synthesis**': the interpretation of assemblages and palaeoenvironmental data in terms of the human utilization of resources in the landscape; human/environment interactions; social organization; Mesolithic/Neolithic transition.

Since 1976, work has gone on throughout the north which has contributed to our understanding of all of these themes. Some projects are rooted squarely within one of these areas; others cut across some or all of the boundaries.

It might be as well, at this point, to remind ourselves what Clack and Gosling said about the region's earlier prehistory in *Archaeology in the North* (1976, 15-16). They made no mention of the Palaeolithic at all, and commenced their survey with 'Mesolithic', with no discussion of the early and later phases of the period. They pointed out that the northern Mesolithic was known by finds of flint and stone artefacts and that only one 'site' at West Hartlepool had been excavated and dated to the seventh millennium bc [uncal] by radiocarbon (Trechmann 1936). The only other, northern, excavated sites that they could point to were the rock shelters of Bowden

*Address: School of Archaeology and Ancient History, University of Leicester, University Road, Leicester, LE1 7RH

Doors and Goatscrag in Northumberland. They suggested that Mesolithic activity was concentrated mainly on the east coast, and they thought that the area between the Tyne and the Tees was important, because over half the known finds had been made there. They also highlighted the scarcity of material north of the Tyne and in Cumbria. The major exceptions in these areas were the finds from Spindleston Crags and Ross Links on the Northumberland coast, and the odd site in Cumbria on the coast between Walney Island and St Bees Head. Their final suggestion was that Weardale in County Durham had been particularly favoured by Mesolithic groups. It is obvious now that there is much more to this distribution pattern than Clack and Gosling suggested, and I will return to consider this below.

Let us turn now to a regional review of Palaeolithic and Mesolithic archaeology, post-1976, using the thematic scheme outlined above.

The Palaeolithic

I want to treat the Palaeolithic as a theme in itself, primarily because prior to 1976 it was argued that there was no definite evidence for such early activity in the region. It is with the Upper Palaeolithic that we have our first tangible data relating to human settlement in the north and, clearly, this aspect of early prehistoric research relates mainly, at the moment, to the typological and stratigraphical sections of my framework.

The caves on the north shore of Morecambe Bay in Cumbria (Fig 3.1) and a paper by Chris Salisbury (1992) on the Pleistocene exploitation of Cumbria are a good starting point for this review. In this short but informative contribution, Salisbury pointed out that nineteenth-century work at Kirkhead Cave and Capeshead Cavern produced possible early prehistoric artefacts, now lost, and that Merlewood Cave and caves in the area around Silverdale and Warton in what is now north Lancashire, excavated by J W Jacks in the early part of this century, may also have produced evidence for Late Devensian occupation. Salisbury also documented his own work at Lindale Low Caves from 1987-9. This has produced the first clear evidence for *in situ*, or at least sealed, Upper Palaeolithic activity in the region. Flint implements of broadly Cresswellian character were recovered from beneath a stalagmite floor, and Salisbury went on to use this information to challenge the notion that the north-west was a polar desert at the end of the Devensian period. He suggested that the Morecambe Bay coast may have been a *refugium*

area with a mild climate, but further work needs to be done to test this idea before it can be accepted without reservation.

If the discussion about Lindale Low Caves has been uncontentious – the lithic material was published without any controversy in *Antiquity* in 1988 (Salisbury 1988) – then the same cannot be said about the debate surrounding the findings from the 1969 excavations at Kirkhead Cave. The 1969 work had produced a group of flints found in layers immediately beneath stalagmite deposits, close to the boss of a *Megaloceros* antler which had given a date of 10,700 ±200 BP (HAR 1059) (Wood *et al* 1969; Ashmead and Wood 1974). Gale and Hunt, in their reassessment of the site (1985), applied a range of analytical techniques to the cave sediments to suggest that human activity at Kirkhead should be dated to Late Devensian Zone III. Their interpretation and methodology, however, drew a barrage of criticism from Salisbury and Richard Tipping (Salisbury 1986; Tipping 1986). Four years later, Gale and Hunt's reply (1990) was no less trenchant, and the arguments, I suggest, rumble on – though the Zone III dating for the lithic material remains unchallenged.

Most recently, Salisbury has rehearsed the background to the Kirkhead debate (1997), but he has also published the results of further work in the immediate vicinity of Kirkhead Cave in the general area of Blenkett Wood. Whitton's Cave was excavated in the period from 1991-92 and produced evidence for possibly Bronze Age lithic artifacts, faunal remains and human burials in some highly disturbed contexts (1997, 8). His work at Kent's Bank Cave, carried out in 1993, may have produced Late Upper Palaeolithic tools, while excavations at the enigmatically named 'Site 17', some 400m NW of Kirkhead Cave, proved inconclusive (Salisbury, 1997, 9-10).

Ongoing work by the Morecambe Bay Archaeological Research Society at another Cumbrian cave, Bart's Shelter in Furness, must be mentioned here as it is also set to increase our knowledge of early prehistoric Cumbria (R Middleton, pers comm). Again, this research fits in with the typological and stratigraphical themes of this review, as over the last five years the society has recovered some 80 complete stone tools from the site, 12 of which may be Upper Palaeolithic and the rest Early Mesolithic in date. They have also discovered an elk bone point, the haft end of a harpoon, a bone ring and a worked horse's tooth. Other faunal remains from the cave include elk, bear, wild pig and,

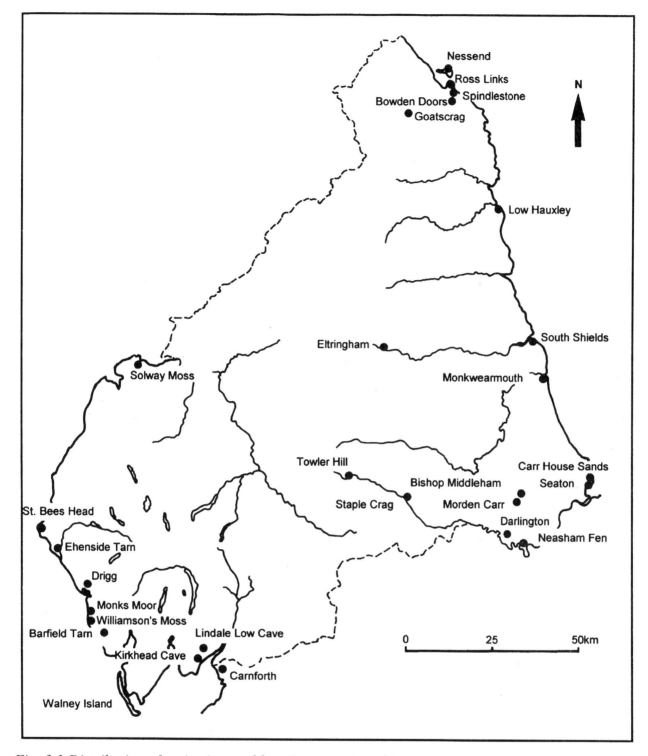

Fig. 3.1 Distribution of main sites and locations mentioned in the text

possibly, reindeer bones. Human remains of Mesolithic and Bronze Age date have also been recorded, with a high number of infants from Mesolithic contexts. The society is still working at the site, and a preliminary publication is pending (D Stables, pers comm).

Open-air locations have also provided possible early evidence. Recent excavations in the Carlisle area have revealed a tanged scraper, identified by Chris Tolan-Smith as possibly of Late Upper Palaeolithic type (M McCarthy, pers comm). Similarly, on the east of the Pennines, one could point to Stephen Cousins' recent find of a backed blade from the Tyne Valley at Eltringham, and also the possible Upper Palaeolithic material discovered by Tim Laurie on the terraces of the Tees at Towler Hill near Lartington in Teesdale (Coggins *et al* 1989).

Recently, Sue Stallibrass has documented isolated finds of northern late glacial faunal remains. These include the well-known elk find from Neasham Fen in County Durham, dated, on the basis of its associated pollen sequence, to c.10,500 BP; and the recent find of an elk mandible from a Late Upper Palaeolithic, or possibly Early Mesolithic, peat deposit on the banks of the River Skerne at Darlington. Plans are afoot to obtain an AMS date for the mandible and also for a bone from the Neasham elk (Stallibrass 1995, 89).

Finds of Giant Irish Elk were made at South Shields and Seaton near Hartlepool in the nineteenth century, and a *Megaloceros* antler was found in a quarry at Carnforth in Cumbria in 1973. Roger Jacobi and Tom Lord are currently studying the dates of late glacial elk and *Megaloceros* finds in Britain, and much of their data comes from northern England and Scotland (*ibid*, 90). In summary, then, there are finds of faunal remains from the region, some tools and a growing body of stratigraphical information that relates to the Upper Palaeolithic. The database is expanding and there must be more to recover, but it is essential that we are pro-active about recovering it if we are to move the discussion of the region's Palaeolithic archaeology beyond typology and stratigraphy.

The Mesolithic

Earlier Mesolithic evidence
Amateur archaeologists have undoubtedly played a vitally important role in keeping up interest in the region's prehistory, and nowhere is this more obvious than in the study of the northern Mesolithic. Certainly, until the development of the Durham Archaeological Survey in 1983, the Tyne-Solway Ancient Landscapes Project in 1992-3 and the North-West Wetlands Survey based in Lancaster in the early 1990s, it would be fair to say that there was hardly any regional, institutional, interest in the earlier periods of prehistory. This is obvious if one looks at an up-to-date distribution map for Mesolithic sites in Durham and Northumberland (Fig 3.2) which clearly reflects where local, and in the main, amateur, workers have been active since the early part of the twentieth century, and which gives the lie to the statements made by Clack and Gosling, quoted earlier.

At the typological/distributional level of research, there has been much activity since

1976. The work of Denis Coggins and Tim Laurie at Staple Crag and Towler Hill in Teesdale, County Durham, has provided us with new information about an Early Mesolithic presence in the Pennine dales, for example (Coggins *et al* 1989). My own work with Deirdre O'Sullivan on Lindisfarne has recorded Early and Later Mesolithic artefacts at the site of Nessend, and I have documented a potential Early Mesolithic site at Monkwearmouth (Young and O'Sullivan 1993; Young forthcoming). As yet, though, we have no published evidence for Early Mesolithic activity in Cumbria.

Later Mesolithic evidence
For the Later Mesolithic, the series of papers published in the *Transactions of the Cumberland and Westmorland Antiquarian and Archaeology Society* from 1983-7 by Jim and Peter Cherry deserves special mention (Cherry and Cherry 1983; 1984; 1985; 1986; 1987a). These documented the results of their Cumbrian coastal fieldwork, and they have highlighted concentrations of material around St Bees, Eskmeals, Drigg and Walney Island; they have also made interesting observations about changes in patterns of lithic raw material procurement and use from the Mesolithic period onwards. In 1987 they also published the results of five years of fieldwalking in the east Cumbrian limestone uplands between Shap and Kirkby Stephen, during which activity they recorded some 30 locations producing later Mesolithic material (Cherry and Cherry 1987b). Again, they observed changes in raw material preference and use over time, and this work has greatly broadened our understanding of Mesolithic activity across the Cumbrian landscape.

Their coastal and lowland concentrations tie in with evidence for pre-elm decline forest interference documented at sites such as Ehenside Tarn, Barfield Tarn and Williamson's Moss at Eskmeals. An oddity in this palaeoenvironmental/archaeological link, though, is the evidence for early interference with the vegetation cover at Blea Tarn in the uplands of the Lake District, where as yet no Mesolithic material has been recovered (Higham 1986, 32).

Most recently the Cherrys have documented a late Mesolithic site at Levens Park (2000, 25-32), thus adding to our scant knowledge of the Mesolithic around Morecambe Bay. The assemblage consisted of 1961 pieces, with microliths being the most prolific tool type (2000, 27 and 31)

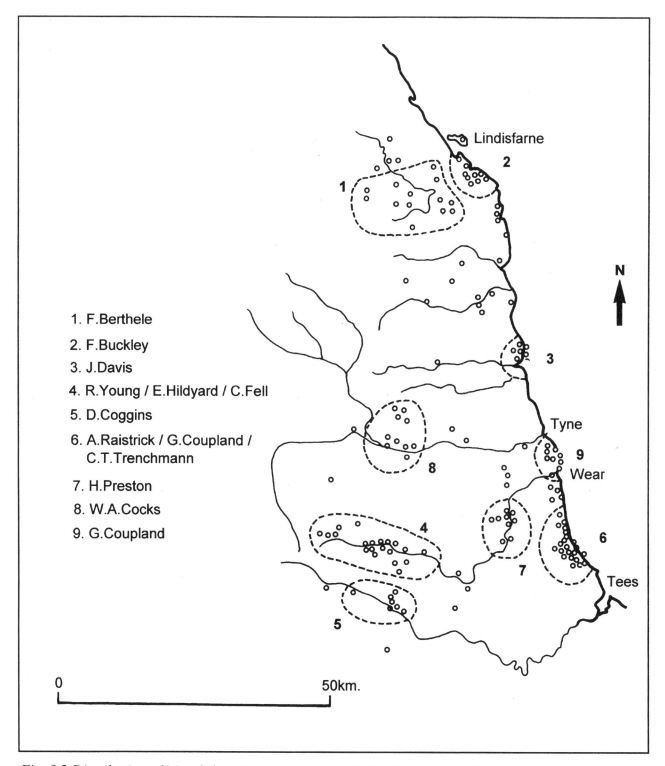

1. F.Berthele
2. F.Buckley
3. J.Davis
4. R.Young / E.Hildyard / C.Fell
5. D.Coggins
6. A.Raistrick / G.Coupland / C.T.Trenchmann
7. H.Preston
8. W.A.Cocks
9. G.Coupland

Fig. 3.2 Distribution of Mesolithic sites in north-east England, showing collectors and concentrations

On the eastern side of the Pennines, published work by John Davies, the late Joan Weyman, Denis Coggins, Tim Laurie and the present writer, in the period 1983-2000, has increased our understanding of later Mesolithic material distributions in Durham and Northumberland, and most of these workers are still actively involved in fieldwalking and survey in the region.

Davies produced a gazetteer of Northumbrian Mesolithic sites in *Northern Archaeology* (1983); Weyman has examined aspects of the north-eastern Mesolithic, particularly raw material type and source location (1984); Coggins produced an excellent summary of his own multi-period fieldwork in Teesdale (1986); and Laurie has published a review of early post-glacial settlement data from the Tees and Swale Valleys (1984). Coggins, Laurie and Young also collaborated to produce a review of the Late Upper Palaeolithic and Mesolithic of the north Pennine dales (1989) and in 1997 Coggins and Fairless produced the report on their excavations at the multi-period site of Middle Hurth Edge in Teesdale (1997). I documented a later Mesolithic flint assemblage from this site (Young 1997). My personal contribution at this level has been to examine potential sources of flint and chert for the north-east of England (1985), to try and assess the formation processes that have produced the Mesolithic and later archaeological record of County Durham and other parts of the region (1986), and to produce a detailed analysis of lithic finds from the Wear Valley in County Durham in particular and the north-east in general (1984; 1987). In 1993, Deirdre O'Sullivan and I published a detailed interim report on our work at Nessend on Lindisfarne in Northumberland, and discussed this in the context of the so-called 'coastal' Mesolithic of north-east England. In 2000 I developed my coastal Mesolithic research in a paper that examined the relationship of so called 'coastal' sites with inland and upland locations of Mesolithic activity (Young 2000). The coastal theme is one that I am still actively researching.

In terms of other, recent, Northumbrian coastal work, mention must also be made here of the Northumberland County Archaeology Section's Coastal Survey (C Hardie, pers comm), and more particularly, the excavations and related work at Low Hauxley (C Howard-Davis, pers comm). This site was examined initially by Clive Bonsall, subsequently by Stephen Speak, and most recently by Lancaster University Archaeological Unit, funded by English Heritage. A series of Bronze Age cairns and cists has been found eroding from the sand dunes at Low Hauxley since 1982. Beneath this was an old land surface and midden deposit, on and in which was an assemblage of lithic material of probably later, but possibly earlier, Mesolithic date. Bonsall's as yet unpublished 1983 excavation, along with Tipping's associated pollen work, showed the importance of the site in terms of its palaeoenvironmental potential. Some 250m to the north of the archaeological exposure there are inter-tidal peat deposits, which have been examined by Innes and Frank (Frank 1982, 24-32), and which have yielded evidence for a well-dated series of environmental changes. Low Hauxley has the potential to tell us much about the later Mesolithic environment and subsequent

marine inundations of the Northumberland coast. Further detailed work is required here before the site is totally lost to the sea.

Most recently Nicky Milner and Clive Waddington of Newcastle University have examined a site at Howick near Alnwick and Craster discovered in the 1980s by John Davies. This is another important 'coastal' site as it has revealed archaeological structures (two clay-lined pits) and a possible occupation area with related timber features in association with large quantities of knapped flint, marine shells, ochre, charcoal and charred hazelnut and acorn shells (Milner & Waddington, 2001, 6). A series of radiocarbon dates concentrating around 7000 Cal. BC has recently been obtained from the hazelnut shells (Milner & Waddington pers comm) making the site comparable with that at Filpoke Beacon on the Durham coast (Jacobi 1976).

Similar work has also been carried out in the last few years by the Cleveland Archaeology Section on submerged peats around Hartlepool. CT Trechmann recorded Mesolithic material here in the 1930s, and the current work has produce a wooden hurdle, radiocarbon-dated to around 3,800 Cal BC (Waughman, pers comm). This date is important, coming as it does from a possible fish-trap. At the conference it was suggested that the hurdle was Neolithic, and if this is the case, then it is very early indeed. It has, in fact, provided one of the earliest Neolithic dates in the region, and as a result this research may prove very important in any discussion of the Mesolithic/Neolithic transition in the area, and we look forward to its full publication.

Archaeological work which has gone beyond field survey and typology in Cumbria includes Bonsall's important excavations at Monk's Moors and Williamson's Moss near Eskmeals, carried out from 1974 to the mid 1980s, and about which three detailed interim reports have been published (Bonsall 1981; Bonsall et al 1987; 1989). The project plotted coastal developments around Eskmeals from the seventh millennium BC, and the Monk's Moors excavations revealed Mesolithic structural evidence as well as lithic artefacts. The Williamson's Moss site provided even more detailed structural data, with the recovery of oak and birchwood structures dating to around 5,500 BP, from a subsequently silted-up drainage channel.

Bonsall discussed the subsistence strategies of the Mesolithic inhabitants of coastal Cumbria, and suggested that sites were ideally situated to exploit seasonally available marine, riverine and inland/upland resources (1981; Bonsall *et al* 1987; 1989). Richard Tipping's pollen analysis at Williamson's Moss allowed the integration of the archaeological features with their past environmental context, with some quite startling results. The first of two elm declines documented at the site is particularly early, and Bonsall has speculated, quite rightly I think, that his findings may have a bearing on the localized transition to agriculture (Bonsall *et al* 1987; 1989).

In this context, one must also note Caroline Skinner's doctoral research, based at Leicester University, which has reinforced the notion of considerable Mesolithic activity in eastern Cumbria. Her work has involved new pollen analyses at five sites in the lowlands, the Pennine foothills and the Pennines proper, coupled with excavation and detailed fieldwalking. She has produced an important radiocarbon-dated pollen sequence from the late Devensian to the early medieval period.

A further development, cutting across all three boundaries of my thematic scheme, is the ongoing English Heritage-funded North-West Wetlands Survey. Bob Middleton and others, based in Lancaster, have been dealing with Cumbria, and while as yet no Mesolithic artefacts have been recovered in the course of their field-walking, environmental work by Huckerby and Wells at Solway Moss has indicated localized woodland burning at around 5,240-4,940 Cal BC (GU-5315), and an early inception of agriculture (Huckerby and Wells 1993, 37-42).

In considering the third of my themes on the eastern side of the Pennines, we should note that as early as 1976, the late Don Spratt and his colleagues had published a discussion of their finds in the Upleatham area of Cleveland which was an important leap forward for regional Mesolithic studies (Spratt *et al* 1976). For the first time, an attempt was made to interpret lithic scatters in terms of potential site functions and landscape and resource use. They introduced the concepts of 'seasonality' and 'base' and 'hunting camps' into the interpretation of the North's Mesolithic archaeology, and this certainly influenced me during the course of my doctoral research on the prehistory of the Wear Valley, which was begun in 1975 (Young 1984).

My work was an attempt to look at landscape, settlement and subsistence development from the Mesolithic to the end of the Iron Age. I tried to move the study of the region's earlier prehistory away from a simple consideration of implement typology, and I was greatly influenced, at the

time, by the old Star Carr seasonality model in my discussion of Mesolithic upland/lowland seasonal movements and game animal and plant availability (*ibid*; Young 1987). In the light of recent work on these subjects, I would suggest that the interpretations that I offered should now be taken with a large bucket of salt! (see, for example, Legge and Rowley-Conwy 1988; Mithen 1990; Spikins 2000).

From 1983-7, however, the Durham Archaeological Survey further attempted to fill gaps in our knowledge about Mesolithic and later activity in the region. The project's broad, multi-period, objectives were to obtain information about settlement pattern change over time, and in the east of County Durham, an area of 1,255 hectares of ploughed land was surveyed. The general results appeared in a monograph in 1988 (Haselgrove *et al* 1988), and the lithic finds were published in 1992 (Haselgrove and Healey 1992). On first consideration, the area walked in this survey seems large, but in terms of the total ploughed land available for study in the region it was still a small-scale survey. Only 882 flints came from 81 of the 207 fields walked, and diagnostic Mesolithic material was very thin on the ground.

This contrasts with the current results from Newcastle University's ongoing multi-disciplinary Tyne-Solway Ancient Landscapes Project, designed to examine the human use of the Tyne-Solway corridor from the earliest prehistoric periods to medieval times. So far 34% of the 400 hectares walked has produced stone artefacts. Tolan-Smith is studying these from a landscape archaeology perspective, rather than simply concentrating on typology, and he has suggested that certain parts of the corridor were more or less important for certain activities at certain times. Indeed, he has argued that contrasting, almost mutually exclusive, patterns of land use were emerging in the area for the Mesolithic and Neolithic periods, with an increase in the amount of the land used by Neolithic farmers. From the distribution of Neolithic axes and other material, he has suggested that this increase was the result of farmers moving up the Tyne Valley, and that evidence for Neolithic activity falls off with distance up the valley from the east coast (Tolan-Smith 1996). This is an interesting approach to the study of the localized Mesolithic-Neolithic transition in the north-east, and as such his ideas find resonance in two of the present writer's recent publications (Young 1990; 1994b).

On-going research by Clive Waddington in the Milfield Basin in Northumberland has further highlighted the important contribution of a 'landscape-based' approach to earlier prehistory (Waddington, 1999; 2000a). In his 1999 volume, based on his doctoral research, Waddington dealt with the Mesolithic and Neolithic of the Milfield area, concentrating on the evolution of the landscape, settlement data, ideology and the changing nature of people's relationship with the 'natural' world. He employed a wide range of methodologies, working closely with geomorphologists among others, and he has developed new fieldwork practices which will benefit all fieldworkers in the region, as well as producing an impressive analysis of the collected lithic data and on overall archaeological synthesis for the area. This I think is the ultimate development of my third research theme outlined above, and along with the other projects outlined it certainly makes the doughnut worth biting into!

Future research

So much for a review of northern Palaeolithic and Mesolithic studies post-1976. 1 hope that anyone reading this would agree with me in that there is much to be optimistic about. But what does the future hold? I would now like to make some suggestions about the direction that regional Palaeolithic and Mesolithic studies might take over the next few years.

In English Heritage's *Exploring our Past: Strategies for the Archaeology of England* (1991), great importance was attached to broadening our understanding of the Palaeolithic and Mesolithic periods, and to landscape studies generally. Obviously, given the changing context of contemporary archaeological practice, with the emphasis on the role of PPG 16 and developer-funded projects etc, there is a need for future research which will have academic aims and priorities, and yet which will also help county archaeologists and planners to manage and protect the available archaeological resource. Such future work must also facilitate the enhancement of the region's five main Sites and Monuments Records which are used to inform the planning and development process. Currently all of theses issues are being discussed under the English Heritage 'Regional Research Frameworks' initiative. I would make the following suggestions:

- **Review of existing northern lithic collections**
  Before further fieldwork can be planned, an up-to-date review of the material already recovered from the region is needed. A number of museums in the north hold lithic material, much of which has never really been examined since it was deposited in the collections. Such an assessment would be timely, and could be tied into the English Heritage review of all English Palaeolithic-Neolithic surface lithic scatters (Schofield 1994a). Besides giving researchers, county archaeologists and planners a better understanding of the regional distribution of material, it would facilitate the planning of future fieldwork projects, and it would probably yield previously unknown artefacts of Upper Palaeolithic and Early Mesolithic date.

- **The study of archaeological formation processes**
  To understand archaeological distributions properly, we need to comprehend the processes of differential destruction, preservation and recovery that have brought these distributions about (Young 1986; 1994a). Such a knowledge would be important for assessing threats to the existing archaeological record, and again it would help in planning future field research.

- **Targeting of areas for future integrated field and environmental survey**
  Exploring Our Past also lays great stress on the identification of locations which will preserve palaeoenvironmental, as well as early prehistoric archaeological, data. There is a real need to identify such areas in Durham and Northumberland. One such would be the south-east Durham/Cleveland carr-lands. This is an area of late glacial and early post-glacial infilled ponds and small lakes, with boulder clay and gravel knolls between the peat basins. It is criss-crossed with drainage channels that cut through the peat, and as such, it would provide an excellent area for detailed dyke survey. The dry land is also regularly ploughed, and pollen analyses from Bishop Middleham and Morden Carr have already demonstrated the potential for identifying evidence of early human activity in this area (Bartley *et al* 1976).

- **Regional register of caves and rock shelters**
  Given their obvious importance in Cumbria, it would seem logical to have an up-to-date record of the location of caves and rock shelters throughout the north which may preserve evidence of Upper Palaeolithic and later activity.

- **Coastal survey in Co Durham, Tyne and Wear and Cleveland, north of the Tees**

This might proceed along the lines of the Northumberland Coastal Survey and the work already carried out for part of the Cleveland coast. The coastal geomorphology of Durham and Tyne and Wear is different to that of Northumberland, but there is a considerable amount of Mesolithic data from the area, and not much is known about its context. There are sites eroding from the Durham/Tyne and Wear cliff-line, and the coast itself is eroding every year. Material is undoubtedly being lost without record.

- **Organization of local fieldwork groups**

The total area of field-walked land in the north is still small, despite the best efforts of individuals and groups. Obviously, professional archaeologists will never have the resources and/or time to survey the majority of the region, so it seems logical to enlist the help of locally organized fieldwork groups. Such groups, once set up, could be trained in artefact identification by the region's County Archaeological and Museums Services, and they could also be trained in field-walking techniques, so that recovered distributions could be compared across the region. Such a networking scheme has been set up and works to excellent effect in Leicestershire. Local groups have an annual meeting at which results are shared, and the end product of their work is fed into the Sites and Monuments Record (P Liddle, pers comm). The benefits of this approach would be obvious, and I know that such work does take place in Cleveland. Archaeological activity would be taken back into the local community, Sites and Monuments Records would be expanded, a broader landscape-based approach to early prehistory could be fostered, and this, in turn, would only be of benefit to anyone charged with managing the general archaeological resources of the region. The regional CBA group could play an active role in co-ordinating such work.

In this review I have tried to examine the Palaeolithic and Mesolithic archaeology of the northern region within the framework of 'Past, Present and Future'. I have suggested that past and present work might best be examined using a thematic approach that highlights typology, stratigraphy and function, and I have made some personal suggestions about what might be done to move our interpretations along in the future. If the above suggestions were to be acted upon, then I believe we would go some further way towards realizing the full potential of the early prehistory of the northern region. As archaeologists we must be pro-active if we want to gain a better understanding of our raw material, and this pro-active approach can only be generated by greater co-operation between professional and amateur archaeologists, especially at a time when resources are scarce. I believe that CBA North can, and should, have an important role in promoting such activity – there is much to do.

Acknowledgements
I would like to thank the following for their willingness to share information: C Hardie, C Howard-Davis, P Liddle, M McCarthy, R Middleton, R Newman, P Rowe, C Skinner, D Stables, M Waughman; without their help this review would not have been possible. Deirdre O'Sullivan and Jane Webster, both of the School of Archaeological Studies at Leicester, read and commented upon earlier drafts of this paper, and it is the better for it. Any errors remain my own responsibility.

Chapter 4: Upland Survey: Neolithic and Bronze Age Sites

*James Quartermaine**

Introduction

In this paper, I want to talk about the recent programmes of survey that have revolutionised our understanding of upland landscapes. It is important to assess the impact of these programmes, and not just those that have identified unequivocal evidence of Neolithic activity. Although this means that the paper does not fit into the carefully designed chronological boxes of the conference, this is not totally inappropriate because upland survey should be about the analysis of the evolution of the landscape, not just trying to define individual monuments within chronological straight-jackets.

I would like to examine the nature and results of the major upland surveys that have been generated since the Clack and Gosling report (1976) and assess in what ways they have and have not affected our understanding of upland prehistoric land use, and therefore to make suggestions about what the future should be for upland survey programmes, in ways that will maximise the work of the past and provide a new enhanced perspective to examine the evolution of the landscape. I will assess the major upland surveys from throughout the north, but provide a slightly greater emphasis on the Cumbria surveys since this is the area with which I have most familiarity but also because it adequately highlights the changing perspectives of upland archaeology.

Upland Surveys

A series of very significant upland surveys have been undertaken in the last twenty years: The Cheviot survey, the Howgills survey and the Yorkshire Dales Mapping Project, all by the RCHM(E) [now English Heritage]; the Swaledale survey by Andrew Fleming; and last but not least the Lake District surveys by the Lancaster University Archaeology Unit (now Oxford Archaeology North) on behalf of English Heritage and the Lake District National Park. The importance of these surveys is that they have identified the important archaeological resource preserved on the marginal uplands. They have enabled the recording of landscapes fossilised at their point of abandonment, which contain the fields, houses, streets, and burial grounds that characterise settlement. The surveys provide the global perspective but not necessarily chronological and stratigraphic detail. Multi-period occupation of a site inevitably causes some analytical headaches in trying to discriminate the phases, and sometimes cannot satisfactorily be achieved without the use of the trowel.

For the most part the surveys were established to satisfy a management requirement, and so the primary aim is to identify the extent and character of the archaeological resource and as such they are an invaluable conservation tool. The net result is that we have considerable numbers of maps and gazetteers which identify and characterise the monuments but do not provide an adequate chronological or social perspective. This effectively means that all that can realistically be stated is the extent to which the surveys have raised more questions than answers about the Neolithic and Bronze Age occupation of the north.

Yorkshire Dales Survey

A prime example of working to a management agenda is the Yorkshire Dales survey which was undertaken by the RCHM(E) under the guidance of Bob Bewley and Pete Horne. It has used aerial photographic sources, both oblique and vertical photographs, to provide a basic level record of over 3000 km^2 of the Yorkshire Dales, giving only a basic graphic and descriptive record of the archaeological resource. It has been undertaken in conjunction with local surface surveys and provides an invaluable archaeological record for the management of the Yorkshire Dales, one that is now used as the primary SMR by the Yorkshire Dales National Park. It was able to create over 18,000 site records and is one of the more remarkable management surveys that have been undertaken in recent years.

However, only a limited number of the features have been visited on the ground and consequently the ability to interpret and analyse the sites is limited. The survey by itself cannot provide a sufficient level of information to analyse the development of the landscapes, and indeed was never intended for this purpose. Such a survey does, however, provide an

*Address: Oxford Archaeology North, Storey Institute, Meeting House Lane, Lancaster LA1 1TF

effective and broadly consistent launching point
for more detailed survey work which can concentrate on the more significant archaeological
landscapes and provide the appropriate analytical information.

The Swaledale Survey is an example of the
type of survey which was generated specifically
from a research perspective and its extent was
localised in order to address the specific
research agenda (Fleming 1986, 1989 and
1993). There was no attempt to produce the
more wide scale, and consistent survey typical
of the management survey. Unlike its management cousins, these surveys of ancient landscapes were dovetailed with an excavation and
palaeobotanical programme to investigate the
formation of the landscapes. The excavations
produced radiocarbon dates and the programme
dramatically contrasts with the other Northern
upland landscapes in that the landscape has a
chronological perspective, which makes it possible to analyse landscape formation within the
valley.

The southern Cheviot Landscape Survey was
a very significant programme undertaken by
RCHM(E) to record systematically 66 km² of
uplands extending from the Ingram valley in the
north to Alnham in the south (Topping 1992).
Like many of the upland surveys, this was
designed to anticipate future management
requirements in the Northumberland National
Park and the emphasis was on defining the
extent and significance of the archaeological
landscapes. The survey demonstrated a vast
wealth of Bronze Age agricultural landscapes,
and often comprised unenclosed settlements,
usually associated with field systems of varying
stages of complexity and development. Clearly
the main period of occupation of these fells at
altitudes of between 230m and 400m was prior
to the climatic decline of the early Iron Age.
Earlier excavation projects have fortunately provided a limited amount of dating for these landscapes such as the excavation by Burgess of a
platform settlement at Black Law which indicated Early Bronze Age activity. Although the main
period of activity was post-Neolithic, there was
one long cairn at Ewe Hill in the Ingram valley
which was subject to antiquarian activity and
would suggest a limited Neolithic presence in
the area. On the available surface survey evidence it is not possible to establish to what
extent any of the landscapes had their origins in
the Neolithic. However, excavations at Turf
Knowe by a team from Durham University, as

part of the Ingram and Upper Breamish Valley
landscape project (Adams 1995a, 1995b), have
demonstrated a cairn of unusual shape with
three radial arms, a shape not dissimilar to that
of a post-medieval sheep shelter. However, this
cairn produced a Food Vessel urn of Early
Bronze Age type and some flints of Late
Neolithic/Early Bronze Age character.
Significantly, the excavators found no evidence
of a primary interment and this led them to question whether it had a sepulchral function. The
existence of such an early cairn is significant in
that it would appear to reinforce the possibility
that some landscapes may have had origins earlier than the Middle Bronze Age.

Cumbrian Surveys
Unlike the Cheviot surveys, the archaeological
survey record of Cumbria is patchy, and reflects
a disparate approach to the recording of the
landscape. A recent survey of surveys (LUAU
1995), commissioned by the Lake District
National Park and the County Council, has
demonstrated that although there has been a systematic approach in some areas, there are a lot
more less intensive surveys undertaken by different professional and amateur groups within
the region which have helped fill some of the
lacunae within the record. Many of these surveys, such as the LUAU (1996a) Haweswater
survey for LDNPA and NWW, are at a basic
identification level, and although invaluable for
management purposes do not provide an overall
developmental landscape perspective. The next
stage of the Haweswater survey is to develop the
record by detailed level 2 survey of selected
sites and groups, which will provide an analytical perspective to the generalised survey.

Other detailed surveys in the region include
the Howgill survey by the RCHM(E), which
covered a large area of unimproved ground but
produced relatively little evidence of any prehistoric activity, let alone Neolithic; and those by
Leech (1983) and Turner (1987; 1991).

The main programme of survey work undertaken within the Cumbrian region is the Lake
District National Park Survey undertaken by
LUAU with English Heritage and LDNPA
funding, which was started in 1982 and was
designed to provide a detailed record of selected archaeologically significant areas
(Quartermaine and Leech forthcoming).
Although it has only explored a meagre 70 km²,
it has mapped over 13,000 monuments. The
survey programme was not undertaken in con-

junction with an excavation or palaeobotanical programme, but the region has been graced by a considerable amount of palaeobotanical work undertaken primarily by Walker (1965b) and Pennington (1970), which has helped to place the archaeological landscapes within an appropriate context. This, coupled with the scale of the results has provided the opportunity to evaluate the pattern of occupation of the uplands during the later prehistoric period. Like the Cheviot survey, the Lake District has demonstrated a remarkable series of Bronze Age landscapes, which indicate that the main period of upland occupation was during this period. The various landscapes are both complex and simple and the analysis of landscapes abandoned at different stages suggest a form of typological development from the earliest and most simple primary cairnfield which would, on the evidence of a palaeobotanical investigation at Barnscar by Walker (1965a), appear to reflect the pioneer agricultural occupation associated with forest clearance. From this there are innovations with field systems, which become increasingly complex and take on a character progressively indicative of cultivation, to the extent where the cairnfield has become a redundant feature of the landscape. Figure 4.1 shows the main developmental forms of settlement, varying from the simple cairnfield to the arable field system, and is based upon a large number of settlements and carnfields in the Lake District where the development has been fossilised at different stages of the development. The last type is only adequately demonstrated by one settlement from within the survey data set, specifically at Town Bank in West Cumbria (Figure 4.2), but there are other less well documented parallels from outside the region (Quartermaine 1989).

The upland landscapes provide a fossilised record of the settlement at the time of their abandonment, not their conception, and the earliest character of the forest clearance will often have been removed or obscured by the later landscaping. The landscapes which are typologically dated to the Bronze Age may potentially have Early Bronze Age or Neolithic origins, but this can not reliably be established from the surface evidence alone.

Neolithic evidence

Although the surveys have produced a wealth of evidence for Bronze Age settlement, they have produced very little definable evidence of Neolithic activity. This applies particularly to the Cheviot and Howgills surveys. Even the periphery areas of the Lake District have produced only occasional long cairns or Neolithic stone circles; most of the substantiated Neolithic funerary/ritual monuments are on the lowland areas, or on marginal lands immediately adjacent to the lower ground.

The Neolithic monuments are typically not associated with any agricultural features and provide no indication that their presence reflects an agricultural occupation of these marginal lands. A typical example is the Swinside stone circle in south-west Cumbria, and other examples identified within the last twenty years include Street House long cairn at Loftus, Cleveland (Vyner 1984) and also the Long cairn on Lazonby Fell identified by aerial photography during the Shell North West Ethylene Pipeline survey (Lambert 1996). However, there is one significant monument, Sampsons Bratful on Stockdale Moor, which is an impressive, well-constructed, trapezoidal long cairn, spatially associated with a large developed, but otherwise typical Bronze Age cairnfield (Masters 1984; Quartermaine 1989). Its form is typical of a Neolithic long cairn, but no modern excavation has been undertaken to confirm its date. The cairnfield is associated with more typical Bronze Age round cairns and it is possible to suggest, very tentatively, that the agricultural activity maximised an area of forest clearance initiated in connection with the earlier funerary monument. But at this point the argument cannot be continued because of the lack of any specific dating evidence, and this problem highlights the inadequacy of the interpretation and analysis of survey data without the availability of appropriate excavation evidence.

Although palaeobotanical evidence is an invaluable tool and would appear to confirm the evidence from survey that there was little upland clearance prior to the Bronze Age around the marginal upland periphery of the Lake District, this would not identify a hunter-gatherer exploitation of the uplands or even a low-intensity woodland pastoral economy, in which there was grazing with little woodland clearance. The upland surveys are typically concerned with the identification of structural features rather than lithic scatters, and so the evidence of a hunter-gatherer economy would typically not be reflected by the results.

All these generalisations about the Neolithic are, however, completely disrupted by the survey

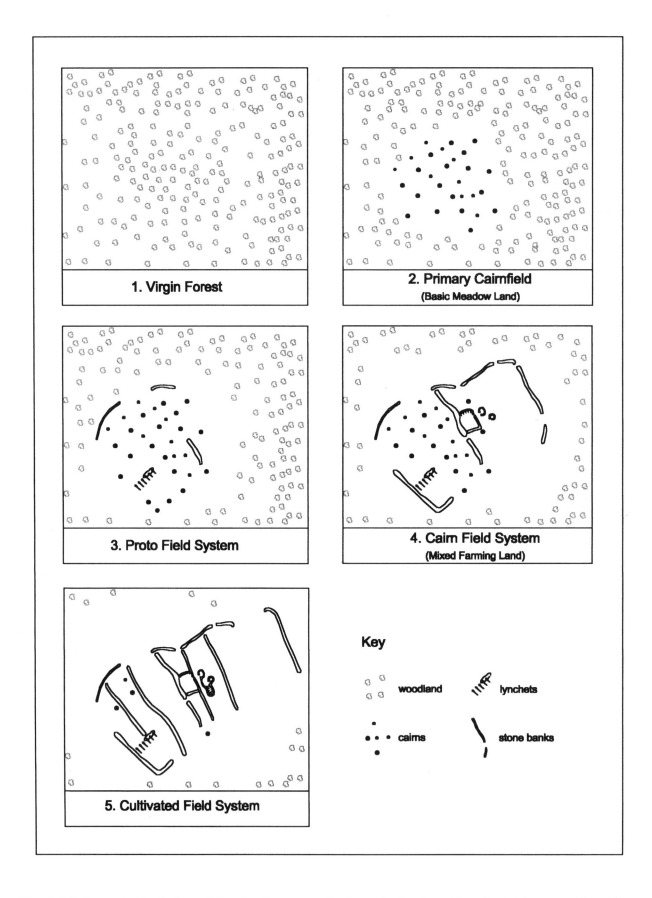

Fig. 4.1 Schematic depiction of the development of a hypothetical prehistoric field system (based on the results of the Lake District National Park Survey)

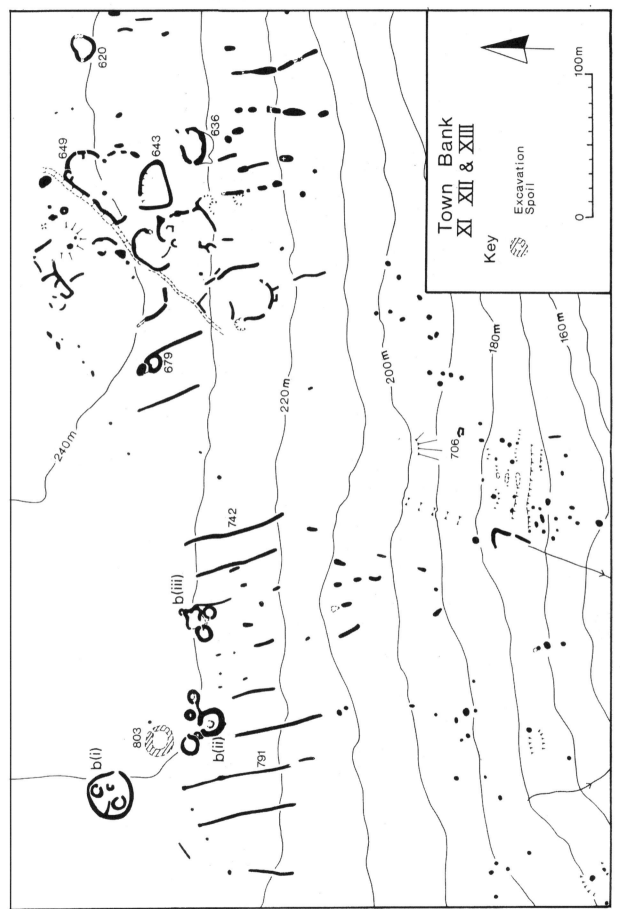

Fig. 4.2 Townbank Settlement groups XI-XIII: plan showing a developed form of prehistoric settlement

Fig. 4.3. General view of the Langdale axe factories, viewed from the opposite side of the valley

of a very significant, and very exceptional site: the Langdale Neolithic axe factories (Figure 4.3) (Claris and Quartermaine 1989). The survey identified vast quantities of lithic material from around the central massif of the Lake District. The survey was undertaken by the Lancaster Unit in conjunction with the National Trust and was undertaken alongside a research programme undertaken by Reading University, led by Richard Bradley (Bradley and Edmonds 1993). The survey identified over 570 Neolithic working floors that used a band of source rock, a fine grained Borrowdale volcanic tuff which outcrops at about 2,500 feet AOD (Figure 4.4). The waste flakes are measurable in hundreds of metric tonnes and some of the sites were found to relate to quarry sites, where the Reading University programme was able to demonstrate the use of fire-setting to extract the rock. The survey demonstrated a typological development of form of the working sites and subsequent excavations by Reading and the Lancaster Unit demonstrated that to an extent these reflected a chronological

development that started as early as 4211 – 3700 CalBC (5080 ±90 BP; OxA - 4212; Hedges *et al.* 1994) at a small, low production working site on an access route, and continued through to the final, most productive quarry phase as late as 3400–3200 CalBC (4590 ±50, BM-2627) (Bradley and Edwards 1993, 128). The survey demonstrated access routes and provided evidence to indicate that this extractive activity was undertaken by communities living in the lowlands and typified by our only substantiated axe finishing site at Ehenside Tarn on the Cumbrian coast (Darbishire 1873)

The significance of these sites cannot be overestimated; the combined survey and research programme has demonstrated the vast productivity of the axe factories, the duration of extraction, and the complex infrastructure involved in both production and distribution of the axes. More than anything else it has confirmed the complexity and sophistication of a Neolithic society that could manufacture on a massive scale and could market throughout Britain.

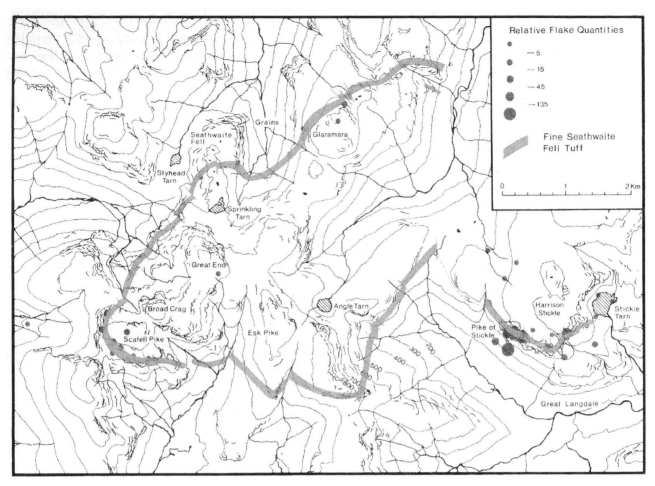

Fig. 4.4. Map showing the outcrops of volcanic tuff and associated Axe Factory groups

The Future

So what of the future? Management surveys need to continue unabated; our first priority must be the conservation of the resource, and if recent surveys are anything to go by there is a vast amount of undocumented archaeological landscape still to be recorded. We need to know about them to protect them. However, these surveys must be undertaken in a cost-effective manner to enable the most efficient use of resources, and should ideally be undertaken as a basic identification survey, that is only dots on maps rather than any more detailed mapping. It will thus be possible to examine large areas of upland, not just limited areas at a higher level of detail. The sort of survey envisaged is that undertaken by the RCHM(E) Yorkshire dales aerial photographic survey or the LUAU/ LDNPA GPS surveys of Haweswater. The net result is that a basic record is produced for very large chunks of the landscape.

The Cumbria Survey of Surveys has demonstrated the number of smaller surveys undertaken in one county and there is a need to collate that information for management purposes; it should be incorporated into the NMR and SMRs. Judging by the success of the Cumbrian survey of surveys there is a case for undertaking similar surveys in other counties of the North.

This proposed programme and the management surveys of the past will, however, not significantly inform us of a non-intensive Neolithic upland presence. The limited evidence suggests that the extensive Bronze Age landscapes may have had Late Neolithic/Early Bronze Age origins, but, because subsequent non-intensive agricultural development has obscured earlier landscapes and because there is still relatively little reliable dating for this pioneer upland agriculture, it is difficult to clarify the extent to which the classic typologically Bronze Age landscapes had earlier origins. These extant prehistoric landscapes have the potential to further our understanding of the exploitation of the marginal uplands, but surface survey by itself, although an essential first stage, only provides some of the answers and indeed creates even more questions.

In addition to the implementation of the management surveys, there is a need for research programmes targeted at some of the questions raised by the basic surveys. In this respect the recording programme of the LUAU/ NT Langdale surveys, was complemented by the Reading University research programme which was able to target the questions highlighted by the earlier work. The consequence is that we have a much clearer understanding of the axe production processes, which has highlighted the archaeological significance of the sites. I believe that there is considerable potential for similar co-operation between the conservation archaeology of the units with the research perspective of the university departments, each maximising the respective strengths to provide an effective complementary research and conservation programme.

Such research programmes need to take on an overall landscape approach, that is not trying to examine specific periods or localised areas, but should examine how the whole landscape has been affected by humans from their earliest presence through to the present. Upland landscapes should not be examined in isolation from lowland landscapes, because they represent the overflow from the better quality lowlands by transhumance or even more permanent migrations. The landscape approach requires the examination of how the vegetational history of the two terrains complement each other and how this interacts with the settlements. The landscape approach would examine the way the natural topography has determined settlement patterns and even defined territorial boundaries. It is significant that certain localities have independently been resettled over the millennia, although there are other nearby terrains which have revealed no evidence of settlement. This evidently reflects the localised topographical advantages by comparison with other areas and is essential to an understanding of settlement patterns.

The important aspect of the approach is to lay the emphasis on the landscape, instead of concentrating on the archaeology; a broad variety of historical, archaeological, palaeoenvironmental and geological techniques are used to establish how the present landscape was formed and the manner in which humans have been instrumental in this process. Because of our past excavation-orientated mentality, there has been a tendency to look at settlements in isolation, but with upland landscapes there is the potential to examine the interaction and complementary development of whole upland communities.

The research techniques to enable this analysis should include a palaeobotanical programme to examine a variety of different pollen catchment areas, although some cores should be taken in association with archaeological monuments to provide the appropriate context. The techniques should also provide a chronological and functional context, which must inevitably involve limited excavation; but any excavations should only sample the sites as there can be little justification in destroying an archaeological resource merely to satisfy an academic requirement. Other techniques such as test pit survey techniques can be applied, but need to be tailored specifically to the research objectives.

To summarise: the major management survey programmes undertaken within the last twenty years should not be viewed simply as a management tool, but as the starting point for major research programmes. This would therefore provide the opportunity to maximise one of northern England's most valuable prehistoric archaeological resources.

Chapter 5: The Neolithic and Bronze Age Periods in the North – Some Matters Arising

*Richard Bradley**

What is my title intended to convey? Every committee follows the same agenda. It starts with a summary of the previous meeting. The minutes are reviewed as a record of those proceedings, and then there follows an item described as 'matters arising'. This is where the issues can be considered again.

In some ways this volume follows a similar format. It takes as its starting point a review of northern archaeology published twenty five years ago (Clack and Gosling 1976) and many of the same topics are revisited. Most subjects are considered by someone with a professional involvement in the archaeology of northern England, and this highlights the changes of approach that have developed over that time.

This paper is perhaps a little unusual as I have not worked in this area for some years, and in any case I do not consider myself to be a period specialist. As a result, I can look back over the major problems with a certain detachment. At the same time, my own research areas have shifted, so that my perspectives have necessarily been modified. I may have started my career in Wessex and the Thames valley but during the last fifteen years my fieldwork has taken me steadily northwards, from Great Langdale to Northumberland, through southern Scotland to Inverness and Aberdeen, and even as far as Orkney. As I made each of these moves, my understanding of northern archaeology changed.

It is as an interested bystander that I make these observations. What are the major issues in the Neolithic and Early Bronze Age archaeology of northern England? And what are the unresolved problems that we need to tackle now? To a large extent it is obvious what has been achieved, but, having read the minutes, what are the matters arising? This contribution should be read in parallel with the reviews edited by Harding and Johnston (2000) and by Frodsham (1996). The latter includes an agenda for Neolithic research in the north (Harding, Frodsham and Durden 1996).

My concern is to identify some of the unanswered questions in northern archaeology: the issues that I find frustrating as a prehistorian with an interest in synthesis. Following my brief from the editors of this volume, I have selected those topics where there is a realistic prospect of undertaking new work, and I shall make some quite specific suggestions as to how this might be carried out.

My first problem is the relationship between field archaeology and environmental science. Here there is a need for integration. There are perhaps four sources for a prehistory of northern England: finds of artefacts, surveys of standing remains, excavations and environmental data. It is my contention that these have still to be brought into alignment. The evidence of portable artefacts is broadly consistent with the evidence of below-ground archaeology, and in certain cases we can integrate the results of landscape survey with those of excavation. But when we do so, our synthesis is frequently at odds with the pollen record. To quote from a paper by Colin Burgess, 'in unravelling the course of exploitation of the northern uplands, the palaeoenvironmental and archaeological evidence is often in direct conflict.... I do not think such difficulties will be resolved by archaeologists being too deferential to scientists, and jumping through too many hoops to accommodate the "scientific evidence"' (1995, 156).

What is his objection to this work? At the outset he disputes the pollen evidence for Neolithic activity in the Cheviots because so few artefacts of that period have been found there. This raises an important issue, for the pollen record from other parts of the north is also at odds with conventional wisdom (Tipping 1996) There are two problems here. First, it is more difficult than we imagine to distinguish between Mesolithic and Neolithic activity. In Cumbria, for example, Pennington (1975) has treated these as chronological terms because there are some sites where she is unable to distinguish between them on the basis of environmental evidence. Much the same happens in Lancashire (Cowell and Innes 1994, table 17) and on the North York Moors where Spratt and Simmons (1976) concluded that the clearances dated to the Neolithic period were more pronounced than those of the Mesolithic, but no different in kind. More recent work has done little to affect this conclusion,

*Address: Department of Archaeology, University of Reading, Whiteknights, P O Box 218, Reading, RG6 6AA

although Edwards has suggested that the amount of charcoal in dated deposits fell during the period of transition (1998, 73-4).

The second problem is that in such cases the pollen record indicates a continuous history of land use in the uplands (Simmons and Innes 1996a), whilst the distribution of dated artefacts often implies a hiatus. The excavated evidence suggests an interval between the Mesolithic sites and the beginning of the Neolithic period. Given the chronological resolution of some of the pollen cores, this must be reconsidered. There is a discrepancy here, but it is a discrepancy between a coarse scale of reckoning (artefact typology) and a more exact one (pollen analysis in fine-grained sediments). At the risk of perpetuating a dubious terminology, are we sure what the latest Mesolithic artefacts might look like? Did they always include microliths? And can we recognise the earliest 'Neolithic' flintwork in the north, apart from arrowheads and axes? A rather similar point has recently been made by Cowell (2000, 116).

Some progress has come about through the computer simulations conducted by Spikins (1999), but there is still too little evidence on the ground. Another way forward would be to reconsider the 'mixed' flint scatters from the uplands published by Young (1989). These are notable as apparently Mesolithic sites with finds of Neolithic arrowheads. Their interpretation has always been controversial, but the discussion would be based on much surer ground if we could identify those examples with the greatest potential for research. Stratigraphic evidence is essential here, and much would be gained if we could compare the distribution of the arrowheads with that of the other artefacts. At present, virtually all our information comes from places which have been damaged by erosion and modified by piecemeal collection. There are problems with the pollen record too, as much of the high resolution analysis has been concerned with Mesolithic activity (Simmons 1996, chapters 1, 2 and 5). It is vitally important to extend this approach to later deposits so that we can see when the character of human activity changed.

Although domesticated resources were adopted in Britain around 4000 BC, can we be sure about the importance of Neolithic agriculture in the north, or, for that matter, the decline of hunting and/or gathering? If these problems affect our reading of the environmental evidence from the Pennines, they are even more apparent in the Cherrys' important work in Cumbria, where

there is a striking contrast between the site-based pattern of the Mesolithic and the more extensive distribution of Neolithic material (Cherry and Cherry 1987b and 1996). Something rather similar may happen in the north-east (Tolan-Smith 1997), and a comparable pattern has been found by field survey in northern and western Scotland (Bradley 2000, chapter 9). Moreover in the Cherrys' study area there is evidence for just two periods of activity, the Late Mesolithic and the Late Neolithic, with little indication of an Early Neolithic phase in between, although the pollen record provides abundant evidence for occupation at this time. Again we have the same paradox: the environmental evidence is at odds with the results of field archaeology. The archaeologists may be those whose interpretations need more careful attention. A similar point has been made by Waddington (2000b).

Burgess would take the opposite view. As we have seen, he believes that archaeologists should not be 'too deferential to scientists' (1995, 136). The second area in which their results appear to be in conflict is the Early Bronze Age. Burgess (1992) favours the large-scale colonisation of the uplands during this period, despite the limited evidence for that process in the pollen record. Similarly, he envisages the abandonment of the uplands during the first millennium BC, when pollen analysis suggests an increasing impact on the natural environment (Fenton-Thomas 1992; Mercer and Tipping 1994).

This is an influential interpretation. At a national level there can be little doubt that the extent of the settled landscape increased significantly during the Early Bronze Age. This is most clearly evidenced by the distribution of dated monuments. Mortuary mounds or cairns are the commonest of these and often preserve environmental evidence in their buried soils. It is likely that some of the cairnfields also result from piecemeal clearance at this time (Johnston 2000), but Burgess (1992) extends this interpretation to the creation of many of the unenclosed settlements of the northern uplands, which are normally accompanied by field systems. He postulates a major period of colonisation, contending that there is no evidence for settlement in the adjacent lowlands.

Burgess's hypothesis is not supported by the results of new fieldwork in the Milfield Basin (Waddington 1999, chapter 7), nor is it is not clear why he should suppose that such fertile soils would have been abandoned in favour of more marginal locations. It is a fundamental premise of his argument that such sites became uninhabitable during the Later Bronze Age as a result of deteriorating conditions brought about by the eruption of the Icelandic volcano Hekla. There is much dispute about the long-term consequences of such events (Grattan and Gilbertson 1994) and it is by no means clear that areas of northern England were deserted (Young and Simmonds 1995). Suffice it to say that it is because Burgess believes that the uplands were unsuitable for sustained occupation during the Later Bronze Age that he considers the unenclosed settlements to be so early in date. To a large extent this is a circular argument.

In fact it is difficult to sustain the case. For a start, the absence of Early Bronze Age occupation in low-lying areas may be more apparent than real (Waddington 1999, chapter 7). That is because it is difficult to identify surface finds of this period anywhere in the British Isles, for pottery rarely survives and the lithic artefacts lack many diagnostic features. Occupation sites are more likely to be exposed in the course of commercial development.

There is a further problem. Whilst Burgess stresses the importance of these early settlements, the dating evidence that he quotes in his most recent paper (Burgess 1995) does not support his thesis. Of the four sites that he mentions, three have produced radiocarbon dates in the *Middle* Bronze Age – precisely the period that sees the appearance of archaeologically visible settlements in other parts of the country. The one apparent exception is his own site at Houseledge, for which there are no dates at all. The pottery may be older than the finds from the other settlements, but this has not been demonstrated on any objective basis, and the excavation remains unpublished after more than twenty years. Until there is a much sounder basis for dating the unenclosed settlements to the *Early* Bronze Age there seems little reason to suppose that the majority were significantly older than the Deverel-Rimbury complex in the south. If so, there need be no disagreement between the sequence suggested by pollen analysis and the results of survey and excavation.

One effect of lowering the dates of the unenclosed settlements would be to emphasise how slowly the high ground might have been settled on a lasting basis. This is more consistent with the environmental evidence from northern England which, in common with that from other

areas, does not seem to show much evidence for intensive or widespread farming before the middle of the Bronze Age (Mercer and Tipping 1994). By implication this might also suggest a context for the cairnfields in the earlier stages of the agricultural colonisation of these areas. What is needed now is the publication of outstanding work. including the former Royal Commission's surveys in the Cheviots, and a much more intensive programme of radiocarbon dating aimed at measuring the extent and history of occupation in variety of different areas. Without that work, the results of any field survey will remain in a chronological vacuum.

I have considered the role of pollen analysis in some detail, for this is a luxury that not all archaeologists enjoy. It also introduces my other main theme, for one implication of these arguments is that the importance of mobility may have been seriously underestimated. There need not have been the stark contrasts between the Mesolithic and Neolithic periods that many writers once supposed, and the onset of large-scale agriculture in the uplands need not have taken place any sooner in the north than similar processes in southern England. Until the later part of the Early Bronze Age there is little to suggest a stable pattern of settlement in many parts of Britain.

But this is to take too limited a view of mobility, for it merely emphasises what is absent. Are there any ways in which a more positive approach to this question might improve our understanding? Two topics are especially important here: the creation and operation of monuments, and the development of long-distance exchange. These may also have something to tell us about the distinctive character of northern prehistory.

One indication of the extent of mobility is the use of lithic raw materials, but this has only been studied systematically for the Mesolithic period. After that time, discussion is virtually limited to the movement of stone axeheads. This does not do justice to the complexity of the situation. Just as work at Great Langdale over a decade ago showed that the scale and character of stone working had changed during the use of the quarries (Bradley and Edmonds 1993), the evidence from lithic scatters on the Shap limestone (Cherry and Cherry 1987), and to a lesser extent in the Yorkshire Dales (Cherry 1998), seems to indicate major changes in the selection of other raw materials. For example, the proportion of east coast flint crossing the Pennines may have changed during the Neolithic period. So far such work has been concentrated in the north-west, but Durden's research close to Flamborough Head has shed considerable light on the organisation of artefact production on the North Sea coast. Here she has identified a series of sites overlooking the modern shoreline where flint artefacts were tested and prepared before they were taken inland to settlements on the Yorkshire Wolds, The latter sites include specialised workshops where some of the cores were turned into knives and arrowheads (Durden 1995). Although we know that these finished artefacts were distributed over a wider area, we have less information about the movement of raw materials. On Ilkley Moor, however, two concentrations of lithic artefacts, associated with Grooved Ware, seem to originate from a similar source, even though this is located some 90 km away (Edwards and Bradley 1999). This collection includes a number of cores which are exactly like those found on the coastline.

It is easier to interpret the movement of finely finished artefacts than that of raw materials, yet both processes involve a greater degree of long-distance interaction than we often consider in studies of northern prehistory. Such questions have been the province of lithic analysts for too long, and could shed important light on the changing intensity of contacts between communities on the North Sea coast and those nearer to the Irish Sea. Again it possible to propose some specific questions for research: to what extent was the eastward movement of Langdale tuff matched by the westward movement of chalk flint? How far did the movement of both these materials change during the Late Neolithic period? And were such processes embedded in more basic patterns of movement between upland and lowland that might have been practised since the Mesolithic period?

If northern England is fortunate in providing a detailed pollen record, another feature that it enjoys is a rich variety of surface artefacts, many of which are in areas of ancient grassland. Again the credit for locating many of these goes to the Cherry family. If the number of lithic artefacts is drastically reduced because so many have been recovered from molehills, the importance of these discoveries is that few of them come from areas in which pottery is destroyed by the plough. This means that, even in the absence of chronologically sensitive forms such as arrowheads, we can establish an outline sequence for these finds (Cherry and Cherry 1987; Cherry 1998). I suggest that such discoveries should be investigated on a larger scale, for some of the findspots provide an opportunity of calibrating the movement of raw materials across the country as a whole and even of relating it to a well-researched ceramic sequence. This is perhaps a rare case in which the investigation of lithic scatters might extend beyond the techniques of landscape archaeology and provide a means of researching the long-distance links established between different parts of northern England. We need to 'section' the country from east to west, combining surface collection with sample excavation, ceramic studies and radiocarbon dating.

That is not suggest that such processes can be divorced from an understanding of the social background to these exchanges. Here there is further scope for creative fieldwork. We still have no idea how the creation and operation of major monuments was related to the movement of people about the landscape. Still less is it possible to show whether these sites played a role in structuring these patterns of exchange. That is because so few have been investigated by modern fieldwork. This has serious consequences.

In the first place we cannot tell how closely the monuments were related to the process of artefact production. Roger Mercer, working in Cornwall, was able to suggest a connection between the production of greenstone axes and the creation of the walled enclosure at Carn Brea (1981, 187-98). The same seems possible in Cumbria, where Fell and Davies argue that a number of stone axes originated on Carrock Fell, for just above the source in question there is a massive hillfort with an interrupted wall which in my opinion looks very like those found at Neolithic sites in south-west England (Fell and Davies 1988, 74; Collingwood 1938); Oswald, Dyer and Barber take a different view (2001, 88 and 159). Mobility is important again here. Carrock Fell is 650 m high and, like the axe quarries at Great Langdale, it is most unlikely to have been visited in winter. In the latter case, we can even show that axes were prepared at the stone source but were polished at more hospitable locations in the lowlands (Bradley and Edmonds 1993). Some of those areas are close to the positions of monuments. The same pattern is found in east Yorkshire, where polished knives and arrowheads were made from coastal flint on sites close to the Rudston cursus complex (Durden 1995).

Such equations may be tempting, but at present they fail to convince. There are problems of two kinds to consider: the chronology of these monuments is quite inadequate; and in any case we do not understand how closely they were articulated with the wider pattern of settlement. I referred to Rudston, but the cursuses in northern England are effectively undated, although slightly more is known about examples in Scotland (Brophy 1999). I mentioned Carrock Fell, but there is little agreement whether causewayed enclosures or their equivalents were a general feature of the landscape. Even where candidates exists, as they do at Long Meg or Duggleby Howe, they lack any dating evidence (Oswald, Dyer and Barber 2001). The large henge monuments pose exactly the same problems. They may be as extensive as well-dated examples further to the south, but they often take a quite different form; and in any case it might be just as appropriate to compare them with sites north of the border where earthworks of this kind may be significantly earlier in date (Harding and Lee 1987). Some light on all these questions comes from Jan Harding's work in the Thornborough complex (Harding 2000), but there is much still to do. There is also the question of stone circles. It is often claimed that the largest of these are the counterparts of major henge monuments, with all this implies for their chronology (Burl 1988), but whilst I am inclined to support this argument, there is no convincing field evidence for or against the proposition. It is unfortunate that the excavation planned at Castlerigg in the 1980s failed to win wide enough support. In the absence of an agreed chronology, it is hardly surprising that it is so difficult to integrate these monuments into any real understanding of exchange.

The obvious answer to the problems of chronology would be a programme of small scale excavation similar to Anthony Harding's work in Northumberland (Harding 1981) and Jan Harding's research in North Yorkshire (Harding 2000). We could also approach a second, related question. Were the main groups of monuments really the central points in the settled landscape, where they might have been built and maintained by a resident population? This is certainly the premise of the territorial schemes proposed by Burl (1988) and by Barnatt (1989), but there is another possibility. Perhaps, rather like markets, they were located at the most accessible points for a wider audience. That is a question that could be studied by systematic fieldwalking, but if it is to provide useful results, such an undertaking must not be confined to the vicinity of the largest earthworks, as happened so often in Wessex. We need to discover whether the intensity of human activity around these sites was any greater than it was in other areas of the landscape. We also have to decide whether the same range of activities is evidenced in monument complexes and in regions where structures of the same kind are absent. Who visited and used these sites? Were they an entirely local population? And were some of those locations set apart from the main areas of everyday activity? Some information comes from the Milfield basin and the Thornborough complex (Waddington 1999; Harding 2000). Until we know more about the situation in other areas, we cannot be sure how the henges and stone circles of northern England were integrated into the pattern of movement about the landscape.

Once again I have had to be critical of the state of knowledge in the north, and I am only too aware of the financial and practical considerations that stand between these objectives and their realisation. That does not mean that they are impossible to achieve. But that will not happen until we admit that we know less then we once seemed to know about earlier prehistoric communities in this area. We would do well to rebuild our ideas from the foundations up, for it would be worse to borrow fully formed interpretations from prehistorians working in the south, where the archaeological record is very different and the opportunities of studying it are greater. I have suggested some priorities – some 'matters arising'. There could be many more, for every agenda that starts with 'matters arising' concludes with 'any other business'.

Section 2: Later Prehistory

Introduction

*Richard Hingley**

There has been a perception in the past that later prehistoric remains in the north of England are scarce and of low quality. This session allowed a consideration of whether Northern England really is poor in contrast to the neighbouring areas of Midland England and Scotland. In both Midland England and Scotland there are particular areas for which the later prehistoric archaeology is comparatively well known (for instance the Western Isles of Scotland and the Nene Valley of the English Midlands) but very restricted information exists for large parts of both. The papers in this session suggest that the later prehistoric archaeology of some areas of Northern England is beginning to be comparatively well known; for instance, parts of the north-east. The information that has been collected for the north-east also indicates that any suggestions in the past that the northern Iron Age was poor related to lack of information, or to intellectual bias (see Bevan 1999), rather than to the nature of the archaeological evidence itself. Information for the later prehistory of the north-west of England, however, remains very incomplete and a major effort is required before any comprehensive understanding of this area will exist.

Two of the papers in this section – those of Welfare and Haselgrove – focus on the later prehistoric period, while Huntley's paper is about environmental evidence from the Mesolithic to the Roman periods. My introductory comments will relate to later prehistory, with a brief excursus into the Roman Iron Age.

The papers raised a number of issues which are of broad relevance. Of these, two are of particular significance:
• the need for more explicit research strategies, and
• the potential of regional research frameworks.
In relation to the requirement for explicit research strategies, Jacqueline Huntley stresses their vital importance with regard to environmental archaeology. This derives from the 'market place'-driven nature of modern excavation work. Her paper presents a research framework for environmental archaeology (bone, pollen and cereal analysis) in Northern England. The

main limitation affecting Huntley's account is the scarcity of excavation and connected environmental analysis in Cumbria. Her question toward the end of the paper:
'..what was going on in the west of the region for any of the periods discussed ...?'
raises the problem of the comparison of the environmental record for the north-west with that for the north-east.

Bob Bewley's suggestion (1994) that Stuart Piggott's 'footloose Celtic Cowboy' economy is valid for the later prehistoric period in Cumbria appears startling in view of the increasing evidence for arable agriculture across most areas of Northern Britain during the Iron Age. If it was possible to grow crops at this time on the West Coast of Scotland, an area in which the environment is wetter and harsher than Cumbria, surely arable was also important to later prehistoric communities in the Solway Plain? McCarthy (1995) has stressed that Bewley's work fails to draw upon valuable research which has been carried out since 1984, work that indicates the importance of arable agriculture in later prehistoric Cumbria. One hopes that this recent research will soon begin to address the limitations of our understanding of the north-west of England and allow Huntley's research frameworks to be extended and supplemented.

The regional potential of the research framework outlined by Huntley emerges from her summary of the research undertaken by van der Veen (1992). This project demonstrated differing cultivation regimes during later prehistory to the north and south of the River Tyne. The potential of the regional approach is also evident, to stray slightly outside my specific area of concern, from Huntley's account of the contrast between the differing dates at which oats became available in North Yorkshire and in Tyneside.

Humphrey Welfare is also aware of the value of explicit research strategies in his analysis of later prehistoric settlement patterns of the uplands. His problem in providing such a framework appears to be a combination of the structural complexity of the surviving earthwork evidence and the lack of detailed excavation

*Address: Department of Archaeology, University of Durham, South Road, Durham, DH1 3LE

work. The problems of establishing a chronology of site development to replace the discredited (or partly discredited) Hownam sequence derives from the lack of excavation and the scarcity of available radiocarbon dates. It is ironic that the uplands have the best surviving archaeological evidence but may also have been fairly marginal in economic terms for much of later prehistory. The lowlands, with poorer survival, appear to have been more densely settled and may be more fundamental to our understanding of later prehistoric society.

Some regional contrasts do emerge from Welfare's account and his recommendation that local landscape-based surveys are required is sound. One major issue which must be addressed is how such work is to be funded, as developer funding will presumably require that most of the evaluation and excavation continues to occur in the lowlands where the major threats to the archaeological sites exist. As Welfare stresses, the next cycle of work in the uplands may need to be research led.

Colin Haselgrove's review is a far-ranging and creative summary which stresses the originality and importance of the evidence for later prehistory in Northern England. He begins his survey of the lowland evidence by attacking the simplistic upland/lowland division. Evidently patterns of transhumance and inter-site exchange will often have meant that upland and lowland formed part of a single economic system. Haselgrove also draws attention to the chronological problems presented by his material. There are over 100 radiocarbon dates available to help to date later prehistoric settlement in the north, but these contrast dramatically with the 70 dates from the hillfort of Danebury (Hampshire) and the 60+ dates from the recently excavated Bronze Age/Iron Age hut circle settlement at Lairg (Sutherland, Highland). The scarcity of radiocarbon dates demonstrates the limitations of the evidence for site form and sequence in Northern England.

Nevertheless, Haselgrove builds a chronological and regional account of the later prehistory of the lowlands. This account is particularly helpful in stressing the complexity of later prehistoric society. Gone are the over-simplistic interpretations of site morphology and sequence. The excavated sites pass through complex changes in form, as at Thorpe Thewles, West Brandon and Dod Law West. There appears to be a contradiction in this account, however, as the alternative model which is based on the radiocarbon dating of site sequence does not appear to be very much more complex than the Hownam sequence itself (open settlements replaced by palisaded settlements, replaced by univallate enclosures replaced by multivallate enclosures). Some of the settlement evidence for northern Britain actually suggests that all sites/regions do not show the same simple sequence of change. For instance, the contrast between the enclosure dominated landscape of East Lothian and the open settlement landscapes of Fife, to either side of the Firth of Forth (Macinnes 1982) cannot easily be explained in terms of a simple sequence from open settlements to enclosed settlements of various forms. It is possible that Haselgrove's model is regionally specific to the areas in which most of the recent excavation has taken place and perhaps we should conceive of different regions as having differing settlement histories which will be uncovered during future research (see, for instance, Armit 1999).

Haselgrove's reference to Gill Ferrell's important research (1995) indicates the recognition of difference in settlement patterns that mirror van der Veen's observations about crop patterns to the north and south of the Tyne. Additional research should result in more complex regionally based interpretations of site form and development. Regional differences at various levels of scale are likely to emerge from the more detailed understanding of the settlement evidence which will result from further research.

The session, like the conference as a whole, stressed the importance of the archaeology of the north. The area has been neglected in comparison to some other areas of Britain in the past, but a fuller understanding is beginning to emerge. However, the clearest regional contrast to emerge in this session is the scarcity of information for the later prehistory of Cumbria (and Lancashire). This scarcity may, in itself, suggest that contrasts exist between the east and west of northern England; why else is the later prehistory of Cumbria and Lancashire so difficult to locate? However, any more detailed account of contrast between the east and west requires the collection of more information for the whole of the north, particularly the north-west.

The papers in this session of the Northern Archaeology conference should assist with the preparation of the research agenda for future work. The recent development by English Heritage and others of a programme of research agendas for the various regions of Britain should help to provide further insight into the potential and limitations of current knowledge in northern England. It will, however, be necessary to find new sources of funding if we are to undertake some of the more imaginative work that these three authors consider to be important.

Chapter 6: The Later Bronze Age and the Iron Age in the Lowlands

*Colin Haselgrove**

Introduction

This paper reviews our current understanding of later prehistoric settlement and society in the lowland areas of northern England and seeks to identify particular topics requiring more work. I should however begin by stressing that drawing too rigid a distinction between lowland and upland areas is bound to be unsatisfactory. Both are part of the same wider picture of settlement and land use, and the most appropriate classification often depends purely on the local context. For this survey, I have taken the 183m

contour as the divide. Less than half the region falls into the category of lowland thus defined, essentially the Solway Plain and Eden Valley in Cumbria, and the coastal land east of the Pennines, from the Tees in the south to the Tweed in the north (Fig 6.1). Only a small proportion of this area is under 60m OD, principally around the larger river estuaries; much of the rest of this landscape is of undulating character. The chronological focus is from *c* 1300-1250 cal. BC – the approximate starting date of the later Bronze Age in metalworking terms – to the

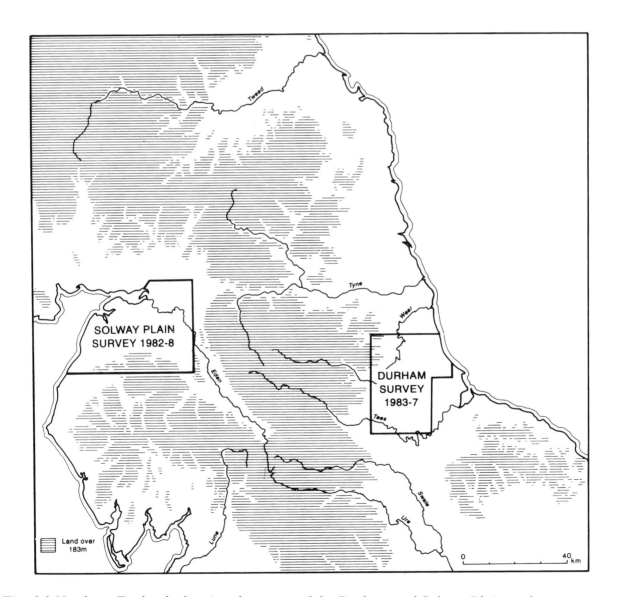

Fig. 6.1 Northern England, showing the extent of the Durham and Solway Plain study areas

*Address: Department of Archaeology, University of Durham, South Road, Durham, DH1 3LE

start of permanent Roman military occupation in AD 72-73, although the majority of known sites belong to the later part of this period. I have included sites on the North Yorkshire bank of the river Tees in this review, as this is where my own work is currently focused.

A number of other general points should perhaps be made at the outset. First, even a region as large as northern England should never be viewed in isolation. Many local developments can only be fully comprehended in a much wider spatial and temporal context. The changing pattern of metalwork deposition during later prehistory is a good example (Bradley 1990), while at certain times northern England evidently formed part of much larger cultural provinces with its neighbours to north or south. At others periods, however, there seem to be genuine differences between it and neighbouring regions. During later prehistory, these include the absence, south of the Cheviots, of souterrains and brochs, or of Scottish style ring-ditch houses and platform settlements, apart from sporadic examples like the ring-ditch houses at High Knowes A (Jobey and Tait 1966) and the Millfieldhill souterrain (Jobey 1975). Given the mountainous topography of large areas of northern England, it would be surprising if there were not significant internal cultural and geographical divisions as well, whilst certain changes during later prehistory evidently affected some parts of the region more than others.

A second issue relates to the idea of lowland and upland as landscapes of very different archaeological potential. Today, upland areas with their excellent preservation of earthwork sites are widely looked on as *zones of survival*, whereas lowland areas with their high incidence of urban expansion, extractive industry and intensive agriculture are seen as *zones of destruction*, where sites survive only as battered cropmarks. As a result, they are frequently all but written off. It is true that many of the most spectacular advances in our knowledge since 1976 have come in the uplands, for instance Topping's (1989a, 1989b) demonstration of the later prehistoric context of cord-rig cultivation in the Cheviots. Nevertheless everything is relative, and informed understanding of the past requires a knowledge of both zones. There were probably seasonal movements and other close links between upland and lowland at most periods in prehistory, while the concept of marginality itself needs to be used with care (Young and Simmonds 1995). Much of the surviving upland

evidence relates to specific strategies of subsistence and land use, while population levels were almost certainly higher in the more fertile lowlands throughout later prehistory, although the heavier, damper soils were probably not exploited to their full potential before the later first millennium BC. It is essential therefore that we seek to maintain a proper balance between the two, both in our conservation strategies and in conducting archaeological research.

This links into a third issue: the outmoded view of the later prehistoric population of northern England as culturally impoverished and conservative, inhabiting an environment largely unsuited to cereal agriculture. This perception is of course embedded in Fox's (1932) famous dichotomy between the Lowland and Highland zones of Britain, which now needs to be extensively qualified. Although almost all of northern England falls technically within the Highland zone, localized climatic and environmental variations are likely in practice to have presented more significant constraints on agricultural potential in lowlands and uplands alike (Higham 1987). In many respects, a more useful general distinction is that between east and west. The west suffers a significantly damper climate, while the east has warmer growing conditions to support cereal cultivation, but is also at more risk of drought (Huntley and Stallibrass 1995). During the later Bronze Age, this ensured that the effects of the worsening climate were differentially experienced east and west of the Pennines, as shown by the more rapid growth of peat in the north-west (Lamb 1981). Nowadays, this affects our recovery of archaeological evidence – more lowland is under pasture west of the Pennines, making site discovery harder, while drought can help cropmark formation in the east.

The blanket view of the north as a conservative backwater in later prehistory is just as ill-founded. Between the tenth and eighth centuries BC, northern England was firmly in the mainstream of cultural and technological innovation, as shown by the objects from Ewart Park and Heathery Burn, and isolated finds like the Irish-British sheet bronze bucket uncovered at Ravenstonedale, Westmorland, in 1774 (Turnbull 1995). At the start of the first millennium AD, the Tees valley was at the forefront of agricultural innovation in Britain, as we shall see below. With regard to the apparent paucity of later prehistoric material in northern England, we need only recall an old adage: absence of evidence is not the same as evidence of absence. Certainly, in many cases a previous lack of evidence can now be put down to failures of archaeological technique (Haselgrove 1999). The classic example is Piggott's (1958) hypothesis that cereal agriculture was unimportant in northern England during the Iron Age. By the early 1980s, few archaeologists working in the region still believed this model, given the plentiful indirect evidence for arable farming in the form of pollen diagrams and rotary querns (eg Hayes *et al* 1980; Haselgrove 1982). But it was not until a decade later that van der Veen (1992) finally put the matter to rest by collecting abundant cereal remains from several Bronze Age and Iron Age settlements.

On other occasions, the absence of evidence is real enough, but part of a much wider pattern. The rarity of early Iron Age metalwork in northern England and the lack of Iron Age burials are good examples. At the end of the Bronze Age, hoarding and other forms of metalwork deposition ceased over virtually the whole of north-western Europe (eg Bradley 1990), while the peoples of Iron Age Britain normally disposed of their dead in ways which are archaeologically unrecoverable. In each case, the principal change is a loss of archaeological visibility; fine metalwork was still used, while the settlement evidence, if anything, suggests a rising population. The particular interest of such situations resides in the subtle regional and chronological variations which we can perceive between one area of Britain and another (eg Taylor 1993), along with any major exceptions to the rule, such as the well-known Iron Age inhumation tradition which developed in east Yorkshire in the late fifth century BC (Stead 1979).

In yet other cases, our expectations may be the real problem. As Ferrell (1992) and Young (1994a) have both noted, the lack of later prehistoric material culture may be partly due to the way we excavate settlements. Houses are targeted, rather than enclosure ditches or other areas. At Houseledge, Burgess recovered quantities of discarded pottery from the field system in front of a house (Young 1994a), while 90% of the pottery found at Doubstead came from the fill of a sunken yard, which lay partially within the excavation (Jobey 1982). The quantity of cereal remains recovered from beneath the collapsed stone ramparts at Dod Law West and Murton High Crags (van der Veen 1992) shows that the occupants of both sites were dumping waste outside the defences. Middens may well have existed outside what we take to be the settlement boundary. In the lowlands, such deposits may well have been destroyed by subsequent ploughing, but we cannot be sure since we virtually never excavate outside the enclosures. Similarly, the number of querns found in sectioning the boundaries around southern Scottish settlements implies a significant total deposited in such contexts (cf Hingley 1992).

The north of England has often been cast as virtually aceramic during the Iron Age, but as Willis (1999, 85-86) has shown, east of the Pennines at least, this is far from being the case. Fewer than 10% of excavated Iron Age sites in north-east England have failed to yield some pottery, although it is rarely present in great quantity. There was evidently an awareness of pottery, but not a habit of everyday use. Whatever the reason for this – perhaps vessels were employed only in certain restricted practices; chronological and depositional factors may be relevant too (*ibid.*) – the technological capabilities of Iron Age societies to manufacture pottery is not at issue. We need instead to rethink our expectations of what its limited presence might signify.

In other cases of apparent scarcity or absence, it is possible that the evidence already exists, but has yet to be recognized at face value. Later Bronze Age settlement is a good example (Young 1994a). Rectilinear ditched enclosures are considered to be an Iron Age cultural phenomenon, so sites like Burradon and Hartburn which have yielded hand-made, finger-tipped pottery are ascribed to this period. On the other hand, Eston Nab in Cleveland, which yielded broadly similar pottery, has been given late Bronze Age origins in keeping with the pattern displayed by similar escarpment edge forts elsewhere (Vyner 1988). Both views may be quite correct but it does underline the problem. Although over 100 radiocarbon dates are now available from 28 later prehistoric settlements in northern England (two-thirds of these are in the lowlands), the nature of the calibration curve between 800-400 cal. BC means that even when we learn to exploit radiocarbon and other dating

1. It is to be hoped that the results of the extensive programme of luminescence dating undertaken by Barnett (2000) on later prehistoric pottery from eastern England will open the door to more widespread application of this technique in northern England. Her programme found excellent agreement between the luminescence and archaeological ages on 24 known-age samples.

methods like luminescence to their full potential – as we must (Haselgrove 1999)[1] – some areas of chronological uncertainty are inevitable

The following sections will examine the respective contributions of aerial reconnaissance, surface survey, excavation, and artefact studies to our understanding of economic and cultural behaviour patterns in the lowlands. None of these approaches should be viewed in isolation and every opportunity should be taken to integrate the results with the exceptionally rich pollen data available in the region (eg Wilson 1983). There is as yet relatively little information about later prehistoric settlement in coastal and estuarine areas, or from the region's wetlands, although these areas evidently have high potential for the future, especially in the west (Huntley and Stallibrass 1995).

Aerial archaeology in northern England

Without doubt, aerial archaeology has made the single most important contribution to our knowledge of lowland settlement since 1976. Those who have been particularly active in this field of research include McCord (eg 1991) and Gates (eg 1983) in Northumberland; Harding (1979) and Selkirk (1983) in County Durham; Still and Vyner (1986) in the Tees Valley; and Higham and Jones (eg 1975) and Bewley (1994) in Cumbria.

The main impact of this work is apparent in the dense distribution of potentially pre-Roman and Roman Iron Age sites now known in areas like the Solway Plain and the Eden Valley (eg Higham 1980). In approximately 1100 km^2 of the Solway Plain, Bewley (1994) has inventoried nearly 300 sites, of which 38 are considered potentially prehistoric (excluding barrows) and another 152 are undated. Of the 113 enclosures used in his detailed study of cropmark morphology, 44 rectilinear examples and 32 curvilinear ones are very similar to types attested east of the Pennines. This compares with a total of 57 rectilinear and 10 curvilinear enclosures known in 825 km^2 of the Durham survey area (Fig 6.1). For the two types of enclosure taken together, these translate into very similar densities of 7/100 km^2 and 8/100 km^2 on either side of the Pennines. The percentage of curvilinear sites in the Solway Plain (42%) is, however, significantly higher than in the Durham lowlands (15%).

The original density of sites must be *far* higher, if we take account of the proportion of ground under crop, although not all of them will have been contemporary. In the five areas examined in detail during the Durham Survey (Haselgrove *et*

al 1988), which were located to avoid urbanized and open-casted areas, arable averages only 45%. In the Wear valley transect, where the landscape is more built over than the rest, the window available for air survey is only 30%. Even so, nine sub-rectangular enclosures are now known, representing one site for every 1.6 km^2 of arable. When *Archaeology in the North* (Clack and Gosling 1976) was compiled, only two cropmark enclosures were known in County Durham. In the Solway Plain, only 14% of the land is under arable (Huntley and Stallibrass 1995), representing an overall density of nearly two cropmark sites per km^2 of cultivated land.

The particular difficulties of the cropmark evidence have been discussed at length (eg Bewley 1994; Still *et al* 1989). Coverage has been variable, and some soils and crops are significantly less susceptible to cropmark formation than others. In the Solway Plain, Bewley (1994) was able to demonstrate that the overall aerial coverage has not been biased in terms of particular areas or soil types. Certain soils were nevertheless favoured for cropmarks, which he argues genuinely reflects past agriculture and settlement practice. It is also apparent that aerial coverage in Cumbria has been more intensive than in the heavily urbanized lowlands of Durham and southern Northumberland. As the latter areas possess similar expanses of well-drained soils *and* a potentially higher soil moisture deficit, in the right conditions they should eventually produce cropmark results as good as – if not better than – those in Cumbria, as the exceptional density of cropmarks already recorded south of the Tees shows (Still and Vyner 1986). This area has received exceptional coverage due to the presence of the Stanwick earthworks and the Roman fort and *vicus* at Piercebridge, but a long-term strategy is needed to realize the potential of other zones (Still *et al* 1989).

Much of what has been written about lowland settlement hinges on morphological comparisons between cropmarks supported by relatively few excavated examples (Young 1994a). Apart from Shadforth, where only the enclosure ditch was sampled (Haselgrove 1980), West Brandon and Coxhoe are still the only excavated rectilinear enclosures in County Durham and only 25% of each site was investigated. Morphology can be taken only so far as a guide to chronological and cultural context. Several excavated sites have turned out to be far more complex than the cropmarks suggested, notably Thorpe Thewles (Heslop 1987) and Holme House (Harding

1984). Equally, cropmarks of rectilinear ditched enclosures are much more readily recognized from the air than those produced by palisades or open settlements, while isolated features like ring ditches are often impossible to classify with any certainty. As Gates (1983) notes, over half the open settlements known in upland Northumberland show traces of a single, circular structure, and very few possess more than five. Some of the isolated circular cropmarks found in the lowlands undoubtedly represent drainage ditches of timber buildings associated with open settlements (Haselgrove 1982), as recent excavations have confirmed. At Melsonby, a pronounced circular feature revealed by geophysical survey proved to belong to a late Iron Age building forming part of a more extensive site (Fitts *et al* 1999) (Fig 6.2). The Iron Age roundhouse and cultivation plot recently excavated beneath South Shields fort (Hodgson *et al* forthcoming) can also be directly compared to many upland sites recorded by Gates (1983).

The potential of surface survey in northern England

Since 1976, surface survey has developed into an increasingly quick and effective means of compensating for some of the lacunae of aerial survey. Geophysical survey is usually regarded as a second-stage investigative technique, providing additional information about the character of known sites. However, on certain subsoils, it is proving invaluable for recognizing sites seemingly inscrutable to aerial survey. At Melsonby, the magnetometer survey was undertaken to investigate the context of the so-called Stanwick hoard of late Iron Age metalwork found there in 1843 (Fitts *et al* 1999). The work covered just under one hectare and took four people a single day. None of the network of ditches and other features revealed has ever shown up as cropmarks, although the area has been overflown on several occasions.

At nearby Scotch Corner, a five-hectare magnetometer survey which took less than a week has provided a detailed plan of an extensive complex of ditched enclosures and droveways (Casey *et al* 1995) to the north of the recently excavated late Iron Age settlement (Abramson 1995). Previously, only indistinct cropmarks had been observed. A similar complex of enclosures has been detected by geophysical survey east of the Roman fort at Greta Bridge (P J Casey, pers comm), presumably predating the civilian *vicus*. The enclosure of Iron Age type found outside High Rochester Roman fort is another example (Crow, this volume). Geophysical survey is now sufficiently rapid to be routinely used for finding

Fig. 6.2 Excavated Iron Age circular building and drainage gully at Melsonby, North Yorkshire

sites and has the extra advantage that it can be used on pasture and arable alike, although rig and furrow can impede the identification of underlying features. In northern England it is likely to be a much more effective technique for site discovery than test pitting.

Geophysical survey can also provide crucial additional data about the character and extent of sites discovered from the air, either as a preliminary to excavation, or as an alternative. Recent work at Gardener's Houses Farm, Dinnington (Biggins *et al* 1997) provides an excellent example. Aerial photographs showed a fairly typical rectilinear enclosure, with traces of a single external hut circle and possible field boundaries, but a combination of magnetometer and resistivity survey revealed the existence of several more circular buildings and rectilinear enclosures of various sizes, extending over a much larger area (*ibid.*). The traditional strategy of excavating in the interior of the known cropmark enclosure would not even begin to characterise this complex. At Ingleby Barwick (Heslop 1984), a recent geophysical survey suggests that the second phase of field system is directly associated with a Romano-British villa building (ASUD 2000).

Conventional fieldwalking has proved less useful for finding later prehistoric sites. This is partly because systematic coverage is limited to ploughed fields, although the monitoring of erosion surfaces and molehills should not be discounted as a means of finding sites under pasture. The other major problem is the friability of later prehistoric pottery (Swain 1988), unless walking is undertaken immediately after the site is first ploughed, as at Roxby (Inman *et al* 1985). Fieldwalking is therefore unlikely to be of major significance for the discovery of first millennium BC sites in northern England, unless we can first define a contemporary lithic industry, comparable to those recognized recently in East Anglia and elsewhere (eg Gardiner 1993; Young and Humphrey 1999). This is not impossible. At Dod Law West, Smith (1988-9) saw no reason why the collection of chipped flint, chert and quartz recovered in the excavations should not be associated with the later prehistoric occupation, and several other sites, including Catcote, Huckhoe, Murton High Crags and South Shields, have yielded sizeable lithic assemblages. For the late Iron Age, isolated finds of beehive querns can provide valuable indications of settlement (eg Hayes *et al* 1980; Gwilt and Heslop 1995). At Potto, in Cleveland,

one such discovery led to the recognition of a settlement with open and enclosed phases dating to the first and second centuries AD (Inman 1988).

The Durham Survey carried out by an MSC team between 1983-87 is so far the only fully published field survey (Haselgrove *et al* 1988). Five study areas covering some 250 km² of the Durham lowlands were selected for investigation, and 5% of each area was fieldwalked at 10m intervals, amounting to over 10% of the available arable land. Only three diagnostic sherds of later prehistoric pottery were found in the entire survey, although the results for Roman pottery and especially lithics were significantly better (Haselgrove and Healey 1992). In north Cleveland, where 109 fields were walked systematically in 1983-4, only two sherds of Iron Age pottery were found out of 3,416 sherds of all periods, together with a fragment of Iron Age glass bangle (Smith 1984). This contrasts with south Cleveland, where fieldwalking has led to the discovery of over 20 Roman Iron Age sites (Inman 1988). The clear lesson of the latter project is that surface survey in northern England is likely to be most valuable when carried out very intensively over a long period by experienced fieldwalkers in optimal conditions. Parts of the Cumbrian lowlands fall within the scope of the current Tyne-Solway Programme and the North-West Wetlands Survey. It remains to be seen whether these projects prove more informative about later prehistoric settlement than the Durham Survey.

Intensive surface collection has been used to help date cropmarks in the Solway Plain (eg Bewley 1986; 1993), although there are dangers of circularity. Due to its friability, the absence of later prehistoric pottery may not be significant, while pottery of Iron Age tradition continued in any case to be used in the Roman period. Similarly, the presence of Roman pottery at a given cropmark site does not necessarily date the entire occupation and may be entirely fortuitous. Ideally, surface collection on known cropmark sites should be complemented by off-site survey to assess the background frequency of material in the landscape. Ironically, the Durham Survey did not target known cropmark sites, while only a trial sample of 38 fields was walked as part of the Solway Plain project (Bewley 1986). In lowland Durham, the occurrence of Roman pottery is closely linked to known sites (Haselgrove *et al* 1988), implying that its presence on some Solway sites, but not others, is significant. In south Cleveland, a number of sites at Hutton Rudby and Stokesley have yielded locally-made pottery with quartz and igneous grits, indicating occupation in the first and second centuries AD (Inman 1988). The changeover to predominantly quartz-gritted fabrics occurred in the mid first century AD (Willis forthcoming a), opening up the possibility that some of these settlements had pre-Roman origins.

Geochemical techniques such as phosphate analysis and magnetic susceptibility can also be used to enhance our knowledge of lowland settlements, both on their own and in conjunction with excavated evidence. In Cumbria, Bewley (1986; 1992) has successfully used phosphate analysis in the investigation of several sites. At both Ewanrigg and Oughterby, high external phosphate concentrations were recorded, which could either support the idea that midden material was indeed deposited outside enclosures or relate to unenclosed phases of settlement. Similar work in Northumberland suggests that phosphate analysis can be used to increase our understanding of the internal organization of sites and even the function of individual buildings (Clogg and Ferrell 1990-1). The Roman Iron Age settlement at Woolaw displays an elevated phosphate concentration over the whole site, with a further increase in its southern half, between the entrances and the central building, which are themselves highlighted as positive residuals.

Later prehistoric settlement in Cumbria

Knowledge of later prehistoric settlement in the lowlands obtained through modern excavation is decidedly uneven between west and east. Although the pollen evidence (eg Turner 1981; Wells 1991) and other factors such as the distribution of late Bronze Age metalwork – which unlike the middle Bronze Age is noticeably confined to the Cumbrian lowlands (Annable 1987) – indicate that the Eden valley, Furness and the Solway plain were intensively settled in later prehistory, excavated settlement evidence is still lacking, as it is in Lancashire. As Richard Bradley observed at the conference, the archaeological invisibility of the Iron Age in these counties is reminiscent in many ways of Ireland (cf Raftery 1994) and implies that the majority of later prehistoric settlements may have been open. In south Cumbria, Kirkhead Cave has yielded pottery ascribed to the later Bronze Age (Gilks 1987), while at Skelmore Heads, near

Ulverston, a palisade was succeeded by a dump rampart (Powell 1963). The excavator rejected the idea that possible postholes at the front and rear of the bank belonged to a timber-framed box-rampart. Crannogs could well turn out to be a feature of the later prehistoric settlement pattern in the Lake District (Welfare, this volume).

In north Cumbria, Higham and Bewley have sampled a number of 'native' settlements, usually on a small scale (Fig 6.3). At Dobcross Hall West, the outer enclosure is interpreted as pre-Roman, largely on the basis of its size, while the inner compound is considered to be a Roman farmstead (Higham 1981). This sequence recalls Burradon and Hartburn in Northumberland (Jobey 1970; 1973), where smaller homesteads seem to have been established within pre-existing enclosures, possibly after a break in occupation (Haselgrove 1982). In the Eden Valley, the enclosed settlement and associated field system at Yanwath Wood may not have been occupied wholly within the early Roman period (Higham 1983). The sites sampled by Bewley yielded a diverse range of dates. The Ewanrigg excavations uncovered late second millennium BC occupation, as well as confirming a later Roman date for the main enclosure (Bewley 1992; Blake 1960). No Roman material was found at Plasketlands, but an arrangement of post-pits outside the enclosure yielded three Neolithic radiocarbon dates (Bewley 1993). Only at Swarthy Hill did material from the inner ditch produce a radiocarbon date in the mid first millennium BC (Bewley 1992). A major Bronze Age settlement has recently been discovered at Crosby-on-Eden near a former course of the river (Huntley and Stallibrass 1995) and other Bronze Age remains are reported from Botcherby Nurseries, near Carlisle, on a hilltop which overlooks the confluence of the Eden and the Petteril (Barkle 1998).

The enclosures at Boustead Hill and Oughterby were both Roman (Bewley 1986), mirroring Blake's (1960) experiences at Jacob's Gill and Wolsty Hall, and those of Higham and Jones (1983) at Crossfield Farm and Silloth Farm. Of twelve 'native' settlements sampled in all, nine have thus proved to be Roman. Only one enclosure, the cliff-edge site at Swarthy Hill, is positively dated to the later prehistoric period, although at two others (Plasketlands and Dobcross Hall) the excavated ditch sections were barren of finds, which makes a pre-Roman date not unlikely. The later Bronze Age occupation at Ewanrigg was apparently unenclosed. On

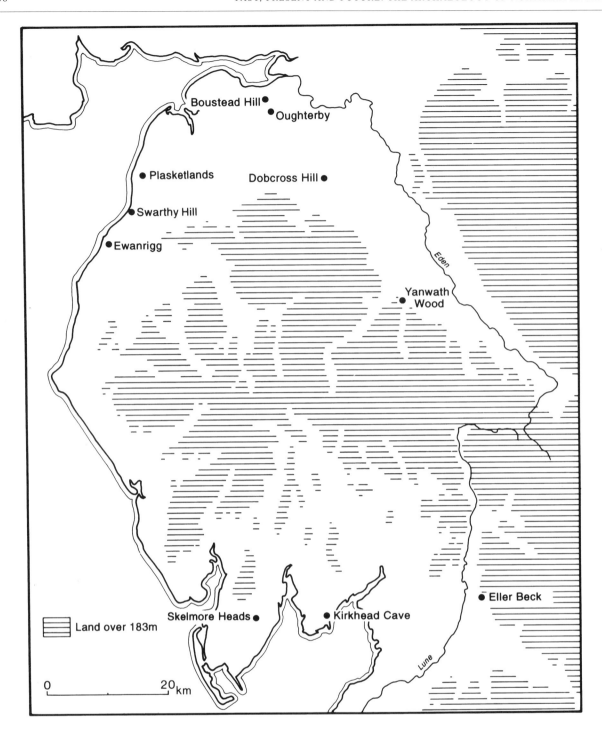

Fig. 6.3 Excavated later prehistoric and Roman Iron Age settlements in lowland Cumbria

balance, the limited evidence available for low-land Cumbria suggests that enclosed sites were predominantly – but not exclusively – a feature of the Roman landscape, making later prehis-toric settlements difficult to detect unless – as at Ewanrigg – the location was later reoccupied.

Recent excavations at Scotby Road, Durranhill, just to the east of Carlisle, have how-ever uncovered the remains of two partly super-imposed palisaded enclosures, one ovoid, the other an irregular square, both apparently with associated internal features (Hirst 1998); until

radiocarbon dates are obtained, the exact period of occupation is uncertain, but while some of the pottery resembles food vessels or collared urns, the other fabrics are strongly reminiscent of Iron Age wares found in north-east England, sug-gesting that at least one of the two enclosures dates to that period. Small palisaded enclosures, if widespread, would be as difficult to detect from the air as unenclosed sites. A third phase at Scotby Road is represented by a ditch thought to be a field boundary or another enclosure, and attributed to the Roman period on the basis of pottery and a quern found in the fill (*ibid.*).

It is not improbable that other Roman sites in north-west England succeed earlier phases of occupation. Eller Beck Site C, in the Lune Valley (Lowndes 1964), is a good example. Although the settlement and field system is normally dated to the Roman period, none of the pottery from the small-scale excavation was securely stratified. As Marriott (1991, 9) notes, there is more than one phase of construction and the site could be re-interpreted as an Iron Age settlement with subsequent Roman occupation. Alternatively, the Roman pottery could relate to the use of the field system, after the settlement was abandoned. Equally, while some of the Eller Beck sites are probably more recent (Lowndes 1963), the overall density of remains suggests settlement over a long period. The enigmatic curvilinear enclosure on Castle Hill, with its external bank, has counterparts east of the Pennines, where they are normally given an Iron Age date.

Marriott's analysis of the Lune Valley data provides several insights into the possible character of later prehistoric and Roman Iron Age settlement in Cumbria. The surviving earthworks include rectangular, sub-rectangular and curvilinear enclosures, and also unenclosed hut circles (Marriott 1991), most of which are below 240 m (88%). Generally, the curvilinear enclosures are smaller and occur at higher altitude than rectilinear ones; as on the Solway Plain, they are also more prominent in the overall settlement pattern. By and large, open sites occur at lower altitudes than enclosures (*ibid.*), which might support the idea that they predominated in the lowlands. The only indication of major changes during the late Iron Age like those in north-east England (Haselgrove 1984) comes from pollen diagrams, although the undated site at Ewe Close (Collingwood 1908) could be interpreted as an Iron Age rectilinear settlement which subsequently expanded into an open settlement complex, as happened at Thorpe Thewles (Heslop 1987). However, until more extensive excavations have taken place on later prehistoric settlements in Cumbria, we can do little more than speculate.

Later prehistoric settlement in north-east England

By comparison, our knowledge of lowland settlement east of the Pennines has developed substantially since 1976. Jobey's pioneering work at Burradon, Hartburn, Huckhoe, Marden and West Brandon has been followed up by further excavation in Northumberland (Fig 6.4) – at Chester House (Holbrook 1988), Doubstead (Jobey 1982), Dod Law (Smith 1988-9), Murton High Crags (Jobey and Jobey 1987) – and especially south of the Tyne – at Coxhoe in County Durham (Haselgrove and Allon 1982); at Catcote (Long 1988; Vyner and Daniels 1989); Eston Nab (Vyner 1988); Ingleby Barwick (Heslop 1984) and Thorpe Thewles (Heslop 1987) in Cleveland; and at Melsonby (Fitts et al. 1999), Rock Castle (Fitts *et al* 1994), Scotch Corner (Abramson 1995), and Stanwick (Haselgrove *et al* 1990) in the Tees valley. Few areas of Britain boast a comparable record of publication, although some important older excavations do remain unpublished, notably Fenton Hill and Houseledge (Burgess 1984).

The nature of the later prehistoric settlement pattern has been discussed in detail, both by Jobey in his excavation reports, and by subsequent authors (eg Annable 1987; Burgess 1984; Ferrell 1992; Haselgrove 1982; 1999; Higham 1986). In general terms, north-east England evidently experienced the same two major periods of transition in later prehistory as other parts of Britain. The first of these was during the middle Bronze Age (*c* 1500-1200 BC), when the communal ceremonial sites and burial monuments which had hitherto dominated the archaeological record disappeared (Barrett *et al* 1991). A very different cultural tradition took their place, in which semi-permanent farming settlements and their cultivation plots became a prominent feature of the archaeological record, and communal effort focused increasingly on control and organization of the landscape. The second transformation occurred in the late Iron Age, when the southern part of the region at least underwent a further series of changes, some of them probably linked to rising population (Haselgrove 1984). These included agricultural intensification and the colonization of heavier, less well-drained claylands, increased interregional exchange, and more overt signs of social and political hierarchy, epitomized by the development of the massive fortified site at Stanwick.

Between these two chronological horizons, a diversity of settlement traditions evidently coexisted, including palisaded settlements, ditched enclosures and unenclosed settlements, whose specific chronology will be considered below. As Annable (1987) has indicated, the terminology used to discuss these sites is often not

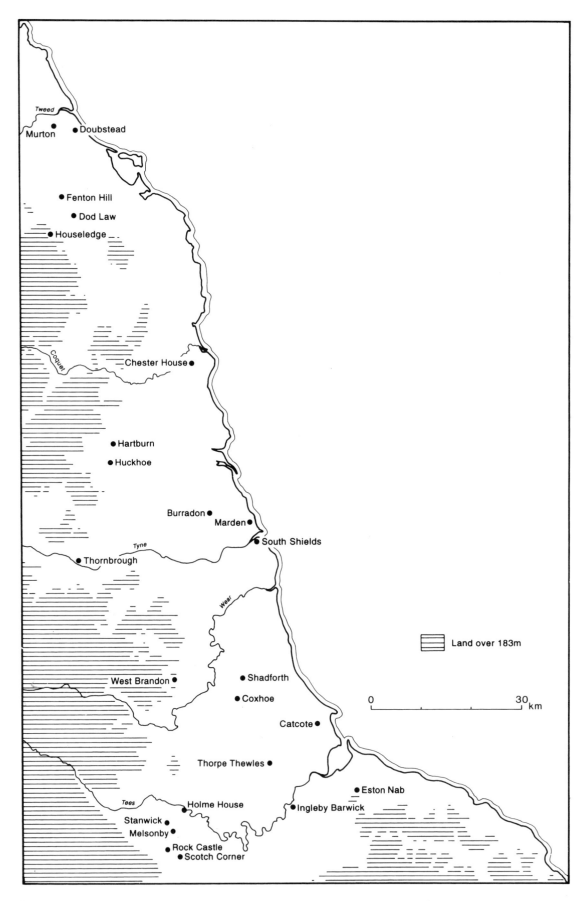

Fig. 6.4 Excavated later prehistoric settlements in lowland north-east England

particularly helpful. Many settlements in fact passed through a range of states, both open and enclosed, as at West Brandon (Jobey 1962) and Rock Castle (Fitts *et al* 1994). At both places, unenclosed sites were succeeded first by palisaded enclosures and then by sub-rectangular ditched enclosures of similar extent. At Dod Law West, the embanked palisade of Phase 1 was replaced by a stone-retained rampart, which was itself surmounted by a palisade (Smith 1988-9). So-called open settlements like Thorpe Thewles which developed in the Tees Valley during the late Iron Age are actually aggregates of smaller enclosures and compounds, quite different in character from simple hut clusters like Roxby on the adjacent uplands. We habitually group together the ubiquitous rectilinear ditched enclosures without any real thought as to their original appearance. Yet some of them were only ever enclosed by small external banks or medial ditches, while others evidently had very substantial ditches and internal banks, which have subsequently been completely levelled, like Caesar's Camp, Heathrow (Grimes and Close-Brooks 1993). It makes little sense to distinguish such sites from surviving earthwork enclosures which happen to be on hills, calling one group 'homesteads' and the other 'hillforts'.

A more relevant distinction is that between enclosures occupied by a single household, and those which contained larger communities (cf Hingley 1992). Lowland rectilinear enclosures actually fall into three distinct size ranges, comprising sites less than 0.2 ha in extent; a majority between 0.3-0.5 ha, and rather fewer over 0.7 ha, including Burradon, Hartburn and Thorpe Thewles (Haselgrove 1982). While the smaller and medium-sized enclosures both seem to have been inhabited by single households – the difference could well be one of status or farming practice, rather than chronology – the larger sites were evidently inhabited by larger residential groups. A similar distinction can be drawn between some curvilinear enclosures. At High Knowes, for instance, the smaller palisaded enclosure A, containing four house foundations, overlooks the slightly larger enclosure B, just over 100 m away, into which as many as sixteen house foundations are crammed (Jobey and Tait 1966). If the two sites are contemporary, a difference in status appears the only reasonable explanation. Ferrell (1997) has taken this kind of analysis further by considering the ratio of built to unbuilt space on different types of settlement and in different areas. She concludes that

significant variations exist, with curvilinear enclosures usually displaying a higher density of internal structures than rectilinear sites.

The primacy of the rectilinear enclosure in the lowlands has tended to inhibit discussion of other types of site with which it may well be contemporary. Open settlements of varying date are known throughout the region, and crannogs may perhaps have existed in formerly wet areas like the carrlands of south-east Durham. Bronze Age features have recently been found along the Seaton Carew sea front (Huntley and Stallibrass 1995), while Iron Age occupation has now been uncovered beneath several major Roman or medieval sites, including Bamburgh, Tynemouth (Jobey 1967) and South Shields (Hodgson *et al* forthcoming), and Dunstanburgh has produced late Iron Age metalwork (MacGregor 1976). Although no trace of prehistoric defences has so far been found at any of these sites, it is quite conceivable that several of the medieval castles of the region made use of existing earthworks. This certainly happened elsewhere, as at Barwick-in-Elmet (Ramm 1980), Dover, and Thetford. Durham, where early samian has been found, is another possible candidate.

Careful re-examination of surviving earthwork castles throughout northern England should be high on the agenda for future research, while the discovery of late Bronze Age occupation beneath Edinburgh Castle (Driscoll and Yeoman 1997) shows that development at such sites should be preceded by archaeological investigation. If larger fortified sites did exist in the lowlands during the Iron Age, they need not have been major centres of population but may instead have served as occasional refuges and ceremonial centres, if the fort at Eston Nab (Vyner 1988) and Scottish sites like Eildon Hill North (Owen 1992) and Traprain Law (Hill 1987) offer any guide. It remains to be seen whether any of the circular cropmark sites known in the North-East turn out to be late Bronze Age fortified sites comparable to those excavated at Thwing (Manby 1980) and elsewhere in eastern England.

The known rectilinear enclosures in lowland Durham tend to cluster around the 125m contour (Haselgrove 1982), presumably because this enabled their occupants to exploit both the well-watered lowlands (for cattle and cultivation) and the drier plateau soils (for grazing sheep). Pollen diagrams confirm that arable indicators are indeed more prevalent in the lowlands and pastoral indicators on the plateau (Fenton-Thomas

1992). It also seems that many of these sites were abandoned earlier than the lower-lying settlements, presumably because the latter occupied better soils. The structural longevity of many lowland sites is worth stressing: Hartburn has a minimum of twelve house replacements (Jobey 1973) and Burradon has five (Jobey 1970). The regularity with which different settlements follow each other on same location is another telling point, as is the proximity of many enclosure cropmarks to Medieval farms (B. Vyner, *pers comm*). Although this need not imply continuous occupation, it can be contrasted with the uplands, where the density of sites might imply that many of them were comparatively short-lived. In some lowland areas, definite pairs or groups of enclosures seem to occur, like those on Cockfield Fell (Roberts 1975). Investigation of the chronology and social relations of one of these 'neighbourhood groups' (Haselgrove 1999) is an obvious priority for the future.

A significant number of rectilinear enclosures found from the air appear to be associated with linear boundaries or trackways. At Rock Castle, for example, the ditched enclosure overlies an earlier ditch on the same alignment, but seems to be integrated with two other boundaries, one of which may be a redefinition of the first (Fitts *et al* 1994, fig 2). At Manfield, North Yorkshire, two rectilinear enclosures are attached to linear features over 900 m apart which run parallel to one another. Possible earlier land divisions have been detected at many other excavated Iron Age sites (eg Heslop 1987; Haselgrove *et al* 1990). This implies that we would be wrong to think of enclosed sites as pioneer settlements established in a thinly-populated and heavily-wooded territory; instead, they probably formed part of a well-ordered and largely open landscape, of which at present we have only limited knowledge. From work elsewhere (eg Williamson 1987), it is even possible that elements of the pre-Roman landscape survive fossilized in the pattern of medieval land divisions. Trying to uncover this organization and establish how different Iron Age settlement types fit within the overall pattern of landscape development is among the more difficult challenges facing us in coming decades.

Over 60 radiocarbon dates are now available for lowland settlements in north-east England, most of them obtained as part of or following on from van der Veen's (1992) study of later prehistoric crop husbandry. The calibrated dates ranges show no sign of a chronological gap between unenclosed and enclosed settlements (cf Jobey 1985), while the earliest dates for the various categories do in fact reflect the structural priorities encountered on many excavated sites – first open settlements, then palisades, then univallate enclosures and finally multivallate sites (Fig 6.5). This must not, however, be allowed to deflect attention from the difficulties of arriving at a satisfactory absolute chronology, either for individual sites or for the different settlement categories. A crucial point to emerge from van der Veen's dating programme is that where charcoal and carbonized seeds from the same context were both dated, the former generally yielded much older dates. She attributes this discrepancy to the fact that grain and chaff are unlikely to survive reworking and transport, whereas on settlements which were occupied or re-occupied over long periods, much of the charcoal is probably residual or comes from old wood (van der Veen 1992, 62-3). In the most extreme case, two charcoal samples (GrN-15678-9) from the rectilinear enclosure at Thornborough in the north Tyne valley yielded radiocarbon dates in the first millennium BC, whereas four cereal samples (GrN-12607- 8, OxA-2130-1) gave consistent dates in the late and post-Roman Iron Age (*ibid*, 61). Grain and chaff are much less likely to be significantly older than the deposit in which they are found, although there is perhaps a greater likelihood of their being intrusive. So far, Catcote and Thorpe Thewles are the only sites in the region where the pottery has been dated by luminescence (Heslop 1987; Vyner and Daniels 1989).

Pottery and querns – the elements of material culture most commonly found on settlements – provide only limited assistance with site chronology prior to the arrival of Roman imports in the mid first century AD. There are obvious difficulties in relying on the presence or absence of Roman material, and the net effect is to pull the chronology towards the historical period. At several sites where datable Roman material appears midway through the sequence, occupation has now been shown to extend back significantly into the first millennium BC; these include the complex open settlements at Catcote – where the luminescence dates centre on 300 BC – and Stanwick, with four radiocarbon dates in the range 200 cal. BC-20 cal. AD (OxA-3377-80; one sigma). The typological dating of prehistoric pottery is often little more than guessing in the dark; discussions of one key site,

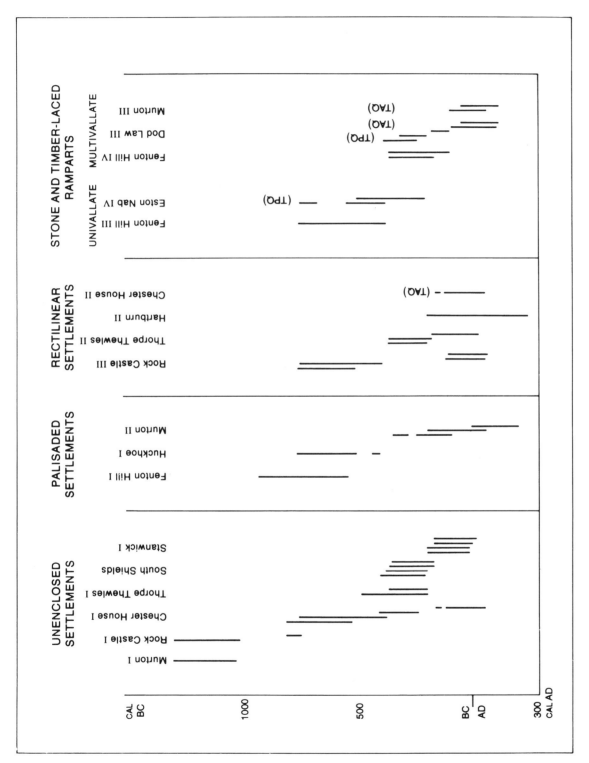

Fig. 6.5 Calibrated radiocarbon dates (one sigma) for later prehistoric settlements in lowland north-east England. Since this was compiled, seven radiocarbon dates have been obtained for the open settlement at Melsonby (period 1), spanning the period 400-1 cal. BC (source: van der Veen 1992, with additions)

Burradon, almost invariably overlook the fact that over half the pottery supposedly dating to the sixth or fifth centuries BC came from the latest context on the site, which is no earlier than the late first century AD (Jobey 1970, Pit A).

The date for the replacement of the saddle quern by rotary varieties offers little more help and is likely in any case to have been a gradual process.[2] Rotary querns were certainly in use in southern England by the fourth century BC (Brown 1991) and perhaps as early as the fifth century BC, but the date of their introduction in north-east England remains vague. At Thorpe Thewles, they may have been present when the ditched enclosure was first established, which could be as early as the fourth century BC (Heslop 1987). A beehive quern came from the bottom of the enclosure ditch, which also contained spelt dated 170 cal. BC-30 cal. AD (OxA-1733; van der Veen 1992). The occupants of Catcote and Stanwick made almost exclusive use of beehive querns, implying that by the late Iron Age they had all but replaced saddle querns in the south of the region. The only radiocarbon-dated saddle quern comes from Rock Castle, where charcoal from the same context – the primary ditch surrounding the central building – is dated 770-520 cal. BC (GrN-15669; Fitts *et al* 1994).

Sites where only saddle querns and rubbers come from contexts unequivocally associated with a particular structural phase include the curvilinear palisaded enclosures at Huckhoe and Murton High Crags; their rectilinear counterparts at West Brandon and Coxhoe; the ditched enclosures at Rock Castle and West Brandon; and the early (ditched) settlement phases at Burradon and Hartburn. The ditched enclosure at Thorpe Thewles has equal quantities of saddle and rotary querns, while rotary querns may have come into use at Hartburn when the long-lived larger enclosure was still occupied. Ditched enclosures with rotary querns only include Coxhoe, Doubstead and Marden, where a quern in the top of enclosure ditch was the only stratified find. Due to its sunken yard, Jobey (1963) dated Marden to Roman period, but the site may well be late Iron Age. Pre-Roman occupation is also stratigraphically possible at Doubstead (which also has a sunken yard) and for the homestead phases at Burradon and Hartburn. By time these sites were occupied, rotary querns were in widespread use north of the Tyne, main-

ly of bun-shaped rather than of beehive form. The same is true of the stone-walled settlements like Huckhoe and Murton.

The evidence, such as it is, implies that many palisaded settlements predate the adoption of beehive querns. The construction of the larger types of rectilinear ditched enclosure also commenced earlier than, but overlapped with, the introduction of beehive querns, both processes occurring after the mid first millennium BC. However, the smaller rectilinear homesteads found north of the Tyne do not seem to be occupied until the very end of the Iron Age. Figure 6.6 attempts to summarize the chronology of the different settlement categories based on the various strands of dating evidence, underlining the increased emphasis on enclosure during the middle Iron Age. It is perfectly possible that the occupation of stone-walled settlements like Huckhoe and Murton followed directly on from their palisaded predecessors, as Jobey (1959, 1968) suggested for the former. On the other hand, if there was a break in the occupation, the earlier boundary would still have been readily apparent centuries later. The same arguments apply to the homestead phases at Burradon and Hartburn.

A key point to emerge from recent work is the under-representation of unenclosed Iron Age settlements in the archaeological record of north-east England. More and more evidence is emerging to suggest that the ubiquitous rectilinear ditched enclosures are merely the tip of the iceberg, being much more easily detected due to their visibility from the air. The existence of what appears to be an open settlement beneath the Roman fort at South Shields and the discovery of other unenclosed sites like Melsonby by geophysical survey has already been mentioned. Other recent finds include a roundhouse at Newby (R. Fraser, pers comm); the presence of several Iron Age features underlying a later Roman enclosure complex at Newton Bewley (Platell 1999); and the re-use of an earlier ringwork for Iron Age settlement at Catterick Racecourse (Moloney *et al* forthcoming). So far this evidence is consistent in suggesting that the extensive complexes found in the Tees lowlands such as Catcote, Ingleby Barwick, Melsonby (Period 2), Scotch Corner, Stanwick (Periods 1-3) and Thorpe Thewles (Period 3) are essentially of late Iron Age date, many of them continuing to be occupied in the Roman period.

---

2. Not all archaeologists take such a position. Armit (1991), for instance, argues that the transition from saddle to rotary querns in Atlantic Scotland was a relatively short-lived process.

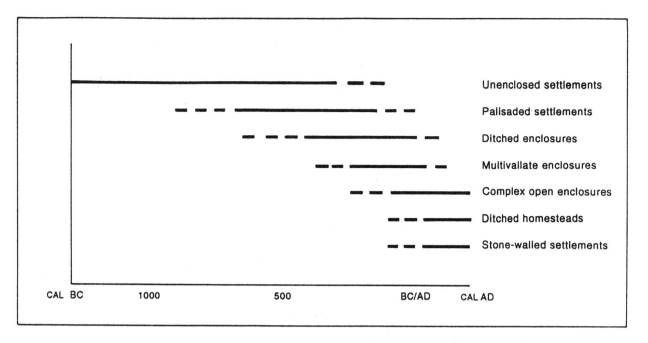

Fig. 6.6 Approximate chronological spans of various categories of later prehistoric settlement in lowland north-east England

It is however equally clear that many smaller open sites like South Shields or Melsonby, which existed in the fourth or third centuries cal. BC, may overlap the *floruit* of the rectilinear enclosures. A similar picture emerges from the nearby uplands (Inman *et al* 1985). This raises interesting questions about the social and economic relationships between different categories of open and enclosed sites. At the same time, recent excavations at Pegswood on the Northumberland coastal plain have revealed a substantial Iron Age open settlement, which was succeeded by a enclosure (J P Huntley, pers comm), reversing the pattern usually found in the Tees lowlands. The sequence at Burradon and Hartburn can be interpreted in the same way (Haselgrove 1982), a timely reminder of the differences in settlement history that can exist even within an otherwise homogenous region. As in Cumbria, developing better means of predicting and detecting different types of open (and palisaded) settlements is clearly one of the major challenges facing archaeologists working in north-east England if we are significantly to advance knowledge of the Iron Age settlement pattern (Haselgrove 1999).

Social and economic trends north and south of the Tyne

In her rank-size analysis of settlement, Ferrell (1992; 1997) detected significant differences between the lowlands south of the Tyne – where sites display a greater size range and a higher level of integration, potentially symptomatic of a more developed social hierarchy – and Northumberland, where the picture is reversed. Here sites are often isolated and lower levels of interdependence prevail. This contrast between the two regions, she suggests, reflects different kinds of social structures, one consisting of small, competitive household groups with a strong emphasis on individual ownership and status; the other focused on larger residential groups for whom communal ownership and group identity were more important. In this context, we might conceivably interpret rock motifs, like those found at Dod Law West (Beckensall 1988-9) and other Northumbrian sites, as a way of marking long-established claims to the ownership of particular site territories. Conversely, the best evidence for the association of Iron Age settlements and potentially contemporary land divisions comes from south of the Tyne.

The nature of the initial settlement of the two regions may well be relevant to these perceived differences. In the upland margins and other areas where land was plentiful, a 'contagious' pattern of expansion seems to have occurred around the initial holdings, whereas in the lowlands, competition for good quality agricultural land produced more regular settlement spacing

(Bradley 1978). Although Ferrell's data for north of the Tyne derives principally from settlements located above 200m, the majority of excavated lowland sites conform to her model of communal settlements and single unit settlements only appear in the area right at the end of the Iron Age, later than in the south of the region.

Ferrell (1997) goes on to link these contrasting social systems to the different agricultural regimes deduced by van der Veen (1992). In the Tees lowlands intensive cropping was the norm, reflected in the high labour input applied to wheat fields in particular, whereas further north the evidence suggests small-scale husbandry, soil fertility being maintained by regular soil disturbance and manuring. Van der Veen regards the low-input regimes found south of the Tyne as consistent with arable intensification during the late Iron Age,[3] whereas farming communities in Northumberland are seen as maintaining small-scale, conservative and labour-intensive husbandry practices. Settlement expansion on the coastal plain was curtailed at a noticeably lower threshold than further south (Bradley 1978). We may conclude that the Tyne itself formed an important cultural boundary. The distinction between the two zones persisted after the Roman Conquest, as shown by the proliferation of small enclosed homesteads north of the river, quite different in character from rural settlements like Catcote and Ingleby Barwick. West of the Pennines, enclosure seems to be the norm in the Roman period, both north and south of Hadrian's Wall.

Another consequence of this internal division was that innovations spread more easily through the south of the region, where communities were more highly integrated (Ferrell 1997). Further north, innovations were slower to take root, owing to the greater degree of isolation, as the archaeobotanical record shows. Despite the pollen evidence for more intensive clearance during the late Iron Age throughout northern England (Wilson 1983; Tipping 1997), emmer wheat remained dominant north of the Tyne. This compares with the Tees valley, where a group of farmsteads which includes Rock Castle and Scotch Corner were apparently amongst the earliest in Britain to experiment with bread wheat. Interestingly, both are located on poorer-quality soils on the exposed higher ground fringing the river valley, recalling the pattern in areas like the Thames Valley where newly founded farmsteads were noticeably more innovative than the long-established sites which occupied the best soils (eg Miles 1984). On current evidence, the beehive quern was also adopted earlier in the south of the region.

Brief mention may be made of the fortified settlement at Stanwick in the middle Tees valley, at 300 ha one of the largest Iron Age sites in Europe (Wheeler 1954). The 1980s excavations have traced the start of occupation back before the first century BC (Fig. 6.7), although the massive fortifications were not added until the mid first century AD (Haselgrove *et al* 1990; forthcoming),. At this period, Cartimandua, the ruler of the Brigantes who inhabited the region, seems to have made a treaty with the Romans (Tacitus, *Histories* 3, 45). The scale of the earthworks led Wheeler (1954) to view Stanwick as a focus of Brigantian resistance to Rome, whereas the nature and range of Roman imports found in the more recent excavations suggests that the site was probably the seat of Cartimandua herself. The assemblage includes an Italian obsidian cup and types of imported pottery that are rare in north-west Europe, let alone Britain (Haselgrove forthcoming). Such finds are easier to reconcile with diplomatic gifts and subsidies of the kind to which Tacitus alludes than with commercial exchange.

The character of the occupation within the complex also changed significantly in the mid first century AD, with the erection of massive timber roundhouses and a rapid build-up of deposits, while the fortifications can be interpreted as above all an expression of the exceptional prestige of the ruler who had them constructed. Until Cartimandua's rule collapsed in AD 69, Stanwick presumably served as the political and economic focus of the territory under her control. At the core of the earthwork complex is a large boggy area, which may well have provided an important ritual and ceremonial centre; given the close link which exists in most traditional societies between the enactment of religious rituals and the reproduction of political power, this – and the strategic location of the site close to important north-south and east-west routes through the region (followed by the A1 and the A66) – helps explain why Stanwick suddenly rose to prominence in the short period when the territory of the Brigantes formed a

---

3. There also signs of changes in animal husbandry in the Tees lowlands at the end of the Iron Age, with certain sites showing increases in the proportion of sheep being kept (Hambleton 1999; Haselgrove 2000). This would accord with arable expansion: sheep require less grazing than cattle and their manure can be crucial in sustaining arable production.

Fig. 6.7 Successive Iron Age circular structures associated with the pre-earthwork phases at Stanwick, North Yorkshire

buffer state on the boundaries of the area under direct Roman military control.

Artefact archaeology and contextual analysis
During the last twenty years, the potential of artefact studies in northern England has – with certain exceptions (eg Hayes *et al* 1980) – been comparatively neglected, although recently there has been a welcome revival of interest. Qualitatively, the character of the surviving artefact record has little which distinguishes it from the rest of Britain that cannot be explained simply by different regional attitudes to the manufacture, use, and discard of material culture. The only significant exception is the lack of decorated pottery assemblages comparable to those found in southern England and Atlantic Scotland in the late Bronze Age and the Iron Age. More than any other single factor, this absence of finewares has helped to create the impression of a materially impoverished society, which the prevalence of acid soils and their effect on the survival of bone and metal artefacts has done little to reverse. Ironically, as already noted above, there are very few sites which have yielded no pottery at all

(Willis 1999), while some lowland settlements have produced substantial faunal assemblages (eg Rackham 1987), although more are required if we are adequately to investigate animal husbandry practices in the region (Huntley and Stallibrass 1995; Hambleton 1999).

Finds of later Bronze Age metalwork are comparatively common in the lowlands (Fig 6.8). Prior to the Wallington phase, only three multiple finds are known, including the important late Penard hoard from Ambleside, but the volume of deposits then started to increase, as elsewhere reaching a peak during the Ewart Park phase (tenth-ninth centuries BC). In common with the rest of Britain and Europe, bronze metalwork deposition then falls off almost completely between Hallstatt C and the end of the Iron Age when the practice resumed, producing a scatter of isolated finds like the swords from Brough, Carham and Sadberge (Piggott 1950), and occasional larger deposits like the Melsonby hoard (MacGregor 1976; Hunter 1997). Both in the late Bronze Age and in the late Iron Age, much of this material (including the eponymous finds from Wallington and Ewart Park) was

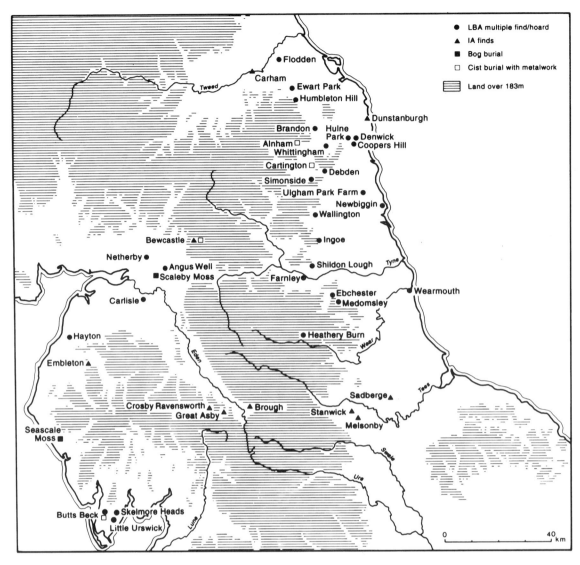

Fig. 6.8 Later prehistoric metalwork and burial finds in lowland northern England (sources: Annable 1987; MacGregor 1976, with additions)

deposited in rivers and bogs, and at other significant natural locations such as mountains and caves (notably Heathery Burn), presumably as offerings.

From the recent excavations, it would appear that that the Melsonby hoard was originally buried near a large depression running through the middle of the site, which resembles the smaller sunken yards excavated at sites like Hartburn (Jobey 1973). Although its function is obscure, the place-name 'Pond Dale' implies that area was originally wet and virtually all the items in the hoard can be paralleled in other northern votive deposits of late Iron Age date (Fitts *et al* 1999). As well as probable offerings, a number of prehistoric boats have been found in the region's rivers; these include two dugout canoes found in the Wear at Hylton (Whitford

1968), and a smaller canoe found in the Tyne at Ryton at the same level as a wheel of Iron Age type (Piggott 1949).

Occasional poorly recorded discoveries of human remains in bogs, such as those from Seascale Moss and Scaleby Moss (Turner 1988; 1989), presumably represent a further facet of the practice of deposition in wet places, comparable to the celebrated bog body found in 1983 at Lindow Moss, Cheshire (Stead *et al* 1986). While these Cumbrian finds are undated, the tradition was at its height during the first millennia BC and AD, and bog bodies of later prehistoric date should certainly be expected in the wetlands of north-west England. A small number of cist and cairn burials accompanied by metalwork are also known (Fig 6.8), mostly of late Bronze Age date, but including one of later Iron

Age date, from Alnham, Northumberland (Jobey and Tait 1966). It now seems that the Melsonby metalwork was associated with a large iron-bound wooden vessel (Fitts *et al* 1999, Fig. 26), similar to one found at Marlborough (Wiltshire), which contained a cremation burial. The burning and discolouration on many of the items from Melsonby would be compatible with their having passed through a funeral pyre, providing a possible alternative explanation for the deposit. Otherwise, apart from a few burials found in the ditches and pits of late Iron Age settlements (Long 1988; Haselgrove *et al* 1990), the inhabitants of northern England adhered to the same archaeologically invisible rites for the disposal of the dead as most of the rest of Britain.

Unless archaeological finds derive from a context clearly labeled ritual or burial, we tend think of them as either accidental losses or as rubbish, leading on to the assumption that their absence from settlements indicates poverty. This is an attitude we need to reconsider. There is mounting evidence from all over Iron Age Britain that discard of household rubbish followed strict cultural or even religious rules, and that there were proper places to dispose of certain items and materials (Hill 1995). Some of these remains probably derive from communal feasts and other periodic activities such as exchange, marriage and death which brought different communities together. Boundaries, entrances and building thresholds were all frequently selected for ritual offerings of artefacts and disarticulated human or animal bone. The sword and skull found at the north-west entrance to the Stanwick complex (Wheeler 1954) is one possible example, but most 'special deposits' are less eye-catching, such as the hinged bracelet, finger ring, and broken quern found at Doubstead in the entrance ditch terminal (Jobey 1982) or the probable horse burial in entrance terminal at Coxhoe (Haselgrove and Allon 1982). Pit A at Burradon (Jobey 1970) with its archaic pottery contents is another candidate. Ferrell (1992) and Willis (1999) discuss other likely examples. The probability of such deposits occurring on Iron Age settlements has important implications both for the design of excavation strategies and for how we interpret the material recovered (Haselgrove 1999).

The beliefs of Iron Age communities also governed matters like the orientation of entrances to buildings and enclosures. Many settlements in northern England have east-facing entrances, an orientation which they share with

Iron Age sites throughout Britain (Hill 1995). This preference does not seem to respect local topography, indeed it sometimes goes against it. A minority of sites have opposed eastern and western entrances, again a pattern familiar elsewhere. Roundhouse entrances display a rigid orientation towards sunrise at midwinter or the equinoxes which has nothing to do with functional considerations such as the direction of the prevailing wind (Oswald 1997).

In the 1960s, metal analysis made a major contribution by showing that the Wallington metalwork tradition (in common with those of Scotland and Wales) differed from the contemporary Wilburton tradition in southern England in lacking lead (Tylecote 1968), as well as in its more conservative typology (Burgess 1968). In the subsequent Ewart Park period, technological developments ran in parallel with the rest of Britain (Northover 1988). More recently, a programme of analysing copper alloys has provided similar insights into Iron Age metalwork in northern England, demonstrating that it follows the same compositional trends as further south (Dungworth 1995; 1996). This is shown by the rapid adoption in the first century AD of brass (which ultimately originated in the Roman world) in place of bronze for the manufacture of weaponry and other prestige metalwork. Four of a possible five sets of horse harness and chariot fittings in the Melsonby hoard were made of alloys containing a significant quantity of zinc (Dungworth 1999). The same applies to the late Iron Age swords and scabbards of Piggott's (1950) Group IV, unlike those of the earlier Group III which were made of tin bronze (Dungworth 1996). A billet of good quality brass was found at Stanwick, along with other metalworking debris. Thus, although the region has yielded minimal evidence of pre-Conquest penetration by Roman imports, it was clearly open to outside innovations where these were culturally acceptable. Conversely, Dungworth (1995) has shown that many items of typologically Iron Age metalwork found in Roman forts (cf MacGregor 1976) are manufactured from mixed alloys which almost certainly post-date the Conquest.

Recent studies of both querns and pottery have provided valuable insights into the organization of production and the nature of regional exchange. In Teesdale, analysis of quern lithologies suggests that most beehive querns were locally made, but the greater range of types found at larger settlements shows that such sites were procuring querns of good quality milling stone from considerable distances (Gwilt and Heslop 1995). Stanwick, the largest and most complex settlement in the region, displays the greatest variety of lithological and morphological types (Heslop forthcoming). In Cumbria, too, specialist quern-producing centres evidently existed, although their scale and period of production cannot yet be assessed (Ingle 1987). There is similar evidence for limited movement of dolerite-tempered and calcite-tempered pottery within the region (Evans 1995; Willis 1999; forthcoming a), while the standardization of certain forms suggests the output of an established workshop. Willis (1999; forthcoming b) has also recently identified briquetage containers for transporting salt at several north-eastern sites, implying the existence of yet another regional exchange network and perhaps also of a hitherto unknown salt industry in the Tees estuary.

Stanwick is still the only site to have yielded significant numbers of pre-Conquest Roman imports, serving yet again to underline its quite exceptional status. These include South Gaulish samian, Gallo-Belgic ware, flagons and amphorae. Although the quantity of samian (13%) seems modest at first glance, comparison with other broadly contemporary assemblages from further south shows that the figure is exceptionally high (Willis 1998; forthcoming a). Other unusual features of the samian assemblage include the high ratio of decorated to plain ware and the number of rare types including handled flagons, while the grand total of forms exceeds that on any other contemporary site in eastern England without known military occupation (*ibid*). The arrival of Roman pottery imports seems to have stimulated a marked increase in local manufacture; indeed, some vessels display an affinity with Iron Age pottery forms from further south. By the end of the Iron Age, the amount of pottery being deposited at Stanwick was similar to that on many southern sites (Willis 1999), whereas prior to the mid first century AD it was present only in small quantities.

The Gallo-Belgic imports to the site display a marked preference for drinking vessels over platters, an emphasis which accords with the exotic assemblage of amphorae. Assuming that the contents were intact, these demonstrate that Stanwick was in receipt of wine and other commodities from as far afield as Spain, Italy and the eastern Mediterranean. Compared to other contemporary assemblages from eastern England, Stanwick displays a strong bias towards wine amphorae, distinguishing it from

Roman military and civil sites, where the Dressel 20 olive oil amphora forms the major component (Willis 1996; forthcoming a). Most of these imports were evidently consumed at Stanwick. Apart from Melsonby, which has produced Neronian samian (Fitts *et al* 1999), and a scatter of vessels from sites like Catcote, Scotch Corner and Thorpe Thewles, pre-Conquest imports are generally absent from local Iron Age sites (Evans 1995), implying that Roman objects were only very rarely incorporated into local social and economic networks following their arrival in the region.

Conclusions

One of the most interesting aspects of the later Bronze Age and the Iron Age is how poorly material culture is represented in the settlement record in most parts of Britain, not just in northern England. Even at the richest and most extensively excavated sites, there is often far less pottery and animal bone than there should be (eg Grant 1991; Hill 1995; Willis 1999). This trend is thrown into sharper relief by the relative profligacy of the subsequent Roman period. While the lack of settlement finds does not make archaeological studies any easier – even basic chronology is a real problem – it is time to accept that understanding later prehistoric societies requires every scrap and source of evidence we can muster. It also entails adopting the unfashionable stance that far from being repetitive and relatively uninformative, later Bronze Age and Iron Age settlements in northern England are unique and significant. Where they cannot be protected, they deserve extensive investigation in their wider environmental setting, as well as careful recording and comprehensive publication of the finds and their depositional context. It is also important that new long-term programmes of research are instigated in lowland areas on both sides of the Pennines to complement those already undertaken in the Tees Valley, or in progress in upland areas like the Ingram and Upper Breamish Valley (Adams 1995a, 1999).

A number of more specific priorities for future work have been noted in the course of this paper, most of which have a bearing on conservation strategies as well as on the long-term research agenda. They can broadly be summarized as follows:

• maintaining an appropriate archaeological research balance between lowland and upland areas;

- developing long-term strategies of aerial coverage to obtain a more accurate picture of cropmark sites in lowland areas where this is particularly lacking;
- employing geophysical survey as a method of finding new sites and instigating intensive long-term fieldwalking projects, targeting pasture as well as arable;
- using a full range of surface investigative techniques, backed up by problem-orientated excavation, to characterize cropmark sites and looking outside as well as inside enclosure boundaries;
- analyzing lithic assemblages from later prehistoric settlement sites to characterize the nature of any contemporary lithic industry;
- undertaking a major programme of research excavation on Cumbrian cropmark sites to investigate the nature of the later prehistoric settlement pattern;
- using multi-disciplinary techniques to establish the potential of coastal and wetland areas for enhancing our understanding of later prehistoric settlement;
- continuing to develop an absolute chronology of lowland settlement in north-east England, and fully exploiting the potential of radiocarbon and especially luminescence dating;
- examining surviving earthwork castles in northern England for the likely re-use of later prehistoric defensive earthworks;
- developing our knowledge of later prehistoric cultural and economic practices through further settlement excavation and environmental sampling;
- excavation of one or more 'neighbourhood groups' of cropmark enclosures in the lowlands to investigate their socio-economic relations and chronology;
- developing effective means of predicting and detecting different types of open (and palisaded) settlements in arable and pasture
- assigning high priority to the large-scale investigation of one or more open settlements in the region;
- exploiting the full potential of the artefact record through contextual analysis of off-site discoveries and detailed study of material from excavated sites;
- integrating the settlement data with other archaeological and palynological evidence for land use and landscape organization
- undertaking regular regional syntheses and developing new interpretative models to guide future research.

This list of priorities should not be seen as comprehensive, nor is it intended to be prescriptive. Rather, by setting out a broad framework and drawing attention to particular gaps in our understanding, it is hoped to ensure that best advantage is taken of the opportunities provided by archaeological interventions in northern England over the next few years, while at the same time stimulating wider debate about how future research into later prehistory should develop. Since this paper was first delivered in 1996, various other papers have appeared which enlarge on the methodological issues and questions set out here. Willis (1999) discusses the cultural practices and exchange patterns of Iron Age societies in north-east England, while Haselgrove (1999) reflects on research priorities throughout central Britain. The volumes edited by Bevan (1999) and by Harding and Johnston (2000) contain several other relevant papers. At a more general level, some strategic research priorities for Iron Age Britain as a whole are outlined in Haselgrove *et al* (2001), which also provides a review of recent research.

Acknowledgments
I am grateful to Pam Lowther for her help with the text and bibliography and to Yvonne Beadnell for drawing the illustrations. Anthony Harding, Richard Hingley, Jacqui Huntley and Rob Young all kindly commented on an earlier draft of the text, but responsibility for any errors remains mine alone.

Chapter 7: The Uplands of the Northern Counties in the First Millennium BC

*Humphrey Welfare**

Background

Research and the growth of understanding do not progress at a uniform speed, nor are they woven from a single strand. Archaeology is no exception to this rule, and in the study of the uplands of the northern counties of England in the first millennium BC this staccato advance is abundantly apparent. Gordon Barclay (1995, 5) has pointed to 'the archaeological equivalent of the boom/bust economic cycle' in research, characterizing it as the 'peak of effort/stagnation cycle'. One of the examples that he had in mind was the innovative work that was undertaken in the 1940s and 1950s by Peggy Piggott on the settlements of south-eastern Scotland and by the officers of the Royal Commission (particularly Richard Feachem and Kenneth Steer) in the compilation of the *Inventories* of Roxburgh, Selkirk and Peebles (eg Piggott 1948; 1949; RCAHMS 1956; 1957; 1967). In the course of these campaigns, the excavation of one particular site – the hillfort and overlying settlements known as Hownam Rings – led to the formation of a model of the morphological sequence of late prehistoric settlement in that part of the Borders. This model, the 'Hownam sequence', proved to be comparatively robust and durable.

In the adjacent land on the southern side of the Border, the boom in research continued through the 1960s with George Jobey's brilliant and simple strategy of detailed survey and selective excavation (eg Jobey 1960; 1964; 1965; a full bibliography, up to 1980, was assembled by Mitcheson, 1984). In the uplands of Northumberland he concentrated his analyses on the hillforts and on the settlements of the Iron Age and the Romano-British period, producing distinctive models, especially for the Cheviots and for North Tynedale. Jobey's work was enormously influential, and has been held up as an epitome of the archaeology of the northern uplands (eg Cunliffe 1974, 209-15). Subsequently it seemed as if research activity had entered the second half of the boom/bust cycle. Jobey's single-mindedness and his capacity for hard work – he was famously described as 'virtually a [Royal] Commission in himself' (Stevens 1966, 116) – may have daunted those who might have wished to follow, elsewhere, in his methodological footsteps.

When this paper was first drafted, in 1996, research activity seemed to be relatively quiescent. Since then, however, a considerable number of relevant publications have appeared.

By the 1970s the 'Hownam sequence' had been consolidated and elaborated by Jobey, and by others. Extending the model backwards, the excavations at Green Knowe in Peeblesshire showed that the unenclosed platform settlements of the Southern Uplands should be dated to the second half of the second millennium BC (Jobey 1980), and although the precise morphological type found in Peeblesshire and Lanarkshire was not identified elsewhere, their counterparts, at Standrop Rigg in Northumberland (Jobey 1983) and at Bracken Rigg in County Durham (Coggins and Fairless 1983), were found to be broadly contemporary. The Hownam sequence was more or less intact: palisades had been found (by survey or by excavation) to enclose many hilltop settlements, and had been succeeded by a greater intensity and breadth of defences; a univallate phase (whether a dump rampart or a wall) had been identified at many sites, to be followed by multivallate ramparts, before the superimposition of an enclosed but unfortified settlement or homestead, or unenclosed huts and associated yards (Burgess 1984).

Very little of this broad and variable sequence was dated. The artefacts discovered in excavation were sparse and simple, providing only the most general chronological indications. In the later phases of a site, the most that could be expected might be a fragment of a glass bangle, a melon bead and an abraded scrap of Roman coarse pottery. In the earlier phases there might be nothing. (Almost all of the Iron Age pottery was of very poor construction and was desperately undiagnostic.) The soil conditions usually determined that there was little organic material to be recovered, and the opportunities (and finance) for radiocarbon dating were few and far between. Some of the dates that were generated were singletons, increasing their statistical uncertainty; worse – for those envisaging a

*Address: English Heritage, NMRC, Kemble Drive, Swindon, SN2 2GZ

purely linear development – some dates appeared not to be significantly different from one another, which, in the case of the hillfort on Brough Law and the nearby settlement on Ingram Hill (markedly different in character but, on this basis, apparently contemporary in occupation), gave rise to serious problems of interpretation and extrapolation (Jobey 1971, 92-3).

However, even the well-established Hownam model was beginning to fray at the edges. The excavations at Green Knowe and at Bracken Rigg, and at Houseledge in the Northumberland Cheviots (Burgess 1984, 144-9) demonstrated that the easy equation 'stone-founded circular hut = Romano-British' was a chronological and cultural fallacy (cf Hill 1982a); the dating evidence available placed these newly excavated stone-founded buildings in the second half of the second millennium BC, and subsequently it became clear that such sites may have begun even earlier in the millennium (Terry 1995). The over-reliance on an undated morphology had made the Hownam sequence fragile; the forms of settlement that were its framework were too simple – and too simplistically perceived – to bear such chronological conclusions. The model had received further bruising from the results of the excavations on the hillfort at Broxmouth in East Lothian (Hill 1982b; 1982c), but the lack of any full publication of this site inhibited the dealing of more serious injuries to the theoretical framework. The savage downturn in the number of excavations in the uplands after the late 1970s slowed the introduction of new interpretations. For the want of further hard evidence, some speculative suggestions were advanced (eg Burgess 1984; 1985; 1995), but these were challenged, not least from the viewpoint of climate change and marginality, and over the use of radiocarbon dates (Young and Simmonds 1995). Nevertheless enough radiocarbon dates had become available to stretch the chronology and to demonstrate that the successive designs that were fundamental to the Hownam sequence were not due to a series of invasions from the South, as had originally been envisaged (Armit 1999, 70). In Scotland, the state of research in the early 1990s was summarized by Hingley (1992).

However, in 1997 there appeared a volume of analytical fieldwork and synthesis that surpassed anything that had gone before. The subject was not the English uplands but was immediately adjacent: the work undertaken by the Royal Commission on the Ancient and Historical Monuments of Scotland in Eastern Dumfriesshire (RCAHMS 1997). Detailed fieldwork there made it abundantly clear that the Hownam sequence was too simple: sites could not be conveniently pigeon-holed and, time and again, the 'sequence' could not be correlated with what was visible on the ground (RCAHMS 1997, 118-67: particularly 151-67). The presence or absence of an enclosure of a particular type could now be seen to have little direct chronological significance. Fortified sites were constructed over most of the first millennium BC, and timber structures were not confined to the earlier phases but were widespread up to the beginning of the Roman period. Without excavation, therefore, no individual fort can be assigned a date. In contrast to most earlier studies it was the forms of the *houses* within a settlement (rather than that of the enclosure) that held the greater significance for interpretation (RCAHMS 1997, 152, 156).

Aspects of the current state of knowledge

The Hownam model can still be helpful for the interpretation of sites in the Borders, even though it must be used with caution and clearly cannot be universally applied: the results of fieldwork – let alone those of excavation – often turn out to be much more complex than the theoretical structure would suggest. Examples of this are the analysis of the hillfort and settlement at Lordenshaws in Coquetdale (Topping 1993), the sequence revealed under the hillfort at Fenton Hill, near Milfield (Burgess 1984, 156-9), and the successive palisades at Gibb's Hill in upper Wauchopedale (RCAHMS 1997, 122-5). Further, it is worth remembering that our very ability to perceive and to understand the complexity of sites has itself increased with each generation; eg the successive plans that have made of the fort at Braidwood on the eastern flanks of the Pentlands (Gannon 1999), the analytical survey work being carried out by English Heritage on a selection of the hillforts in Northumberland, or the work at Edin's Hall, Berwickshire (Dunwell 1999).

In the northern counties of England, for more than a generation, it has been Northumberland that has stolen the limelight in the study of the first millennium BC and of the early first millennium AD. To the south of the Tyne, and in the west, fewer defensive sites have been identified (Challis and Harding 1975, figs 87-90, still provides an outline), and there seems to be a huge diversity in the size and morphology of settlements, and in the topographical choices made. The broad understanding acquired in the Border hills can be applied here, albeit with some diminished confidence, and the models that have been developed elsewhere can aid recognition and interpretation (eg the settlements at Forcegarth Pasture in County Durham; Fairless and Coggins 1980; 1986). Detailed characterization, area by area, has yet to be done, but a few scattered examples of the diversity that is apparent may suffice as illustrations.

In the heart of the Lake District – the prehistoric settlement of which is all too little understood – there is a clutch of small defended sites; these include the fortifications on Castle Crag above the narrow valley of the Shoulthwaite Gill, just to the west of Thirlmere (NY 299188; NMR NY 21 NE 2), and on another Castle Crag in Borrowdale (NY 249159; NMR NY 21 NW 2). Although they are undated, in their construction, size and the use of natural defences they appear to have much in common with the duns and forts of western Scotland. In gentler surroundings, the settlements and field systems on Aughertree Fell, on the skirts of the Caldbeck Fells (Higham 1982), would not be out of place, in their form and topography, in mid Northumberland. However, in the extreme south-eastern corner of Cumbria, in the Howgill Fells, the picture is less clear. There the topography offers few good locations for settlement; in consequence, it seems likely that the prehistoric sites are usually masked by their post-medieval and modern counterparts. In only a few cases, such as the oval embanked settlement in the Cautley valley, have earthworks survived (Bowden 1996, 3, 5, 6).

Across the Pennines, in County Durham, the ubiquitous landscapes of industry have overlain many of the earlier phases; the presence of extraction scars and of tips may have discouraged research. Where circumstances have ensured the survival of earthworks, however, the evidence is rich and diverse. On Cockfield Fell, near Staindrop (Roberts 1975; Welfare and Everson 1984), the earthworks of a rectilinear enclosure, apparently of a type familiar from the coastal plain and from North Tynedale (eg McCord and Jobey 1968; Jobey 1960; 1970), may be tentatively dated (but only by analogy) to the late first millennium BC or to the early centuries AD. A larger and much more irregular enclosure nearby cannot be so readily pigeonholed, but a 'fort' a couple of hundred metres away, defended by an outwork on the skyline,

might be classified *morphologically* as a hillfort, except that it lies in a hollow. (For more such non-defensive sites, see below.) These contrasts intrigue but the diversity does make it difficult to identify convincing patterns. Much more constructively, a distinctive type of undefended settlement seems to be emerging in Upper Teesdale, exemplified by the sites at Dubby Sike and Bleabeck Washfold (Coggins and Gidney 1988; Coggins and Fairless 1995), the first of which was dated to the last three centuries BC. These may, conceivably, be analogous to the unenclosed forecourt settlements of Northumberland (Charlton and Day 1978, 77-83; cf Jobey and Tait 1966, 7).

The flaw in trotting out these examples – with the exception of the Teesdale sites – lies in the old assumption that all earthwork enclosures are, almost by definition, most likely to fall into the morphological dustbin that we call the Iron Age (Welfare 1980). This is all too easy but it is a trap that the work in Eastern Dumfriesshire should warn us of. Nevertheless, despite the continuing paucity of chronological benchmarks, the broad trends do seem to be reasonably clear. From the late Bronze Age onwards, defensive palisaded enclosures seem to have become established (eg Eildon Hill, Roxburghshire: Owen 1992; Fenton Hill, Northumberland: Burgess 1984, 156-9). A later development – and probably existing in parallel to some extent rather than being simply successive – was a complex, idiosyncratic sequence of defended sites ('forts'), the forms of which seem to have varied enormously. For social and political reasons that we do not understand, more of these forts have been identified in the northern half of Northumberland than anywhere else in northern England. In considering the variety of their forms, the influence of the topography (which, at least, can be readily assessed) should not be underestimated, nor should the contemporary availability of materials – timber and stone – the estimation of which is more difficult. Before the end of the first millennium BC the defensive imperative seems to have waned – as Jobey (1978) established in his series of excavations in North Tynedale – although it did not disappear completely (RCAHMS 1997, 164).

That said, it is no longer safe to assume that the surviving earthworks of every hillfort hide an unenclosed-palisade-wall-univallate-multivallate-undefended sequence, even though one or more elements may be present. Even more importantly, it is clearly wrong to assume a *linear* progression tied to chronology. Such self-deception is often tempting in our efforts to make this infinite variety comprehensible, and the archaeological labels that we devise sometimes (if not always) become simplistic and may hinder us. Thus, for instance, we know that timber palisades were not only set up late in the Bronze Age and in the early Iron Age, but also towards the end of the first millennium BC in the homesteads of North Tynedale (eg Jobey 1978), and in the second half of the first millennium AD at Yeavering, in Glendale (Hope-Taylor 1977). Further, in considering the form and evolution of settlements, we should also expect to find (in every age that was not subject to crushing centralized and ultimate power) some expressions of radicalism and of conservatism in design; of some regression; the effects of strong localized traditions; and the pendulum swings of fashion. Archaeology deals with these with varying, and largely unknown, degrees of success.

In the debates of the 1960s and 1970s, the emphasis was laid on the defensive/non-defensive character of settlements. Since then, the political and religious aspects have come to the fore, especially with regard to hillforts (Bowden and McOmish 1987; Hingley 1990); the prestige that may have been attached to a particularly prominent topographical position or to the choice of building materials has come to be regarded as a factor of great potential potency. These ideas have been extended to emphasise the importance of the activities that took place *within* the enclosure. As in any modern settlement, especially those above subsistence level, the hillforts would not have been exclusively places in which to live, but they were also where the inhabitants and their visitors chose to do business, to settle disputes, to marry, to celebrate, and to mourn, over many generations. The everyday ritual of life within the settlements has been difficult to identify in the uplands, not least because of the paucity of artefacts. Some of those that have been found in excavation have been identified as 'special deposits' (Willis 1999, 99) although they could also be interpeted more simply as domestic rubbish. Looking back at the sites themselves, McOmish (1999, 120) has suggested that the ritual importance of the interior may have led to a desire actually to be overlooked and that in some cases this may have been a key consideration in the choice of location. Some earthwork enclosures certainly seem to have had little or no defensive potential but, instead, appear to have had strong ceremonial

functions. At Over Rig, beside the White Esk and close to the complex fort of Castle O'er, the presence of these specialist functions was demonstrated by excavation (RCAHMS 1997, 78,79, 84-6) – although as the site lies in the bottom of a natural amphitheatre the indications of its particular nature were evident from survey alone. It will be important to have this site in mind when considering the roles of sites elsewhere for the whole question of non-defensive 'forts' in the northern uplands requires more examination. Beyond the southern border of the region there is Maiden Castle, at Harkerside, in Swaledale (SE 022981), a site set on a terrace in the hillside which is completely overlooked and which seems to have been approached down a ceremonial avenue (Bowden & Blood forthcoming). The enigmatic earthwork in Fozy Moss, an island in the bog just to the North of Hadrian's Wall, near Sewingshields (NY 817707) may conceivably fall into this non-utilitarian category. It is increasingly recognised that it is important to investigate the ground immediately adjacent to locations where artefacts have been deliberately deposited in wetlands (Hunter 1997, 113-14, 119-23). In this context it is frustrating, for example, that nothing is known of the findspot or associations of the early 1st millennium BC bucket from Ravenstonedale (Turnbull 1995; cf Hunter 1997, 118-19; Green 1998). At Fozy Moss we may perhaps have an instance in which the associated structure is recognisable before any artefacts are discovered.

In the settlements, the importance of house-types as chronological indicators has already been mentioned. The longer timescales that are now envisaged for the various designs may help to explain the diversity of house-types which is apparent on the surface in a site such as the large hillfort on Yeavering Bell in Northumberland (Jobey 1965, 31-2, 34; Pearson 1998; cf also Hill 1982a; 1982b; Reynolds 1982; Halliday 1999). However it has also been argued that the type of house that is visible as an earthwork on the surface in a settlement or fort can be used as a pointer to the date of the final abandonment of the site (RCAHMS 1997, 156). The same reasoning could be applied to the changing fashions of building in an extensive site, such as Yeavering, to put forward the case that abandonment was only gradual, leaving behind a variety of relict house-types from successive phases of the site's history. In this, Yeavering Bell is unusual. The massive rubble wall of the fort there is also morphologically atypical and has an uncertain relationship to the details within the interior, but the surrounding landscape does contain field systems and settlements that may not be out of place in a contemporary context, and which might have provided economic and social support. The same does not seem to be true of some other massive forts on even less habitable summits, such as Ingleborough in North Yorkshire (Bowden *et al* 1989), and Carrock Fell, in the Caldbeck Fells of northern Cumbria, both of which would be included in any discussion of the topographical siting of forts for non-utilitarian purposes – ie for the symbolism of political dominance and prestige, or for cultic reasons. Strictly speaking all of these sites are undated, although, as with the massive fort on the summit of Eildon Hill North (Owen 1992), their origins may have preceded the Iron Age.

The speculative suggestion that the site on Carrock Fell may be much earlier in date stems as much from its isolation from a recognizable contemporary landscape as from the likelihood that in the immediate vicinity there was a (unlocated) source of rock for Neolithic polished stone axes (cf Oswald *et al.* 2001, 88, 159). However, other aspects of the site's context are less than clear: despite pioneering environmental work, all too little is yet known about upland prehistoric settlement patterns (in distribution, morphology and chronology) in the former Lake counties. Were these valleys really abandoned because of climatic deterioration at the Late Bronze/Iron Age transition? There seems to be little evidence for it. Burgess (1984; 1995) envisaged wholesale abandonment and recolonisation but continuity in the landscape is a very powerful factor, and there may be other viable models. As in the Howgill Fells, the sites suitable for settlement in the Lakeland valleys are few and far between, and are probably still occupied. In the face of such restricted choices, the archaeological sites that do survive may not have been at all typical of their contemporary landscape, and they are perhaps more likely to have been the out-and-out failures.

During the 1990s there was a significant surge in the dissemination of the environmental evidence for later prehistory in the North (eg van der Veen 1992; Tipping 1994; Huntley & Stallibrass 1995; Huntley 1999). It is now apparent that in the 1st millennium BC there was a long phase of forest clearance that grew in intensity towards the end of the period and which seems to have coincided with a compara-

ble increase in the numbers of small settlements, many of which lasted into the Roman period (eg in North Tynedale, the Cheviots, and Eastern Dumfriesshire: RCAHMS 1997, 161-7). This is Richard Tipping's 'Late Iron Age agricultural revolution' (1994, 33) in which there was a major expansion into the uplands. Where these new settlements overlie hillforts the defences seem to have been abandoned for some time before the sites were reoccupied (RCAHMS 1997, 160). The picture is, however, still sketchy and much more fieldwork and analysis needs to be undertaken if the vegetational and demographic histories are to be adequately correlated.

Since the 1970s there has been a marked shift of emphasis away from treating the site itself – almost in isolation – to seeking to understand the site within its landscape; this approach tends to reveal evidence that may be readily visible to those able to see it (eg at Lordenshaws, on the flanks of Simonside; Topping 1993) and to appreciate that it is the relationships between the various elements in the landscape that are crucial to the overall interpretation. An outstanding example of this is provided beside Greenlee Lough, just to the north of Housesteads, where the remains of a curvilinear, stone-founded settlement with a droveway, fields of cordrig cultivation, a small hillfort and a Roman camp all survive in close proximity to one another; some elements overlap and have to be mentally prised apart (Welfare 1986; Welfare and Swan 1995, 104-5).

Some complexity, at Greenlee and elsewhere, will be masked and will only be recovered in the research excavations that are now all too rare. In those that have taken place in recent years the value of shifting some of the focus away from the settlement itself to its immediate vicinity has been amply demonstrated (Adams 1999; Topping & McOmish 2000). Less intensively, the complexity and the articulation of landscape is best supplied from the air. Aerial photography by Tim Gates (1995; 1999), in the Otterburn ranges and in the area of Hadrian's Wall within the Northumberland National Park, has shown how great the potential is for a radical increase in data. The extension of the National Mapping Programme to the whole of the Wall corridor is especially welcome and should provide some new insights into the extent and time-depth of the landscapes of later prehistory there.

In passing, it would be difficult to underestimate the sea-change to the economic model of the uplands in the first millennium BC and the first few centuries AD brought about by the reconsideration of the agricultural base (Halliday 1982), and by the recognition of the organization and planned exploitation of the landscape, and its effects (Mercer and Tipping 1994). The most graphic illustration of the changes in our perception may still be the identification of the exceptionally narrow ridge-and-furrow known as cordrig (Halliday 1982, 82; Topping 1989a; 1989b), the distribution of which is now known to be widespread. The intensity of arable agriculture – and the potential for further discoveries – may be further illustrated by the recognition of cordrig at an altitude of over 450m OD on Ward Law, below Windy Gyle, close to the head of Coquetdale. Agricultural activity at such an altitude prompts the question whether the cultivation may not be associated with the unenclosed settlements of the second millennium BC, which seem to have been established further up into the hills than the later settlements in the Cheviots (Gates 1983; Jobey 1985, 179). A great deal more work needs to be done on cordrig, especially in the definition of its associations, formation and chronological limits; the known distribution will be expanded further through fieldwork, and – more bravely – the higher 'tide-lines' of medieval ridge-and-furrow should be tested to ascertain how much of the later cultivation overlies and masks the ridged fields of later prehistory.

Future research

In looking forward to the pathways for future research, it is important that the focus should be upon those sites and landscapes that were normal for their time. This is a desirable aim, even though in many areas the basic fieldwork has yet to be done, or brought to a consistent standard. In particularly fruitful areas, such as North Tynedale and the Cheviots, Jobey demonstrated how effective local studies can be. Many more of these are desperately needed, throughout the region. Local syntheses – perhaps of a single valley – are very effective in taking knowledge forward. They should be based upon field survey and on comparative morphologies, with some selective excavation to provide the essential chronological pegs. Dennis Coggins' work on Upper Teesdale is an example of what can be done (Coggins 1986). Areas for examination include the Fell Sandstone ridges of Northumberland, South Tynedale, East and West Allendale, Weardale, northern Cumbria (where the environmental record is at odds with the

sparse distribution of known settlements; Dumayne 1995), and the heart and flanks of the Lake District. The well-known settlements on the limestones of the upper Eden valley, around Crosby Ravensworth, would certainly benefit from a new scrutiny and analysis, which is long overdue.

In tackling the whole of the local picture, in pursuit of the normal, some exotics should also be expected. It should not be any great surprise if it can be confirmed (as in the possible Lakeland examples mentioned above) that a few duns have strayed over the Border from Dumfries and Galloway (although none was identified in Eastern Dumfriesshire). There may be more souterrains to be discovered, even though they are predominantly (but not exclusively) a lowland type (Welfare 1984). The identification of crannogs may be expected; one contender is the island in Devoke Water, on the edge of Eskdale, in western Cumbria. (Although the basic form of construction is too simple to be a firm chronological indicator, two-thirds of the Scottish crannogs that have been dated have been confirmed as belonging to the Iron Age; Crone 1993.)

There is no doubt that the old models of interpretation should be looked at more critically. (For instance, there is still no confirmation of the date of Jobey's curvilinear homesteads in the Cheviots.) Influential sites, often quoted, may also be worth a second, more searching, look. A case in point is the clutch of 'hengiform enclosures' – with no ready parallel – that was identified near the settlements on High Knowes, above Whittingham Vale in Northumberland (Jobey and Tait 1966, 23-5, 37, 40-1, 43-5; cf Harding and Lee 1987, 213). These can now be seen to be fairly conventional ring-ditch houses, an identification that is even more interesting, given the immediate proximity of the Iron Age burial excavated there (Jobey and Tait 1966, 25-33). Despite the intensity of the settlement record and the recognition of widespread arable farming, both of which would imply significant levels of population in the uplands, the growth of knowledge of contemporary burial customs seems to be painfully slow (Welfare 1983); as was the case at High Knowes, and also with the cremation of BP 2210±80 (uncalibrated: HAR 2918) under a cairn at Middle Hurth in Teesdale (Coggins and Fairless 1997, 6, 16-18), our understanding seems to advance only through serendipity. Some new thinking is urgently required here. Perhaps the examination of other 'cairnfield cairns' in the vicinity of ring-ditch houses would prove to be worthwhile.

There are also lessons to be learned from the later landscapes. The potential underlying the medieval and post-medieval ridge-and-furrow has already been mentioned. In addition, given that (without major technological changes) the requirements for defence and settlement alter only slowly, many 'later' sites may bear examination. One fruitful topic is the origin of castles; in the archaeology of Northumberland it is now well known that the castles at Bamburgh, Dunstanburgh and Tynemouth were occupied in the Iron Age. Less obvious – although it was staring us in the face – was the recognition that the earthworks bounding the inner ward and the bailey of Harbottle Castle in Coquetdale, nominally of the mid twelfth century, represent an economical adaptation of a much earlier hillfort (Welfare *et al* 1999, 58-9). Excavation there, which had other questions in mind (Crow 2000), has not yet confirmed this. A critical trawl through the castles of the northern counties is producing other examples.

The emphasis in this paper, as in so many others, has been on the settlement evidence. Although the uplands have not proved to be rich in material culture it does merit more attention. The samples are comparatively small but there do seem to be some regional contrasts in, for instance, the deposition and survival of contemporary pottery (Willis 1999, 83-90). Much more work also needs to be done on the exploitation and the use of metals in the area. There is now some tentative evidence that the extraction and the processing of copper – and thus perhaps of other metals as well – may have taken place in the Borders during the Iron Age (cf Hunter 1999, 339-40).

Priorities for the future include: more local studies, based upon analytical fieldwork; selective excavation, in pursuit of material that may provide chronological pegs which will reduce the reliance on morphology; more specialist aerial photography and cartography of the uplands; further research on the environmental context of the period, on the economic bases of society, on the non-utilitarian functions of some 'forts' and 'settlements', and – crucially – more synthesis of the results. The information available in the uplands is enormous; we need to maintain some momentum if we are to unlock it and thus to remain in the 'boom' section of the research cycle.

Chapter 8: Environmental Archaeology: Mesolithic to Roman Period

Jacqueline P. Huntley[*]

The past

In the past the only environmental evidence recovered from excavations was in the form of hand-recovered animal bones, occasionally with collection from caches of hazelnut shells or burnt cereal grain, for example. References to straw and wood deposits can be found, but with no indication of the types of cereal. Plant remains were, by and large, ignored, as were the smaller mammal, fish and often bird bones, and the invertebrates in general. In the 1960s people started wondering more about this smaller material, and consequently methods were devised to sample deposits and process them by some means or other in order to undertake microscopic investigation of the contents. Sampling became routine in the late 1970s, and this has allowed much more information about the diet and economy of sites, as well as environmental aspects, to be determined, interpreted and discussed.

The excavations of the past concentrated upon the structures rather than related activities, and this is especially clear from the work on the numerous Roman forts of the region, and the very detailed surveys and excavations of native sites by Jobey in particular (Jobey 1965; 1985). Again in the 1970s, the emphasis changed subtly and at least some archaeologists became interested in the activities themselves. This can be seen as the development of a holistic approach.

Many of the excavations themselves were undertaken as a result of urban revival – the rescue excavation, for example in Newcastle (O'Brien *et al* 1989), Hartlepool (Daniels 1988; 1990) and Carlisle (McCarthy 1991) – and thus much of the material from those excavations reflects medieval and later town developments, plus the underlying Roman deposits where present. Such urban sites often produced deep, well-stratified and waterlogged deposits, and thus the potential for preservation of organic material was extremely high (and the material was obvious during excavation – it smelt!).

With major rescue-funded excavations under way, vast numbers of samples were taken, although in general there were not the specialists available to cope with the volume of material being produced. The inevitable backlog was produced.

Environmental archaeology therefore became a regular part of excavation in the 1970s, with the 1980s and early 1990s largely being spent producing detailed archive reports upon specific sites. Environmental archaeology was excavation-led, and in the rare instance of synthetic work being undertaken (notably van der Veen's 1992 analysis of later prehistoric sites), it was as a result of large bodies of site data having being individually accrued.

The present

At present much of that backlog has been completed, although regrettably not published. Backlogs do not apply only to *environmental* archaeologists. There has, therefore, been time to sit back and review the work of the past – what has been achieved, where spatial and temporal lacunae remain – and to start developing a research framework for the future.

Today, few excavations are rescue-driven; the majority are undertaken as a result of planning policy, and hence are small and rarely allow full excavation or post-excavation work to be carried out. In such a market-place it is vital that research frameworks are in place, and reviewed at regular intervals, to allow the best to be achieved in terms of environmental (and other) archaeology in what is inevitably an unsatisfactory situation.

Environmental archaeology: status today

The Mesolithic period

Cultural evidence for the Mesolithic has been found throughout most parts of the region. A hunter-gatherer culture is not going to leave behind well-stratified deposits of domestic refuse, however, and so evidence for the Mesolithic comes mainly from palynological work and spot finds of animal bones. The latter are relatively common (Fig 8.1), and at least some have associated tool marks suggesting human presence. The region has been well studied in respect of the palynological work,

*Address: Department of Archaeology, University of Durham, South Road, Durham, DH1 3LE

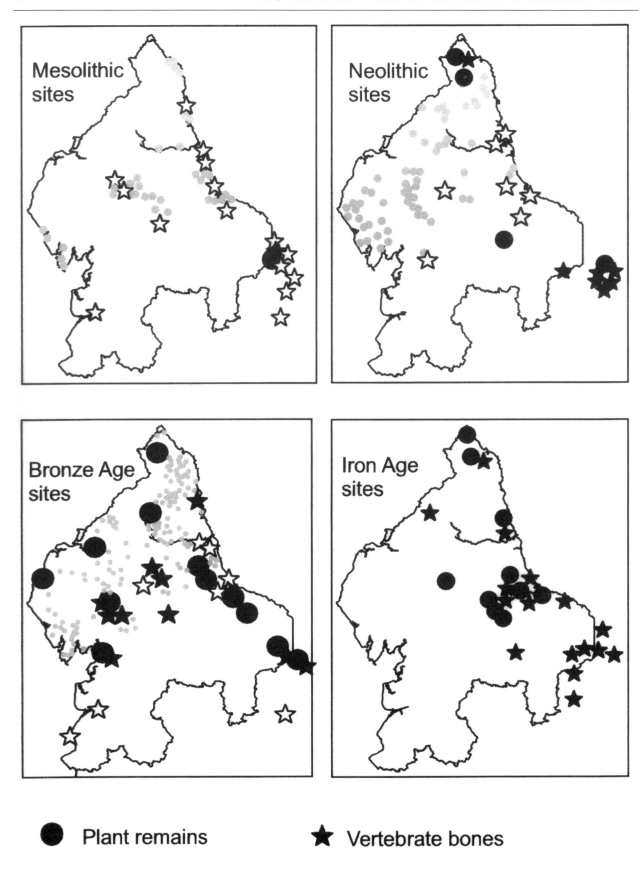

Fig. 8.1 Distribution of archaeological sites with assemblages of plant remains and animal bones (after Huntley and Stallibrass 1995)

although most pollen diagrams were produced with questions of vegetational history in mind, not specific archaeological questions. In addition, the older diagrams were neither dated nor of sufficiently fine resolution for short-term fluctuations in the pollen to be perceived. By analysing pollen from very thin slices of sediment in conjunction with radiocarbon dating, it is possible to produce pollen counts representing only a few years of accumulation. Using contiguous samples allows the definition of short-term changes. Such modern techniques of fine-resolution work have enabled Simmons and Innes (1996a; 1996b) to investigate the spatial effect of Mesolithic people upon the vegetation of parts of the North York Moors. Although at some of their sites fire (evidenced by charcoal fragments) evidently initiated forest clearance, at others it did not, instead being used to increase a grass component in a clearance. This, they surmise, could have been the result of Mesolithic activity to encourage grazing animals.

The region (more broadly defined) contains arguably the most important Mesolithic site in Britain, Star Carr, where detailed analyses of bone remains have shown that it was a year-round settlement site (Legge and Rowley-Conwy 1988). Palynological work here (Day 1993; Day and Mellars 1994) has demonstrated two periods of clearance and activity. Ongoing work in the Eskmeals area of Cumbria suggests a similar settlement, although of considerably younger date (Bonsall et al 1990).

What has become clear in some pollen diagrams is the presence of cereal-type pollen grains from early to mid-Holocene deposits (see, for example, Williams 1985), and this could be linked with Clarke's (1976) hypothesis that flint artefacts could be related to cereal-based activities as well as to skinning animals. No one, however, has produced evidence other than the ubiquitous hazelnut shells for usage of plants, let alone cereals. This probably reflects the lack of investigation of macrofossils other than fruits and seeds. The starchy roots and tubers of many plants are edible and were probably collected, but they are not likely to have been preserved other than by charring, and suitable sites have not been found, let alone excavated, sampled or analysed.

The Neolithic period

Environmental evidence for the Neolithic has taken great strides forward in the last 20 years, although the region still contains only four well-

sampled sites (Fig 8.1). Pollen evidence again suggests moderate clearance phases throughout the region during this period. Animal bone studies show that there was probably quite a rapid adoption of the three main domesticated species (cattle, sheep/goat and pig), but that there was still a heavy reliance upon wild resources such as aurochs and red deer. Metrical data from cattle bones throughout eastern Yorkshire suggest at least three broad size categories, generally ascribed to aurochs (the larger bones), domesticated cattle (the smaller bones) and an intermediate category (Manby 1988). The species exhibit sexual dimorphism, however, with the result that female aurochs are indistinguishable from domestic bulls on size grounds, and the possibility of domestic castrates being present simply adds further complication. The nature of domestication itself remains unclear. What seems reasonable is that size reduction in domesticated cattle is likely to have taken several generations to stabilise, and that the early domestic forms may be expected to be larger and more variable in size than the so-called 'Celtic shorthorn' typical of the Iron Age.

With respect to plant remains all of the evidence is from charred assemblages from the east of the region (Fig 8.2). Wild plant resources are the most important, and include mostly hazelnuts and apples; this is in accord with evidence throughout most of Britain (Moffett et al 1989; Robinson 2000). Where cereals are present, emmer wheat and barley are recorded, and at Marton-le-Moor both hulled and naked barley occurs (Huntley 1994a). Whilst numbers of grains can be significant (over 1,000 each at Marton-le-Moor and Caythorpe; Huntley 1993; 1996), their occurrence is limited to about 10% only of the Marton-le-Moor samples (only one Neolithic sample was available from Caythorpe). Cereals may not, therefore, have been a major contributor to the diet of the people. Recent stable isotope work on material from central and southern England also suggests that plants were of considerably less importance than animal-derived foods (Richards 1996). However, the suggestion by Richards that 'sites where grain has been found generally seem to have been used for ritual purposes and it is possible that... cereal was grown... only for ritual purposes' is debatable in that most of the excavated sites have been ritual in nature; few settlement sites have been excavated and extensively sampled. Evidence from such sites, for example Balbridie in Scotland (Fairweather and Ralston

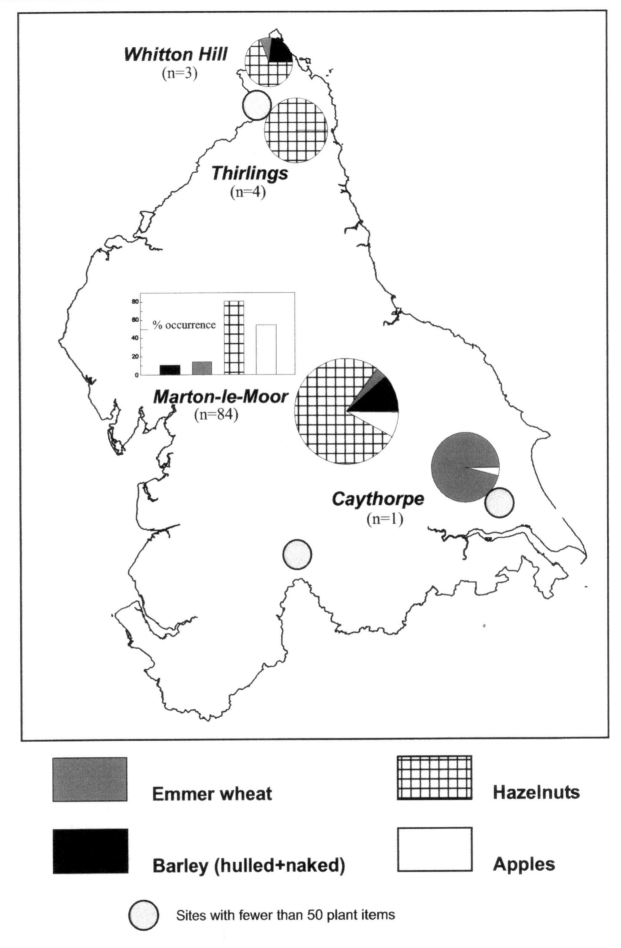

Fig. 8.2 Neolithic sites with plant remains. n = number of samples. Size of circles gives an indication of overall numbers of 'seeds' found, but circles are not to scale. Data after Huntley 1993 (Caythorpe); 1994a (Marton-le-Moor); van der Veen 1982 (Thirlings); 1984 (Whitton Hill)

1993) and Lismore Fields, Derbyshire (G Jones, pers comm), do demonstrate almost certain local cultivation of considerable amounts of cereals by inference from the associated chaff and weed assemblages, representing considerable effort on the part of the population.

Very few chaff remains have been recovered from the north, and the implications are that the cereals recorded represent either a fully cleaned crop or discard. Given that much of the grain is emmer wheat, a glume wheat, chaff would perhaps be expected, since the species is typically stored in the spikelet and is only parched and pounded to loosen the grains themselves at the time of use. Weed seeds are likewise not common, most representing grassland communities with some evidence for more nitrophilous vegetation. This, however, would not be too surprising given that cultivation was in its early stages.

The Bronze Age
Considerably more Bronze Age sites have been excavated and, indeed, sampled (Fig 8.1). Disappointingly few have produced even reasonable amounts of data, however. This must partly be due to the nature of the sites, burial cairns, which are unlikely to produce much in the way of plant remains, but also due to the adverse burial environments, acidic soils, precluding animal bone survival. The best bone assemblages, not surprisingly, have been recovered from sites on the Carboniferous limestones of the region. Thwing (Manby 1980) and Caythorpe (Stallibrass 1996) are the only two settlement sites to have produced bone; both sites are in North Yorkshire. Cattle, sheep and pig bones are present in almost equal proportions at Thwing, with a wide range of other animal bones and marine shellfish shells, although the material has never been fully published. Caythorpe produced bones from mature cattle but young sheep – a contrast to the Neolithic material from the same site – but the assemblage was very small.

Material from burial cairns gives indications of perhaps funerary feasts, but has also provided detailed evidence for local small mammal populations (and by implication local environments) because large-scale sieving programmes were undertaken. Hardendale (Stallibrass 1991a) and Manor Farm, Borwick (Jones *et al* 1987), both produced considerable numbers of bones from frogs, toads, watervole, fieldvole, all three British shrew species, fieldmouse and bank vole. In addition, Hardendale produced large numbers

of small immature bird bones showing signs of acid etching (Allison 1988). These were interpreted as the remains of pellets from a diurnal raptor rather than owls. What is clear is that the sieving programme enabled small bones to be recorded, which added considerably to the overall interpretation of the site (Stallibrass 1991b).

Only three sites have produced moderate amounts of plant material (Fig 8.3). Hallshill, Northumberland (van der Veen 1992), has the most samples, and shows that emmer wheat was dominant in terms of both numbers and frequency of occurrence. Spelt wheat was recorded, as was a small amount of both hulled and naked barley. Thwing likewise produced evidence for emmer, spelt, bread-type wheat and hulled barley (Carruthers 1993). Chaff suggested that emmer was, again, the most commonly used cereal. Measurements of both spelt and emmer glume bases indicated large, well-grown plants, perhaps benefiting from the warm chalk soils of the area. Ewanrigg in Cumbria produced a different picture, although only three samples were available. One particular pit was full of hulled barley grains with moderate numbers of culm nodes, possibly reflecting a storage pit lined with straw. Spelt glume bases were also quite common, although no wheat grains were recorded (Huntley 1988; Bewley *et al* 1992).

In terms of the weed seeds present, grassland communities are, as for the Neolithic, the most commonly represented. Surprisingly few weeds overall have been recovered; only 7% of the grain/chaff/weed seeds from van der Veen's (1992) Hallshill data are from weed taxa, for example. Whilst this may, of course, relate to context types analysed, it could represent well-cleaned crops, or low levels of cultivation in terms of manuring and so on – the traditional weeds of intensively farmed fields having not yet invaded.

The Bronze Age, therefore, may be seen as an intensification of the Neolithic in terms of both domesticated animals and crop plants. Emmer and barley remain most common, but spelt occurs at several sites. What is clearly different is that the cereals are more commonly represented by their chaff than their grains. This probably reflects the different natures of the archaeological sites, with settlements from the Bronze Age but storage/disposal features (pits) from Neolithic sites. Cereals have certainly taken over from natural food resources such as apples and nuts.

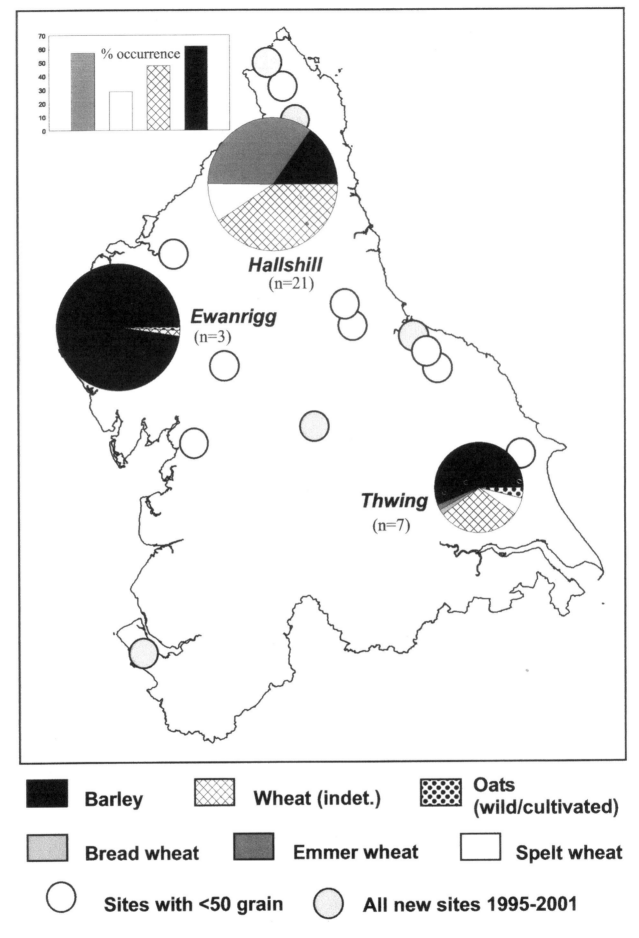

Fig. 8.3 Bronze Age sites: proportions of cereal grains (excluding indeterminate). n = number of samples. Data after Carruthers 1993 (Thwing); Huntley 1988 (Ewanrigg); van der Veen 1992 (Hallshill)

The Iron Age

From the botanical point of view the Iron Age is the best represented, with major assemblages analysed, although only from the east of the region. Animal bone assemblages, too, are only from the east and south of the region, soil status precluding bone preservation at many of the upland and northern sites (Fig 8.1).

Sites are largely settlements, and at least some have their origins in the Bronze Age, as well as continuing in use through to the Romano-British period. Comparisons of occupation between these cultural periods are therefore possible.

Animal bones are predominantly from the three main domestic species; wild animals as an economic resource have become considerably less important. Whilst cattle seem to have been the major animal at all sites, at least at Thorpe Thewles in Cleveland there is a greater emphasis on sheep in the later deposits (Rackham 1985; 1987). Ageing data also suggest a change from a dairy- to a beef-based economy during the second phase of activity, which is nonetheless still pre-Roman conquest. Occasional cattle bones indicate particularly large animals; whilst these may simply represent bulls, Rackham notes that they are comparable with some of the largest bones from Romano-British sites and bigger than the Thames Valley material. He therefore suggests that regional differences may have been present during the later Iron Age.

Several sites, notably Thorpe Thewles (*ibid*) and Kennel Hall Knowe in Northumberland (Rackham 1977), have produced bones from domestic fowl. These are early records, and the sites are not clearly 'Romanised'.

Ironically, evidence for the main areas within the region, the uplands, is minimal, and this is perhaps the area where the greatest effect of the Romans upon the natives may have been felt. As Stallibrass states, '...yet we are still almost totally ignorant of the pre-existing Iron Age economies and faunal environments for the region' (Huntley and Stallibrass 1995, 131).

Evidence for crop husbandry practices is considerably greater, due to the work of van der Veen (1992). Whilst her data were originally collected as a result of predominantly rescue-funded excavations, she used the individual site data to investigate regional-scale patterns of variation. Analyses of the charred plant remains and environmental parameters led her to conclude that it was, in fact, cultural parameters between populations north and south of the Tyne which had probably determined the different cultivation regimes, and not the environmental parameters themselves. She concentrated upon the wheat remains, which showed species differences, although from the cereal grains alone, barley was almost always the most common species. Figure 8.4 shows this well.

Although the emphasis above has been upon the cereal grains themselves, it is without doubt the cereal chaff, the ear and straw fragments, that can provide the detailed evidence for crop husbandry practices. Presence of grain simply reflects usage of that crop, not how it was grown and harvested, the nature of soils in which it grew, and so on. Figure 8.5 shows a very different picture from that of the grain in that wheat chaff of one sort or another overtakes the importance of barley, although the latter remains common on the more northerly sites. Such an implication, however, overrides in particular differences in processing which could affect the proportions of the various cereals. For example, the product of threshing glume wheats is spikelets, which traditionally are supposed to require fire to parch them to separate out the grain, leaving spikelet and rachis fragments which survive in the archaeological record. Whilst barley lemmas too are tightly adpressed to the grains, threshing removes grains+lemmas leaving behind complete rachis units (ears), that is to say that barley acts more like a free-threshing wheat. The grain+lemmas are then ground, thus producing the barley flour or meal plus a coarse bran element. Interpretation must therefore take into account a wide variety of taphonomic factors as well.

Nonetheless, of the wheats, spelt is the more common in the south and emmer in the north. Bread wheat and rye have appeared in the south of the region too during the Iron Age, but with an early occurrence of rye at Thornbrough Scar.

The Roman period

The occupation by the Roman military left a considerable structural mark on the landscape in the form of forts, roads and, not least, Hadrian's Wall. Whilst excavation has been undertaken at such sites for a very long time, surprisingly few have had well-sampled assemblages recovered. The animal bones from military sites suggest a diet of beef more or less throughout the occupation, but with some greater emphasis upon mutton at South Shields, for example (Stokes 1996).

Many of the cattle bones were from aged females, suggesting a long life for breeding and dairy purposes. However, several of the forts

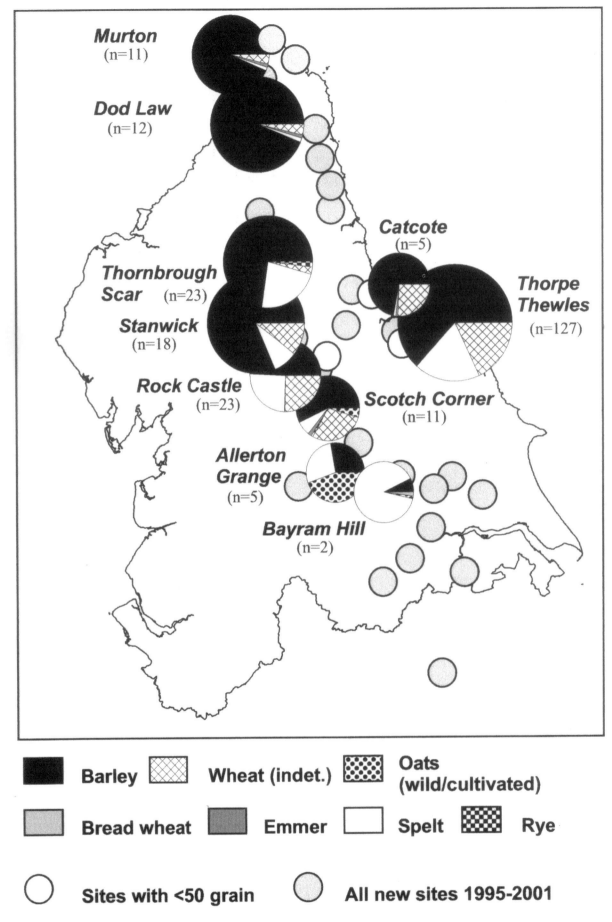

Fig. 8.4 Iron Age and Romano-British sites: proportions of cereal grains (excluding indeterminate). n = number of samples. Data after Huntley 1989b (Catcote); 1994b (Bayram Hill); 1994c (Allerton Grange); 1995 (Scotch Corner); van der Veen 1992 (Murton, Dod Law, Thornborough Scar, Thorpe Thewles, Stanwick and Rock Castle)

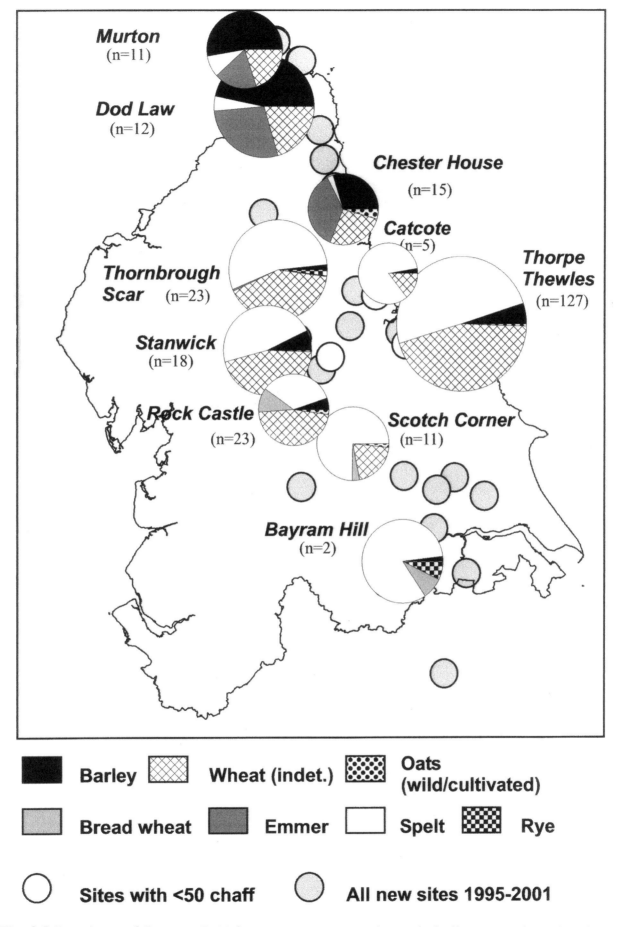

Fig. 8.5 Iron Age and Romano-British sites: proportions of cereal chaff. n = number of samples. Data as for Fig 4, plus van der Veen 1992 (Chester House)

clearly bought in joints, judging from the numbers of 'extra' shoulder bones, and prime beef certainly found its way to the officers' tables (Stallibrass 1991c). There is very little evidence for eating fish, or indeed wild fowl or other hunted species. With respect to the plant remains, barley remains the most commonly occurring cereal, with spelt wheat also being important. Many sites have produced very small amounts of either emmer or bread wheat, although bread wheat was being stored in quantity in one of the South Shields granaries (van der Veen 1988). The majority of the military sites have produced only grain or very small amounts of chaff, perhaps one or two contexts only with much chaff, usually spelt glume bases. This may partly relate to the fact that Roman deposits are often waterlogged, and the sampling procedures have been such as to sample inadequately the charred material, which is only ever at relatively low concentrations.

Waterlogged data show that exotic taxa are commonly recorded at some sites but rare at others; for example, vast quantities of fig seeds, grape pips and olives occur at Carlisle (Goodwin and Huntley 1988; Huntley 1989a) but very few at Ribchester (Huntley 1996b; Huntley in Buxton and Howard-Davis 2000). This could relate to the different origins of the men garrisoned there, and may suggest that Roman soldiers retained their ethnic origins, at least in part. This does not seem to have happened with the meat side of their diet, though, since beef remains dominant throughout the occupation at both sites.

Samples from native sites of the Roman period are disappointingly rare, and have only been collected in the east of the region. In general they show similarities with both the Iron Age and Roman military occupation, but further work is clearly needed.

The future
Excavation in the foreseeable future is, I believe, going to continue as relatively small-scale developer-funded work, rarely passing beyond assessment level. It is to be hoped that research excavations can attract funding, and no doubt some developer sites will be fully excavated (as was the Marton-le-Moor site in advance of projected improvements to the A1), but project designs will need to be both concise and precise in order to succeed. There will be continuing pressure to produce results in less time, but this must not equate to less quality.

Given that many sites are likely to receive only assessment funding, what the environmentalist produces as an assessment will almost certainly need to contain more information than at present; it will become, in effect, the archive. Not only will qualitative data be needed, but short statements regarding the location and nature of the site should be included. Although not necessary for the client, the latter are essential for other specialists in order to make the reports usable. To ensure that adequate levels of data are recovered, excavation specifications must become more precise, although not prescriptive, which would prevent the subject from advancing. Statements such as 'environmental evidence must be considered' are academically inadequate in what is essentially a money-led exercise.

The sites themselves will rarely produce enough data for statistically significant interpretation, and therefore the major analyses of individual sites possible in the past, for example Thorpe Thewles (Heslop 1987) and Carlisle (McCarthy 1991), will become rare. Group value will become far more important and will force environmentalists to look at a broader scale, perhaps more than was possible and certainly more than was favoured before, itself allowing wider interpretation of changing economic practices. Such assessment work should also enable research proposals targeting specific problems to become more focused and, it is to be hoped, enable them to attract what is a very limited resource – money.

An example of potential group value can be seen from a study of plant remains from Roman to Romano-British sites in the east of the region (Fig 8.6). It is unclear when oats were cultivated, and this is not made easier by the inability to distinguish reliably the cultivated from wild grains. The chaff is identifiable, but rarely preserved. Oat grains do, however, regularly appear in deposits of the first century AD in North Yorkshire, but it is not until the third century that they become apparent in the Tyneside region, or indeed abundant in North Yorkshire. A combination of detailed sampling from a variety of sites, plus morphometric work on modern oat grains, could help determine the status of oats – arguably the most important local species by the medieval period. This is also a clear example of how the relatively small assessment sites (all of these except Roecliffe) have great potential to develop research questions.

Investigation at a population level rather than

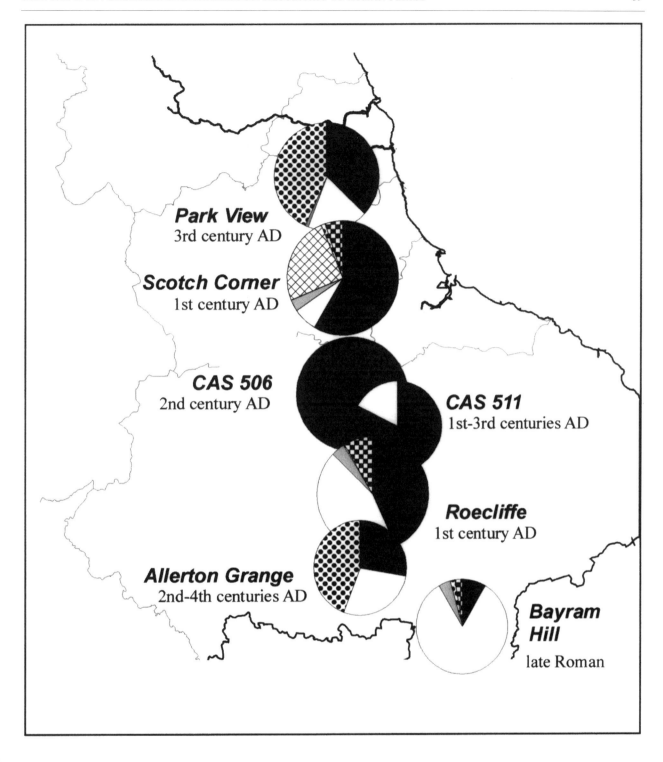

Fig. 8.6 Proportions of cereal grains (excluding indeterminate) from Roman sites, predominantly military, in County Durham and North Yorkshire, demonstrating increasing importance of oats in the third century AD. Data after Huntley 1994b (Bayram Hill); 1994c (Allerton Grange); 1994d (Park View); 1994e (CAS 506 and CAS 511); 1994f and forthcoming (Roecliffe); 1995 (Scotch Corner)

the individual grain level could considerably improve interpretation as well. For example, at Bayram Hill metrical analysis of wheat grains indicated that a third of the material was probably bread wheat (Huntley 1994b).

A second example of group value suggests the possibility of different crop husbandry practices in the North Yorkshire area by the regular occurrence of achenes of *Anthemis cotula* (stinking mayweed), a species characteristic of heavy clay soils, on Romano-British sites. It has not been recorded from any of van der Veen's sites on Teesside and northwards (Iron Age or Romano-British), irrespective of their soil status. Such group value is again leading to the generation of hypotheses, themselves the subject of testing. Environmental questions can therefore lead excavation for a change.

More emphasis will need to be placed on the charred plant remains and the smaller animal bones. The former in particular are the only categories of plant remains to be preserved in the majority of both urban and rural sites. These are not visible during excavation, and sampling still needs to be undertaken more widely. The days of 'I can't see it so it isn't there' must disappear, and it is clear that the environmentalists must become more pro-active. Selling ourselves becomes the name of the game.

In more specific terms: Mesolithic evidence from flints suggests that the Cumbrian coast around Eskmeals has equally high potential for investigation as the North York Moors, and pollen sites are present too. Such an area would compare well with the upland work. Sites such as Star Carr, where macrofossil, pollen and bone evidence all survive, must be examined in detail, but their discovery is likely to be by chance, although potential areas are being suggested through survey work – the North West Wetlands Project, for example.

Neolithic settlement sites need targeting to investigate the nature of domestication of plants and animals, and to test the hypothesis that Neolithic culture spread rapidly through Britain, but not necessarily from north to south (witness the fact that Balbridie has more similarities to mainland European sites than to other British sites). Synthesis of existing pollen work, as well as new fine-resolution work, would also assist this debate. Metrical analyses of bones and modern DNA work could assist too.

For the Bronze Age, more work needs to be carried out at an archaeological level on a variety of site types which may or may not be Bronze Age; this would aid investigation of the changing nature of agriculture. For example, we have both naked and hulled barley from this period, but by the Iron Age nearly all barley is hulled; when did this transition occur, and how? It is, indeed, a nationwide transition, and there are surely potential sites in the region to address the questions. However, sites need to be well-dated as well as excavated and sampled in order for this question to proceed. From surveys it is clear that field systems still survive from the Bronze Age, and the region therefore has high potential to investigate sites within their landscape. Given that seed concentrations are low in many cases, particularly large samples should be taken in order to produce statistically significant results.

The Iron Age has the most well-analysed data, but only from the east of the region. Such analyses show very well what can be done with palaeobotanical data in terms of crop husbandry in relation to environmental parameters. It is probably the only prehistoric period so far where specific sites could be targeted in order to address detailed environmental questions. For example, further comparative work between high status sites, such as Stanwick, and local farms, such as Scotch Corner and Rock Castle, is needed. Landscape studies remain important, not only for comparison with the Bronze Age material, but also to investigate the effect of the later Roman military occupation on the area's agriculture. As for the Bronze Age, a series of different types of sites should be fully investigated from the environmental point of view; whilst their typology has been well studied, their biological remains have largely been ignored.

Weed assemblages from all periods provide the potential to investigate changing usage of local vegetation: when particular types of soil were (could be) cultivated, for example. There are clear differences in a north-south transect through the east of the region for the Iron Age to Romano-British periods.

In geographical terms, what was going on in the west of the region for any of the periods discussed above? Pollen evidence demonstrates that people were present and clearing woodland, but what they were then doing is almost completely unknown; environmental evidence from excavation of any type of site is very rare.

Conclusions

Environmental archaeology has been accepted (more or less) as a routine part of excavation, and has achieved a great deal, particularly with regard to the plant remains for certain limited periods and parts of the region. However, given that we do not actually know even what the main cereals were or the favoured meat was in the west of the region, we cannot rest on our laurels. We need to be more focused and pro-active to march into the twenty-first century; the first aspect is already being addressed by producing reviews of existing material (Huntley and Stallibrass 1995), as well as developing research frameworks for the region. It is time for excavation to be led by environmental questions. It is also time to integrate more with the traditional palynologists working on material not directly related to excavation. 'Landscape archaeology' is a popular concept; environmentalists in the broad sense are essential to its investigation. Perhaps it is even time to forget the pottery and relegate *it* to the spoil heap for once; after all, its potential for dating has largely been superseded by radiocarbon and other independent means. It is certainly time to concentrate on the environmental evidence, to put archaeology in its place and to see how people were living in all the marvellous sites we have in our region.

Future (Im)Perfect?

The above was written in 1996 and has not been changed other than to update the bibliography and to add dots on the maps to show where new sites have been at least assessed. Whilst this is not the place in which to update fully the data and the story itself, it does provide an opportunity to look back five years.

It has proven true that the majority of excavations are a result of the planning process and thus developer-led. In addition, they are, by and large, small sites with relatively small-scale sampling (Fig. 8.7). This figure presents the post-1995 sites which have samples that have at least been evaluated, compared with those pre-1995 sites which were either evaluated or, in many cases, went straight to full analysis without detailed assessments – as was the norm at that time. 50% of recent sites have fewer than five samples investigated compared with thirteen samples for the earlier sites, with only 5% producing more than 25 samples compared with more than 200 samples for the earlier sites. Thus the group value of sites has, indeed, become the most important aspect since, at this level of sampling, hardly any sites are producing statistically valid data-sets of themselves. There has, however, to be more than "adding dots to the map", and time is needed to look at sites in more detail with respect to numbers of samples taken on site as opposed to those being evaluated, to the numbers and types of context, the area/nature of excavation, and the data obtained. Such an overview may allow targeting of some site types or periods, thus making more effective use of limited resources. It may also allow us to demonstrate whether the present level of sampling is appropriate or not. Group values should also lead into the Regional Research Frameworks which are, at last, actively being developed for the North-East, the North-West and, separately, for the Hadrian's Wall World Heritage Site, although this latter should draw heavily upon, and integrate with, the others. English Heritage is providing some funds to enable these to progress but they are being managed by, and will belong to, the Regional Community as a whole. Such frameworks should, we hope, then provide impetus to design research projects as well as act as a formal background against which funding bodies can judge project designs.

The pressure to produce more in less time (ie money), but with no concomitant loss in quality, is being addressed through the implementation of a series of posts, funded by English Heritage, of Regional Advisors in Archaeological Science. The Advisors (North-East Region plus Hadrian's Wall based in Durham, and North-West in Liverpool) provide impartial and free advice on scientific matters to Local Authority curators, EH Inspectors and independent contractors. They are also developing, at the national level, "Model Briefs and Specifications" for scientific work to assist curators in providing a level playing field against which contractors tender – another area into which the overview of sites and sampling would feed – although these may need fine tuning to specific regional criteria. The advisors are contributing, as appropriate, to the English Heritage guidelines for specific materials in collaboration with staff from the Centre for Field Archaeology at Fort Cumberland. Provision of training for local archaeologists in a variety of materials is proving both popular and useful as well as an effective means of keeping people up-to-date with recent techniques and advances. Such sessions also demonstrate what specialists do 'behind the scenes' in the laboratory thus demystifying the specialist areas and, one hopes, demonstrating value for money.

Synthetic research was suggested as one way

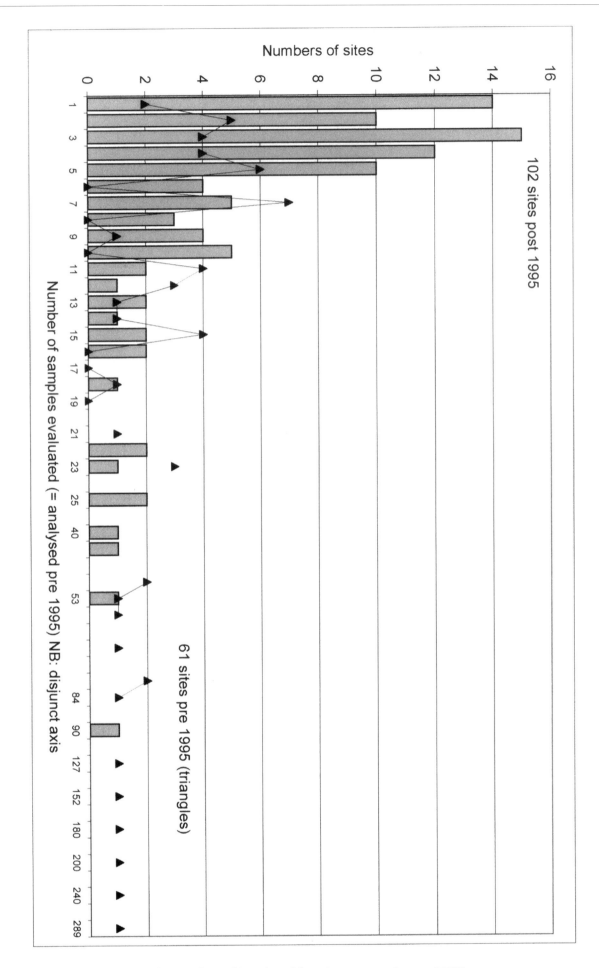

Fig. 8.7 Numbers of samples evaluated/analysed by site pre- and post-1995

forward in 1996. Some has been completed, notably that of Pratt (1996) and demonstrates the potential for such work, although it was not, in reality, associated with any aspect of the planning process. As well as looking at archaeological data, she extracted pollen data at 500 year intervals, from the many published pollen diagrams for the Tyne-Tees region, presenting the latter as a series of maps. She demonstrated intriguing changes in cereal pollen, for instance, suggesting intense cultivation in the north-east of the region during the early part of the Neolithic, with a subsequent retreat and then expansion from two discrete directions, northeast and south-east, during the Bronze Age. These sort of patterns challenge considerations of cultural or social change or of environmental parameters, and are beginning to be tied in with charred plant remains too.

Other data requiring synthesis are probably now available and suggestions would include the macroplant and animal/fish remains from excavations in both Berwick and Durham. Such syntheses would feed into the Urban Database projects and, again, inform the better use of limited resources in future developments.

However, for such syntheses to be undertaken, comparable data need to be available and we return to the details given in curatorial briefs and specifications. Inevitably in the market-led world some specialists will simply say "charred cereals present" rather than identify to species unless that level of detail is required from the outset and monitored adequately. Even presence/absence data can be acceptable, but, more usefully, identifications need to be made and the criteria used for those identifications presented. Without them data can be unreliable as witnessed by some recent blind tests using fish bone (Gobalet 2001). Here, experienced specialists were given an assemblage for analysis and their results compared. The conclusions indicated that a specialist with narrow expertise was more reliable than the often more favoured "general environmentalists", that local knowledge and experience reduced a regional bias, that access to (and use of) good reference collections is critical and that methods and criteria plus the data themselves must be presented. The latter would enable other workers to judge for themselves if necessary. The reports clearly need also to be in the public domain.

In terms of the 1996 'dark hole of the west', one large assemblage has now been studied – that from Irby on the Wirral by the author

(archive reports in preparation) – and inevitably has raised more questions than it has answered. The site dates from perhaps 400 BC to 400-500 AD and is essentially an extensive rural settlement. The economy is dominated by emmer wheat and naked barley until perhaps the 3rd century AD when it switches to hulled barley with bread wheat and oats. Spelt is minimal although it would be expected given the well-attested Roman military activity in the area. Were these farmers actively conservative, ignoring or being allowed to ignore the Romans, or were there other reasons why they didn't adopt a Roman economy? Were they typical of the area or simply an 'odd bunch'?

So, in summary, we have moved on in that there are rather more sites, albeit small with few samples and little data, than there were in 1996. We have started the process of synthesising existing data and are just about starting production of the Regional Research Frameworks. We have developed a system to try to improve quantity and quality of work from developer-led interventions, where this is appropriate. Perhaps the most important aspect is that we have recognised, dare I say accepted, the changed fate of the majority of archaeological funding, have recognised many of the potential problems that that has brought and are now trying to address those problems in order to take our subject forward.

Acknowledgements

I would like to thank Sue Stallibrass for many discussions about the animal bone assemblages in particular during the reign of the 'Regional Review' – Mark 2 is on the way. I also thank archaeological colleagues in departments and units across the region for years of supplying samples for analysis. Without them this paper would not have been possible. I also gratefully acknowledge English Heritage who, besides funding many of the earlier rescue-type excavations and my work on their plant remains, allowed me time to produce both the original paper and this somewhat updated version.

Section 3: Roman

Introduction

David J Breeze[*]

It is remarkable that discussion of military structures forms such a small part of the four papers which cover the Roman period. One suspects that this would not have been the case twenty years ago. The period from 1976 onwards has seen major work on Roman forts – Wallsend, Housesteads and Birdoswald on the Wall, South Shields, Vindolanda and Carlisle. Excavations at all these sites have significantly changed our understanding of the planning of forts and cast light on the history of the North. But all such work has been undertaken within a much wider framework than before. Lindsay Allason-Jones has emphasised this for the finds and Jacqueline Huntley for the environmental evidence, while James Crow has placed the work on military sites within a different, but equally wide, framework: archaeological resource management. We are long past the days when guide-books to military sites gave a bare nod towards the 'natives' and ignored the environment altogether as Jacqueline Huntley and Mike McCarthy show. This is important for it is indicating that Roman archaeology, after some years in the doldrums, or perhaps rather Coventry, is coming back into the mainstream of British archaeology.

This is illustrated in another way. The Roman period, for its practitioners (and not withstanding the comments of Richard Reece), has long held a certain fascination in the interplay of literary sources and archaeological evidence. The Vindolanda writing tablets have given a fillip to the study of archaeology in the north for, I think, two reasons. Firstly, for the evidence they contain in themselves and through that our ability to understand the Roman army and life on the northern frontier in the early years of the second century AD. Secondly, because they validate the use of the Eastern documents for the north-western frontiers of the Roman empire. Hitherto, there has always been an element of doubt as to the relevance to the northern frontiers of the material relating to the more sophisticated Eastern society with its longer history of civilisation. Although there are unique documents in the Vindolanda archive, there is also much that is very similar to the Eastern material and demonstrates that 'evidence by analogy', as Rivet puts it, is an important source of information for the study of Roman Britain. This itself has encouraged the interest of theoretical archaeologists such as John Barrett, who sees Roman Britain as a testing ground for his views of archaeology.

Another reason, I suspect, where Roman Britain is coming back into fashion is the sheer wealth of material which can now be manipulated through excavation reports. Again, as Lindsay Allason-Jones points out, there has been a flood of publications on small finds. Major reports have been published on work on Hadrian's Wall, at South Shields and elsewhere, all providing comparanda and rich mines of data for analysis and synthesis by other scholars.

Finally, the Roman period in the North continues to provide an important dated horizon. The building of Hadrian's Wall (and the Antonine Wall) can be dated very closely, as can other events in the north. This is not only of general importance to the prehistorian or early medievalist, but of especial significance when so much of the Roman period falls within a period when radiocarbon dates are so problematic. The four papers which consider the Roman period are thus not only important in themselves, but they point us towards a more interesting future for Roman archaeology in northern England where its wider significance and value is more widely appreciated.

[*]Address: Historic Scotland, Longmore House, Salisbury Place, Edinburgh EN9 1SH

Chapter 9: Roman Military Sites

*James Crow**

To the world beyond the north of England, the monuments of the most northerly fringe of the Roman empire are probably the most celebrated and certainly most familiar aspect of the archaeology of the north. The region can boast two of England's World Heritage Sites: one, the Romanesque architectural grandeur of Durham, and two, Hadrian's Wall, from the urban edge of Newcastle across the Tyne-Solway Isthmus and down the Cumberland coast as far as Maryport. Before outlining the successes and triumphs of the archaeological campaigns of Roman military archaeology over the past two decades, it is useful to recall briefly how the Roman Wall has been perceived by at least some of its immediate neighbours over the past twelve months.

In April 1995, English Heritage launched a draft management plan for the World Heritage Site of Hadrian's Wall. At the initial meeting, filled with councillors, planners, tourist board managers and academics, the plan met with general, if guarded, approval. For the first time in many years, a positive effort was being made to coordinate planning and tourism, and aspects of archaeological management, for the benefit of the monument. Responses to the draft plan were not anticipated before the end of the summer, and initially there seemed to be a limited response after a glittering launch of the draft plan at Birdoswald, and English Heritage's commitment to the Wall with the appointment of Dr Christopher Young as Director for Hadrian's Wall. Like Varus' legions descending into the Teutoburgerwald, the Wall's protectors had gravely underestimated the local opposition to the plan, and the influence of the local Tynedale weekly newspaper, the *Hexham Courant*. By the end of the summer, local opposition began to emerge, and week by week the local hostility to the management plan was vocalized in the columns and letters pages of the *Courant*. Many of these responses were misinformed, and were ignorant of fact and detail about the history and archaeology of the Roman Wall and the objectives of the draft plan, although with hindsight many of the recommendations could have been expressed more tactfully. Of greater concern to the archaeologists than to the managers was that these responses showed little or no sympathy with the archaeological importance of Hadrian's Wall, or the academic and international significance of the World Heritage Site. The more vocal opponents to the plan, they can be termed 'Murosceptics', continued to express extreme views throughout the autumn months, although none was as extreme as a Tynedale District Councillor, who likened the proposals to 'Ethnic Cleansing', a jest seen to be in extremely bad taste shortly after news of the massacres at Sebrenica.

Only after a vigorous public relations campaign by Dr Young were many of the original concerns and fears of the scheme's opponents calmed, and a revised plan was finally launched in July 1996. Many of the original objectives have been met, and the overall proposals have been slimmed down and simplified. The process of democratic consultation has been shown to work, and it is to hoped that future management can be achieved through 'consensus and partnership' (English Heritage 1996, 5). But at the same time this process exposed the lack of sympathy towards the archaeological remains of the Roman past from some of the extreme 'Murosceptic' views. Little seems to have changed in two centuries since the destruction of Castlesteads, or the levelling of part of Chesters by John Clayton's father. Generations of antiquarian study, public information and international repute seemed to be of no consequence to some members of the local farming and land-owning communities on either side of the Roman Wall. The archaeology and its study are still seen by some as an interference into the processes of their daily livelihood, worthy of notice only if there is an instant economic benefit. This is a rather bleak view of what is probably a minority, yet that minority has certainly become more vocal than earlier this century. When the Central Sector of the Wall was threatened by quarrying in the 1930s, the Establishment sprang to the defence of the Wall, bringing with it some local support (Crow 1995, 110-14). Today these actions are reserved for bypasses and SSSIs; ecological and environmental agendas predominate over cultural and historical issues, and as archaeologists we need to win back some of this lost ground, and to make more of the discoveries and new evidence which continue to emerge about the structures and garrisons of Hadrian's Wall. In short, Hadrian's Wall needs not to be just a

*Address: Dept of Archaeology, The University, Newcastle upon Tyne, NE1 7RU

'resource' for managers, but we need to regain some of the 'excitement' which it generated in earlier generations of scholars and visitors.

In many respects, it is inevitable that there should be a paper concerned with the Roman Military archaeology of the four northern counties covered by the CBA region at a conference such as this; at the very least, the Roman remains provide such a usefully dated benchmark for the more diffuse societies before and after the Roman occupation. But how inevitable was the Roman presence in the north? In southern Britain, centuries of close ties across the English Channel ensured that many of the developments in material culture, tribal organization and settlement were predetermined and inevitable, closely following patterns in continental Europe. But in the north this was not necessarily so, and there remained a fundamental difference between the north and south parts of Roman Britain, defined approximately by the M62 and the two most northerly permanent legionary fortresses at York and Chester. The pre-existing differences between north and south conditioned a different response from the Mediterranean invaders, so that the Roman presence retains an artificial character which hardly became integrated into northern Iron Age society. This different response meant that throughout three and a half centuries of Roman rule, two parallel and unrelated systems of native and Roman co-existed. Crucial for the effective running of the Roman provincial system was the engagement of the local elites – the *devotio* of the upper classes. Yet there is simply no evidence for this system taking root in the northern part of Britain, with the exception of the artificial military towns of Corbridge and Carlisle. Elsewhere in the frontier zone, the forts and their garrisons were paradigms for the provincial mosaic of cities which was the Roman imperial norm. It is important therefore to remember that the Roman Wall and its military garrisons were not inevitable in the long-term history of the region, and that they represent a distinct imprint on the northern scene, with a character unique in Europe, to be interpreted as potent symbols of power or failure.

It is useful to take stock after twenty years, not simply because of the anniversary of the publication of *Archaeology in the North*, but also because it is *more than* twenty years since the publication of the first edition of David Breeze and Brian Dobson's *Hadrian's Wall*, a work which remains, now in a fourth edition

(2000), the most useful modern synthesis of the history of the Wall and its garrisons. The period under review has seen major and extensive excavations and fieldwork, much of it financed either directly or indirectly from government funds, and we should acknowledge the support from the Department of the Environment and English Heritage, as well as other agencies and local authorities, especially the Manpower Services Commission. Whether Roman archaeology will fare as well in an age of Developer Funding and Lottery Grants is less clear.

A review of the achievements of the past two decades needs to recognize the major advances in our knowledge of the principal structures of the Wall, as well as developments on the Wall forts and posts to north and south. One vital aspect of the Roman occupation that is not considered in detail is that of the native population. One major development has been the air reconnaissance carried by Barri Jones and Nick Higham in Cumbria, which has drawn attention to the diversity of settlement in the uplands and on the coastal plain of the Solway (Higham and Jones 1975). East of the Pennines, since the retirement of George Jobey and his one-man 'Royal Commission', the past decade has seen little further research into this question, which remains fundamental to our understanding of the period and which poses the biggest challenge for future scholarship. A major disincentive for the study of the native population and settlement is the imprecision of the chronology of non-Roman sites. A radical new approach, perhaps involving high precision radiocarbon dating or some such method, is needed to allow a correlation with the dated contexts and structures in neighbouring Roman military sites, otherwise one data-set will remain in the shadow of proto-history and no proper synthesis can be achieved.

A number of the forts, particularly to the east and in the centre of Hadrian's Wall, have been subject to major excavations. The most extensive of these is Wallsend, excavated by Charles Daniels from 1975-84. Threatened redevelopment of the site occasioned the almost total excavation of the fort and the eventual preservation and partial display of the remains. The scale of the excavation is unique for a stone fort in Britain (comparable only with the recent work at the turf and timber Flavian fort at Elginhaugh, south of Edinburgh), and although the remains were less well preserved than at forts such as Birdoswald, it gave the opportunity to examine the anatomy of a fort in plan, and to see how that plan evolved over three centuries (Daniels 1989, 77-83, figs 39-42). The basic plan is that of a conventional *cohors quingenaria equitata*, including stables and a courtyard building in the central range almost identical in plan to the so-called hospital at Housesteads (Crow 1995, 50). In the second phase, rebuilding and additions included a substantial cross-hall built across the front of the headquarters and the granary; but the major changes in plan did not occur until the fourth century, when the northern third of the fort (*praetentura*) appears to have been largely empty of structures, and chalet-type buildings replaced the earlier barracks to the south. The implications of the changes are discussed below.

Very extensive work has been carried out south of the Tyne at South Shields since 1977, initially directed by Roger Miket, and latterly by Paul Bidwell. It has long been recognized that the remains at South Shields were more than just another hinterland fort, but could be related to long-distance trade and communications with the Hadrian's Wall system as a whole. The recent excavations, now published in part (Bidwell and Speak 1994), suggest that the earliest stone fort, similar in size to the Hadrianic fort at Wallsend, was constructed in the middle of the second century AD. Excavations to the south of it revealed an extensive cobbled area, which may have been a parade ground or vehicle parade, beneath which were discovered traces of a pre-Roman Iron Age circular house and earlier prehistoric finds (Hodgson 1994).

This mid-Antonine fort was drastically altered in the late second or early third century when fifteen new granaries were built in the interior including part of the headquarters building. In the next phase, dated to the early to mid third century, a new headquarters was constructed, and additional granaries brought the total up to 23, with an estimated capacity of 3,200 tonnes, sufficient to feed 15,000 men for six months, or else to fill the granaries of all the Wall forts from Wallsend to Carvoran (Bidwell and Speak 1994, 30). Formerly this phase was considered to represent a campaign base for Septimius Severus' expedition into Scotland; the recent excavations have suggested that rather than being a base for a single expedition, it was the supply base for the garrisons on Hadrian's Wall throughout. Of particular importance was the discovery and analysis of charred grain which could be identified as bread wheat with a probable continental origin (*ibid*, 243-60). The implications of these finds are very considerable

for our understanding of long-distance trade and the impact of the Roman garrisons on the native communities. Ever since Manning argued that locally farmed resources could adequately supply the Roman garrisons in northern England (1975), it has been accepted that local supplies were sufficient for this purpose. However, it is clear from pottery and other evidence that large quantities of material were transported for the northern military market (eg Funari 1991). The evidence from the South Shields granaries would imply that grain was also a staple that was transported, although how the imported foodstuffs were handled and stored before the third-century structures were built is not known.

Parts of the fort seem to have been damaged by fire in the late third or early fourth century, and some of the granaries were converted into barracks, possibly for a naval detachment with the exotic name of the Tigris Bargemen. The form of the barracks does not resemble the plan of the chalet units which are present at the same period across the river at Wallsend, but follows a pattern already known at Vindolanda and South Shields from the mid third century. By making what he calls 'selective comparisons', Bidwell has recently argued that there is no real difference between this barrack plan and the so-called chalets (1990, 9; *contra* Daniels 1980). In reality, individual barrack units or chalets appear to represent a distinctive development (Crow 1995, 85-8), which is mainly found on the Wall forts, and may indicate that there was different status between those units on the Wall and those set behind it (see Hodgson 1991). Daniels argued from the fourth-century evidence for Wallsend and Housesteads that there was a significant reduction in the size of the militarily effective population in the forts (1980), including perhaps 'married quarters' (see however his cautious observations in Daniels 1989, 83). This interpretation has been followed in recent general accounts of the late Roman army in Britain (including Cleary 1989, 59, which favours a rather drastic reduction to 10% of the second-century garrison). The evidence from South Shields, and a reassessment of the Housesteads structures and the small finds evidence (Daniels and Rushworth forthcoming), should cause some of these extreme views of fourth-century 'downsizing' to be challenged. The late Roman army was certainly different from its second- and third-century predecessors, yet at South Shields the recent excavations have revealed a large fourth-century house with an internal bath suite in the east corner of the fort, which is best identified as the new '*praetorium*' for the prefect of the Tigris Bargemen (Bidwell and Speak 1994, 35-9). The sort of garrison reductions which have been proposed would not only have had a drastic impact on the military strength of the Wall army, but also a very visible effect on the economic life in the Roman north, and this is not represented either in the artefacts or in the barrack buildings, or in the public structures of forts such as South Shields and Housesteads.

The excavations at South Shields and Wallsend represent the largest-scale archaeological projects on Hadrian's Wall since the excavations of Corbridge before the First World War, but there have been many other investigations, partly determined by modern pressures and developments or, like Birdoswald and Housesteads, by a combination of research and presentation. One, however, stands out by the nature and importance of the discoveries. Excavations at Vindolanda have continued throughout the period, a unique example of a private excavation by Robin Birley for the Vindolanda Trust. The remains of the waterlogged deposits from the pre-Hadrianic forts provide an archive of unique importance for the study of the Roman army and Roman social history. The archive of written material (Bowman 1994) can only be compared to the finds of papyri from Egypt or from Dura Europos in Syria (Fink 1971), The documentary evidence provides an insight into peoples' lives and language in Northumberland not available again for another 1400 years.

Other works, on a smaller scale than these enterprises, have provided important evidence for the location and character of the Wall and forts such as Newcastle, Bowness and Burgh-by-Sands (see the summaries in Daniels 1989 and Breeze 1991). More extensive works at Housesteads have already been noted, and the excavations from 1974 to 1981 provided the opportunity for a detailed study of the barracks and the fort defences in the north-east angle, as well as a reassessment of earlier works (Crow 1995; Daniels and Rushworth forthcoming). One important development has been the extensive surveys carried out on the Wall and on the temporary camps in the north by the Royal Commission for Historic Monuments for England from its Newcastle Office (Welfare and Swan 1995). This corpus provides for the first time a comprehensive record of those fragile field monuments, many of which survive best in the upland pastures of Cumbria and Northumberland.

Although a great deal of attention has been shown towards the detailed investigation of the forts on Hadrian's Wall over the past two decades, one significant change in attitude came in 1978 when the then DoE Inspector for the Wall, Ian Stewart, embarked on a programme of detailed recording of the curtain of Hadrian's Wall before consolidation. Previously, long stretches had been cleared and restored with little or no detailed record, and archaeological recording was reliant on the interest, good will and experience of the DoE charge-hand or foreman. The first work was associated with the excavation of milecastle 35 (Sewingshields), and although little was published from that excavation (Haigh and Savage 1984), it set a precedent for work in the 1980s, both in the Central Sector and in the suburbs of Newcastle, with significant consequences for our understanding and perception of the mural barrier. The period under consideration has also seen extensive recording by English Heritage of the Wall and other monuments in guardianship (Whitworth 1994), and a detailed analysis of two of the most imposing stone structures along the line of Hadrian's Wall, the bridges at Chesters and Willowford (Bidwell and Holbrook 1989). This study showed that the bridges were, in their second phase at least, massive stone structures carrying the military road and Wall, indicative of the new road system created to service the Wall in the late second century.

As a result of serious erosion to the fabric of the Wall caused by walkers between Steel Rigg and Housesteads, a programme of excavation and recording began in 1982. Eventually over 500 metres of Wall were excavated, recorded and consolidated during the next seven years and a number of important observations were made (Crow 1991a). An unexpected tower was located in Peel Gap additional to the known system of turrets, and it could be seen that the Wall had been extensively rebuilt and restored in the early third century throughout the length examined. As part of the same programme, milecastle 39 (Castle Nick) was fully excavated and the north gate of milecastle 37 (Housesteads) was investigated before consolidation. From both milecastles it was clear that there was minimal provision for access through the Wall: the north gate of 37 was blocked after an early collapse, and at 39 buildings were allowed to encroach across the central roadway. It would appear that the milecastles functioned to allow Roman troops access to the north of the Wall, but did not provide convenient crossing points for the native communities as has been claimed in the past.

The overall impression from these excavations was that Hadrian's Wall was intended and maintained as a barrier; it could certainly control movement, even if it might not repel a sustained assault. It is possible to draw similar conclusions from work at the east end of the frontier. Immediately to the west of Wallsend fort, excavations by the Tyne and Wear Museums Service before the construction of a replica length of Hadrian's Wall revealed not just the line of the curtain wall with evidence for repairs, but a series of regular pits cutting into the berm (Cleary 1993, 284). These would appear to be the remains of *lilia*, intended to provide additional warning and protection for the Wall curtain. An additional system of ditches at right angles to the Wall may have served as a defence for a *vicus* or an annexe west of the fort. At West Denton, work by Paul Bidwell in advance of the construction of the new A1 revealed a length of broad curtain wall with clay bonding. Traces of plaster indicated that the inner face of the Wall had been rendered (Bidwell 1996, 22), a discovery which supported the suggestion that part of the Wall in the Central Sector was whitewashed (Crow 1991b, 46). The same excavation at West Denton also revealed a section through the Vallum which was found to be cut through the sandstone bedrock and with almost vertical sides (Frere 1988, 433). None of these excavations have been fully published, yet the results certainly justify the new resources directed towards the wall and the lesser structures of the system. In addition to the investigation at milecastles 35, 37 and 39, work has been undertaken to completely excavate milefortlet 21 (Swarthy Hill) on the Cumbrian coast. The results revealed a single phase of Hadrianic occupation (Frere 1992, 270-1) with huts and stores for the garrison. Significantly the main Hadrianic phase was not at all similar to the primary phase identified at Sewingshields (35), and there does not necessarily appear to have been a uniform blueprint for these structures as is sometimes proposed.

Other results from excavation at Carlisle and elsewhere in the north-west are discussed in Mike McCarthy's paper in this volume. For the remainder of this paper, attention will be directed towards three themes: new evidence for pre-existing Iron Age settlements, what happened after the Romans, and forts in the hinterland and beyond Hadrian's Wall.

Pre-Roman activity is best documented from the recent survey of early cultivation marks found below Roman structures (Topping 1989), to which can be added evidence from recent excavations at Wallsend and West Denton. At South Shields, excavations below the possible parade ground revealed a circular house of early Iron Age date, and other structures may be expected in the vicinity (Bidwell and Speak 1995, 13). Geophysical survey at High Rochester Fort has identified a geomagnetic anomaly to the west of and partly below the late first-century western annexe (Crow 1994). The survey revealed a D-shaped enclosure, comparable in size and shape to the nearby Iron Age settlement of Manside Cross, classified by Jobey as a rectangular multivallate fort (1965, 45-7). The use of Iron Age hillforts is well established from a number of sites in southern England and on the Welsh Marches (Frere 1986), but is not known from the north. Rather than adapting the existing defences, at High Rochester the Roman army was simply taking over the site of a pre-existing centre of local power. At Birdoswald, however, where ditches on the promontory were formerly considered to be of pre-Roman date, recent study of the environmental evidence indicates that the site was not cleared of primary vegetation before the construction of the Turf Wall (Wilmott 1997).

The principal new discussion of the sub-Roman period has arisen from Tony Wilmott's work at Birdoswald. Excavation of the granaries and the west gate provided clear evidence for post- Roman usage of the earlier structures, and the construction of a possible timber hall on the site of the north granary. Wilmott has argued for continuity of settlement, and in particular for the importance of the site as a centre of local authority in the immediate region after the withdrawal of Roman rule (1997). The post-Roman period poses some of the most intriguing, and at the same time most frustrating, questions concerning the history of the Wall. Churches have been recently suggested at South Shields (in the *principia*) and at Housesteads (Bidwell and Speak 1994, 45; Crow 1995, 95-7), and it is to be hoped that future excavations will continue to reveal more about the latest Roman and post-Roman deposits; this problem should be a priority for future research.

Forts and military settlements north and south of the Wall have received less attention. It is to be hoped that the extensive excavations at Piercebridge and Ribchester will soon be published, but another of the Durham forts, Lanchester, has been the subject of a detailed topographical and geophysical survey (Casey, Noel and Wright 1992). This has revealed the barracks and central buildings of the fort; a few later structures are apparent, but significantly there are no signs of 'chalet'-type barracks. On the line of Dere Street to the north of the Wall, a similar survey has been carried out at High Rochester. The geophysical evidence from the interior is less impressive, but in part confirms the results of the nineteenth-century excavations. Pre-Roman occupation has already been noted, but in the west field the plan of the late first-century annexe was identified by resistivity survey, and limited excavations have revealed traces of the turf bank. Further research will seek to investigate the relationship between the early fort and annexe and the pre-existing native enclosure. To the east of the fort, geophysical survey has identified structures beside Dere Street, but it remains unclear whether these represent a formal *vicus* or external workshops along the Roman road (Crow forthcoming). Survey at High Rochester and Chesters Bridge Abutment has also demonstrated the value of Ground Penetrating Radar, and another geophysical method using seismic refraction has been used to investigate the Vallum near Rudchester (Musty 1995, 394).

A preliminary study of the internal plan of High Rochester has indicated that the internal structures were more closely arranged than at the forts on Hadrian's Wall, a response to the isolated and vulnerable location of these forts with their mixed garrisons. Further research into these forts and their environs will be able to draw out some of these themes, since in their isolation they provide a useful contrast with the better-known Wall forts and their garrisons.

Conclusion

Hadrian's Wall and its associated structures and collections of finds and inscriptions represents a vast archive for the study of a vital aspect of the Roman world. The extent of the subject and the diversity of the evidence may appear intimidating, but new developments and technological advances in data collection and retrieval provide an opportunity to approach old problems in a new way, and furthermore to ask quite different questions. Two examples will suffice here: Geographical Information Systems can be used to examine questions about the location of the structures along the Wall, and to test rigorously

some of the claims concerning signalling and observation on the frontier system (cf Wooliscroft 1989). Similar techniques can be used to look at new ways of investigating existing data-sets. One possibility, using GIS, is to consider the Sacred Landscapes of Hadrian's Wall; to investigate the location and origin of shrines and sacred objects from the military zone, with the potential to understand more about the ideologies and beliefs of the Roman and native populations.

Author's note:
The text is presented here as it was submitted in 1997 with limited editorial revisions. Work has of course continued on the Roman remains in the North and in certain areas, notably air-photography (Tim Gates) and geophysical survey (Timescape Surveys) some very significant advances have been made. Bidwell's handbook for the 1999 Pilgrimage (1999) provides a comprehensive and insightful review of work over the past decade. A more popular, but well illustrated account, appeared in the special issue of *Current Archaeology* on Hadrian's Wall (No. 164, August 1999). The late Roman period has merited special attention, see the collected papers edited by Wilmott and Wilson (2000). The Wall figures also in a recent attempt to provide future research agendas for Roman archaeology (see the papers by James and Esmonde Cleary in James and Millett 2001) although the outstanding issue of 'Romans and natives' remains to be fully addressed. The potential of an intensive and detailed landscape survey has been revealed in the recent study of Eastern Dumfriesshire by Scottish Royal Commission (RCAHMS 1997). It presents new surveys of Roman military sites set in the continuing cultural landscape of the late Iron age. The opening of the site and visitor centre at Wallsend in 2000 with a spectacular reconstruction of Roman baths (based on Chesters) is a major new National Lottery initiative at the east end of the Wall.

Chapter 10: The Archaeology of Roman Non-Military Sites

Mike McCarthy*

Introduction

There are two possible starting points for this assessment. One is the publication in 1976 of *Archaeology in the North* (Clack and Gosling 1976), but the other could be 1965 when Peter Salway published his *The Frontier People of Roman Britain* (Salway 1965). As one would expect after more than thirty years, much of what Salway wrote, based on research carried out prior to 1961, has been overtaken by events, but it remains a fundamental work for the study of so-called non-military sites in northern England. Taking the evidence of epigraphy, plans of buildings and other matters concerning daily life, Salway attempted to define the evidence for civilian settlement and to breathe some life into the peoples who inhabited the northern frontier under Roman occupation.

My present aim is first to look at the range of information that is now available. I will then examine aspects of recent work in more detail, and these two points will provide an indication of how much progress has been made in the past three decades. I will then conclude with a look forward to possible research aims that could be addressed in the next twenty years.

The range of recent work

The past thirty years or so have seen an impressive increase in activity on many fronts. Aerial photography, notably the work of Higham and Jones (1975) and Bewley (1994), has substantially increased the numbers of 'native' sites, especially, but not only, west of the Pennines. Were we to agree with Higham and Jones's, but not Bewley's, contention that many of these new sites are Roman, we would concur with Daniels, who observed that this explosion of new data argues for 'the presence of a *considerable* population... and significantly increasing in size' (1979, 361). Even supposing that some of these sites are prehistoric or post-Roman in date, as Bewley would argue, it nevertheless remains the case that their discovery adds greater chronological depth to many landscapes in the north, and in some areas necessitates a reappraisal of the density of settlement in pre-medieval times.

Excavation has also proceeded apace in over a dozen *vici* and larger settlements, and in some cases this has had the fortunate effect of uncovering well-preserved waterlogged remains with all that entails, as well as useful ceramic and artefactual assemblages (Birley 1977; Austen 1991; McCarthy 1991; Padley 1991a and b; Hird forthcoming). To this can be added the recent growth of archaeological evaluation whereby potential development sites are examined to determine the presence or absence of archaeological remains prior to development taking place. Although the academic value of evaluations is clearly limited, they can identify settlement and land use patterns broadly attributable to pre-medieval periods. To that extent they are a useful additional tool.

It is difficult to quantify the amount of excavation and evaluation on non-military, as opposed to military, sites not least because the distinction between the two is not always clearcut. Nevertheless, a crude analysis shows just less than 100 major entries in the Roman Britain section of *Britannia* between 1976 and 1994, of which about half relate to Cumbria and half to counties in the north-east. The distribution of investigations east and west of the watershed is itself a significant advance on the mid-1970s, but although the number of projects appears to give cause for encouragement, the numbers are a result of the boom in rescue and developer-funded archaeology since the early 1970s, and it has to be said that many of these projects recorded in *Britannia* were very small in scale and, as with evaluations, of limited academic worth. The extent to which the frontiers of knowledge have been pushed forwards as a result of conventional excavation is, therefore, somewhat patchy.

One of the most important advances has been made in the field of environmentally-based work, arising out of the discovery of rich waterlogged deposits in places such as Carlisle, as well as in the study of carbonized plant remains, insect fauna and vertebrates by Huntley, Stallibrass and Kenward from a wide range of northern sites, building on Keeley's review (Keeley 1984; Huntley and Stallibrass 1995). Of particular interest is the work of van der Veen on carbonized material from late prehistoric sites in the north, which provides an invaluable starting point for evaluating Roman land use and crop husbandry (1992). A number of studies have

*Address: Department of Archaeological Sciences, University of Bradford, Richmond Road, Bradford BD7 1DP

looked at land use and climate through palyno-logical analyses combined with radiocarbon dates on cores taken through peat bogs (eg Dumayne and Barber 1994; Dumayne *et al* 1995; Barber *et al* 1994).

There has also been an increase in the numbers and range of publications including syntheses, general articles and conference proceedings (Chapman and Mytum 1983; Wilson *et al* 1983; Breeze 1984; Higham 1986; 1987; Bewley 1994), and site- or subject-specific volumes or excavation reports (Birley 1977; Charlesworth 1978; Bowman and Thomas 1983; Bishop and Dore 1989; McCarthy 1990; 1991; Caruana 1992; Bowman 1994; McCarthy 1995b). A large number of other wider-ranging articles which have a significant bearing upon the Roman landscape have appeared (eg Macklin and Passmore 1992; Macklin *et al* 1994; Dumayne and Barber 1994; Barber *et al* 1994; Dumayne *et al* 1995). Such works demonstrate the value of looking at the landscape from a much broader point of view, and illustrate Higham's point (1986) that the Roman occupation was but an interlude. In addition to the national and period journals there have been new publication vehicles in the north, including the journal of the Arbeia Society and the CBA's *Archaeology North*.

Recent work in the west
Until Higham and Jones commenced their work in Cumbria, knowledge of Roman non-military sites was largely confined to the limestone uplands and a few *vici* outside forts. In a series of papers they have demonstrated that lowland settlement was much more extensive in the west than was hitherto known. This led Jones and Walker (1983) to advance the idea that rural settlement developed to the rear of, and in the shelter of, Hadrian's Wall, whilst to the north of the Solway, in Annandale and Nithsdale, the aerial survey evidence seemed to indicate not just a lower density of settlement, but a greater proportion of defended, bivallate, sites. They concluded that settlement expanded under the protection of the Roman frontier and as a direct consequence of the needs of the army.

The evidence on which this model was based was slender in the extreme, and the dating evidence was virtually non-existent. Despite this they persist in viewing these new sites, numbering over 250, as being Roman. Both Young (1994a) and Bewley (1994) have exposed some of the difficulties with this, not least the circularity of the argument. In the first place, there is

so little archaeological data derived from excavation that any sweeping arguments founded on aerial photographs alone, and without any serious analysis of the data, must remain in the realms of pure speculation. Secondly, whilst we may well expect an increase in farming activity after the establishment of the frontier, we cannot know what form this may take, nor do we know whether Roman influence would necessarily be detectable in settlement morphology. Roberts's recent demonstration (1993) of the extreme complexity of landscapes in parts of the Eden valley conducive to above-ground survival casts serious doubt on simplistic conclusions based on aerial photography in areas where preservation is much poorer. Thirdly, much more off-site palynological work is required before we can begin to understand the mosaic of landscapes both faced by the incoming Romans, and modified by them.

Bewley's much more thorough analysis (1994), and to a limited extent the work of Carlisle Archaeological Unit, has shown that despite the superficially unpromising terrain, not only is there much diversity of enclosure form, but there is also considerable chronological depth in the landscape of north Cumbria. Bewley attempted to work out the theoretical exploitation territories of settlements. Abandoning the old MAFF Land Classification maps whereby soils were graded 1-5 as being inappropriate to a consideration of ancient agricultural practice, he looked instead at field capacity and workability using techniques developed by the Soil Survey. Taken with the distribution of prehistoric artefacts, he was able to conclude that there must have been much more Neolithic, Bronze Age and Iron Age activity in the region than had been supposed, and that the Roman element had been overstated. Carlisle Archaeological Unit's work tends to support this view, but with the caveat that Dumayne and Barber's palynological sequences in the central sector of Hadrian's Wall and in the Borders show no significant decreases in arboreal pollen prior to the first and second centuries AD (Dumayne and Barber 1994).

Jones and Walker's model, interesting though the essential idea is – the expansion of agricultural activity following the arrival of the Romans – must remain on hold. We certainly cannot accept it as it is currently stated, but we should not throw the baby out with the bathwater. What is required is much more high-quality fieldwork of the kind that both Jones and

Higham have published, as at Silloth Farm and Crosshill Farm, Penrith (Higham and Jones 1983), as well as a more intensive programme of palynological work.

Aspects of vici *and small towns*
Much work has taken place at many sites outside the defences of Roman forts, including Ambleside, Burgh-by-Sands, Stanwix, Low Borrow Bridge, Papcastle, Kirkby Thore, and Nether Denton, Rudchester, Vindolanda, South Shields, Wallsend, Piercebridge and Chester-le-Street.

At South Shields and Wallsend, Bidwell and his team have located buildings, roads and burials outside the forts (Snape 1993, 55-9) whilst Jones has photographed Nether Denton from the air revealing a network of roads and boundaries. At Burgh-by-Sands, excavation, aerial photography and geophysical survey have revealed an extensive and extremely busy *vicus* outside the Hadrian's Wall fort on its eastern and southern sides.

One of the impressive factors about many of these sites is their physical extent and apparent intensity of usage. At Old Penrith (Austen 1991) and at Vindolanda (Birley 1977), for example, the archaeological deposits were in excess of 3m in depth and were as complex as at any urban site. Some of these sites are of considerable size, and the extent of *vici* at South Shields, Kirkby Thore and Old Penrith, when plotted out, may eventually be similar to those sites such as Corbridge and Carlisle, normally thought of as small towns (see Postscript). Where do we draw the line here? How real is the distinction between the *vicus* and a small town in archaeological terms? Unfortunately, despite the list of *vici* that have been examined in recent years, we are still not much further forward in understanding the street layouts or building positions, let alone defining their chronological development from origins to abandonment. It is possible that the distinction may prove very difficult, if not impossible, to draw in pure archaeological terms.

A common feature of the two kinds of site is the strip building. Rectangular structures with one or two internal divisions, and in some cases with open fronts as at Burgh-by-Sands, they are known in stone and timber. The strip building is a very simple multi-purpose architectural form. Excavated evidence suggests that they were used for a variety of purposes, ranging from workshops for industrial activities, as in the case of bronze- and iron-working at Burgh-by-Sands

(G D B Jones pers comm.), to agricultural or food-related purposes, as assumed at Old Penrith or Carlisle where there are ovens associated with a great deal of burning, but no evidence for residues (Austen 1991; McCarthy 1990). As both vici and small towns must have been intimately linked in with farming activities, strip buildings may also have served for storing grain or as hay barns. Some could have been used for storing equipment, as places to smoke joints of meat, and doubtless for domestic accommodation or as shops.

We have hints at floor and foundation level for the shape of strip buildings, but what did they really look like? The size of the stones used in the foundations is sometimes such that we must surely envisage buildings with at least one upper floor, as was revealed at Redlands Farm, Stanwick, Northamptonshire where a complete collapsed gable end was found (Frere 1991, 253). Perhaps we should be thinking of these buildings as large barn-like structures, in some cases comparable in size to medieval tithe barns, and not as modest-sized bungalows.

Other elements that may be expected as important components in *vici* have either not been investigated, as is the case with *mansiones* and bath-houses, or so little work has taken place in recent years that no significant comments can be made, as is the case with cemeteries. The question of whether *vici* were defended has also not been widely addressed in the Hadrian's Wall zone. The two sites for which defences might be expected, Corbridge and Carlisle, still lack substantive evidence, but they are known at Malton and Bainbridge, and recently at Wallsend a 6-7m wide bank and substantial ditches have been discovered (Snape 1992, 62). It is possible that the apparent absence of permanent defences at Corbridge and Carlisle is an accident of discovery, but if not, the fact that some sites have them and others do not suggests that the question of defence provision may not be straightforward.

At the upper end of the settlement scale, Corbridge and Carlisle have long been regarded as pre-eminent in the Roman settlement of the north. Both may have been promoted to cantonal status perhaps in the late second or early third centuries.

At Corbridge (*Corstopitum* or *Coriosopitum*), where excavations first started in 1906, the most important advance has been the publication of the post-war excavations. Bishop and Dore (1989) have done a fine job with data of very variable quality. Although the well-known remains in the guardianship area are impressive, it is the site plan, Figure 5, which provides a dramatic picture of what a small town on the northern frontier looked like from the mid to late Antonine period. The settlement, extending over more than 40 acres, was centred on the junction of the Stanegate and Dere Street on the north bank of the River Tyne. It was divided into square to rectangular *insulae* by metalled streets fronted by densely packed buildings, including gable-end-on-street strip buildings, corridor houses, shops, workshops, a possible *mansio*, the enigmatic Site 11 variously described as a forum and a store building, walled compounds, and granaries, whilst epigraphic evidence implies the presence of temples.

As Bishop and Dore readily admit, our knowledge of the Severan and later settlement is sadly deficient in a great many respects. Indeed, we are still left with the picture of Corbridge which is not dissimilar to that which we had of Silchester before Professor Fulford's recent work. At Corbridge, despite the sequence of forts, and the plan of the later town as updated by the Royal Commission on Historical Monuments, major questions remain unanswered. Of these, the transition from fort to town in the later second century, the function of the two compounds, and the development of the settlement in the third and fourth centuries presumably through phases of gradual desertion, fragmentation, and abandonment, are amongst a host of problems. Within the guardianship area some of these questions may now be beyond answering, but opportunities in areas of pasture outside may still exist and should be sought.

Curiously, Carlisle, thought by Salway (1965, 204) to lack any real archaeological potential because of the presence of the modern city centre on the south side of the River Eden and on the main western route north into Scotland, may yet provide a model for Corbridge. Here, large-scale sustained investigations in the late 1970s and 1980s have now revealed the skeleton of the road system, the position of a major fort is known for certain and others are attested or suspected from other evidence. Many buildings are known, and long stratified sequences spanning the entire Roman period and beyond have been recovered.

As with Corbridge, where the later settlement overlies a succession of forts, Carlisle (*Luguvalium*) also began as a fort with an annexe on its southern side. The fort, established by Cerialis in AD 72-3 (Caruana forthcoming),

continued to be occupied throughout the Roman period into the mid fourth century, but the area of the annexe, containing a variety of repair, maintenance and provisioning functions (McCarthy 1991), was gradually encroached upon during the second century as the fort defences were rebuilt further south. Recent work has provided hints of other forts at a short distance to the east, as well as at Etterby on the north bank of the Eden.

Beyond the fort and annexe, a variety of sites excavated in the city centre have provided quite different pictures. In the late first and second centuries at Blackfriars Street, there is a pattern of strip buildings placed cheek by jowl (McCarthy 1990), not unlike some medieval burgage tenements developing in towns where space was at a premium. By contrast, at the southern end of The Lanes, large enclosed properties, each with a building and yards, resemble small farms, whilst at the northern end of The Lanes was a large complex of buildings, incorporating features reminiscent of military timber buildings, attributed to the Hadrianic to mid-Antonine periods. These appear to merge into a sequence closer to what one might expect in a domestic context (Zant forthcoming). What exactly was going on here is by no means clear, although a picture of zoning within second-century Carlisle seems to be emerging.

It is a fascinating sequence, made even more interesting by hints that Carlisle, like Corbridge, appears to have been upgraded at some point perhaps in the late second or early third century. The upgrading included new metalled streets and some fairly substantial buildings, amongst which is a building near Tullie House with massive foundations (Frere 1988, 438), and another on Scotch Street (Frere 1991, 235) which incorporated a large bath-house. At about this time there is a suggestion that earthen defences were thought necessary, but were left unfinished (McCarthy, 2000, 44-7). With the exception of large diamond-broached stones observed on the line of the medieval walls in 1972, and which could be Roman work *in situ*, this constitutes the only evidence for defences around the Roman settlement at Carlisle (Charlesworth 1978, 117-pre8).

Other buildings include at least two, possibly domestic, late structures incorporating hypocausts. The plan of one resembles a simple villa-like structure, but the majority of the buildings identified to date are strip buildings. There may have been several temples to judge by the epigraphic evidence, including one dedicated to Mithras, but no conclusive structural evidence has yet emerged.

Inevitably, perhaps, recent work in the small towns and the *vici* has raised many more questions than it has settled. One conclusion to be drawn is that the distinction clearly drawn by Salway in 1965 between on the one hand, the *vici*, unwalled and dependent upon the forts, and on the other hand, the towns such as Carlisle and Corbridge, both arguably civital capitals, defended and purely civilian (1965, 41), is becoming impossible to sustain. Notwithstanding the epigraphic sources referring to *vici* and *canabae* and their inhabitants, in archaeological terms the line between military and civilian cannot easily be drawn. Moreover, it is fair to add that that we do not yet understand any of the processes of settlement growth and decline, and we have little idea as to their function. Did a *vicus* develop out of an annexe? – and can we recognize the transition from one to the other? Were the processes of settlement accretion around forts usually the same? – or did different mechanisms operate, and if so what were they? What happened to these settlements that were seemingly alien in the Iron Age landscape of the first century AD, in the fourth and fifth centuries? How can we recognize the processes of settlement decay and metamorphosis at a time when cultural assemblages were also changing?

Future research directions

Where do we go from here? The easy answer, is of course, more excavation followed by publication. Excavation will undoubtedly expand our database with more buildings, defences if we are lucky, pottery, finds and some dated sequences, and this will take place anyway where the planning process impinges on such sites. We should not rely on such opportunities, however, because rescue archaeology, an unfashionable term these days, invariably operates to a different agenda and funding base to that of research. In the present writer's view, developer-led archaeology is unlikely to provide us with the tools for making a quantum leap in knowledge in the next twenty years. We need to complement planning-based archaeology with research, and here I wish to air two approaches, defined as the macro- and the micro-approach respectively.

The macro-approach

At the macro-level, a major issue concerns the environment within which settlements, *vici*,

native farmsteads, the towns and forts, existed. The potential for off-site and on-site environmental archaeology is now evident (Huntley and Stallibrass 1995), and a clearer understanding of the ecosystem within which all settlements operated is desperately needed. Without this dimension, archaeological projects concentrating entirely on settlement morphology and artefacts, as is conventionally the case, will inevitably fail to shed light on anything very much except perhaps aspects of architecture and material culture.

Research at the macro- or landscape-level could usefully focus on the relationships between settlements and the natural environment in all its forms. Following the work of both prehistorians and geomorphologists, research is needed into how environmental factors moulded life within the settlements, whether isolated native sites or semi-urban communities such as Corbridge, as much as the way human activity made use of the natural resources.

In doing this, we should put the distinction between forts and other sites to one side. The concept of the military site as being something separate and distinct from the non-military site is worth challenging. Whilst not doubting the primary purpose of the fort, which was military, and the substantial realignment of the economy that must have followed from the arrival of the Romans, to suppose that they existed apart from the rest of the community and its landscape would be mistaken, and the Vindolanda writing tablets provide a graphic illustration of the network of social, economic and official relationships that bound Roman military personnel together at the turn of the first and second centuries AD. To a significant degree, fort life was necessarily rooted in the agricultural cycle, and in the ability of the locality to produce the raw materials essential for the repair and maintenance of buildings and equipment. It is worth recalling that the medieval castle was also overtly military in function and concept. Abbeys served a specifically religious function, but castles and abbeys also had several key roles within the wider community as well as depending for their existence on their estates, their *territoria*. Roman forts and their *vici* were settlements in the landscape.

In parts of the north where settlement had been relatively sparse, the arrival of the Romans may have substantially upset the balance between different parts of the ecosystem, the meadows, open grazing, woodland pasture, uncleared woodland and wildlife including invertebrates, and contributed to longer-term effects on water flows and rates of incision of fluvial systems. Having arrived, the inhabitants of the *vici*, perhaps in combination with the military at certain times, may then have been responsible for establishing and maintaining a new equilibrium geared to the needs of an enhanced population.

In order to understand such issues, as well as fundamental problems underlying the relationships of native farmsteads, *vici*, forts and small towns, their economic base, or the dynamics of demography, it is necessary to invest time and resources into researching the context of settlement, of the kind that the RCAHMS and Historic Scotland undertook in the north Cheviots in the Bowmont Valley, near Kelso (Mercer and Tipping 1994). The argument here is not one in favour of environmental determinism, but it is a plea to swing the balance of research away from a political and military interpretation of the frontier region of Roman Britain, towards other factors which must have played a critical part in daily life.

The micro-approach
At the micro- or site-specific level, there is a need to adopt a more rigorous and analytical approach to the archaeological data themselves, especially site formation processes and cultural assemblages. The need to be aware of such matters is fundamentally important and can hardly be overstated, since the requirement to to date the deposits, and therefore frame a chronology for the site, is a paramount objective of any excavation.

A recent assessment of one of the largest excavations in Carlisle has shown that for some phases, the minimum residuality rate for pottery is around 30%, and for others it is as high as 90%. Some periods produce no finds at all. Samian ware vessels and mortaria can be shown to have joining fragments from tens of metres away, showing substantial dispersal patterns (Hird forthcoming). We are accustomed to thinking of residuality as an urban problem, but what about 'native' sites where finds are rare occurrences? Does the discovery of the occasional glass bangle or potsherd on rural sites have any evidential value at all for the history and dating of the sites?

Arising out of a close attention to site formation processes could be the creation of a series of phased spectra encompassing all finds, bones, seeds and other material, expressed perhaps in tabular or seriographic form. Such spectra will help us to compare like with like, phase by phase, site by site, and will enable us to see what, if anything, is typical at different points in time. Variability in the data will become apparent. At Carlisle, it is apparent that every site of first- and second-century date is different from every other. It raises the question, for example, as to whether the people who inhabited Carlisle between the Flavian and Antonine periods were not so much one community or one settlement, but more an agglomeration of communities, each of which had its own identity and its own reason for being there? Were these differences obliterated, or at least masked, by the imposition of other features in the townscape in the late second or early third centuries? Was this also the case at Corbridge, Old Penrith and other vici? – and what effect did turning the fort at South Shields into a supply base, perhaps during the Severan campaigns, have on the size and structure of the extra-mural settlement? One message that seems to be emerging from Carlisle, and which may well apply elsewhere, concerns the dynamic nature of settlements responding to a variety of pressures, including at one extreme Imperial frontier policy, and at the other, environmental factors.

Another aspect of the micro-approach concerns an alternative means of analysis, specifically that of archaeo-entomology. Kenward and Allison have recently examined the question of the origins of urban insects (1994, 55-6). They note that urban species did not evolve to take advantage of towns. Rather, a great many species in Britain are indigenous, and the immediate origin of the town insect fauna was in farm nuclei, usually in buildings of varying kinds and in mucky yards. The question is, can we use insects as a means of ranking settlements? In terms of their biota, can settlements be viewed as points on a continuum in which indices of diversity, specifically those of synanthropic species, that is to say those generally associated with human activity, may be used to measure the intensity and duration and nature of occupation, as well as lengths and breaks of abandonment, in the same way that proximity and numbers of buildings and artefacts are used to determine settlement function, size and social status? If this is the case, the eastern side of Carlisle in the late first and early second centuries AD would score differently from the western side. Some *vici*, or parts of *vici*, may show a similar score to an enclosed native site containing just two or three buildings. Unlike artefacts and structures, insects require their habitats to be continuously replenished on very short timescales if they are to survive. It follows, therefore, that a stratigraphic succession of insect fauna could provide an alternative means of measuring change. To test this we need other waterlogged sites comparable to Carlisle, or Deer Park Farm, Co Antrim.

Conclusion

Since Salway's review in 1965, and that of Clack and Gosling in 1976, a very great deal of new data has been recovered and several new syntheses have been produced. As a result, we are now better equipped to assess Roman settlement in the north. It nevertheless remains the case that our knowledge of most settlements of this period is woefully inadequate. In many specific cases we know little more about the grammar of settlements, the buildings and spaces in between, than we did twenty years ago, and artefact studies are only slowly moving out of the trainspotting or stamp-collecting mode.

Archaeological opportunities arising out of the planning process will undoubtedly add more to the plans of some settlements, and will provide us with better datasets for assessing individual sites. It is not likely, however, to facilitate research on the big questions, the first of which concerns a clearer understanding of the landscape, which is at least equal in importance to political, military and cultural considerations. This is the area in which we have probably made the most important advances in the past twenty or thirty years.

The other major question concerns the need to extend our appreciation of the ways in which archaeological deposits with their artefactual and ecofactual components accumulate. This might then lead to a clearer grasp of the nature of the data at different levels of magnitude, from which may emerge a new view about Roman settlement and its impact on the landscape.

Postscript

A number of important geophysical surveys on *vici* have taken place in the period between the conference that prompted this paper in 1996, and its publication. Attention is drawn in particular to important work at Halton Chesters, Carvoran, Castlesteads, Birdoswald and Maryport some of which is published (Biggins and Taylor 1999; Taylor, Robinson and Biggins 1999). In addition further work has taken place by Carlisle Archaeology Ltd on the *vici* at

Brougham, Papcastle, (Burnham 2000, 393), Kirkby Thore and Bowness-on-Solway. Essentially these works support the point made earlier in this paper that *vici* could be extensive and very complex settlements. At Maryport the geophysical survey has located a relatively large number of large stone buildings, compared with sites such as Birdoswald and Carvoran. Zonation within the *vici* can also be seen in some instances with the main road out of the forts forming the main street against which are clustered large numbers of buildings, whilst to the rear can be seen lanes and fields. Close study of some of the geophysical plots may well reveal chronological depth with some features overlying others, and perhaps, new blocks of land being taken in and added on to a pre-existing pattern of buildings and boundaries. Such surveys are immensely useful and should facilitate further targeted work in *vici* whereby questions of chronological growth, building type, population density, industry and technology amongst many others can be addressed in the next 20 years.

At Carlisle one of the most significant new additions has been the recognition of an extensive suburb along Botchergate to the south of the main built up area (Zant and Giecco 1999, 306-7; McCarthy 1999a, 170-7). Further comments on vici can be found in Bidwell 1999.

Acknowledgements

Thanks are due to colleagues at Carlisle, especially John Zant, as well as to Paul Bidwell and Paul Austen for discussions and comments. I also thank Jacqui Huntley, University of Durham and Harry Kenward, University of York, for many stimulating discussions over a number of years on the environmental remains and what they may, or may not, mean.

Chapter 11: Review of Roman Small Finds Research

Lindsay Allason-Jones

Historical review

The purpose of this paper is to review the research carried out on Roman small finds in the north of England over the last twenty years. To avoid confusion it might be as well to start by defining terms – what exactly is a Roman small find?

As a rough description the term 'small find' covers any artefact which is easily portable. Thus it excludes architectural fragments, sculpture and altars. Unfortunately, this simple definition does not reveal the full story, as pots, glassware and coins are rarely classified as small finds whilst querns are invariably classed in such a way. Recording methods are often the deciding factors in dividing the small finds from the rest of an assemblage. Pottery and glass are usually found in bulk and recorded in bulk, not each separate sherd as a separate find. The small finds, on the other hand, can be dealt with individually: can be given a 'small find number'. What is classed as a small find, however, can often be related to the specialists to whom an excavation director has access when writing the report. No doubt there will be a pottery specialist, a glass specialist and a numismatist; the architectural fragments might be regarded as part of the structure and therefore the responsibility of the excavation director, while the soil samples and other scientific elements will be dealt with by suitable scientists. The rest of the material will then be designated as 'small finds' and sent to the 'small find specialist'.

The study of small finds over the last 100 years if plotted on a graph would produce a line like a section through the Lake District: all peaks and valleys. Back in the dawn of archaeological time, when the public was starting to become interested in their past, it was the artefacts which caught their attention. In the excavations of Ur, the Valley of the Kings and the British Bronze Age barrows, it was the artefacts which were sought, whilst the structures received cursory attention. Floor levels were features which one's labourers hacked through to get to the aesthetically pleasing objects in the cellars. This was treasure hunting, and it was the artistic quality of the objects which appealed. Only complete objects were kept, for two reasons: firstly, they were the objects which had the greatest appeal to the public – and almost everything found would be displayed – and secondly, they had a certain intrinsic toughness which would ensure survival; anything needing complex conservation was not worth keeping.

By concentrating on these objects, the nineteenth-century archaeologists produced their picture of life as they thought it was lived in the past. This picture was biased by their use of only the more opulent pieces and by their own contemporary attitudes, but to give them their due, within the limits and constraints of the time they did well, and certainly drew the attention of the public to archaeology and artefacts to the extent that almost every stately home, vicarage and farm in the nineteenth century had a small collection of artefacts.

There was then a backlash. All of a sudden it was the structures which provided the focus for excavations and wall-chasing started in earnest. The deposits in the centre of the rooms were ignored in the search for the plan of the building. The usefulness of the finds was seen to be proportional to the extent to which they could provide dating evidence. The study of pottery and coins became paramount; brooches, weapons and domestic artefacts were treated with scorn as mere museum fodder, and their study ceased to be respectable. Small finds were only included in an excavation report to cheer it up for public consumption. These items were not expected to reveal anything about the site, but a few erudite paragraphs (preferably giving the objects typology numbers), accompanied by elegant drawings of the more complete items, would raise the tone of the exercise and encourage sales. Sites which are popularly believed to be fully published, such as Corbridge, Richborough and Woodeaton, in practice have a large quantity of material languishing in museum stores which has never been mentioned on a printed page. As a result, to attempt a distribution map of any class of object from published sources alone is a very dangerous undertaking.

The art of small finds reporting then moved on to giving everything a mention, but in such a way as to leave the reader none the wiser. The reports of the 1960s and 70s were usually written by the excavation director in order to save money and time, and consisted of bald lists. A

Address: Museum of Antiquities, University of Newcastle, Newcastle NE1 7RU

quotation from a Hadrian's Wall site report published in the mid 1970s reads: 'an iron object', whilst another object is later described as 'an unidentified bronze object'. The latter turned out on investigation to be an elaborately decorated snake's head bracelet. There was no mention in the report of the decoration, nor were any measurements given or drawing published. Any scholar trying to find a parallel or compile a catalogue of the type would have missed this example. The general view of the site which one gets from reading the report is that the finds were of poor quality and mostly uninteresting scraps – with all that this implies. If a site needs to be reassessed and the excavation report is the only source, it is as well to bear in mind the historical context in which the specialist reports were written and the site excavated, otherwise it is easy to be led astray.

By the time the period under review is reached, only 2% of the small finds from Hadrian's Wall and its surrounding area had been published, and most of these were the more impressive pieces, such as the Aesica Hoard. These statistics are surprising; Hadrian's Wall, after all, could be considered to have had a large share of archaeological attention over the past 200 years. In the last 20 years, however, the picture has changed dramatically. Some sites have yet to be formally published but most have a written small finds report. Some, such as Halton Chesters, are currently in the press stage (Dore and Allason-Jones forthcoming). There are also a number of sites, such as Carlisle (McCarthy 1990; McCarthy 1991) and South Shields (Allason-Jones and Miket 1984; Bidwell and Speak 1994), which are well published and up-to-date. This is an opportune time, therefore, to sit back and reflect on what is now known about the small finds of the Roman north and what the future might hold.

The discussion will be divided into four main groups: military studies, gender studies, industry and technology, and domestic artefacts.

Military studies

It is probably true to say that it is the military artefacts which have received the most attention of any group of small finds in the north of England. Even if many of the finds specialists in the area were not keenly interested in Roman military equipment, the growth in re-enactment societies, determined to keep attention on the subject, has ensured that spearheads, *lorica segmentata* and similar artefacts have all been studied in depth. Roman re-enactment societies all over the world have come to rely heavily on the research carried out in the north of England. The International Roman Military Equipment Conference has met twice in Newcastle upon Tyne during the period under review, and no doubt will return in the future (Coulston 1988; *J Roman Milit Equip Stud* 1992).

Specific areas of study have included Jon Coulston's work on archery equipment (Coulston 1985) and Bill Griffiths' study of slings and other airborne weaponry (Griffiths 1989). The Corbridge Hoard, although found before our review period, was published more recently and has added greatly to our knowledge of Roman armour, particularly *lorica segmentata* as pieces of 12 cuirasses were included in the chest (Allason-Jones and Bishop 1988). All three studies have one thing in common, and that is the use of sculpture and classical texts in the discussion of the artefacts. The Roman period has an advantage which the preceding periods do not have, and that is that pictorial sculpture and written texts do survive to aid our understanding. Whilst it is always as well to treat such evidence with caution, it is remarkable how often it is ignored. In the north of England there is a tradition of using every source of information.

Rather than look at the results of a number of specialized studies, it would be profitable to consider for a moment the broader canvas. Is it now possible to give an opinion on the range of material which might be anticipated from an excavation on a northern fort? The answer appears to be 'yes'. Whilst the estimates may not be statistically accurate, it is now possible to anticipate the range of material to be expected from a barrack block or a headquarters building. Curiously, on these sites the military equipment is likely to form one of the smaller groups in the assemblage; most finds from a Roman fort relate to the day-to-day life of the soldiers rather than military parades and battles. However, or possibly because of this, it has proved to be impossible to use the finds to suggest which unit was in residence, or even if a fort had legionaries or auxiliaries present. Whilst it might be presumed that each unit would have distinctive elements to their armour or weaponry, in practice it would appear that most soldiers looked remarkably similar – any variation tending to be local to the fort they were living in rather than the area they had been recruited from. Nor does the average fort produce enough harness to indicate which had cavalry and which infantry troops. This may not be totally surprising; a cavalryman would take great care of his harness, so discarded items would be rare, whilst even infantry forts would have had a great number of horses.

The recent work on forts in Scotland has provided a comparable database, and it has become increasingly clear that a Scottish fort was very different to a fort on Hadrian's Wall in the quality, quantity and type of small finds present. Precisely what this difference means requires more work before clear conclusions can be reached.

An unexpected bonus for military studies throughout the Empire has been the discovery of the Vindolanda writing tablets (Bowman and Thomas 1994). It might, of course, be argued that these are inscriptions, not small finds, but their interest for small finds specialists has been in what they reveal about the supply and cost of some of the objects. References to 12 shoemakers confirm the theory that cobblers were working in the *fabricae*, so hobnails and shoemaking equipment can be expected (*ibid*, no 155), whilst a letter which mentions a dealer called Gracilis sending hobnails worth 2 asses adds information as to the probable cost of a pair of shoes in first-century Britain (*ibid*, no 186). Tablet 309, on the other hand, implies that some requisites which we might have expected to have been made on site were being imported ready-made or in kit form: Metto tells Advectus that he has sent him wooden items, including 34 hubs, 38 cart axles (including one turned on a lathe), 300 spokes, 26 bed planks, 8 seats and 6 benches as well as 6 goatskins, through the agency of Saco.

On a more domestic front, Tablet 194 gives an inventory of kitchen equipment which includes a bronze lamp, and tends to list items such as bowls and cups as being in boxes. All box-fittings, therefore, should not be labelled in future as military chests or jewellery boxes. The tablets also provide evidence for objects which by their very nature are unlikely to survive, such as bedspreads, coverlets and blankets (*ibid*, nos 192, 167).

Gender studies

Recent studies have revealed that the use of the words 'military' and 'civilian' can be misleading and inaccurate. Most of the items mentioned in the Vindolanda tablets could be used by soldiers or civilians, whilst the finds from the excavated turrets on Hadrian's Wall included nail-cleaners, needles and tweezers, despite the fact that the turrets were only occupied for forty years in two clear-cut stages and then only for military purposes (Allason-Jones 1988). These items are traditionally categorized as being evidence for a civilian or even female presence, but civilian and military populations have many of the same needs: second-century soldiers would have had to mend clothes, clean their nails and remove splinters, whilst civilians may have required arrows and knives for hunting, hobnails for their boots and chapes for their knife scabbards. To further confuse the issue, men would no doubt have taken civilian objects with them into military service and then taken military objects into their civilian retirement. The work of the last twenty years may have cleared up many questions about equipment in the military zone, but has also shown that the usual separation of finds into 'military' and 'civilian' by use alone is invalid.

The conviction that it is possible to tell which artefacts were used by women and which by men has also come under attack. The traditional indicators of a female presence have been such articles as brooches, earrings, finger-rings and bracelets; but recent research has shown that brooches were rarely gender specific, that the Roman army included many men from the eastern provinces and Africa where it was not considered improper or unusual for men to wear earrings, that size and type are not sufficient to indicate whether a finger-ring belonged to a man, woman or child, and that bracelets were worn by men of many ethnic groups, including the Celts (Allason-Jones 1995). Pins which can be firmly identified as hairpins as opposed to cloak or shroud pins, on the other hand, appear to have been confined to female use. It also seems that jet artefacts had a special significance for women, as jet is rarely found in a male context (Allason-Jones 1996). In identifying objects and their purpose, our use of modern values and biases will invariably introduce errors into our research, and this must be kept in mind when sites are being evaluated or re-evaluated.

The excavation of Barrack Block 13 at Housesteads has added greatly to the discussion about objects and gender (Daniels and Rushworth forthcoming). The recording method allowed the artefacts to be attributed to a specific room or chalet, and to specific periods. This has revealed that of the ambiguous material, only brooches were used or lost in the barrack rooms or chalets during all the periods of the fort's occupation, whilst the artefacts which may have been worn by women alone, such as the hairpins and jet artefacts, were confined to the centurion's quarters. Centurions appear to have always been allowed to marry, and there are many inscriptions around the Roman Empire which record the presence of centurions' wives at forts (Allason-Jones 1989). There has been much debate, however, as to the precise location of the accommodation of these women and their children. The Housesteads finds confirm the theory that they were housed within the centurions' quarters.

Technology and industry

Less glamorous than military equipment research or gender studies, work on Roman technology and industry has not hit the headlines, but this is where the north of England has been leading the field and where the most interesting results have been obtained. Much of this work requires modern technology to get to the answers, and archaeologists have needed to work with specialists from many other disciplines.

As was discussed above, jet and shale artefacts are likely to have been used by women rather than men. This observation has derived from a joint project between the Museum of Antiquities and the Fossil Fuels and Environmental Geochemistry Institute at Newcastle University. The problems of differentiating between the various black shiny materials used for making jewellery and domestic objects in Roman Britain have been acknowledged for a long time, but the analytical techniques which did not destroy the object being analysed were limited to distinguishing merely between jet and non-jet. In recent years, the financial interests of the oil companies have directed research into oil-bearing rocks. The Newcastle University project has employed the methods used in finding oil and fossil fuels to analyse Roman artefacts and this has produced some unexpected results (Allason-Jones and Jones 1994). Firstly, the sources of material used by craftsmen during the Roman period for the manufacture of black jewellery were remarkably varied. The local coal measures were occasionally used; in the case of two armlets from Halton Chesters, coal measures within a mile of the fort were exploited, which suggests a very localized industry, although the measures in the immediate vicinity of South Shields – the fort which has produced the largest group of black shiny objects in the area – have so far produced no evi-

dence of exploitation in the Roman period. Comparative work at the Yorkshire Museum has shown that black artefacts from Roman York are likely to have been carved from locally derived jet, shale and cannel coal, with, curiously, a few items which appear to have been made from Spanish jet (Allason-Jones 1996). The objects from the military zone, on the other hand, might be carved from Yorkshire jet, but are just as likely to be carved from Derbyshire or Dorset shale, Midlothian torbanite, or cannel coal from Alston or the North Tyne Valley. The conclusion has been reached that South Shields was a centre for black jewellery manufacture, not because it was close to a source of raw material but because it was a port, receiving the raw material from a variety of sources, and was in a prime position to exploit the markets of the frontier zone with the finished products.

The variety of materials used for artefacts of mostly third- or fourth-century date is interesting. This was an unsettled period in Scottish history when it is unlikely that official Roman commercial activities were taking place in the area, yet raw material from Midlothian was finding its way to the craftshops of South Shields. Rock from the ambiguous area immediately to the north of Hadrian's Wall was also being exploited at this time. This variety of sources would have provided materials which would have had to be handled differently in order to be carved successfully. Roman craftsmen did not have sophisticated analytical techniques at their disposal, so we must presume that they knew by experience that black material from Yorkshire needed to be treated differently to that from Midlothian or Derbyshire, or from a more local source.

This research is continuing and has now been expanded to include the analysis of black artefacts from Germany, France, Hungary, Wroxeter and London, and is a prime example of archaeologists making progress by collaborating with other specialists. Another example is in the work of David Dungworth, with his analysis of Iron Age and Roman metalwork (Dungworth 1995).

Evidence for metalworking has been found at Turrets 26A and 18B, at Sewingshields Milecastle, and in the forts of Housesteads, Vindolanda, Stanwix, Carrawburgh, South Shields, Newcastle upon Tyne and Piercebridge (Allason-Jones and Dungworth 1995). Dungworth has analysed much of this evidence as well as the products, and has revealed that most of the bronze artefacts produced in the area in the second and third centuries were made of leaded bronze or gunmetal (Dungworth1995). This is a different result to that produced by the analysis of first-century military equipment, which was invariably of brass. The difference may be because of the different manufacturing techniques employed: *lorica segmentata* fittings, for example, were made by hammering and cutting sheet metal, whilst openwork mounts and the like were cast in moulds. The presence of zinc in the second- and third-century objects also suggests that they were being made from scrap metal as this type of alloy is likely to have been the result of melting brass and bronze together. Fragments of scrap metal, neatly folded into little bundles to fit into crucibles, have been found, particularly at Piercebridge, Turret 26A and Newcastle, but enough survives elsewhere in the military zone to suggest that this recycling was a widespread practice.

The analysis of the resulting objects suggests that the artisans were being careful about what they included in this recycling, and that small quantities of new metals were being added to make the molten alloy able to flow easily into the moulds.

The study of bronze scrap and mould fragments may not grip the imagination, but it has revealed much. For example, it has shown that much of the bronze-working on Hadrian's Wall was on a small scale, despite the military nature of some of the products and the manufacturing sites. None of the pieces studied required complex equipment or techniques to be produced successfully. In fact, each could easily have been made by one person using the most basic equipment and recycled scrap. The analysis also indicates that some understanding of the properties of the different alloys was being applied – knowledge which is unlikely to have been common to the average soldier. Possibly the authorities were providing the raw materials and the 'recipe' for the alloys to be used for each type of object, but the final metalworking was being carried out in a variety of locations rather than concentrated in fort *fabricae*. Finally, and possibly most importantly, this study shows that even the most unpromising fragments of metal or clay found on a site can produce useful evidence for activity on that site, and contribute to our discussion of the Roman army – a topic which some authorities have declared to be already exhausted.

Domestic life

Small finds are often the best evidence for revealing the details of everyday life in the past. Vindolanda has produced brushes and brooms, for example: rare examples of the archaeology of housework, an area where too often little remains or is ambiguous. After all, who can say if a scrap of fabric comes from a vest or a duster, particularly as many vests finish up as dusters at the end of their useful lives? Some of the Vindolanda textile scraps have been analysed at York University where they have been shown to have been dyed with the local bedstraw, an alternative to French madder (Taylor 1983). This would seem to imply that the local soldiery were being clothed in locally produced garments. Research by the various re-enactment societies mentioned earlier has shown that a soldier's tunic does not last very long, so a local source of replacements would have been sensible.

Vindolanda and Carlisle have both produced some outstanding leather. Both sites have contributed the evidence which has allowed Carol van Driel Murray to reveal the pattern and shape of a Roman army tent (Driel Murray 1990), whilst at Vindolanda the shoes have survived so well that she has been able to trace the footwear of the Commanding Officer's family to the extent that we now know that his son had a problem with his feet (Driel Murray pers. comm.).

In looking at domestic artefacts, the native sites should not be ignored. Admittedly these are not renowned for their massive artefact assemblages, and Professor George Jobey always expressed himself as being satisfied if his excavations uncovered half a quern and a piece of glass armlet. But progress has been made even in this unpromising field. Professor Jennifer Price's research into the glass armlets of Yorkshire has shown that the Northumbrian examples are not the most southerly examples of a Scottish artefact (Price 1988), although it is not yet clear whether the ubiquitous glass armlets of the Northumberland settlement sites came down from Scotland, up from Yorkshire or were being produced locally. Possibly the true picture is a mixture of all three ideas; as they are made from recycled glass, analysis is unlikely to shed much light on the question.

On the other hand, the comparison of native products on fort sites on Hadrian's Wall and Roman objects on native sites in Northumberland has not revealed a local populace eager to become Romanized, but seems to suggest a shrewd group of people producing trinkets specially aimed at Roman military taste (Allason-Jones 1991). In other words, the invading army was not exploiting the downtrodden locals but the Brigantian and Votadinian tribesfolk were doing quite well out of the army. This does not fit neatly into the picture which the traditional literature paints. It may be a case of the Romans having the best advertising executives but the native Northumbrians having the best marketing strategies.

Kilbride-Jones (1980) put forward a theory that Hadrian's Wall permitted southern-made objects to be exported to the north but would not allow movement south. The evidence, however, would seem to suggest that, on the contrary, trade was brisk from north to south but negligible from south to north. Even so, the indigenous peoples to the north of the Wall do not seem to have judged success in monetary terms. Similar sites south of the Wall, such as Thorpe Thewles in Cleveland, seem to have far richer assemblages, including gold and silver jewellery (Heslop 1987). Possibly the tribes north of the Tyne-Solway line displayed status by intangible indicators, such as the size of their cattle herds. Exactly what an individual object meant to its owner is one of the great imponderables of small finds research, and it is important not to fall into the error of presuming that modern indicators of high status had the same meaning for communities in the past. Nor should it be presumed that an object of high status for a Brigantian tribesman would have equal value to a southern tribesman, or indeed for an African or German auxiliary.

Future work
What needs to be done in the future? Firstly, although it is a widely held belief that Roman military equipment has had more than its fair share of attention, more needs to be done. The bulk of the material from the Roman north is now catalogued and accessible, and Mike Bishop has started cataloguing the Russell Robinson archive and transferring the data to the Internet, so that researchers all over the world can contribute parallels and information (Armamentarium: www.ncl.ac.uk/antiquities). This is important because military equipment from Hadrian's Wall has tended to be studied in isolation due to the lack of comparative data. It is important for these assemblages to be compared with others from Britain and the other provinces in order for knowledge of the Roman army to develop. It is possible that the finds

from a fort occupied by a specific unit might show some affinity with the material from the area where the unit was first raised. Only when the local assemblages are compared with those from further afield are we likely to be able to put Hadrian's Wall truly into context.

Secondly, very little is known of the funerary habits of the population of the Roman north. The cemeteries of Petty Knowes and Lanchester were disappointing in their finds (Charlton and Mitcheson 1984; Turner 1990), the soldiers apparently having been buried only in their tunics and boots. Recent excavations at South Shields suggest that there is much to be learned about the religious beliefs and burial customs of both civilian and military populations (Snape 1994). A large synthesis of the burial evidence for the whole of Roman Britain by Robert Philpott (1991) has provided a basic framework against which to judge newly excavated material. It is already known that there were people from every province of the Roman Empire living in the north of England, but it is still impossible to identify these people by their graves or their artefacts. Gender studies, also, may derive useful evidence from cemetery excavations.

Thirdly, comparatively little excavation has been carried out in recent years on the *vici*. Excavations in the 1960s at Housesteads in the buildings outside the south gate and on Chapel Hill (Birley and Charlton 1934; Birley *et al* 1932) produced some unexpectedly high-quality objects, a coin forger's mould, religious sculpture and murdered bodies, but more prosaic information is still required about the life and times of the *vicus* dwellers. Much of the discussion about the third- and fourth-century history of Hadrian's Wall is based on the premise that the *vici* were abandoned, and this has added fuel to the theory of married quarters inside the forts, but the material from the *vici* of Roman Britain has not been surveyed as a whole to confirm that they were abandoned. Possibly the populations in the *vici* were from the same ethnic groups as the surrounding native settlements; if this is so, then they may not have had many material possessions to indicate their presence. If, on the other hand, they came from different stock, did they come from regions which had a distinctive material culture which might be recognizable?

The situation at the time of writing, as far as the Roman small finds in the north of England are concerned, is reasonably comforting. From a 2% publication record, the latest estimate suggests that 92% of the material is either published or in the process of being so. With this plethora of facts, contradictions, paradoxes and oddities are beginning to emerge, and it is now the time for syntheses to be produced, although the north may claim to be well advanced in this area as well. Before complacency sets in, however, a plea must be made for reassessment. New techniques are being applied all the time, which are leading to new ideas about sites and the dating of those sites. Small finds specialists need to take note of the changes, and look again and again at their evidence for dating a particular type of brooch to the fourth century, or calling one sort of artefact a foreign import. It is important to keep an open mind all the time; as Mr Mailey says in one of Sir Arthur Conan Doyle's Professor Challenger stories, 'we must fit our theories to the facts. Up to now we have fitted the facts to our theories' (Doyle 1902). Advantage must be taken of the scientific techniques of other disciplines. The limited analysis done so far has reaped an enormous harvest, but the possibilities are endless. For example, metal vessels, of which there are many in the area, would bear re-evaluation in the light of Pliny's comment that copper vessels were coated in *stagnum* (a silver compound) so that the contents had a more agreeable taste and lasted longer (Pliny, *Nat Hist* XXXIV.48.1). No doubt there are many other technical questions which can now be answered.

Finally, the standards which have already been achieved must be sustained. At the start of this paper, the newness of small finds research as a discipline was mentioned; it would be regrettable if the progress which has been made in the last twenty years was to lose pace: if it was decided that certain types of object had been done, ticked off, and need be given no further attention. To describe a particular object by its type alone is not enough – a proper description, including measurements and illustrations, must be included so that not only can the initial identification be tested, but the full information, which never goes out of date, continues to be accessible to everyone.

Section 4: Anglo-Saxon

Introduction

Rosemary Cramp[*]

As the authors below have described, at the beginning of the period under consideration the region with which we are concerned was a political and cultural entity, Bernicia, and, as Loveluck noted, this embraced an area which had been located both within and outside the Roman provinces. Although Hadrian's Wall and its hinterland was no longer an important frontier, the nature of the Roman occupation of this area may have shaped its later settlement pattern and the major lines of communication, whilst the nature of the terrain, in which the high ground created barriers around the major river valleys probably encouraged the survival of the native population more readily than in the southern province of Deira. In the Roman period no large towns developed in this area and no villas north of Durham have been discovered, and in the Early Medieval period likewise there is a significant lack of urban centres. Cumbria, an area which continued to border Celtic speaking peoples, seems to have shared a common culture with the rest of the region during the eighth and ninth century, (at least as far as the church was concerned), but its interests were re-orientated after the Scandinavian settlements of the tenth and eleventh centuries. The important way in which this region demonstrates the process of acculturation between the native and invading peoples in the first millennium AD is only just beginning to be understood, as is more fully pointed out in the succeeding papers.

If small pockets of Anglo-Saxon settlers established themselves within a predominantly British population, initially the archaeological picture of the acculturation which ensued is not much different from western Wessex – Dorset, Somerset, and Devon- where there is likewise thinly dispersed evidence for early Anglo-Saxon cemeteries, and a paucity of settlements. By the eighth century the region had become part of greater Northumbria and there were close links with the continent through diplomacy and missionary activity, whilst the population seems to have favoured the same types of architecture and artefacts as other kingdoms. But, during the ninth century, as numismatic evidence has shown, the economy declined, and the settlement of a new Germanic peoples (Norse and Danes) in the tenth through eleventh century in

Cumbria and Yorkshire fragmented Northumbria yet again, and cut off the northern territory from the revival of art and learning in southern England. From the earlier period there is a little evidence in the form of imported pottery for external contacts, but this area must have been cut off from cross channel trade in the tenth century and even to a certain extent from the east to west trade which linked Dublin and York under the Viking hegemony. Throughout the period the location of markets, whether on beaches, at royal centres, or monasteries remains a mystery, and the possible eleventh century development of towns and fortifications, which has begun so much earlier in other kingdoms, is only hinted at in the excavations in Durham, Newcastle and Carlisle. The papers below comment illuminatingly on the archaeological evidence for this general picture, and the following remarks are meant to complement this, particularly in the light of the lack of a paper on the later period of Scandinavian settlement in the north.

The 'furnished' burials of the sixth to seventh centuries, which have been discovered between the Tyne and the Tees, with dress fastenings of West Germanic type are fully discussed by Loveluck, who convincingly concludes that this form of display must signal membership of a common elite group, along the north-east coast, whilst as O'Brien has stated, 'in the region between the Tweed and the Tees the native British population continued to practice whatever 'invisible' rite had prevailed throughout Britain during the later Bronze Age and early Iron Age (O'Brien 1999, 62). If we had in the north the extensive Roman cemetery excavations conducted elsewhere in England and on the Continent, then it might be possible to chart mortuary practice from the Roman into the Anglo-Saxon period in a more illuminating fashion. As it is we have no knowledge of how far Christian custom had affected late Roman burial rites, and no perceived relationship between Roman and Anglo-Saxon burial grounds. It is possible that some Anglo-Saxon burial grounds were sited in derelict Roman forts, such as Binchester, just because this was ground unsuitable for agriculture, and with no deeper significance, but in some cases as with

[*]Address: Department of Archaeology, University of Durham, South Road, Durham DH1 3LE

the mounds at Yeavering or henge at Milfield North, prehistoric monuments may have been deliberately chosen as a suitable focus for the incomers' burials. How many of the North Britons lapsed into paganism in the post-Roman period or, like *pagani* in other provinces, had never been converted, is unknown, but the ephemeral nature of any sacred foci surrounding woods, trees, wells or springs, which could have been common to pagan Britons and Anglo-Saxons alike, ensures that they are difficult to detect archaeologically. With the exception of a few cist burials (which may or may not be Christian) there has been little to substantiate sub-Roman Christianity, save the recently discovered apsed building and its associated cross-marked slabs from Chesterholm, (pers. comm. Robin Birley), and with which to supplement the few inscribed grave markers and small finds marked with a Chi Rho which have been long known in the North. Links between burial grounds and settlement sites are only revealed by intensive field prospection followed by large scale excavation, as at Heslerton in Yorkshire and nothing like that has been attempted in Bernicia.

Whether the burials in Roman forts such as Binchester (unfurnished), or Newcastle (with some dress furnishings), signify continuity of occupation nearby, or, since they are of Middle Saxon date, a later fortuitous location of a church somewhere in the site, must await the answers from further post-excavation analysis. Nevertheless the extensive excavations at South Shields which have demonstrated no continuity of occupation in the fort may indicate that any continuity of occupation must be looked for in the *vici*. The churches which do exist in Roman forts, particularly around Carlisle such as at Brampton or Brough, are, above ground, much later structures, but there has not been the full excavation of a church in this region although sites such as these are prime candidates for research.

The possible siting of some monasteries, such as Rachel Newman has discussed, along side or over earlier secular burial grounds remains unfortunately only a supposition since dating of the earliest burials at sites such as Wearmouth, has not been confirmed by radio-carbon dating. Nevertheless the relationship between the ecclesiastical and the lay settlements which surrounded them (possibly with a client status), is an important field of research, and the publication of volumes in the *Corpus of Anglo-Saxon Stone*

Sculpture (Cramp 1984) which cover the area of Northumberland and Durham, Cumbria and parts of Yorkshire has provided evidence for monumental links between sites which seem significant. The pattern of distribution of sculptured monuments is currently one of the best indicators of important ecclesiastical centres and their cultural or economic satellites in the region, whilst Deirdre O'Sullivan's excavation of the site of Green Shiels on Lindisfarne (in prep.) is the only example we have for illustrating such economic links. The importance of the royal site at Corbridge, with its surviving Anglo-Saxon church fronting the market place, has recently been affirmed by the discovery of a large mill – a find unique in the area- but unfortunately because of the limited brief for the excavation, its context (whether lay or secular) has not been explored.

Excavations on ecclesiastical sites such as Hartlepool and Whithorn have proved important not only in establishing comparative house types, but also in demonstrating a fact which as archaeologists we often overlook, namely that sites can significantly change their function, and their cultural and economic orientation, through time. This was most clearly demonstrated in the Whithorn excavations, but the changes noted by Newman of increased evidence for metalworking from the ninth century at Dacre and Jarrow also indicate changes of function for these sites.

The ninth century is a key period for charting change, but the lack of pottery, particularly dateable pottery, for the region is a severe inhibitor to understanding that period. In fact every chance should be taken in the region to discover and excavate pottery kilns which can be reasonably supposed to be pre-Conquest. Without this evidence reliance has to be placed on radio carbon dating for deciding whether a site phase can be assigned to a period before or after the watershed of the Viking Age settlements, and field walking to find settlements is rendered very difficult, as David Austin found in his concentrated field work which resulted in the excavation of the deserted village of Thrislington (Austin 1989). Upland sites are particularly difficult to identify, and the important excavation of the Teesdale site of Simy Folds (Coggins, Fairless and Batey 1983) which was dated by radio-carbon to the second half of the eighth century is a case in point. The simple rectangular drystone buildings were probably a normal type in the uplands for a considerable period of time, and would have been equally acceptable to Anglo-Saxon and

Scandinavian inhabitants. In fact the very similar houses excavated by Alan King at Gauber High Pasture Ribblehead (King 1978) were hailed enthusiastically as the first excavated 'Viking' houses in the north, but are probably of a date earlier than the Scandinavian settlement.

The Scandinavian settlement in the north seems to have affected this region differentially, if one judges by the evidence of place-names and sculptures with Scandinavian influenced iconography and ornament. In Cumbria and along the Tees valley such evidence is common, although no settlement site where such evidence is provided has been excavated. Sites such as Sockburn or Gainford in the east where there is documentary evidence for an earlier ecclesiastical settlement and a major Viking Age burial ground are obvious candidates. But such evidence may be difficult to find under later settlements. Penrith was obviously an important Viking Age centre, but so far limited excavations in the town have failed to reveal this period. The area between the Wear and the Tweed seems, relying on the same non-archaeological evidence to have stubbornly maintained its earlier culture, but as stated above, the excavated evidence from Newcastle is beginning to show the development of the town and port there, and although the pre-Conquest defences of Durham are still to find, it is possible that it, and other centres such as Morpeth, grew swiftly in the period of stability and increased southern influence in the eleventh century. The basic outlines of our present settlement pattern were laid down in this Early Medieval period and as such it is of great importance to discover them. The omens are more hopeful than they were when *Archaeology in the North* (Clack and Gosling 1976) was written, but the fragmentary and fugitive evidence for this period will not be discovered by small scale interventions of limited scope but by targeted and large scale excavation.

Chapter 12: 'The Romano-British to Anglo-Saxon Transition' – Social Transformations from the Late Roman to Early Medieval Period in Northern England, AD 400-700

*Chris Loveluck**

Introduction – concepts, objectives and a framework of analysis

Any study of the social changes which took place in northern England between the fifth and early eighth century AD is immediately faced with the problem of defining terminology, particularly with regard to whether it is appropriate to view these changes as a 'Romano-British to Anglo-Saxon transition'. The geographical area defined as the north of England for the purpose of this volume is exceptional in that it encompasses regions which were located both within and beyond the late Roman provinces of Britain. At the end of the fourth century, the Roman Iron Age confederacy of the Votadini occupied Northumberland, while the military zone of Hadrian's Wall lay immediately to its south, and the areas of County Durham and Cumbria housed societies which exhibited a varying degree of Romanization, with minimal Roman influence in upland areas. The general culture-historical term 'Romano-British' is therefore highly inappropriate, and gives the impression of a false uniformity within the study area. Instead, the changes between AD 400-700 must be viewed as products resulting from the actions of independent British, partially Romanized civilian, and military elements within the social fabric of northern England. A similar problem of inappropriate culture-historical labelling also exists with regard to the general description of the Early Medieval successor societies in this region as 'Anglo-Saxon'. The longevity of distinct native groupings within the period covered by this paper, and the influence of their social, political and settlement organization, may render the term 'Anglo-Saxon' highly misleading without reference to the specific regional circumstances of the development of Early Medieval societies in Durham, Northumberland and Cumbria.

Despite the problems of terminology, the excavations and publications of the past twenty-five years have enabled the identification of Early Medieval settlement patterns, building techniques, mortuary practices and patterns of material culture use across the north of England – although not to a uniform extent throughout the region. The potential varies, however, for explaining the formation of different Anglo-Saxon societies, according to the extent of archaeological work, the presence of diagnostic artefacts, and hence the identification of closely datable deposits. When diagnostic artefacts are rare or are highly residual, evidence for post-Roman social and economic developments must be gleaned through an understanding of excavated stratigraphic sequences, often subject to complex site formation and taphonomic processes, and from pollen evidence. Both of the latter sources of information need to be linked to radiocarbon dates for the provision of absolute chronological indicators. As a result of the different circumstances within the study area, the framework used below to analyse the emergence of Early Medieval societies, from their late Roman and Roman Iron Age predecessors, reflects the varying nature of the archaeological remains across the region. These variations result from a bias in archaeological fieldwork, and differences in terrain and land-use, in conjunction with a real variation in the media of cultural expression in the archaeological record.

This paper has three basic aims: first, to review the physical evidence of the development of Early Medieval societies in northern England; secondly, to put forward some explanatory frameworks to account for the varying characteristics of these societies; and finally, to suggest some future research priorities which would help further our limited understanding of the mechanisms of social change between AD 400-700. Following a brief overview of the evidence for the character of occupation across northern England at the turn of the fifth century, investigation of post-Roman changes proceeds via the analysis of their varying manifestations in different geographical areas, specifically Durham, Northumberland and Cumbria. The results of these case studies are then used to examine the extent to which the developments of the fifth to seventh centuries can be explained as a 'transition', or as a combination of both sudden and long-term transformations which

*Address: Department of Archaeology, University of Southampton, Southampton SO17 1BF

produced societies with different characteristics, depending on specific regional circumstances. The paper will then conclude with some suggestions for new avenues of research into the formation of an Anglo-Saxon population in northern England.

Northern England at the turn of the fifth century

In order to assess and interpret the reasons behind the changes of the immediate post-Roman period, it is first necessary to summarize the evidence for the effects of the collapse of the late Roman state infrastructure, both for areas within the former diocese of Britain and immediately beyond its northern frontier. As a starting point, it is perhaps most appropriate to consider the changes in the character of occupation in the forts on Hadrian's Wall, since they represent the most obvious manifestation of the late Roman state in northern England (Fig 12.1).

The issue of the fate of the fort garrisons has been a subject of recent study both at the levels of detailed site-specific research, and wider landscape and synthetic analysis. In a general review, Casey noted stratigraphic evidence for continued phases of occupation after the deposition of the latest datable Roman artefacts, namely coins of the house of Theodosius, and pottery such as Crambeck and Huntcliff wares. Fifth-century refurbishment of fort defences with earth banks is seen at Chesterholm and partial repair is evident at Housesteads, while ditches were also re-cut at South Shields and at Piercebridge, in the southern hinterland of the Wall (Casey 1994, 259-60; Crow 1989; Bidwell and Speak 1994). Evidence of undoubted occupation within some of the forts throughout the immediate post-Roman period has also been uncovered through careful interpretation of the complex stratigraphic sequences associated with the former granary area at the fort of Birdoswald, in Cumbria; and a courtyard house at Binchester, County Durham (Wilmott 1997; Ferris and Jones 2000, 1-3). At least two phases of large timber 'halls' were uncovered at Birdoswald by Tony Wilmott, on behalf of English Heritage. All were built as non-earthfast structures on stone footings, and in the first of these phases the footings of the northern granary were used as foundation bases (Wilmott 1997; Wilmott 2000, 13-14). At Binchester, Rick Jones and Iain Ferris uncovered a similar sequence of continued occupation through the fifth century and beyond, focused on a mid fourth-century courtyard house, with subsequent fifth-century smithing and butchery activity, prior to abandonment and use for a sixth-century Anglo-Saxon burial (Ferris and Jones 2000, 3).

The stratigraphic sequences now being recognised certainly suggest continuity of occupation on at least some forts into the fifth century. In 1994, Casey put forward the hypothesis that the former garrisons of predominantly frontier forces (*limitanei*) retained a military character into the fifth century, supported by a system of food and raw material renders from the population living in the hinterlands (*territoria*) of individual forts. The term 'military character' is used to cover both martial elements, their families and dependent artisans, and their suggested means of support is viewed as the continuity and further development of the system of levies that had existed for the support of fort garrisons in the fourth century. With the disappearance of all payment in coin, it is assumed that greater mutual dependence would have resulted between the former garrisons and their surrounding populations, due to almost total reliance on local resources and a potentially greater need for protection in uncertain political times (Casey 1994, 262). If the former military units of the previously united command of Hadrian's Wall fragmented into a series of warband-based fiefdoms reliant on localized resources, it is conceivable that the result of poor harvests could have resulted in warfare over resources, between former late Roman regiments. Indeed, in the absence of a recognizable late Roman tribal or civilian aristocracy within the northern military zone, south of Hadrian's Wall, any nascent fifth-century warbands which developed from the late Roman frontier regiments are likely to have been the precursors of some of the British warbands that figure in the heroic poem, *the Gododdin*, thought to have been written down for the first time in the seventh or early eighth century (Wilmott 2000, 17-18; Koch 1997, lii &cxxxiv; Griffen 1994, 21).

The changes in the character of occupation on non-military sites are more difficult to assess. At the Roman town of Carlisle, the *civitas* capital of the Carvetii, and the smaller urban focus at Corbridge, evidence for occupation in the fifth century is extremely sparse. Nevertheless, despite this paucity it appears that Carlisle did remain a settlement focus in the fifth century, the *caer-* element in the name possibly reflecting a fortified centre, but the former town was certainly not urban in character (McCarthy 1990; Cramp 1995b). The loss of its urban

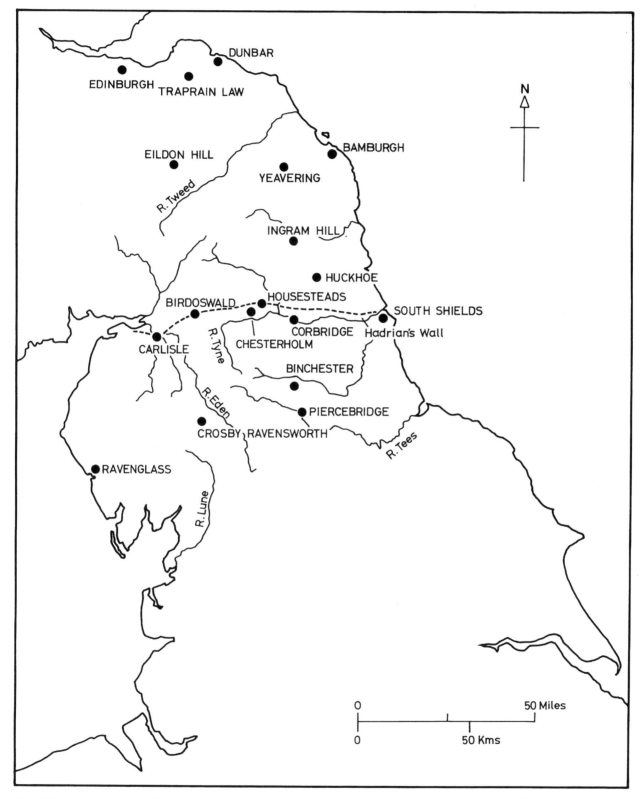

Fig. 12.1 Late to post-Roman and Late to post-Roman Iron Age sites in northern England, discussed in the text.

characteristics, however, may already have occurred during the fourth century – a trend observable in many Roman towns in Britain, which have been characterized previously as 'administrative villages' in the late Roman period (Reece 1980). Similarly, it can be assumed that Corbridge remained a settlement focus, together with other settlements formerly associated with forts, whose garrisons may have been withdrawn prior to the late fourth century. The absence of the physical manifestation of a civilian elite resulted in an almost total lack of villas in the area under study, with the exception of isolated examples from Old Durham and Piercebridge, and neither of these sites has yielded evidence of occupation beyond the fourth century. In contrast to the villas, it seems sensible to assume continued occupation of farmsteads and hamlets after the disappearance of non-residual, diagnostic Romano-British artefacts to date occupation horizons. Excavations on upland farmsteads have uncovered rectangular buildings in their latest phases, examples coming from Huckhoe and Ingram Hill in Northumberland, and Crosby Ravensworth in Cumbria (Jobey 1959, 250; Higham 1986, 247). It is not possible to date these latest phases in most cases, but at Huckhoe the rectangular buildings were demonstrably occupied into the post-Roman period (Jobey 1959, 251). Consequently, the occurrence of rectangular buildings in the latest phases of occupation on upland settlements may well reflect occupation in the fourth and fifth centuries, despite the lack of dating indicators.

The changes that occurred in the early decades of the fifth century on Hadrian's Wall, and in Durham and Cumbria, have been viewed as a 'de-Romanization' process, involving both a sudden and more gradual disappearance of the physical trappings of Romano-British culture. The refurbishment of fort defences with embankment ramparts indicates an inability to replace existing fortifications in kind, as do the latest attempts to maintain the baths of the courtyard house at Binchester; and the absence of fifth-century imported pottery and coin issues reflects the collapse of long-distance state distribution networks (Ferris and Jones 2000, 2; Evans 2000, 41). The major undertakings exhibited, however, in the construction of ramparts and re-cutting of ditches do not suggest a collapse in the authority of fort garrisons at a local level, and this maintenance of local power is consistent with the model of a gradual devolution of administration to the level of garrison-/warband-based fiefdoms during the fifth century. At the same time, however, as this localization of power and the growing inability to display a 'Roman' identity in traditional forms, there are also potential indications of the display of a new 'Roman' identity in the adoption and use of Christianity, which would expand across much of western and northern Britain during the fifth century. Possible late Roman churches have been identified at Chesterholm and at Housesteads, the latter in suggested association with an inhumation burial placed in a stone cist (Wilmott 2000, 15; Crow and Jackson 1997, 66-69).

Recent surveys of the pollen evidence in northern England, for the fourth to sixth centuries AD, have been used both to corroborate theories of continued agricultural exploitation in support of fort garrisons and to refute them, in favour of ideas of abandonment and subsequent re-occupation. Largely on the basis of the work of Turner and Fenton Thomas, Casey suggested the maintenance of levels of cereal pollen and therefore production, during the fifth century, with subsequent re-afforestation taking place during the sixth century (Fenton-Thomas 1990; Casey 1994, 261). In contrast, Petra Dark suggested a reduction of agricultural activity in the vicinity of Hadrian's Wall during the fifth century, on the basis of the same pollen evidence (Dark 1996, 39). Both Petra and Ken Dark, have suggested that this pollen evidence reflects the abandonment of the forts by their garrisons, prior to later re-occupation (Dark *ibid*; Dark 2000, 84-85). It is proposed that the excavated occupation sequences at Birdoswald and Binchester do not provide conclusive evidence for a wider continuity in occupation of forts by former garrison communities. Jaqui Huntley, however, has provided an important cautionary note against the wide-scale use of cereal pollen as an indicator of the extent of cultivation, and as a corollary continued occupation of forts. She points out that the dispersion of cereal pollen would always be under-represented in the mire and bog sources of pollen diagrams (Huntley 2000, 67). At the same time, Petra Dark's use of radio-carbon dates at only one standard deviation of error may also give a misleading impression of decline and re-afforestation within a short timescale; whereas at two standard deviations of error (i.e. at a 98% level of confidence) any decline could have taken place at any point within a longer timescale (Dark 1996, 41).

The pollen evidence, however, does indicate a phase of re-afforestation on marginal land between the fifth and seventh centuries, which may have resulted from a combination of local factors and a short period of climatic deterioration (Higham 1987, 39-43; Baillie 1999, 85-88). The evidence for this re-afforestation is seen particularly in pollen diagrams east of the Pennines. At Bolton Fell Moss in Cumbria, however, there is evidence of the maintenance of cereal cultivation, with a subsequent rise in production in approximately AD 880 (Barber 1981; Dark 1996, 42). Evidence from the pollen diagram at Burnmoor Tarn, in Cumbria, also indicates increased agricultural activity during the fifth and sixth centuries (Dark 1996, 43). Bearing in mind this contrasting evidence east and west of the Pennines, it is possible that the use of climate change as an explanation for re-afforestation in north-eastern England has been over-emphasized, to the detriment of social and political factors at work during the first post-Roman centuries.

Unlike northern England south of Hadrian's Wall, the area of Northumberland appears to display continuity in all the physical aspects of the pre-existing Roman Iron Age society in the region. In the late Roman period, Northumberland comprised a major part of the territory of the tribal 'confederacy' or 'kingdom' of the Votadini. The origin of this polity is uncertain; it may have evolved from the coalescence of existing tribal units as a response to the presence of the Roman military frontier zone. Alternatively, Breeze and Dobson have suggested that the confederacy was promoted by the late Roman state in the fourth century, as a buffer zone beyond the northern frontier (Breeze and Dobson 1987, 230). It is possible that both these hypotheses are partially correct, in that the elite of an emerging kingdom could have been supported via luxury gifts from the Roman authorities in order to ensure friendly political relations. The gifts could then have been used to reinforce the ruling status of the leaders of the Votadini by rewarding their clients. The hoard from the hillfort of Traprain Law in East Lothian, presumed to be one of the political centres of the Votadini, may represent such diplomatic gifts from the late Roman state. The hoard consisted of scrap-silver tableware from over a hundred vessels, several silver coins and some dress jewellery, the whole weighing over 20 kilograms (Curle 1923; Martin 1997, 51). The items comprising the hoard date from the late fourth-early fifth century, and it is conceivable that it reflects gifts from emerging fifth-century post-Roman authorities as much as the late Roman state. That the kingdom

of the Votadini survived into the sixth century is reflected in the heroic poem named after it – the *Gododdin*, which is the mutated Old Welsh form of their Latin description and is thought to have been written down in its archaic form before AD 750, after a period of oral transmission (Koch 1997, li-lii & cxxviii-cxxxv). By the late sixth century, however, the focal centre of the kingdom appears to have been Edinburgh (*Din Eidyn*), following the development of an 'Anglo-Saxon' polity in Northumberland (Koch 1997, xiii-xiv).

There is no recognizable evidence at present to suggest that the elements of the settlement pattern in Northumberland changed in any way during the fifth century. The characteristics of this settlement pattern are best differentiated by their topographical situation in upland, lowland interior and coastal locations. In the uplands, the previously mentioned settlement at Huckhoe, in the Wansbeck valley, exhibits occupation throughout the fifth and possibly into the sixth century (Jobey 1959, 251; Thomas 1959, 260-1), and there is no reason to suppose abandonment on other upland sites which have not yielded diagnostically datable artefacts. Continued occupation of lowland settlements in the Northumberland interior, in areas such as the Milfield basin, is also largely assumed rather than proven. Although, the situation of Anglo-Saxon settlements on the sites of Roman Iron Age farms at Milfield and Sprouston, near Kelso, suggests that the native farmsteads influenced the location of succeeding Anglo-Saxon settlements (Gates and O'Brien 1988, fig 1; Smith 1984, 185). Fortified coastal centres such as Bamburgh also show an unbroken occupation sequence from the Roman Iron Age into the Early Medieval period, and consequently it is sensible to assume continuity of settlement function in the fifth century and beyond (Hope-Taylor 1977, 370). Indeed, it will become evident that this settlement pattern also survived in its Anglo-Saxon form during the seventh and into the eighth centuries.

In summary, therefore, archaeological evidence of fifth-century societies in northern England presents a picture of both continuity and sudden change. A sequence of actions that can be described as 'de-Romanization' occurred on Hadrian's Wall and in Durham and Cumbria, resulting from the collapse of the late Roman state infrastructure and a disappearance of most physical aspects of Romano-British material culture. The former military garrisons were probably forced to rely on the resources of their hinterlands, continuing a trend from the fourth century, which is likely to have resulted in a series of warband-based authorities. The coalescence of these authorities can be seen as the origin of British kingdoms such as Rheged. There is no incontestable evidence to show that local agricultural economies of the late Roman period were affected by the collapse of the central government, and surpluses and taxation renders in kind were probably able to support the development of new British polities in the fifth century. In contrast to this radical change in political authority in the northern military zone, however, the developing Roman Iron Age kingdom of the Votadini evolved in an uninterrupted manner in the post-Roman period, until its division and emergence as part of an 'Anglo-Saxon' polity with an overtly indigenous character. It is within the context of these developments that the invention of a distinctive post-Roman British material culture should be viewed, as a reflection of a new social and political situation. Although the evidence is sparse, this involved the elaboration of certain dress accessories such as penannular brooches and the adoption of Christianity and epigraphic monuments to reflect a continuum with the religious beliefs of Rome (Loveluck in press). This use of Christianity and the traditions of what has become known as the 'Celtic' church would paradoxically set the insular British medium of expressing a Roman legacy against the actual Roman church, during both the Pelagian heresy of the fifth century and the Easter debate of the seventh century.

The appearance of an Anglo-Saxon population in County Durham, between the Rivers Tees and Tyne

From the late fifth or early sixth century, users of Anglo-Saxon material culture and burial practices began to be interred in newly founded cemeteries on the River Tees and in County Durham. The closest parallels to these predominantly inhumation burials, often described as 'Anglian' in character, are to be found on the Yorkshire coast, and especially in East Yorkshire (Lucy 1998; Loveluck 1998; Loveluck in press). Unfortunately, the settlements that must have been associated with these cemeteries have not been excavated. As a result, the evidence of the development of Anglo-Saxon society in County Durham must be viewed almost exclusively through the medium of burial ritual.

The two cemeteries with the greatest degree of similarity to those found in East Yorkshire are located on or within the immediate hinterland of the River Tees at Greenbank, in Darlington and at Norton on Tees, nearer to the North Sea coast. Six furnished inhumation burials were recorded at Greenbank in 1876. A range of dress accessories and weapons associated with both male and female graves were recovered, including two swords, spearheads, great square-headed brooches, cruciform brooches, small-long brooches and amber and paste bead necklaces (Miket and Pocock 1976, 65-7). This collection of artefacts may in reality represent the finds from more than six graves, and it is likely that the Greenbank burials constitute part of a much larger cemetery. At Norton, 120 graves were excavated between 1982 and 1985. All were inhumation burials apart from three cremations, which constitute the only Anglo-Saxon cremation burials yet discovered north of the River Tees (Sherlock and Welch 1992, 30). Many of the burials were furnished with grave-goods which can be described as 'Anglian', although a large number of graves were also unfurnished. As with most Early Anglo-Saxon cemeteries, the majority of the artefacts recovered were items of female funerary dress costume, including annular, cruciform, small-long, and great square-headed brooches, together with wrist clasps and silver scutiform pendants among other artefacts. A range of weapons was also recovered from male graves, comprising spears, knives, and an early seax (*ibid*). On the basis of current artefact chronologies, the use of the Norton and Greenbank cemeteries spanned the sixth and early seventh century. Graves exhibiting a similar range of grave-goods have also been found in the recently discovered cemetery at Easington, in County Durham. Again, the small number of graves excavated appears to belong to a larger cemetery, represented by a large number of unassociated items of dress jewellery (Hamerow and Picken 1995).

An especially notable trait in the Norton and Greenbank cemeteries is the interment in wealthy female burials of a particular form of great square-headed brooch of the Leeds type C2 series (Leeds 1949). Two examples were retrieved at Greenbank and four were recovered from three graves at Norton. Other C2 square-headed brooches have also been found in graves or as chance finds between the Tees and Tyne: at Piercebridge, Benwell and Whitehill Point, Tynemouth (Baldwin Brown 1915, 269; Pocock 1971, 408). The vast majority of these brooches have a coastal or riverine distribution, and the

County Durham examples form part of a group stretching along the North Sea coast from Tynemouth to north Lincolnshire, with particular concentrations along the Rivers Tees and Tyne and in East Yorkshire (Fig 12.2). The better cast and finished examples from Norton (Grave 61) and from Benwell are best paralleled in the East Yorkshire cemeteries of Hornsea (Sheppard 1913), Staxton (Sheppard 1938, 10), Driffield-Kelleythorpe (Mortimer 1905, 282) and Sewerby (Hirst 1985, 60). The more poorly finished examples found at Norton, Piercebridge, and Catterick, North Yorkshire (Pocock 1971, 407), and Fonaby, north Lincolnshire (Cook 1981, 36-7), may reflect the desire to emulate the better made pieces using the same design and motifs. As a type, these brooches have been recovered from graves which have been dated to between the mid sixth and early seventh centuries AD. The east coast location of the majority of these brooches, with several outliers further inland, has previously been interpreted as a reflection of a Deiran advance north and westwards from East Yorkshire and the York area (Pocock 1971, 409), but Martin Welch and Stephen Sherlock have now demonstrated that such a distinction cannot be made on stylistic grounds (Sherlock and Welch 1992, 38). The linkage of this brooch type to an expansion of the power of the southern Northumbrian kingdom of Deira is also inappropriate, since burial ritual is not likely to have been a direct reflection of political fortunes. Nevertheless, the distribution of C2 great square-headed brooches may reflect the development of a common medium of display among wealthy women along the north-east coast by the mid to late sixth century, possibly displaying membership of an extended clan or elite status within a larger social group (Loveluck 1994, vol 1, 151).

The furnished burial practices present in the Greenbank, Norton and Easington cemeteries do not reflect any direct legacy from native antecedents in eastern England between the Tees and the Tyne. Instead, the graves indicate adoption of traditions whose ancestry lay ultimately in western Scandinavia and the Low Countries, though the amalgamation of these new fashions into the 'Anglian' furnished burial practice must be seen as an insular development. Despite the intrusive nature of these cemeteries, however, post-Roman 'British' dress accessories are recovered from predominantly wealthy female Anglo-Saxon inhumations. They are found in the form of penannular brooches, and all are variants of Fowler's type G (Fowler 1963, 99). Two

examples were recovered at Norton, one from a female in Grave 65 accompanied by a knife, and the second from an extremely wealthy female burial (Grave 40) which also contained annular brooches, wrist clasps and silver bracelets paralleled at Long Wittenham, Oxfordshire, and Holywell Row, Suffolk (Akerman 1860, 335; Lethbridge 1931, 8). The occurrence of penannular brooches in wealthy female graves is another trait shared with cemeteries in East Yorkshire, where type G penannular and pseudo-penannular brooches have been found in burials at Driffield- Kelleythorpe and Londesborough (Mortimer 1905, 282; Swanton 1964, 273). The Norton and East Yorkshire penannular brooches were all produced between the fifth and sixth centuries, but opinions differ over the interpretation of their presence within an Anglo-Saxon burial practice (Dickinson 1982, 53). They have been seen as heirlooms, providing an indication of British ancestry, but Sherlock and Welch view them as curios buried for their rarity and unusual nature (Sherlock and Welch 1992, 104). The latter dismissal, however, of any symbolic role for these native brooches is paradoxical to the view that the 'Anglian' dress jewellery was an overt expression of identity. The recurrent trend of the deposition of penannular brooches in some female Anglo-Saxon graves does suggest some symbolic significance, despite the fact that its nature is unclear. It is also interesting to observe that penannular brooches are found only in female Anglo-Saxon graves, whereas sculptures from Early Medieval Ireland also show them being used as display brooches by men, suggesting their use by both genders in post-Roman British societies (O'Floinn 1989, 89).

In a few instances, isolated graves with demonstrable native traits are found in County Durham, although they are exceptional and cannot be interpreted as evidence for large-scale native influence on burial traditions from the end of the fifth to seventh centuries. Unlike the deposition of post-Roman penannular brooches within the context of a new Anglo-Saxon burial ritual, the accompaniment of stone cist burials at Castle Eden, East Boldon and Cornforth with a fifth- to sixth-century claw beaker, a late sixth- to seventh-century garnet-inlaid buckle and spears respectively, appears to reflect a further development of this late Roman burial tradition (Baldwin Brown 1915, vol IV, 810; Cramp 1995a, 26). Other late to post-Roman inhumations in stone cists have been found across the north of England and into the Peak District

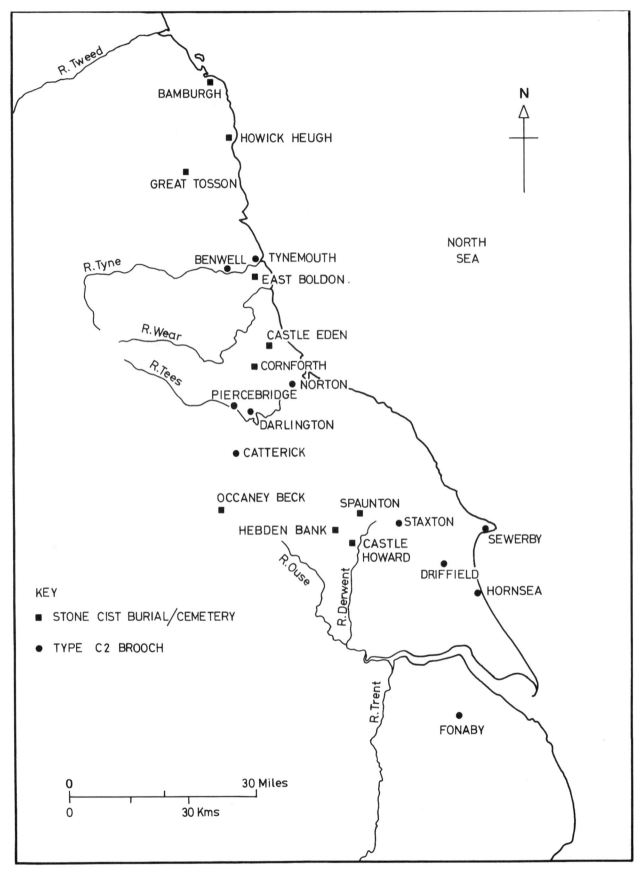

Fig. 12.2 Distribution of fifth- to seventh-century stone cist burials and Anglo-Saxon cemeteries with Type C2 Great square-headed brooches in north-eastern England

(Faull 1977, 26-30; Loveluck 1995, 85-7); and items of Anglo-Saxon dress jewellery or exotic luxuries began to be interred within cist graves, during the course of the sixth and seventh centuries. This occurrence probably reflects the development of new Anglo-Saxon fashions through a fusion of indigenous and 'Germanic-derived' practices. Such a demonstrable fusion of cultural traits is very rare in County Durham and further south along the North Sea coast, but it is more common in Northumberland and the upland interior of Yorkshire and the Peak District. In this context the phenomenon of the mutation of cist burial from a native to Anglo-Saxon tradition is discussed in more depth when considering the development of Anglo-Saxon society in Northumberland.

Unlike the fifth-century population of County Durham, the Anglo-Saxon society which developed between the Rivers Tees and Tyne over the course of the sixth century exhibited evidence of wide-ranging exchange contacts with southern England and north-western Europe. These links were no doubt facilitated by seaborne communications along the North Sea coast, and the distribution of the already mentioned C2 great square-headed brooches is probably a reflection of these links and the consequent promotion of a unifying identity. The majority of imports recovered originated ultimately from 'Frankish' areas of northern France, Belgium and Germany; although they may also have been procured via contacts with intervening regions, such as Kent. They include a shield-on-tongue buckle and probably the seax from Norton, the glass claw beaker from Castle Eden, and the buckle from East Boldon. Many of the amber and polychrome glass beads from the Anglo-Saxon cemeteries are also likely to have been imported, having been derived from the Baltic Sea region and Frankish areas respectively. Although the presence of these objects demonstrates long-distance exchange links, the limited number of imports indicates that contacts with continental Europe were limited, whether they were maintained directly or indirectly through 'middleman' regions. The imports were recovered from wealthy furnished inhumations, and can be seen as reflections of high status. The possession and ritual disposal of these rare luxuries probably reflects to a certain extent the wealth and by implication social position of a dead individual or clan group. In this context, it is interesting to observe that these luxury imports, often viewed as 'prestige' goods, were utilized in burial ritual

in both the Norton cemetery and the stone cist graves, containing 'Anglo-Saxon' material culture. It is possible that this reflects a similar disposal of rare luxuries in order to emphasize what may have been a tenuous social position, on the part of both any immigrant and established indigenous elites, seeking to display status and a new choice of identity in a mutually understandable 'Anglo-Saxon' form (Arnold 1982, 126; Lucy 2000, 185-186).

It is not possible to demonstrate any relationship between the fourth-fifth century settlement pattern and any Anglo-Saxon developments, between the Rivers Tees and Tyne, due to the lack of excavated Early Anglo-Saxon settlements. Nevertheless, it is possible to make some suggestions relating to the assumption of continued occupation and the metamorphosis of existing centres, with particular reference to settlements associated with former forts. During the course of the sixth to early seventh centuries, Anglo-Saxon dress jewellery and furnished burials appeared both within and adjacent to a series of the former forts. In 1908, the remains of an Anglo-Saxon female inhumation burial was excavated at the site of the Roman fort and small town at Corbridge. The burial contained two non-identical cruciform brooches, beads and a ceramic accessory vessel, but unfortunately the skeletal remains had decayed or were not recovered (Baldwin Brown 1915, vol IV, 811-12). The grave appears to date from the early-mid sixth century. Another female grave, dated to the mid sixth century, was found in 1978 within the former *praetorium* of the fort at Binchester. The woman was furnished with an S-shaped brooch, a necklace of amber and glass beads, and an ivory/antler purse ring. Other isolated finds, some of which may have come from disturbed graves, include the already mentioned mid to late sixth-century C2 great square-headed brooch from Piercebridge; another C2 brooch and an additional cruciform brooch from Benwell; and two seventh-century annular brooches from Chesterholm and Chesters, paralleled at Uncleby and Garton-Green Lane Crossing in East Yorkshire, (Miket 1980, 291-7).

The occurrence of Anglo-Saxon material culture and graves seems to reflect continuity of settlement foci at the sites of former forts, albeit with some possible settlement shifts through time. This is certainly suggested at Binchester, where both Early and Middle Saxon graves have been excavated, and fashioned Roman masonry from the fort is likely to have been used for the seventh-century church at nearby Escomb (Ferris and Jones 2000, 3). Organic settlement shift through the Early-Middle Saxon periods may also be evident at Corbridge, accounting for the different locations of the Roman and Saxo-Norman towns. Indeed, the late Roman and Early Anglo-Saxon remains, together with the Mid-Late Saxon evidence in the form of a watermill (Bidwell and Snape 1996) and church, suggest a continuing settlement focus at Corbridge throughout the Early Medieval period. Unfortunately, at the present moment in time it is not possible to make inferences on the character of the Early Anglo-Saxon settlement pattern in areas away from the former forts.

The development of an 'Anglo-Saxon' society in Northumberland

In contrast to the archaeological remains from County Durham, the area of Northumberland north of Hadrian's Wall has yielded unparalleled evidence of an 'Anglo-Saxon' society which appears to have taken over the existing Roman Iron Age settlement hierarchy. This region is exceptional within the area which became Anglo-Saxon England in that the legacy of the pre-existing native society is immediately evident. The merging of demonstrable native and Germanic influences produced an Early Anglo-Saxon society with an undoubted indigenous character. Nevertheless, new architectural styles in the form of *Grubenhäuser*, with their origins in 'Germanic' Europe, were adopted in the lowlands of the Milfield Basin and at coastal centres, such as Dunbar (Gates and O'Brien 1988, 3-4; Holdsworth 1991, 315). The area also witnessed the appearance of new burial practices of a recognizable 'Anglo-Saxon' character and the further development of existing burial practices, where Anglo-Saxon material culture was buried within the context of the native cist burial tradition. Unlike the Anglo-Saxon cemeteries on the River Tees, however, excavated Anglo-Saxon burial grounds in Northumberland are poorer in terms of the quality and quantity of grave-goods accompanying the dead. This paucity of portable wealth may reflect a real poverty in terms of access to raw materials and luxuries – a trend which seems to continue from the Roman Iron Age in this region. However, it is equally possible that the relative poverty of Anglo-Saxon graves in Northumberland could indicate the use of alternative media for expressing wealth, particularly media which may have had more meaning to a population that adopted new methods of physical expression to a lesser extent than their counterparts in eastern England.

Since Clack and Gosling's survey of *Archaeology in the North* (1976), the excavation of the settlement at Thirlings in the Milfield basin, the publication of Hope-Taylor's Yeavering excavations, and the discovery of new Anglo-Saxon settlements through aerial photographic survey have resulted in the identification of a diverse series of settlement forms for the Early Medieval period, and what became the 'Anglo-Saxon' settlement hierarchy in Northumberland (Fig 12.3). The range of settlements within this hierarchy can be characterized within the three environmental zones identified earlier, namely coastal, lowland and upland areas.

On the North Sea coast, evidence for pre-eighth-century settlement has been found at the coastal promontory sites at Bamburgh and further north at Dunbar. Both of these settlements were pre-existing fortified sites which continued to be occupied by the emergent Anglo-Saxon population. As a settlement form, they are most akin to the Early Medieval British fortified sites at Edinburgh Castle, Dumbarton, and the Dalriadan centres of Dunadd and Dun Ollaigh (Nieke and Duncan 1988, 11-16; Lane and Campbell forthcoming). At Edinburgh Castle, the nearest of these centres to Dunbar and Bamburgh, the settlement also seems to have been occupied continuously from the Iron Age, if not slightly earlier (Yeoman 1990, 24; Driscoll and Yeoman 1997). Early Anglo-Saxon occupation of this type of settlement appears to be unique to Northumberland, and represents the wholesale take-over of pre-existing native centres. This may imply continuity of the function of these settlements, and probably continued occupation by at least elements of the existing populations of these sites. The archaeological evidence for 'Germanic' influences and the creation of a new Anglo-Saxon identity is reflected by the adoption of diagnostic Anglo-Saxon material culture, and in the case of Dunbar, the appearance of *Grubenhäuser* (Hope-Taylor 1977, 370; Holdsworth 1991, 315). At present, the earliest datable Anglo-Saxon artefacts recovered from these sites appear to be belong to the seventh century. Notable among these artefacts are a gold plaque with style II zoomorphic decoration from Bamburgh (Bailey 1991, 58-59), and a fragment of a gold and cloisonné garnet cross from Dunbar, bearing close similarities to the seventh-century pectoral cross of Saint Cuthbert from Durham Cathedral (Holdsworth 1991, 317;

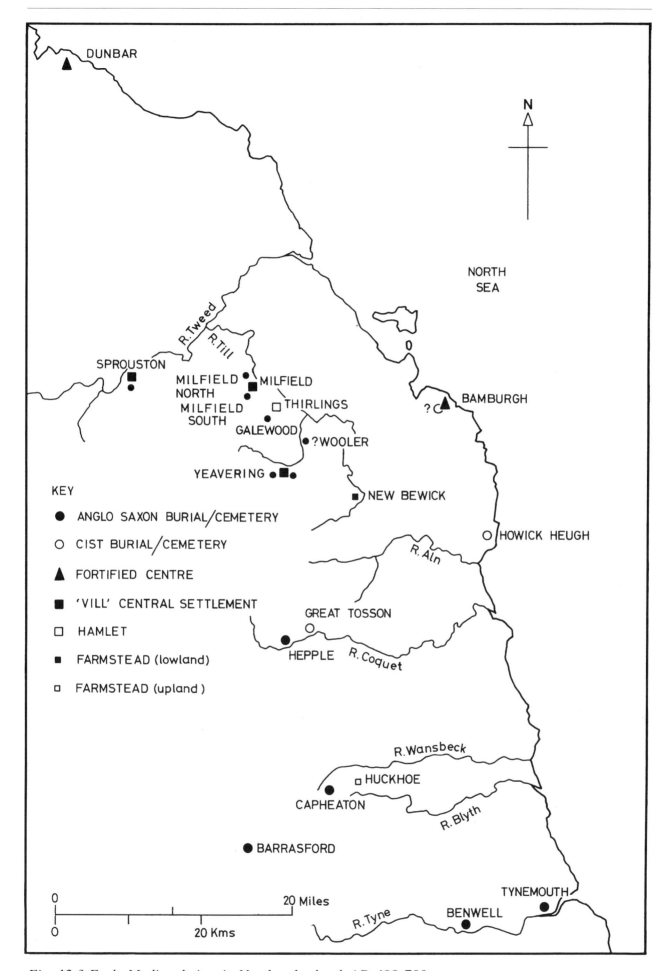

Fig. 12.3 Early Medieval sites in Northumberland, AD 400-700

Kendrick 1937, 283-5). The artefact evidence therefore suggests that the occupants of these fortified centres followed dress fashions which can be described as Anglo-Saxon from at least the seventh century.

The excavations which have taken place at Bamburgh and Dunbar to date have not yet yielded conclusive indications of the function of these settlements, although the recovery of exotic gold and garnet artefacts in a region where such high value commodities are exceptionally rare indicates that they were high-status centres. Indeed, historical sources indicate that Dunbar, and especially Bamburgh, were key royal centres of the Northumbrian ruling dynasties. Dunbar was described as an *urbs regis* by Eddius Stephanus, who described how the Northumbrian king Ecgfrith imprisoned Saint Wilfrid in this royal stronghold (Webb 1983, 145); while Bamburgh is frequently described by Bede as the most important fortified royal centre and 'bolt-hole' in the northern Northumbrian kingdom of Bernicia (Colgrave and Mynors 1969; Farmer 1983a, 173). The relationship between these coastal fortified centres and the high-status settlements identified as royal vills in the lowland interior of Northumberland is currently a subject needing further research. Hints toward the inter-relationship of these sites are likely to be provided only through renewed excavation at these coastal centres. On the basis of evidence from comparable fortified centres such as Dunadd, it is possible to advance the hypothesis that centres such as Bamburgh and Dunbar acted as centres for the storage, processing and consumption of tribute renders, yielded to the Northumbrian kings in Bernicia. Given that such a role appears to be characteristic of fortified settlements in the West and North of Britain in the Early Medieval period, the function of centres like Bamburgh and Dunbar may well have reflected the continued operation of existing post-Roman British mechanisms for supplying an elite in Northumberland.

Inland from the coastal centres, particularly on the gravels in the Milfield Basin and the Tweed valley, archaeological excavations and aerial photographic evidence have presented a picture of a lowland Early Medieval settlement hierarchy, unparalleled in quality except in the upper Thames Valley. The bottom tier of this lowland settlement hierarchy consisted of isolated farmsteads or small hamlets, an example of which has been identified at New Bewick by means of aerial photography and sample excavation (Gates and O'Brien 1988, 3-4). At this site, *Grubenhäuser* were identified from the air and subsequently excavated to check their character. They proved to be identical in form to equivalent examples in other areas of England, although they contained very few artefacts. Nevertheless, among the finds were loom-weights of a diagnostic Anglo-Saxon character. At New Bewick, a native predecessor in the immediate vicinity of the settlement was not indicated by aerial photographic evidence. Consequently, this presumed farmstead unit may represent a sixth- to seventh-century *de novo* settlement foundation, with buildings of a distinctive Anglo-Saxon character. At present, however, no earth-fast timber buildings have been identified on this site. Unlike the coastal centres, the New Bewick settlement does not seem to reflect any relationship with the pre-existing native settlement pattern in the region.

Above the level of the small farming units, the excavation of the settlement at Thirlings suggests the existence of a category of larger hamlets. In the case of this site, the excavated part of the settlement comprised nine rectangular earth-fast timber buildings, often described as 'halls', including one example with an annex (O'Brien and Miket 1991, 60-2). Two of these buildings were also enclosed within rectangular and circular fenced enclosures. The earth-fast foundations took two forms: the first consists of posts and wall panels set into continuous foundation trenches, and the second comprises posts or shaped planks set into posthole foundations. Radiocarbon dates taken from *in situ* charred timbers suggested that the buildings were in use during the sixth and early seventh centuries AD. Internal divisions were represented by postholes within several buildings, and in one instance the location of an internal hearth was indicated (*ibid*, 70). External foundations for roof-supporting raking timbers were also found, running along the exterior of the walls of the larger buildings. Similar foundations for raking timbers have been found on other settlements of a similar date, in association with both posthole and continuous foundation trench buildings, with local parallels at the nearby settlement at Yeavering (James *et al* 1984, 189). *Grubenhäuser* were not excavated at Thirlings, but their absence may be accounted for by the possibility that the settlement exhibited a degree of zoned planning, with halls and *Grubenhauser* located in different parts of the settlement, as at Early Anglo-Saxon West Heslerton, in North Yorkshire (Powlesland 1997). An area occupied by

Grubenhäuser has also been tentatively identified to the north-east of the excavated buildings at Thirlings, beyond a ditch running north-east/south-west which seems to divide the two zones of the settlement (O'Brien and Miket 1991, 59). Their existence was suggested on the basis of aerial photographic evidence showing large pits similar in character to the *Grubenhäuser* identified from the air at New Bewick. Very few artefacts were recovered from the Thirlings settlement, being limited to a small quantity of hand-made ceramics, an annular loomweight fragment, iron nails, a knife, several glass beads, and three glass vessel fragments, including one from an imported bag- or claw beaker (*ibid*, 87).

At the top of the lowland settlement hierarchy in 'Early Anglo-Saxon' Northumberland was a tier of larger settlements which had a partially or completely planned layout. They contained large rectangular buildings, including some with annexes; large enclosures, with elements that can be interpreted as fortified; and in at least one instance, associated religious foci. The two settlements which come into this category have been found at Yeavering, in the Glen valley, and at Milfield, in the adjoining Milfield basin; while a third in the Tweed valley is indicated by aerial photography at Sprouston, near Kelso. Most of the Yeavering settlement was excavated by Brian Hope-Taylor between 1953 and 1962, and a more limited excavation of a Neolithic henge by Anthony Harding to the south of the Hope-Taylor excavations also yielded features associated with the Anglo-Saxon settlement, in the form of pits, crucible fragments and fuel ash slag from copper alloy working, together with animal bones, and an annular loomweight (Hope-Taylor 1977; Tinniswood and Harding 1991, 101-6). Aerial photographs also indicate the remains of at least three additional rectangular earth-fast timber buildings and several possible *Grubenhäuser* adjacent to the Harding excavations (*ibid*, 95-6). In total, the Hope-Taylor and Harding excavations and the aerial photographic evidence at Yeavering indicate a minimum of 24 earth-fast timber buildings. The vast majority of these 'halls' had continuous trench foundations for the timber superstructure of the buildings, represented by posts, shaped planks and wall panels. Several buildings with posthole foundations were also recovered, occurring early in the occupation sequence of the Anglo-Saxon settlement, although the different foundation types need not imply different construction techniques or above-ground

appearance (Scull 1991, 57). As at other Anglo-Saxon settlements, many of the continuous trench buildings also possessed evidence for raking timbers to assist in roof support. The Yeavering settlement also yielded a unique building with a sunken element, uncharacteristic of a *Grubenhaus*, which contained fired clay hearths and butchery waste. This was interpreted as a 'cookhouse' associated with one of the religious and funerary foci of the settlement (Hope-Taylor 1977, 103-8).

The buildings and associated structures at Yeavering seem to have been laid out within units relating to the functional use of different parts of the settlement. The siting of these functional elements also reflects take-over or continuity of ritual and funerary use from the Roman Iron Age and earlier periods. Six functional areas can be defined: the 'great enclosure', incorporating an enclosed building in one of its terminals; a 'major hall' area in the centre of the settlement, with residential zones extending to the north and south; a display area associated with a theatre-like structure; two religious and funerary areas in the west and east of the settlement respectively; and a craft-working area at the southern periphery of the settlement. The two religious and funerary zones do not appear to have been contemporary. The western focus was earlier, and is interpreted as a 'temple' complex and associated cemetery, which may have been sited in relation to a group of Roman Iron Age inhumation burials within a ring ditch (*ibid*, 116). The eastern area has been identified as a Christian cemetery and associated church, and is suggested to have been a development of the later phases of the settlement's occupation sequence (*ibid*, 73-4).

Like Yeavering, the settlement at Milfield also seems to exhibit a planned layout with different functional areas, although these are to some extent assumed, since the site is known only from aerial photographic evidence. The production of a detailed plan of the Milfield cropmarks by Gates and O'Brien revealed three broad elements within the settlement. These comprised a larger double-ditched enclosure than the Yeavering example, with an integral enclosed area of rectangular buildings; a central area of large earth-fast timber buildings with annexes, set within their own fenced area; and an associated settlement agglomeration to the north, with *Grubenhäuser* and small enclosures (Gates and O'Brien 1988, 3). Again like Yeavering, the Milfield settlement also seems to have been focused on the site of previous Roman Iron Age activity. A small double-ditched enclosure, best interpreted as a pre-Roman or Roman Iron Age farmstead is situated to the west of the largest residential buildings at Milfield, and in this respect there is a direct parallel with the large Anglo-Saxon settlement at Sprouston, in the Tweed valley. The latter settlement also developed from a native double-ditched farmstead (Smith 1984, 187; Loveluck 1990).

Both the Yeavering and Milfield sites have been identified as the centres of royal vills belonging to the Northumbrian kings. Yeavering has been identified as the paramount settlement (*caput*) within a royal vill at *Ad Gefrin*, mentioned by Bede, while the Milfield settlement is viewed as the site of the *caput* at *Maelmin*. Based on evidence from Bede, the Milfield settlement has been viewed as the successor to Yeavering, possibly forming the central settlement for the same territory (Cramp 1983, 275). However, even if these historical identifications are correct, there is no reason to believe that a significant settlement did not exist at Milfield prior to any elevation in status to become a royal centre. Indeed, bearing in mind the existence of other comparable settlements like Sprouston, the historical references of Bede may be misleading in the sense that these larger settlements could have been contemporary high-status centres with similar functions within the Bernician resource heartlands of the Milfield basin and the Tweed valley. In their character, there can be little doubt that these sites represent high-status centres. The occurrence of large enclosures and large central hall complexes probably reflects the collection of tribute or tax renders in kind at these settlements, possibly in the form of cattle (Cramp 1988b, 75; Charles-Edwards 1989, 30-1). Similarly, they would also have accommodated a peripatetic royal household, thereby acting as centres for conspicuous consumption on the part of the Northumbrian rulers, and the dispensation of justice etc. In the absence of the royal household, however, settlements like Yeavering are still likely to have remained central settlements for their surrounding territories. By the seventh century, if not before, such rural centres were probably administered by royal representatives, often referred to as *praefecti* or reeves. Despite being a royal centre, however, the range of artefacts recovered from the Yeavering settlement is very limited in comparison with settlements further south – a regional trait that is shared with contemporary settlements such as Thirlings.

Unlike the lowland settlements, which developed over the course of the sixth and seventh centuries into forms which are recognizable in other parts of Early Anglo-Saxon England, the upland settlements in Northumberland do not appear to have changed in character from the Roman Iron Age. In fact, as discussed earlier, it is difficult to prove that many of the upland farmsteads were occupied at all between the fifth and eighth centuries AD. The problems in assessing the pattern and character of settlement in the uplands are twofold: first, those which have been excavated have very rarely yielded diagnostically datable artefacts or radiocarbon samples showing occupation in the Early Medieval period; and secondly, many of the upland settlements may have represented shielings occupied only in the summer, during the movement of livestock to upland pastures. The upland settlements that have produced evidence for post-Roman Iron Age occupation have not grown in number since the previous review of archaeology in the north (Clack and Gosling 1976).

The clearest evidence for continuing post-Roman Iron Age occupation at an upland site is still that yielded by George Jobey's excavations at Huckhoe, in the Upper Wansbeck valley, in Northumberland. During the fourth-fifth centuries AD, this enclosed upland settlement contained a number of rectangular and sub-rectanguar stone huts which had replaced earlier stone round-houses (Jobey 1959, 247-50). These rectangular buildings contained late Roman coarse pottery wares and several sherds of diagnostic post-Roman wheel-made wares in their floors. The post-Roman imported wares are paralleled most closely at Dunadd and Dalkey Island, near Dublin (Thomas 1959, 258-61). The latest datable phase of occupation on this settlement was therefore placed between the fifth and early sixth centuries AD, with the artefact assemblage indicating links with the Irish Sea rather than with any incoming fashions, traditions or settlers from across the North Sea. Other upland farmsteads such as Ingram Hill also contained similar rectangular stone buildings in their final phases of occupation, but unfortunately this site did not yield any dating evidence (Jobey 1959, 250). Currently, therefore, it is exceptionally difficult to assess the extent of the permanent occupation of the Northumberland uplands beyond the end of the fourth century, except on the basis of relative stratigraphic sequences, certain architectural features and the exceptional occurrence of diagnostic post-

Roman artefacts. It is reasonable, however, to observe that artefacts of a distinctive 'Anglo-Saxon' character have not been found on any upland settlements.

In many ways, the Early Medieval burial record in Northumberland reflects the extent of adoption of Anglo-Saxon fashions within the settlement hierarchy, although the quality of the funerary evidence for the period from AD 400-700 is much poorer than that provided by contemporary settlement remains. Inhumation was the predominant burial practice between the fifth and seventh centuries, but two broad forms of inhumation are evident as in County Durham: a new Anglo-Saxon tradition and the existing cist burial practice which gradually incorporated items of 'Anglo-Saxon' material culture (Figs 12.2 and 12.3).

Burials of an Anglo-Saxon character, directly analogous to graves found in eastern England to the south, have been uncovered at Barrasford, Capheaton, Galewood, Hepple, Milfield North, Milfield South, and to some extent at Yeavering (Miket 1980, 290-7). As in parts of England such as the Yorkshire Wolds, the majority of the burials or cemeteries mentioned above were placed within existing prehistoric burial or ritual monuments, such as barrows or henges (Mortimer 1905). It is difficult to date any of the Anglo-Saxon furnished inhumations in Northumberland to earlier than the sixth century, and the vast majority of burials with grave-goods were interred during the seventh century. The Barrasford and Capheaton burials were placed in barrows, the former in an earlier barrow, while the latter may have been constructed to cover the Anglo-Saxon burial. Both barrows housed apparently high-status individuals. At Barrasford, a male burial was accompanied by a sword, shield and knife, and Capheaton burial by a copper alloy hanging bowl, finger ring and other copper alloy fragments. Both barrow burials are directly akin to other such graves dating to the seventh century, with parallels in southern England and the Peak District (Geake 1992, 84-6; Loveluck 1995, 85-7). It is unclear whether these Northumberland barrow burials acted as foci for larger cemeteries.

At Milfield North and Milfield South, cemeteries were focused on Neolithic henges. At the former site, to the north of the Milfield Anglo-Saxon settlement, six badly preserved inhumations were excavated. These graves contained Anglo-Saxon dress accessories consistent with a date of deposition in the seventh century (Scull

and Harding 1990, 11). None of the burials can be regarded as particularly wealthy. The Milfield South cemetery was located immediately to the south of the Anglo-Saxon settlement. A possible 45 burials were uncovered in the area of the Neolithic henge, although only 21 graves were excavated. Very few grave-goods accompanied the graves, and the dress accessories recovered suggest that the cemetery dates from between the mid seventh and early eighth century (*ibid*, 22). Fragments of a pattern-welded iron sword and a spearhead were also found as unstratified finds. The particularly close proximity of the Milfield South cemetery to the suggested *caput* settlement of *Maelmin* has led to the suggestion that it formed at least one of the burial foci for the vill centre. The material poverty of the cemetery in comparison to contemporary cemeteries further south in England has been accounted for by the possibility that additional cemeteries may have served the settlement (*ibid*, 23; Miket 1980, 299). Alternatively, cultural influences working within Early Anglo-Saxon Northumberland may have mitigated against expression of wealth and rank within funerary ritual. The possible under-statement of status within Anglo-Saxon burial practice during the seventh century is also witnessed amongst the datable graves at Yeavering, for example, in the grave group BZ (Hope-Taylor 1977, 185-7). Nevertheless, the wealthy burials at Barrasford and Capheaton do demonstrate that high social status was expressed to a certain degree in burial ritual in Northumberland. The apparent paradox between wealth expressed in settlement features, such as the buildings and large enclosures at Milfield and Yeavering, and the poverty of the Anglo-Saxon graves from these sites will form a major theme for discussion below. At Yeavering, it is the buildings rather than the graves from the settlement which appear to be sited in relation to earlier ritual monuments, although the eastern and western Anglo-Saxon burial foci are also located within an earlier Roman Iron Age funerary complex, due to their association with the buildings. Unlike the excavated cemeteries at Milfield, however, the eastern cemetery at Yeavering is composed of east/west-aligned inhumations in association with a possible church or mortuary chapel. This resulted in its interpretation as a mid to late seventh-century Christian burial ground (*ibid*, 165-7).

The second group of Early Medieval burials in Northumberland reflects a greater degree of overt indigenous influence on burial practice.

Like the examples found in Durham, North and West Yorkshire and the Peak District, Anglo-Saxon dress accessories and other artefacts are found interred within the native tradition of stone long-cist burial (Corder 1928, 19-21; Faull 1977, 6-7; Loveluck in press). Long cists and stone cairns containing inhumations with Anglo-Saxon accoutrements have been found at Great Tosson and Howick Heugh, while a further long-cist cemetery was also exposed at Bamburgh but its date is uncertain (Hope-Taylor 1977, 254). The Great Tosson graves were sited within an earlier prehistoric cist cemetery (Miket 1980, 294; O'Sullivan 1998, 16). The burials at Howick Heugh are more difficult to date, since many were unfurnished. The artefacts recovered, including beads, knives, riding gear, a spearhead and Romano-British artefacts, may represent a cemetery used from the Roman Iron Age into the Early Medieval period. Other cist burials with Anglo-Saxon artefacts have also been found in south-eastern Scotland, in Lothian (Proudfoot and Aliaga-Kelly 1998, 10; Cessford 1998, 50-51). It has already been suggested that the use of Anglo-Saxon artefacts within the context of this pre-existing burial practice reflects the adoption of Anglo-Saxon fashions by the existing population. It demonstrates the fusion of a Roman Iron Age and late Roman burial practice with new influences from across the North Sea. That this burial tradition developed in areas such as the North Yorkshire Moors, West Yorkshire, Northumberland, south-eastern Scotland and to a certain extent in Durham and the Peak District, arguably reflects less extensive influence or adoption in these areas of ideas from across the North Sea, when compared with eastern England to the south. The long-term continuity of elements of existing funerary customs is certainly consistent with the overall take-over of pre-existing native centres witnessed in Northumberland.

Post-Roman societies in Cumbria

When setting out to study the physical attributes and development of the immediate post-Roman society of Cumbria, both Deirdre O'Sullivan and Rachel Newman have drawn attention to the paucity of diagnostic archaeological remains and the small number of excavations as factors which limit the scope of interpretation (O'Sullivan 1984, 143; O'Sullivan 1998, 15; Newman 1984, 155). The problem of a lack of diagnostic archaeological evidence is at its worst for the period between the fifth and sev-

enth centuries – the period under consideration in this paper. Consequently, analysis of any changes that occurred during the immediate post-Roman period must be approached through the interpretation of a small series of excavations and chance finds, often of an antiquarian nature (Fig 12.4). It is important to observe, however, that a total of six secondary inhumation interments in barrows from the Upper Eden valley, and three stray finds of metalwork, suggest that Anglo-Saxon material culture was not discarded in Cumbria before the seventh century; and nearly all of these finds were made on Cumbria's eastern margins (O'Sullivan 1993, 25; O'Sullivan 1998, 16-22).

An assessment of the nature of the post-Roman settlement pattern is forced to rely on an assumption of continued occupation of settlements known to have been occupied at the time when the latest datable Romano-British coinage and ceramics were present. Following the turn of the fifth century, therefore, it is necessary to rely on relative stratigraphic sequences for evidence of post-Roman occupation, in conjunction with rare finds of new post-Roman material culture. The evidence for the continued occupation at the Roman fort at Birdoswald has already been discussed, and there are no indications of subsequent abandonment of the fort as a settlement focus in the immediate post-Roman period (Wilmott 1997; Wilmott 2000, 14). It is also sensible to suppose continued occupation of upland settlements, albeit without any diagnostically datable post-Roman evidence to support this claim. Similarly, it can be assumed that Carlisle was still occupied as a settlement focus in the fifth and sixth centuries, prior to its take-over as an Anglo-Saxon political and religious centre in the mid-late seventh century (McCarthy 1990). Rosemary Cramp, however, has cautioned against the assumption that the former Roman town of Carlisle maintained a paramount position in the lowland settlement pattern around the Solway, within the post-Roman kingdom of Rheged (Cramp 1995b). Instead she has suggested the existence of a series of fortified settlements, akin to centres such as the Mote of Mark (Laing 1975, 32-36), on the basis of a series of place-names with the Welsh element *caer*, meaning fort, eg Caerlaverock, Cardurnock and Carlisle itself. It can be assumed that the settlement within the former Roman fort at Birdoswald also represents one of these fortified sites. Cramp has suggested that these centres formed foci for the consumption of surpluses by an itinerant 'royal' elite within the kingdom of Rheged,

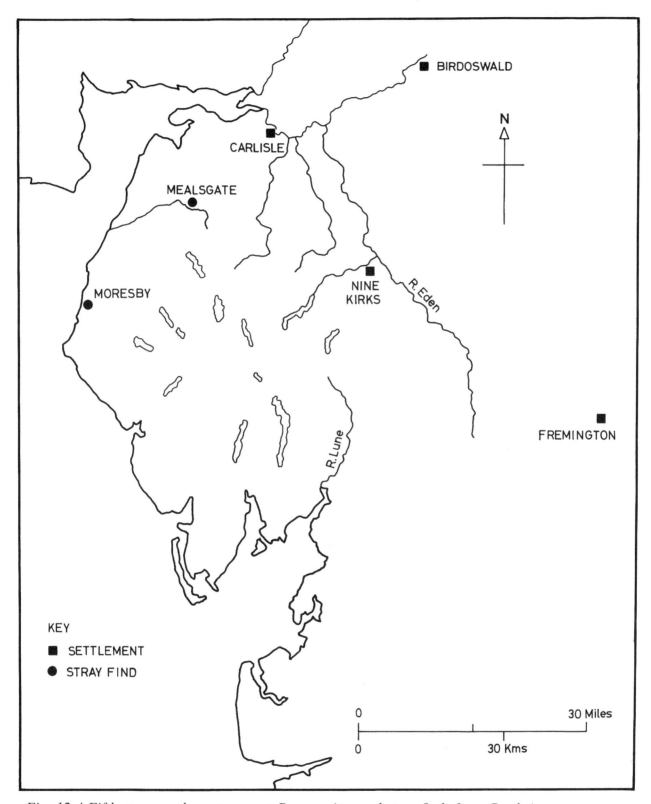

Fig. 12.4 Fifth- to seventh-century post-Roman sites and stray finds from Cumbria

although this may assume a single ruling authority which may not have existed across Cumbria during the fifth and sixth centuries (Higham 1986, 253). It is thought that these centres were supported by 'multiple' or composite estates, exploiting upland and lowland territories (Jones 1961; 1976), but this assumption is supported only by tenuous evidence gained from Old Welsh heroic poetry and the backward extrapolation of eleventh- to twelfth-century estate structures (Koch 1997, xxx-xxxi; O'Sullivan 1984, 146-9; Newman 1984, 157-62).

Despite the use of what may be anachronistic assumptions, the hypothesis of the existence of a conservative settlement pattern in Cumbria, with long-lived tenurial units comprising lowland central settlements (*llysoedd* and *maenorau*) and upland settlements (*hafodau*) can be tested archaeologically, particularly with regard to the lowland centres. In this context it is important to draw attention to the Brougham area of Cumbria, in the fertile central heartland of the Eden valley. Within the parish of Brougham lies the church of Ninekirks – St Ninian's church, the dedication probably indicating an early Christian centre of the post-Roman period (Cramp 1995b). During the course of a renovation of the existing church in 1846, several inhumations were uncovered within the chancel. One of these skeletons, interred in a plain stone cist, was accompanied by a silver-gilt cup mount decorated with Hiberno-Saxon anthropomorphic and knotwork motifs. Bailey has dated this find to the eighth century, based on parallel motifs in the Book of Kells, and has ascribed it a possible Pictish origin (Bailey 1977, 179-80). The indications of an early Christian focus and the presence of a demonstrable post-Roman burial with a luxury grave-good do not constitute strong evidence of a major lowland centre, but crop-mark evidence also shows that the church lies within an enclosure with rectangular buildings. It is possible that this combined evidence represents an Early Medieval settlement complex, and later a monastery, at the heart of an estate. Like the Yeavering Anglo-Saxon settlement in Northumberland, it is located within an area of pre-existing settlement and ritual activity. Just as the Yeavering settlement may have been sited with a view to taking over a ritual centre, so an early Christian focus at Ninekirks may have supplanted the earlier Romano-British religious centre at Brougham, dedicated to a local deity Belatucadrus (Higham 1986, 227).

Other than the archaeological evidence from Birdoswald and the Brougham area, the remainder of the albeit limited diagnostic evidence of post-Roman British society from Cumbria comes from isolated chance finds, often with poorly recorded provenances. These objects have recently formed part of a corpus of Early Medieval stray finds from Cumbria, compiled by Deirdre O'Sullivan. Only two items of distinctive post-Roman manufacture have been found, consisting of a copper alloy penannular brooch of Fowler's type Fl, from Mealsgate in the Ellen valley; and a copper alloy proto hand-pin from Moresby, on the Cumbrian coast (O'Sullivan 1993, 32-4). The penannular brooch is of a type which has been dated between the fifth and sixth centuries, while the hand-pin probably dates from the sixth to early seventh century. Both these pieces of dress jewellery have been viewed as Irish products (Kilbride-Jones 1980, 213-14), imported into a post-Roman Cumbria which probably used very similar display artefacts. If these objects are of Irish derivation, they provide evidence of integration within the long-distance communications routes of the Irish Sea, between the fifth and seventh centuries. In comparison with regions immediately to the north and south, however, Cumbria appears to have been incorporated within these exchange networks to a much lesser extent. The region has not yielded imported Mediterranean and Gaulish ceramics or glass vessels, unlike the centre of Whithorn and the beach sites at Luce Sands, in Dumfries and Galloway, and Meols in the Wirral (Hill 1997; Campbell 1997, 297-322; Griffiths 1992, 63-5; 1994, 184-5). Indeed, with the exception of the two pieces of post-Roman metalwork which may be Irish, Cumbria is conspicuous in its absence of imported luxury commodities. It is possible that this absence of evidence reflects limited excavation in Cumbria, but if this is not subsequently found to be the case, a cultural explanation may need to be sought for the apparent material poverty of post-Roman British Cumbria.

On the basis of historical references, primarily from Bede's *Historia Ecclesiastica* but also from Saints' lives and Old Welsh heroic poetry, a hypothesis has been advanced of the gradual development of Northumbrian Anglo-Saxon hegemony over Cumbria – or rather the British kingdom of Rheged, as the seventh century progressed. This has been characterized as proceeding via raiding and demands of tribute after the

British defeat at *Catraeth*, followed by political overlordship achieved in part by inter-marriage at elite level between the ruling houses of Rheged and Northumbria; and finally by take-over of existing political and religious centres (Cramp 1995b). In contrast, Higham has recently suggested a more direct conquest by Aethelfrith and a consolidation under his successors, although if this was the case it might be considered surprising that diagnostic Anglo-Saxon finds dating from the seventh century are so scarce in Cumbria (Higham 1993, 111-13; O'Sullivan 1998, 22). As already mentioned, only a possible six inhumation burials and three characteristic stray finds of seventh-century date have been found in Cumbria. The burials are all concentrated in the Upper Eden valley – the eastern extremity of Cumbria (O'Sullivan 1998, 22); and the stray finds comprise a horn sword-handle, decorated with gold panels of filigree scrollwork and garnet settings (Smith 1923, 92-3), a gilt copper alloy mount, and an enamelled hanging-bowl escutcheon (O'Sullivan 1993, 27-8). Indeed, it may be inappropriate to ascribe the sword-handle a seventh-century date, since devoid of the undoubted seventh-century gold panels, the form of the handle has been seen as a product of the fifth century. The decoration can be viewed as later embellishment in an Anglo-Saxon style (Bone 1989, 64). Undoubted structural evidence of an intrusive Anglo-Saxon type has been found only at Fremington, again on the eastern margins of Cumbria (Cramp 1995b). This consists of several sunken-feature buildings, although unfortunately they are very difficult to date (R Newman, pers comm; Oliver 1993).

The development of 'Anglo-Saxon' Cumbria seems to have been an exercise in acculturation on the part of the existing British aristocracy. The limited adoption of Anglo-Saxon fashions, primarily relating to display items, may reflect the desire to maintain an existing social position on the part of the native elite by using contemporary Anglo-Saxon methods of expressing high status. Indeed, the Cumberland sword-handle discussed above could demonstrate the adoption of new elite fashions in the decoration of a potential heirloom in the new Anglo-Saxon manner. The take-up of Anglo-Saxon media of display by members of a surviving native elite would also account for the apparent continuity of occupation at existing centres, albeit under Northumbrian political overlordship during most of the seventh and eighth centuries. It is difficult to escape the conclusion that with the exception of elements of the native aristocracy, the period of Northumbrian domination during the seventh century did not precipitate large-scale cultural or linguistic change on the part of the inhabitants of Cumbria.

Conclusions – thoughts towards an understanding of social change in northern England between AD 400-700, and future research directions

The archaeological reflections of the changes that occurred in northern England between the fifth and seventh centuries make it clear that it is not possible to view them as a transitional development along a single trajectory from the Romano-British to Anglo-Saxon period. Instead, it is more appropriate to see the events of the immediate post-Roman period as a series of social transformations, incorporating different degrees of continuity and revolutionary change. It is also evident that regional circumstances exerted such a powerful force on social change that it is difficult to produce a general model for post-Roman development in Cumbria, Durham and Northumberland without dealing with them separately. This is especially true when analysing the development of Anglo-Saxon societies from post-Roman British or post-Roman Iron Age antecedents. Nevertheless, despite their differences, certain common themes can be investigated using evidence from the three regions: namely, the role of acculturation; the inter-relationship of different elements of settlement hierarchies; trade and exchange contacts, and although the evidence is limited, factors influencing linguistic change.

For the purpose of discussion, the series of transformations which occurred between AD 400-700 can be summarized in three phases: first, the period of the fifth century, characterized by both sudden change and long-term continuity; secondly, the emergence of post-Roman polities; and thirdly, the Anglo-Saxon transformation and further development of existing British societies.

There can be little doubt that the collapse of the late Roman central administration, with the consequential disappearance of long-distance transport systems and coin-based taxation, can be viewed as a sudden and revolutionary change. This was probably especially true for the military commands in northern England. Similarly, the inability to maintain Romano-British media of display, if so desired, must also have become gradually evident. Yet despite these sudden changes, there is no evidence of a social or political catastrophe in the former Roman military zone of northern England during the fifth century. The refurbishment of fort defences suggests the devolution of power from unified state control to a local level, with former fort garrisons being supported from their immediate hinterlands, via the existing system of agricultural and raw material renders which had supported most of their subsistence needs in the fourth century. The garrisons and the people within their fort *territoria* therefore became more interdependent, resulting in the emergence of warband-based fiefdoms as the fifth century progressed. In contrast, the situation in Northumberland can be viewed as one of continuity, the confederacy of the Votadini enjoyed a long-term development from the Roman Iron Age. The only sudden change in this area probably manifested itself by the disappearance of diplomatic gifts from the late Roman central administration, possibly forcing rulers of the confederacy to reward followers using other means, such as cattle.

The second period of change can be seen as a linear progression and result of the apparent developments in response to the collapse of the late Roman state. It saw the emergence of new British polities and the consolidation of existing political entities. It is possible that the small warband-based territories centred on forts underwent a process of coalescence between the mid fifth to sixth centuries, possibly by agreement, or alternatively as a result of warfare between the descendants of former Roman regiments. It is by this means that the emergence of larger political units can be explained, such as the kingdom of Rheged in north-western England. In the north-east, further consolidation and development of the Votadini or Gododdin can be assumed, and it is probable that the area known as *Brynaich*, later to become Anglo-Saxon Bernicia, formed the Northumberland component of this social and political entity. It would appear that the onset of the third phase of post-Roman developments, comprising the first appearance and adoption of Anglo-Saxon traits, occurred during this phase of potentially aggressive enlargement of British political units.

The earliest datable Anglo-Saxon finds are reflected by a completely intrusive 'Anglian' burial practice in cemeteries in County Durham, between the Rivers Tees and Tyne, with a particular concentration on the Tees and on the coast. The earliest graves appear to date from the end of the fifth to the early sixth century, based on current artefact chronologies. With a few exceptions, the adoption of new Anglo-Saxon fashions of cultural display was total in County Durham, suggesting a sudden and radical change to the use of dress and media of cultural expression derived from eastern England to the south, which used ideas and traits ultimately derived from the Low Countries, northern Germany and Scandinavia. The closest parallels to the character of the items interred in the Anglo-Saxon cemeteries of County Duham are to be found along the Yorkshire coast, and particularly East Yorkshire. Indeed, by the second half of the sixth century, a common identity began to be displayed in wealthy female graves along the North Sea coast, between the Humber and the Tyne, in the form of Leeds type C2 great square-headed brooches. These large 'display' brooches could be a representation of an emerging social and political unity among the north-eastern Anglo-Saxon elite, or alternatively they could reflect high-status kinship links across this area. The only evidence of the overt maintenance of pre-Anglo-Saxon influences in burial practices is seen in the few stone cist burials, accompanied by imported luxuries from across the North Sea and limited dress accessories of an 'Anglo-Saxon' nature.

In contrast to Durham, the development of an Anglo-Saxon society in Northumberland appears to have been supported by a take-over of the existing settlement hierarchy and its social relations. The physical attributes of the Anglo-Saxon society which developed exhibited a distinct indigenous character due to the evident legacy of its British antecedent. The coastal fortified settlements of Bamburgh and Dunbar retained their role as high-status centres, presumably for the storage of surpluses yielded as renders from the upland and lowland interior. The take-over of high-status and ritual centres is also witnessed in the Milfield Basin and Tweed valley, with the central settlements at Yeavering and Milfield emerging into the historic period as royal vills of the Northumbrian kings, mentioned by Bede as *Ad Gefrin* and *Maelmin* respectively. Nevertheless, new settlements and architectural types of an intrusive Anglo-Saxon form are being uncovered in the Northumberland lowlands and on the coast, indicating the adoption of diagnostic Anglo-Saxon traits to a certain extent. Characteristic Anglo-Saxon cemeteries are also encountered in the Northumberland lowlands, although they were materially poor in comparison with contemporary graves in County Durham. The onset of the appearance of Anglo-Saxon material culture in Northumberland also occurs later than in Durham. The artefacts from Northumberland date predominantly from the later sixth and seventh centuries. The general poverty of artefacts in Anglo-Saxon graves in Northumberland may not reflect a real lack of wealth. Instead, it may indicate the use of different methods of wealth assessment and display, remaining as a legacy from the post-Roman Iron Age period. The presence of the large enclosures at Milfield and Yeavering, together with the predominance of cattle at the latter site, may reflect assessment of wealth based on the possession of cattle. Such an inherited method of displaying wealth would also account for the apparent paucity of imported luxuries in Northumberland, since their possession may not have been as necessary for social display in this region, in comparison with other 'Anglo-Saxon' areas. This would also account for the limited evidence of long-distance exchange contacts. The continuing influence of indigenous traditions is also indicated by the cist-burials, akin to those in Durham. However, despite the undoubted native physical traits in the Anglo-Saxon society which formed in Northumberland, Anglo-Saxon influence was still strong enough to precipitate a linguistic change, involving the abandonment of 'P-Celtic' for Old English – although certain P-Celtic linguistic fossils still survive in place-names.

In Cumbria, archaeological evidence of Anglo-Saxon influence is extremely sparse before the eighth century, and for most of the period between AD 400-700 the development of post-Roman Cumbria was the result of indigenous changes. Indeed, without the existence of historical evidence, it would be very difficult to argue for an Anglo-Saxon identity, presence or element of control in this region before the eighth century, with the exception of its eastern margins in the Upper Eden valley. With the assistance of the historical sources, however, it would appear that Anglo-Saxon control in Cumbria was achieved by the replacement or acculturation of the native British elite, who adopted Anglo-Saxon fashions of display during the course of the seventh century. This acculturation appears to have been limited to the elite alone, and it must be assumed that the bulk of the population remained characteristically 'British' (even when Anglo-Saxon influence is more evident, predominantly in the form of

sculpture during the eighth century). It is also a mistake to assume inevitability in the eventual dominance of Anglo-Saxon material culture and the Old English language. 'P-Celtic' place-names seem to have survived the period of Norse influence, with some associated settlement, during the ninth century. And after the incorporation of Cumbria within the hegemony of the British kingdom of Strathclyde, during the tenth century, P-Celtic place-names seem to have expanded in use again, prior to the consolidation of England under the Anglo-Scandinavian and Norman kings of the eleventh century.

In conclusion, it remains to suggest some future avenues of research which would further our still limited understanding of the fifth- to seventh-century changes which took place in northern England. Recommendations for future research priorities depend largely on specific regional circumstances and the extent of existing archaeological work in Cumbria, Durham and Northumberland. It is abundantly clear that the nature of the archaeological questions which can be asked of the evidence in these three regions must either be different, or they need to be asked within different time frames. Hence, for the study of the first post-Roman centuries in northern England it is perhaps most appropriate to divide research priorities on the basis of landuse, terrain and the archaeological visibility of physical remains.

Taking the pastoral uplands and mountains as a starting point, it is evident that the study of relatively short-term changes relating to cultural transformations is difficult to achieve. This is a function of both landuse and the rare presence of diagnostic material culture. Within the uplands of Cumbria, Northumberland and Durham, research and analysis of changing patterns of settlement, subsistence, and integration within wider society has to be achieved within a wide time-scale; for example, within the first millennium AD as a whole. Our understanding of changing patterns of upland landuse can be significantly enhanced by expanded sampling of pollen cores, and by the greater use of AMS radio-carbon dates for the provision of chronologies of upland occupation sequences, when opportunity allows. Perhaps above all else, adequate sampling and retention of faunal remains is also essential for our understanding of animal husbandry on upland sites, although acid leaching of soils may render such opportunities rare (Stallibrass 1995; Stallibrass 2000,

78-79). Nevertheless, only with such analyses might we be able to understand the complex relationships between upland and lowland settlement patterns, within what were probably composite estate units within the post-Roman north.

The archaeological evidence from lowland interior and coastal areas encourages both the researching of changes which may have occurred over a short period, as well as those of a longer duration. Again the applicability of questions is heavily influenced by the availability and chronological resolution of material culture, coupled with landuse factors. It is essential to examine longer-term trends in settlement, subsistence and material culture use in Cumbria because of the paucity of diagnostic material culture, a point recently stressed for the Tyne-Solway area (Hardie 1994). Again, the use of AMS radio-carbon dates from sites with well understood stratigraphic sequences is of key importance here. The settlement evidence in the Brougham area would act as an ideal focus for such a long-term analysis of cultural changes linked to settlement patterns, arable and pastoral strategies, changing religious beliefs, and patterns of exchange.

In Northumberland, different opportunities arise. The coast, lowland interior and the uplands of this region provide an unparalleled example of a settlement hierarchy, probably dating from the Roman Iron Age into the eighth century. With the publication of the settlement evidence from Yeavering and Thirlings, the publication of Hope-Taylor's excavations of 1971 from the west ward of Bamburgh castle is desperately required to enable us to begin to investigate the probable inter-relationship of the lowland vills and hamlets, and the coastal fortified centres. In this sense, it would be eminently appropriate to co-ordinate any research along these lines with investigation of similar sites in southern Scotland, such as Doon Hill, Dunbar and Edinburgh. The goal should be to understand these sites through the social relations reflected in their structural, artefact and animal bones assemblages.

Within County Durham, the challenge with regard to the settlement archaeology is certainly to expand our knowledge of settlement beyond former Roman forts, for the period from the fifth to eleventh centuries as a whole. The results from both Binchester and Corbridge suggest long-term continuity of settlement foci, with limited shift within large settlement zones. The

challenge for archaeologists in the next twenty years is to appreciate the subtleties of the stratigraphic sequences, which might allow the identification of post-Roman occupation on other sites.

In all three regions included in this review of archaeology in the north, the potential for investigating the way identities came to be expressed in burial practices is also huge, in conjunction with recent developments in sociological and archaeological theory (Jenkins 1997; Lucy 2000). The value of the regions of Durham, Northumberland and Cumbria for such studies lies in the evidence for different forms of burial tradition and the acculturation of burial practices using new forms of material culture. This may have been accompanied by both native pagan and new Christian beliefs, as well as newly adopted pagan Anglo-Saxon traditions, prior to their conversion to the Celtic, then Roman form of Christianity. Sites such as Yeavering and Brougham provide a sense of place and continuous focus for both these changing burial practices and beliefs.

Although these recommendations are limited, in the current climate of scarce resources for archaeological fieldwork and subsequent analysis, they represent attainable goals for the not too distant future, probably through co-operation between universities, research-funding bodies and government agencies, and their fulfillment would greatly enhance our understanding of the emergence of Early Medieval societies in northern England.

This paper was written in 1996 and early 1997 with limited amendment in 2001.

Acknowledgements
Sincere thanks are due to Robin Daniels, Mike McCarthy and Anthony Harding for investing their time into the production of this volume, and I must also thank Rosemary Cramp and Rachel Newman for providing important information on sites published only in interim form.

Chapter 13: Anglo-Saxon Christianity

*R M Newman**

Introduction

Twenty-five years ago, when *Archaeology in the North* was published, it was stated that 'Our knowledge of the Early Medieval Period in this area, in terms of archaeological sites rather than artefactual, sculptural, place-name or documentary evidence, is extremely limited, and this at a time when Northern England was experiencing its political and cultural zenith' (Clack and Gosling 1976, 38). However, the authors also went on to say that 'So far, the North's contribution to the marked progress of Early Medieval studies nationally has been the identification and excavation of its monastic and royal sites, rather than the settlement and burial sites that might be expected to be more common' (*ibid*). In terms of religious sites, they noted that 'It is undoubtedly in this area of study that the greatest advances in our understanding have been made, although the discrepancy between actual and presumptive sites [those identified from documentary, place-name or sculptural evidence] even here remains striking' (*op cit*, 45). In summary, it was suggested that 'The potential for expanding our knowledge of this period is considerable', although 'Major advances... will only be made from *excavation* (related to detailed work on other complementary material), since this process alone can identify and date the sites discovered' (*ibid*).

During the intervening years, the words of Clack and Gosling have certainly been heeded, for several significant excavations have taken place, both as part of the planning process and for research purposes, on the known and presumptive religious sites of Northumbria, not all within the area covered by CBA North (which is small in comparison with the bounds of Northumbria at its zenith). In 1976, excavations had not yet been completed at Jarrow (Cramp in prep a) (although no major work has been undertaken since at Monkwearmouth: Cramp in prep b), and since that time, further excavations at Hartlepool (Daniels 1988) and Lindisfarne (O'Sullivan in prep) in the east and at Carlisle (Keevill in prep), Dacre (Newman and Leech forthcoming) and, recently, at Workington (M McCarthy, pers comm) in the west, not to mention further work at Whitby, N Yorks (T Wilmott, pers comm) and Beverley (Armstrong et al 1991) in what used to be Humberside, Heysham, Lancs (Potter and Andrews 1994), and the Hirsel (Cramp in prep c), Hoddom (Lowe 1991) and Whithorn (Hill 1997) in southern Scotland (all within Northumbria in the seventh/eighth century although outside the present area of consideration), have greatly contributed to an understanding of the religious life of the 'Golden Age' in Northumbria.

Monasticism

According to Bede (*Historia Ecclesiastica* III, 3), 'Many Scots arrived and proclaimed the word of God... to all provinces under Oswald's rule... Churches were built in several places... while the King... gave lands and endowments to establish monasteries and the English, both noble and simple, were instructed by their Scots teachers to observe a monastic life'.

The archaeological evidence gathered for this period in the North supports Bede's contention that there was a blossoming of Christian activity in the area in the seventh and eighth centuries. The amount of surviving church architecture from the pre-Norman period is surprisingly great, certainly in the North-East, although largely absent in the North-West. In addition the presence, in the area of Northumbrian influence, of a corpus of stone sculpture dated to the eighth and ninth centuries which is very large in comparison to that for England as a whole is perhaps the most obvious result of this activity (see for instance Cramp 1984; Bailey and Cramp 1988). It is now increasingly accepted that such sculptural material from the Anglian period denotes a religious community, although whether such a community was in all cases fully monastic as the term is accepted today could be debatable, in contrast with the Scandinavian period, where the presence of sculpture, except in unusual circumstances, tends to be thought of as denoting a proprietorial church (Bailey 1980).

For instance, the amount of sculpture from St Michael's Church, Workington, Cumbria (M McCarthy, pers comm), a headland site as are Whitby, Hartlepool, Wearmouth and Tynemouth in the North-East and Heysham in north Lancashire, has been used to suggest tentatively that this may be the site of an Anglian monastery; interestingly, as at Dacre, the site has

*Address: Oxford Archaeology North, Storey Institute, Meeting House Lane, Lancaster LA1 1TH

also produced significant pieces of later sculpture as well (Bailey and Cramp 1988). Similarly, the presence of two churches at Heysham, one (St Patrick's Chapel) entirely pre-Conquest in date, the other (St Peter's, the present parish church) with substantial elements of pre-Conquest masonry, as well as sculpture with both Anglian and Scandinavian attributes, has led to the suggestion of a monastery there. Excavations around St Patrick's have demonstrated activity commencing in the eighth century and continuing into the twelfth century (Potter and Andrews 1994).

Yet there are considerable questions as to the extent to which the North's undoubtedly great contribution to the study of the development and growth of Christianity during the seventh and eighth centuries is a reflection of the sites available for study, or whether it has been governed by the enormously influential presence of Bede's *Ecclesiastical History of the English People* (Colgrave and Mynors 1969). Also, to what extent can the subtleties demonstrated by Bede be distinguished in the archaeological record, such as the influence of the Irish teachings as opposed to the Roman influence of firstly Paulinus, and subsequently Wilfrid and Benedict Biscop? Undoubtedly, Bede's writings have played a huge part in the work undertaken in the last twenty-five years; many of the sites excavated, particularly for research purposes, were picked as a result of documentary references, mostly in Bede. Indeed, it could be argued, at least in some cases, that they have been interpreted as monastic sites because of this documentary evidence, rather than because they have some feature which can be said to be diagnostically 'monastic'.

Back in 1974, Rosemary Cramp and others at the *Scottish Archaeological Forum* discussed the evidence available that had been used to interpret a site as monastic (Cramp 1974). The aspects that one might think of as diagnostic in actuality can prove difficult to establish beyond doubt; for instance, a church may be constructed of either wood or stone, as can domestic structures of the period, but apart from its orientation, perhaps the presence of a clearly identifiable altar is the only truly unique aspect (Thomas 1971), although the presence of burials within the structure must help the interpretation. In many ways, however, a church may not differ in techniques of construction from large secular buildings, although at the Hirsel (Cramp in prep c) the small, apparently proprietary, church

gained an apsidal east end in the tenth or eleventh century, a feature which is not found in secular buildings of the period.

Similarly, any monastic establishment will be associated with a cemetery, but secular communities are also likely to be associated with all but the most eremitical of monasteries, and it is known from documentary sources that monastic cemeteries were also used for lay burials; Whitby was after all used as a royal burial place in the seventh century (*Historia Ecclesiastica* III, 24), and Tynemouth was similarly used in the late eighth century (*Vita Oswini* IV). Whilst the evidence from Dacre, near Penrith, a site mentioned as monastic by Bede (*Historia Ecclesiastica* IV, 32), demonstrated that the majority of graves seemed to be for adult burials in terms of their size (the bone preservation was so poor there that the sexing of individuals was not possible, and of course, adult skeletal material is more likely to survive than that of a child, so the total dominance of adult material in the assemblage cannot be used as conclusive proof either; Bullion forthcoming), the cemeteries at Monkwearmouth and Jarrow produced skeletal material from both females and children (Cramp 1994).

The excavations at Monkwearmouth and Jarrow identified buildings very different from what may be expected in a secular context, both in layout and in constructional technique (Cramp 1976). Both complexes were largely constructed in stone, which corresponds to Bede's assertion that Benedict Biscop went to Gaul to find masons who could build in stone (*Historia Abbatum* 5), and, in addition, window glass was found at both places, again confirming Bede's comment that Biscop also brought glassmakers from the Continent (*op cit*, 9). In particular the large buildings at Jarrrow have been described by Professor Cramp as both 'Roman-looking', and in shape and size not unlike the timber halls of the secular world (Cramp 1976, 241, 250).

Both sites provided evidence of regular planning, although this differed between them, Monkwearmouth seemingly planned almost in a claustral manner with ranges of buildings to the south of the church complex, whilst Jarrow seemed to have been laid out in a series of tiers, again to the south of the church complex, stepped down the slope towards the river Don (Cramp 1994). Twenty-five years ago, however, the corpus of information was not large enough to be able to speculate whether these were typical or atypical of monastic establishments; indeed, it was not possible to state with any degree of confidence whether there was a monastic style of architecture such as developed in the tenth and eleventh centuries in Europe. As a general principle, it has also been suggested that the density and perhaps also the complexity of structures might be used in the interpretation of a site as monastic (Higham 1986), as at Whitby.

As yet, no site of a known or putative monastery of the seventh or eighth century has been available in its entirety for archaeological study. Inevitably, religious institutions are usually continuously occupied to the present day, and their associated modern cemeteries can effectively sterilise large parts of the site. Even when there has been a revived monastic tradition, such as at Jarrow or Whitby, the ruins of the later structures cover the site, making total excavation physically as well as economically unviable. At Monkwearmouth, where much of the church contains Anglo-Saxon masonry, and at Jarrow, where the present church retains part of the Saxon church complex as a chancel, the buildings have in addition retained a parochial function, and thus only small-scale archaeological work has been possible within these important structures, such as the monitoring of the renovation of the heating system, or the installation of new electricity cables (eg Cramp 1994). Excavation outside has been limited in both cases to the south, at Jarrow in the area of the medieval priory, although it was perhaps not surprising that important elements of the early monastery were identified here, given the statement that Aldwin refounded the site, as did Reinfrid at Whitby, on the ruins of the Northumbrian monastery (*Simeon* 56; 57).

At Dacre, the church is also the parish church, and the area immediately surrounding is part of a continuously used cemetery; indeed, in this case the extension of the cemetery to the north of the church, beyond its medieval bounds, provided the threat leading to excavation and also demonstrated that, in the pre-Conquest period, a large cemetery (more than 234 graves) occupied the area to the north of the present church, apparently focused on some feature to the south, perhaps an earlier church on or near the site of the present medieval structure (which retains features from the twelfth century onwards) (Newman and Leech forthcoming). It also meant, however, that, apart from the cemetery, two timber structures only were excavated in this area, which were not closely datable;

although likely to be pre-Conquest, they may not belong to a monastic phase of occupation. To the south of the church, the presence of a double drain suggests that there may have been buildings on the terrace between it and the church in a position similar to the large communal buildings at Jarrow, now lying beneath the medieval graveyard.

In terms of entire sites available for excavation, the nearest to a complete example is at Whithorn, in Galloway. Whilst this is outside the area encompassed by CBA North, its importance is such that it cannot be ignored when contemplating Anglo-Saxon Christianity in Northumbria. During the last twelve or so years, the area to the south of the medieval cathedral has been subject to detailed excavations (Hill 1997). Whithorn was reputed, even in Bede's time (*Historia Ecclesiastica* V, 23), to have been the base from which St Ninian preached Christianity to the Picts, and it was for a time the seat of a bishop (*op cit*, III, 4). The excavations clearly demonstrated a shift in focus within the settlement, with potentially extremely early structures (unfortunately, like so many potentially early medieval structures, not closely datable) overlain by structures which can be dated on typological grounds, and also from their material assemblage (particularly the coins), to the Northumbrian period (ie eighth/ninth centuries). The most significant conclusion that the excavators came to was the interpretation of structures on a terrace in the northern part of the site (ie closest to the medieval cathedral) as a church complex, with a series of timber halls on the lower slopes to the south (Hill 1997, Ch 4). In terms of the layout, it is not unlike that seen at Jarrow: churches to the north, major communal buildings immediately to the south, and smaller buildings to the south of these. It can also very tentatively be suggested that a similar layout existed at Dacre (Newman and Leech forthcoming), although there it is unlikely ever to be confirmed since little of the site is available for excavation.

It is notable that the small buildings at Whithorn are not unlike those excavated at Hartlepool (Daniels 1988), where a sequence was identified of small, regularly arranged rectangular structures, constructed firstly in timber, of both posthole and wall-trench construction, although a later phase was of stone. These small structures were described as being of a very distinctive type, unlike anything that would be expected on a secular site, leading to the conclusion that these can be regarded as a monastic type of architecture (*ibid*).

The church complex at Whithorn has been divided into a number of phases, apparently growing from a feature identified as a 'platform shrine', later surrounded by a small rectangular timber structure, constructed of spaced vertical planks, which in turn was combined with a structure to the west and modified to form a single large building, apparently surrounded by an arcade (Hill 1997, Ch 4). This was again refurbished before it fell out of use. Internal features have been interpreted as a stone altar set within a timber partition. A further building to the east with stone foundations was aligned with this structure and has been suggested as a burial chapel. If these structures can be interpreted as the religious centre of the complex in the eighth and ninth centuries, their layout is comparable with the known plan of the churches at Jarrow and that posited at Monkwearmouth (Cramp 1994), although it has been suggested that the principal church lies beyond the area of excavation, closer to the medieval church (Hill 1992, 24).

Continuity of layout is a question that should also be addressed, as is the ability to distinguish a common pattern within putative and known monastic establishments. Indeed, the question has arisen more than once as to the validity of whether there is such a thing as a monastic type of layout, given the different traditions being drawn on, both Celtic and Roman, during the seventh and eighth centuries. The differences in layout noted between Monkwearmouth and Jarrow could not be explained entirely by terrain (Cramp 1974, 123), which perhaps suggests that there was no formally predetermined building plan for early sites, as there was in the later medieval period. This is in despite of the fact that both monasteries had been constructed by Benedict Biscop within a decade of each other, not to mention the evidence (above) suggesting that there may be some similarity in the layout of both Whithorn and Dacre.

Those sites that have been interpreted as monastic seem to produce in relative terms a large assemblage of metalwork, and also a disproportionately large amount of coinage, in comparison even with such a prestigious site as Yeavering (Hope-Taylor 1977). They frequently also produce fragments of window glass, a material not to date found on secular sites of the period. Many produce distinctive pieces of roofing lead; for instance, identical material has

been found at Jarrow and Dacre (Trueman 1985; Quartermaine forthcoming a). Coffin fittings help to date the cemeteries but, although distinctive, these do not seem to be limited to graves in a monastic context. Evidence of literacy, in the form of inscriptions or writing implements, and the indication of far-reaching contacts in the artefactual assemblage, have been noted (Cramp 1976) as perhaps the most useful guides to the identification of monastic enclaves. Thus at Dacre, if one tried to be objective rather than unquestioningly associating the site with that mentioned by Bede, it was the identification of a stylus, as well as an escutcheon which may have decorated a book cover (Tweddle forthcoming), that tipped the balance in favour of monastic occupation. At Hartlepool, evidence for the manufacture of metalwork with Christian attributes was identified, in the form of a stone mould of an *agnus dei* (Cramp 1988b). Imported pottery has been found at Whitby, Jarrow and Whithorn (Cramp 1976; Hill 1997), and vessel glass at many sites; in addition, a Merovingian bead was recovered from a grave at Dacre (Quartermaine forthcoming b). Perhaps the most intriguing common find is that of loomweights, not perhaps surprising in a community that was probably self-supporting although no such material was recovered from either Jarrow or Monkwearmouth (RJ Cramp, pers comm), but it does raise questions as to who was weaving, since their presence has been used tentatively to support the idea of double monasteries at Whitby and Hartlepool (Cramp 1994).

After Bede

Following the death of Bede in AD 735, the information available on Christianity in Northumbria decreases dramatically. The Viking incursions of the late eighth century (Lindisfarne was first sacked in AD 793), and more consistently from the later ninth century onwards, are frequently credited as the cause of the decline in monasticism, although it is becoming increasingly accepted (for instance in Higham 1986) that the apparent collapse of monasticism in the ninth century may be linked to the collapse of Northumbrian kingship rather the despoiling of sites by enemy forces. The growth in monasticism, as demonstrated by Bede throughout the *Historia Ecclesiastica*, was closely tied to the royal house, which gave vast wealth and huge estates to the church with which to found and endow religious establishments. This alienation of land not only weakened the crown, but also tied the fate of such monasteries very closely to the strength of that institution. Bede criticized the number of houses that were founded by the aristocracy under royal licence where members of the family continued to live in a style no less secular than the life they had renounced (Higham 1986). It is likely that such communities were amongst the earliest to collapse in the apparently turbulent degeneration of Northumbrian kingship.

This potentially gradual disintegration may in part explain the fact that on several sites, particularly where a nascent parish church developed, not least at Dacre and Workington, there is no clear break between what might be construed as monastic and activity of the later pre-Conquest period. At Dacre, there was no apparent decrease in the amount of fine metalwork in the tenth century, and apparently eleventh-century material was also present (Tweddle forthcoming). Below the west end of the medieval cathedral at Carlisle, bodies within a three-phase cemetery were associated with both Anglian/Carolingian and tenth-century metalwork (M McCarthy, pers comm); the implication here is that this cemetery focused on a church below the medieval cloister, perhaps remaining in use, as has been suggested at Durham (E Cambridge, pers comm), until the medieval church had been constructed slightly to the north. The cemetery at Dacre had been slighted by the construction of a churchyard boundary in the form of a bank and ditch immediately to the north of the medieval church, perhaps originally as early as the eleventh century, certainly enhanced by the construction of a wall on the crest of the bank in the early thirteenth century (Newman and Leech forthcoming). Similarly, at Carlisle the cemetery had been disturbed by the construction of the twelfth-century cathedral (M McCarthy, pers comm).

At Whithorn, apparently secular occupation overlay the timber hall-type structures of the Northumbrian complex, interpreted as a centre of manufacture in a Hiberno-Norse trading post (Hill 1992). At Whitby, the 1990s evaluation of a block of land several hundred metres to the south of the medieval abbey indicated the presence of an 'early medieval centre within a substantial boundary, which includes an extensive cemetery and also timber buildings' (T Wilmott, pers comm). This activity had again been slighted by the medieval monastic boundary; the distance from the dense settlement of small stone structures identified in the 1920s as Hild's

monastery (Peers and Radford 1943) raises intriguing questions as to the size of this community, or perhaps points towards an important physical distinction between the male and female elements of the community, or even of secular activity beyond the monastic complex.

Secular sites

Whilst the theme of this section is Anglo-Saxon Christianity, some brief mention needs to be made of the developments over the last twenty-five years in terms of the secular sites of the seventh to ninth centuries. *Archaeology in the North* stated that 'Our knowledge of the settlement of the region during the Early Medieval Period from archaeology alone is very poor, bearing little relation to the documentary and place-name evidence' (Clack and Gosling 1976, 42). It is notable that it was recommended that 'our best guide... [to such settlement must be] the distribution of surviving churches and religious sites, which appear to have been situated in known centres of population and to have acted as *foci* for settlement' (*ibid*). Using this model, a distribution could be suggested concentrating on the lower-lying coastal plains of east and west and some way up the principal river valleys.

Twenty-five years ago, no sunken-featured structures had been identified in the region, and indeed, of the secular sites excavated, only Thirlings seemed to be non-royal (*op cit*, 42). Since then, sunken-featured buildings have been identified at New Bewick in Northumberland (Gates and O'Brien 1988) and at Fremington, near Brougham, in Cumbria. There, a site containing evidence of the development of a settlement from apparently Roman origins through to occupation in the seventh/eighth century was excavated in advance of pipeline construction (Oliver *et al* 1996). The excavation at Bryant's Gill, in upper Kentmere in the Lake District (Dickinson forthcoming), has also produced evidence of activity in this mid pre-Conquest period; although a single site, it has nevertheless pointed to a distribution of settlement in this period other than that mentioned in *Archaeology in the North* (Clack and Gosling 1976). Whilst few in number, these sites have added to the picture of integrated settlement that is being developed in research excavations such as that at West Heslerton in Yorkshire (Powlesland *et al* 1986).

Future research

This review has demonstrated that recent excavations have reinforced and extended the ground- breaking work of Professor Cramp at Jarrow and Monkwearmouth. These last years have concentrated on gathering information; there is now a great need to synthesise this evidence with a view to establishing whether distinctive traits can be identified, perhaps concentrating on differences that may be perceived between those sites established before the influence of Wilfrid and Benedict Biscop, and those following the introduction of 'Roman' techniques of construction, and whether the feeling can be substantiated that on occasion there is some common layout. In addition, the complex history of Christianity in what had been Roman towns, particularly Carlisle but perhaps also Lancaster, should be considered, and the wider influences of Christian activity, particularly in the realm of trading networks, may be a fruitful area of research; consider, after all, the dissemination of information discernible in Bede's work – he clearly gathered information from many correspondents.

In the present climate of stagnation in terms of research excavation, due often to financial constraints and the fact that work arising from the planning process is dependent on commercial funding and the vagaries of the national economy, it is sadly often a matter of chance, such as at St Michael's, Workington (M McCarthy, pers comm), or Fremington (Oliver *et al* 1996), that allows new work to be undertaken. Where possible, attention should now be turned towards attempting to gain an idea of the distribution and function of minster churches in Northumbria, to complement the knowledge gained from a study of monastic sites. In addition, where possible, there should be an attempt to develop the study of secular settlements, particularly those that are not out of the ordinary (for instance, although it can be argued that we know relatively little about the numerous royal sites of Northumbria, we still have the benefit of one detailed research excavation), and this should be integrated with the picture being gained of religious activity.

Finally, although long-standing psychological prejudices and the present constraints of archaeology provide major hurdles to be overcome, there should be far more strenuous attempts to think in terms of Northumbria as an entity rather than simply in terms of individual counties (as perhaps the present system encourages); this will require some vision, particularly given that Northumbria crosses present national boundaries, but it can and should be achieved when research priorities are being considered.

Chapter 14: Environmental Archaeology: The Post-Roman Period

A.R. Hall and Jacqueline P. Huntley*

When Clack and Gosling's review of archaeology in the Northern counties of England was published twenty five years ago (Clack and Gosling 1976), environmental archaeology as a discrete discipline within archaeology was in its infancy. Today, few archaeological interventions take place without acknowledging the contribution of studies of plant and animal remains and their sedimentary matrix to an understanding of the past, although in practice financial constraints often restrict the scale of recovery of 'environmental' material. In addition, the lack of involvement of environmental archaeologists from the very beginning of many projects is still to be regretted. Huntley (this volume) has outlined something of the history of the subject and there is thus no need to reiterate it here.

In 1995 Huntley and Stallibrass published their "Regional Review" of plant and vertebrate remains for the five counties which are the subject of this conference volume, together with North Yorkshire, Lancashire, Merseyside, Greater Manchester and Cheshire (Huntley and Stallibrass, 1995). Subsequently separate material based reviews (plants, vertebrate bones, invertebrates and soils/sediments) for the English Heritage complete Northern Region (above counties plus the remaining parts of Yorkshire and what (until April 1996) was Humberside have been produced in draft. A considerable body of information therefore already exists although not all yet widely available.

Thus this paper consists of two parts. In the first the scale of work undertaken within environmental studies on post-Roman sites in the Northern counties will be explored in crude quantitative terms. In the second part some broader issues will be addressed as summarised from the updated "Regional Reviews" especially relating to plant remains, providing examples of how such reviews can feed into fund-limited research developing a better understanding of the cultural history of our region.

The scale of environmental studies

To assess the amount of work carried out on plant and animal remains and on soils and sediments in the five Northern counties under consideration in this volume, a convenient starting point is the *Environmental Archaeology Bibliography* (EAB) compiled initially by Philippa Tomlinson at the Environmental Archaeology Unit (EAU), University of York, with funding from the Ancient Monuments Laboratory of English Heritage (Tomlinson and Hall, 1996). It is now routinely updated by one of the authors (ARH) with funding from English Heritage, thus continuing to be an extremely valuable resource. This database contains information about reports (mostly published) on, for example, plant macrofossils, insects, bones and soils, from archaeological sites throughout the United Kingdom and the Republic of Ireland and can be interrogated to provide information by 'material', by country or county, or by period, amongst other criteria. This database is available online at the English Heritage website: http://www.eng-h.gov.uk/EAB/

A first statistic that may be drawn from the EAB is that there are in fact only 72 site reports for the five Northern counties for which there is both post-Roman archaeology and something relating to 'environmental' aspects of the site (Table 1). It is also clear that the division of these sites between counties is very uneven so that it is unlikely that comparison between areas within the region can be made reliably on the basis of either substantial or qualitatively similar datasets, not least because of the great variety of site types represented. However, it is equally clear that the situation is improving with 64 of those sites representing post 1976 publication and more than half of those relating to the last 5 years.

Table 2 presents the numbers and sizes of reports, following the EAB's somewhat subjective scheme of a three-point scale for report size:

1. small, i.e. a few lines to a paragraph with few taxa, perhaps only from one sample, including reports with no discussion/interpretation.
2. medium, i.e. a page to several pages, with lists of taxa, a few to many samples and some interpretation/analysis.
3. large, i.e. detailed, report, with many samples/assemblages, extensive analysis and interpretation.

*Addresses: Environmental Archaeology Unit, University of York, Heslington, York YO1 5DD
Department of Archaeology, University of Durham, South Road, Durham DH1 3LE

Table 1. Numbers of sites with post-Roman archaeology recorded in the *Environmental Archaeology Bibliography* for the northernmost counties of England for which *published* reports on plant and animal remains and sediments/soils exist.

Number of sites	Pre-1976	1976-1996	1997-2001	Total
Cumbria	2	4	5	11
Durham (including Cleveland)	1	17	8	26
Northumberland	1	8	6	15
Tyne and Wear	4	13	3	20
Totals	8	42	22	72

Table 2. Numbers and sizes of 'environmental' reports (excluding those relating to dendrochronology and artefacts of biological origin) for sites with post-Roman archaeology for the Northern counties of England. 1—small, i.e. a few lines to a paragraph with few taxa, perhaps only from one sample, including reports with no discussion/interpretation; 2— medium, i.e. a page to several pages, with lists of taxa, a few to many samples and some interpretation/analysis; 3—large, i.e. detailed report, with many samples, extensive analysis and interpretation.

Report type/Size	1	2	3
mammal bone (may include other vertebrates)	20	28	
fish bone	5	5	1
plant macrofossils (from samples other than 'spots')	7	17	1
bird bone	5	5	
human bone	7	5	
marine molluscs	10	2	
'spot' identifications of plants other than cereals	3	1	
pollen analysis	2	4	
geological reports (non-artefactual stone, etc.)	1	1	
human cremation	1	1	
human teeth (where reported separately)	2	1	
insects (including beetles and flies)		1	2
plant fibres (not textile report)		1	
parasite remains (of animals)		1	
terrestrial molluscs [may include freshwater taxa]		1	
diatoms		1	
wood, both charred and uncharred (not mineral-replaced)	8		
'spot' identifications of cereal remains	1		
animal fibres (hair; not textile report)	1		
crustaceans (marine)	4		
soil analysis (not specified)	3		
soil chemical analysis (e.g. phosphates)		1	
soil physical analysis		1	
human bone pathology		1	
tree-ring studies (not dendrochronology); usually includes identifications			1
Totals	80	78	5

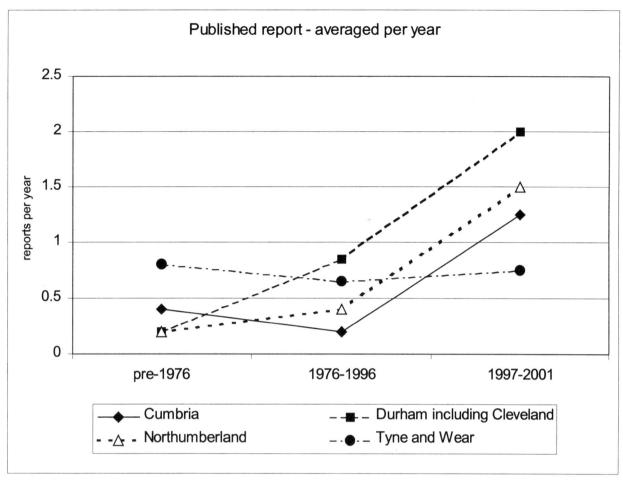

Fig. 14.1 Published reports (totals averaged over year periods from Table 1) demonstrating increased data production over recent years

It demonstrates that, of the 163 individual environmental reports (and the whole range of held in the database), about half are in class 1 thus providing mostly presence/absence data of a very limited extent. Half, however, have some interpretative offerings although less than 7% of these provide large detailed and interpreted datasets. In addition, the distribution of reports by type is very uneven, with the largest categories being those concerned with plant macrofossils and bones of various kinds, especially 'mammal bone' (reports in this category are nearly all dominated by data for large domesticates).

The reports considered in this discussion so far do not, for the most part, include 'off-site' analyses of pollen. A considerable body of data has been gathered from lakes, mires and blanket peat in the region for post-glacial vegetational and environmental history, but for the post-Roman period there are two complications which limit the amount of information available to us from this source: the limitations of dating and the loss of the uppermost (usually including

the post-Roman) part of so many peat sequences through peat-cutting and other human activity. Even where pollen has been examined from a site close to an excavation, as for example at Simy Folds in Upper Teesdale, the results may not be unequivocal: Donaldson in Coggins *et al.* (1983) was unable to date precisely that part of the sequence for which early medieval activity in the vicinity was inferred from other evidence. In addition there has been the focus on the effect of the Romans upon the regional landscape, with the construction of Hadrian's Wall in particular, which has rather overshadowed other periods of activity but which have, perhaps, left less of constructional remains visible. For example, both place name and documentary evidence attests for much activity during the latter centuries of the first millennium AD although structural or even artefactual evidence is limited.

Likewise they do not include the considerable corpus of unpublished data which exists for post-Roman sites in our region especially in relation to PPG16 or older "Rescue" interventions. For example there are at least 157 reports in total on plant remains alone from the Northern Counties on work largely undertaken through the contract laboratory in the Department of Archaeology at Durham and there must be as many if not more through the EAU at York. Whilst many of these reports will be small in extent and detail, those from the urban centre of Carlisle are predominantly major reports dealing with hundreds of samples in considerable detail. It is therefore paramount that all such work enters the public domain as rapidly as possible in order to develop regional strategies for environmental work.

Some broader issues

This section presents some of the possible "future directions", partly as suggested in either the Huntley and Stallibrass (1995) or Huntley and Hall (forthcoming) reviews, using specific sites as examples. Due to the authors' botanical interests all relate to plant remains.

Data for the Saxon-Anglian-Early Christian periods (principally Post-Roman to Post-Conquest) are scarce despite the great cultural changes which occurred in the region. One of the main problems is dating an essentially aceramic period although environmental archaeology can furnish relevant material for use of radiocarbon techniques. Huntley (1999) summarised the botanical data for these periods and concluded that, as yet, we could say little more than that *Triticum aestivum* (bread wheat) had replaced *T. spelta* (spelt wheat) as a cereal staple and that *Avena* sp. grains (oats) were also abundant. *Secale cereale* (rye) is another crop which apparently gains acceptance in the region although, as yet, we are unable to determine whether this reflects cultural influence from the Danes or not. It dominated one context from Lindisfarne (Huntley 1994g) and, more recently, has appeared in several contexts from excavations at Marne Barracks, Catterick (Jacqui Cotton pers. comm.). However, these contexts are undated but presumed 'Saxon' from the coarse pottery and sunken floored features. This is an obvious case where radiocarbon dating of that grain would be appropriate. So, for this period, little can yet be said even for the large ecclesiastical sites for which the region is rightly famous; unfortunately most were the subject of major excavations in days that were pre-environmental sampling. Large samples must be taken from any site where such a period is considered even remotely likely in order to answer even the most basic questions about what was being used for food.

The development of urban centres from the 11th/12th centuries onwards is an important change in social structure throughout Britain and we have both those centres and the continuing rural communities for comparison. However, most excavation has been carried out in the towns producing reasonable information about the consumer society, for example in Newcastle, Hartlepool and Durham. In these the charred plant remains suggest that bread wheat, 6-row barley and oats were the dominant cereals with peas and beans also eaten. Weed seeds are rare, nor surprising in an urban situation. There is patchy evidence for use of other plants – heather for roofing and/or bedding, straw, grass- and peat-rich turves for fuel and/or roofing and rather constant evidence for ruderal weedy communities. As little excavation is undertaken in present day villages we know less of the rural communities of the past. Elton West Garth in Cleveland (Huntley unpublished data) has produced evidence for bread wheat production as well as some quantities of peas and beans but data for the weed assemblages and hence possible technological changes, as outlined by Huntley (this volume) for the later Roman period are lacking.

Waterlogged deposits, often surviving under modern towns, have high potential to provide evidence for diet in the form of cereal bran and other delicate tissues lost in more aggressive burial environments. For example, leek and broad bean have become a quite common recovery from York but are as yet absent from the more northern towns. Pits especially have the potential to produce such faecal material and excavations of whole burgage plots should make the most of opportunities to study such features. What has often been demonstrated is varying preservational conditions and suggestions that a somewhat biassed assemblage of material has survived. This consists of taxa which are especially woody and resistant to decay, such as elderberry, blackberry with buttercups and possibly sedges. Such differential preservation appears to be common in deposits associated with the Medieval quaysides of both Berwick upon Tweed and Newcastle upon Tyne/ Gateshead.

Urban continuity and the enormous expansion of urbanism after the 15th/16th centuries, and especially during the late 18th to 19th centuries, means that almost all post-Medieval archaeobotanical studies have been conducted on material from excavations in towns. However, these studies are woefully thin and most towns have no more than a handful of samples studied. Charred remains are even more scarce presumably as a result of development of centralised mills producing flour which was purchased by the towns' folk rather than their continuing to purchase grain and grind it themselves, and we are therefore more reliant than ever upon waterlogged deposits for survival of plant materials. Unfortunately, such post-Medieval deposits are obviously high in the stratigraphic sequence and therefore often only damp not strictly waterlogged. Thus even more differential preservation is likely. However, appropriate deposits should allow us to target imported fruits and seeds themselves possibly lending to interpretations of status of deposits. In the heavily industrialised parts of our towns we have high potential to investigate the lives of working people when other available sources, for example documentary records, tend to emphasise the higher status. As the region has an extremely strong tradition in industry and heavy manual work samples from such sites must have high priority.

Reports from these urban centres are generally of class 1 or 2, in EAB terms, and have been produced mainly in response to planning interventions and considerable information is available for Newcastle upon Tyne and, indeed, Berwick upon Tweed. The majority is unpublished. Many such reports simply provide small pieces of the jigsaw and it is time to synthesise the existing data to evaluate just how fragmentary they are or whether there are patterns emerging. For example, is the flax retting inferred from debris in a pit in Newcastle an indication of a home industry associated with that house or area or is it a more widespread phenomenon, a cottage style industry even? Carlisle is a major centre in the north-west but there are relatively few data for the post Roman period since effort has very much concentrated upon the Roman deposits. Some material is available from excavations of the last few years and should have high priority during post excavation stages of projects. As this is a city with demonstrable Anglian activity it may also provide the opportunity to investigate the transition from Roman to Anglian occupation.

Overall the evidence for plant remains from the post-Roman period is extremely patchy geographically, spatially and from the nature of the preservation/recovery. In the charred form they do not on the whole suffer from preservational factors as do animal bones and can thus be expected to survive on more or less any site. However, it is more likely that the nature of the deposits leads to lack of comparative data – rural sites are dry and only charred plant remains are likely to survive thus bulk 30 litre samples are taken and processed whilst urban sites are more frequently waterlogged thus 1-2 litres samples only are taken. With charred material mostly at quite low concentrations few can therefore be expected to be recovered from the urban samples. Even if large samples of waterlogged deposits are taken and processed it is not especially cost effective to sort through very large volumes of flot for the recovery of rather few charred remains. What would be useful are improved methods for separation of dried waterlogged organic from charred organic remains, in other words, further separation of the flot into charred versus non-charred.

In spatial terms we have 'hot spots' in some modern urban centres where there is a clear need for synthesis in the first instance as discussed above. We have blank areas especially in the north-west as for other periods too. Other cover is, as stated, patchy and as yet a detailed sampling strategy is probably needed for almost any intervention where post-Roman deposits are likely. We are not yet at the stage of having specific detailed questions to ask.

Section 5: Medieval

Introduction

Barbara Harbottle[*]

The Later Medieval Period is represented by three papers which, while very different in their approach, are all concerned with medieval domestic settlement of one sort or another. Religious houses, once a favourite field of activity for archaeologists, receive no mention here. There is barely a reference to parish churches. Castles and town walls, tower houses and bastles, are virtually absent. These omissions are misleading since all these sites were dependent on one another for their existence. Are we to suppose that their investigation here is now deemed to be unnecessary, positively unfashionable? This is not the case elsewhere. The study of medieval fortifications is promoted vigorously by the Castle Studies Group which has always adopted an international approach, and the Baker-Chitty Report has forced us to consider how to record, and make generally available, the wealth of information about English parish churches.

In their Annual Report 15 (2000) the Medieval Settlement Research Group published an admirably clear statement entitled "Medieval Rural Settlements – A Policy on their Research, Survey, Conservation or Excavation". In looking to the future in the North-East it would undoubtedly be fruitful to adopt some of their recommendations, for example the enhancement of relevant data in the county sites and monuments records, better coordination with current research by the North-East Vernacular Architecture Group, improved annual statements of recent discoveries. Though no North-East evaluations, surveys or excavations are listed in this Annual Report it seems unlikely that none occurred. And it is good news that English Heritage is considering how best to preserve ridge and furrow since, in the past, it has proved difficult if not impossible to persuade planners and developers that such earthworks are important.

Future work, and I admit to personal preference here, might for a time and with advantage be concentrated on areas outside the medieval villages, in particular the marginal land. A research project of the University of Durham, entitled "Settlement and waste in the Palatinate of Durham", is already in progress, and other parts of the region would benefit from a similar approach. Specific topics could include the identification of 'moorland farms', with a clear distinction being made between them and shielings, and the ebb and flow of settlement on the fringe. Work some years ago in the North Tyne valley, for example, produced a hitherto unknown category of site, the late medieval or 17th-century farmstead representing an unsuccessful, if late, attempt to colonise the uplands. Recent, but unpublished, survey and excavation at Glantlees in Northumberland revealed interesting remains of dwellings and arable land close both to the head dyke and to a junction of the boundaries of several commons. An archaeological and historical study of another estate in Northumberland uncovered a rich and little used archive concerning the changing field patterns of the medieval village of Beanley.

While it is useful to have a summary of the medieval boroughs of the North-East such a generalisation inevitably has its limitations. A more specific inclusion of the centres of shires, e.g. Bedlington and Tynemouth, would have been welcome, and it is important to emphasise that town plans are dynamic, and that the larger settlements in particular have an individuality which can be drawn out by a detailed study of the documentary sources. The first edition O.S. maps provide a common base but that is all. They do not show such topographical detail as the underlying watercourses which provided boundaries, determined the lines of roads and required bridges. They do not always show the original outlines of the earlier precincts of castles and religious houses, which also influenced the development of both roads and defences.

There remains the problem of Newcastle. Although it was to be the largest of the medieval boroughs of the region its origin remains obscure. Because of the cemetery, in use from probably the 7th century to the late 11th, and though the contemporary settlement has yet to be found, the town can hardly be described as a post-Conquest foundation. The existence of a single mother church with dependent chapels, both within and outwith the urban core, has led some to suggest that here there was a minster. Another view is that Newcastle was more akin to a Scottish burgh (pers. comm. Geoffrey Stell) in this respect. Could it have been the centre of

*Address: 18 Leazes Crescent, Newcastle upon Tyne NE1 4LW

a shire, sharing its common land, the Town Moor, with the ring of vills which surrounded it? The documentary evidence appears to be insufficient to prove this. What is certain is that we have to investigate the central role of Newcastle in the region. We need to understand what brought people here, and particularly the effect of the town's companies which offered apprenticeships, employment, influence and enormous wealth. From how wide an area did the apprentices come? A cursory study suggests they were drawn more from Co. Durham, the Bishopric, than from Northumberland though there is no obvious explanation for this. And where did they go to invest their commercial gains in rural estates, south rather than north of the Tyne?

There is much to do, and much unpublished material to make available, including all the evaluations, and even watching briefs, carefully filed on dusty shelves.

Chapter 15: Rural Settlement in England: A New Assessment

*Brian K Roberts and Stuart Wrathmell**

Introduction

In the 1980s English Heritage set up the Monuments Protection Programme (MPP). This is designed to accelerate the process of giving statutory protection to the most important archaeological remains. As part of the programme English Heritage have funded a series of projects involving the mapping of rural settlement diversity. This was undertaken as part of a new approach to the concept of 'national importance' in medieval settlement remains. The first phase of the work resulted in new Monument Class descriptions (MCDs) for such remains: these emphasize the regional diversity of both settlement patterns and forms, and established that such regional diversity was itself a matter of national importance. The MCDs incorporated maps showing the broadest of England's settlement regions, three 'provinces' defined by the presence/absence and density of nucleated settlements. A second phase of the project has looked in much more depth at settlement diversity, taking into account not only the distribution of nucleated settlement but also variations in the dispersion of non-nucleated settlement. Parallel activity has involved both the detailed mapping of terrains and other aspects of settlement and landscape, and the result has been the definition and characterization of sub-provincial and local regions within the overall framework of the provinces, and the use of these regions in selecting settlement sites for which scheduling proposals will be prepared. A third phase of the work will involve the preparation of maps for wider dissemination in the form of an atlas of national maps of both terrain and rural settlement.

For English Heritage, concerned with the protection, management and presentation of archaeological and historical sites, this is a severely pragmatic exercise. All archaeological sites need placing within their broader settings: their contexts, both physical and cultural. The medieval period, in contrast to earlier periods, possesses two distinctive qualities: first, there are large amounts of both local and national documentation providing images contemporary or near-contemporary to excavated materials; second, the late twentieth-century settlement sys-

tem is, judging by the large numbers of surviving artefacts, in many senses an adapted version of that which evolved between the Norman invasion and the advent of the Tudors. To generalize about the 'medieval' ingredients of this landscape, to move away from the study of particular sites and the formal structures of mapped interpretations of comprehensive taxation records, it is necessary to seek a framework within which to integrate diverse evidences and begin the process of identifying broad synoptic patterns. How can this be done? What 'elements' or 'indicators' associated with the medieval scene must be taken into account? This was the practical question which initiated this work.

National maps of individual medieval sites inevitably include great areas of 'white space', yet reality is a continuum, a closed mosaic of local regions, where the only voids are water and the most inhospitable of uplands. This is why Phase II involved the mapping of terrains, again encompassing total national coverage. The concept of major settlement provinces evolved from an initial national map of nucleations created by BKR, and appears to be confirmed from many different sources we have now examined. In this paper, originally drafted in 1996, we consider some questions of terminology, briefly describe some of our provisional results (now encapsulated in an atlas, Roberts and Wrathmell 2000a), and, finally, suggest the direction in which our preliminary results lead by describing and commenting on a model which touches practical questions of interpretation and explanation. A brief re-assessment of *Archaeology in the North* (Clack and Gosling 1976) draws our arguments together and focuses upon the theme of this present volume.

Questions of terminology

Countrysides of the present contain complex mixtures of entities, some of which are wholly natural, some of which are artefacts, bequeathed by former generations, entities which are now often relict features, substantively divorced from their original setting. At any point in time past, any given countryside would comprise mixtures of elements inherited from both the

*Addresses: Department of Geography, University of Durham, South Road, Durham DH1 3LE
West Yorkshire Archaeology Service, 14 St Johns North, Wakefield WF1 3QA

immediate past and from even earlier antecedents. Each period possessed a complex cultural landscape in its own right. This would have been as true of the Romano-British countryside as it is of that of today. Processes of creation, decay, adaptation, renewal, sometimes in the context of dramatic transformations over long or short periods of time, generate what the historian Maitland termed 'that complex palimpsest' (Maitland 1897, 38), bearing comparison with an overwritten document. This creates tensions, for the landscape is a *resource*, from which contemporary society must, in part, obtain a living, but it is also today a source for all concerned with the past. In M R G Conzen's words, settlement is the 'geographical record of its own evolution' (in Isaac and Allan 1949, 76).

The use of the word 'landscape' to describe this complex palimpsest has been recently challenged by Tim Darvill in a conference contribution, and this matter demands some consideration. Although most ideas have many roots, for English readers the concept of the cultural landscape was closely defined in a classic paper by Carl Sauer entitled 'The Morphology of Landscape'. Originally published in 1938, this was reprinted by John Leighley (1963), thus making it available to a wider public. In 'The Morphology of Landscape' Sauer reviews what had been and (in 1938) was the object of geographical study, showing that the German roots of the term – *Landschaft* – imply the study of 'the content of areas', both of the entities present and the connections between these. Sauer argues that human activities act upon both unaltered and altered nature to generate cultural landscapes, places and areas, whose distinctive and unique associations of elements (by definition location is always unique) are worthy of study, analysis, comparison and explanation. In this matter, the time dimension can never be excluded, although the duration taken into account may vary from a few decades to several thousand years.

That the word *landscape* was originally introduced into English from the Netherlands as a painter's term, with all that this implies in terms of perceptions, judgments and values, is not in question – indeed, Sauer comments on this link (*ibid*, 322). In philological terms landscape uses two Old English words – 'land' and 'scape' – to integrate two ideas, the first implying 'a tract of land', with the second meaning 'create, ordain or appoint', as seen in *craftsmanship* and *workmanship*, where individuals and artefacts are

involved, but also extending to the collective as in *township* – the territory of a -*tun* or local farming community. Common usage such as that seen in W G Hoskins' *The Making of the English Landscape* (originally published in 1955, but revised in 1976; see Taylor in Hoskins 1988) supports the general use of the term to designate the components of the artefactual scene which, in close combination with wholly natural elements, give distinctive character to tracts of countryside, perhaps even including and embracing *townscapes*. This usage has the sanction of scholarship (Beresford and St Joseph 1979, 3; Aston and Rowley 1974, 21-27; Cantor 1982, 17-23; Everitt 1986, 1-13; Taylor in Hoskins 1988, 7-9; Morris 1989, 3). Of course, such a definition in no way excludes artistic or perceptual approaches. No narrow limits need be sought or accepted (*Landscape Research – Mapping Landscapes*, 19, 1994, *passim*). This argument in no way negates Darvill's core point, that we must attempt precision in scholarly usages, for precision in terminology should accompany rigour in thinking, but here we must argue that to impose any purist specific meaning – 'the visible scene as perceived by the eye' – is not only fraught with dangers, but is impractical – indeed wholly impossible – in the light of everyday accepted usage. The landscape is something that is, and was, *seen* and *experienced* in the real world as well as through pictorial representations. In fact real world experience involves more than sight: touch, hearing, smell and use all play a part, so that reconstructed landscapes, seen as maps, drawings or even models and major reconstructions, are but imperfect portrayals.

A second term which is charged with many possible meanings is the word *region*: there is no simple, single definition, although the common view is of an area characterized by distinctive features, normally a particular combination of physical and/or cultural entities, what may be called *landscape elements*. Many shades of definition are possible: regions can be wholly pragmatically defined in terms of one or more dominant features, for example, a particular type of settlement or land use, or by physical features such as gravel lands or chalkland, or the area dominated by a particular type of economic system. These simple examples emphasize both the contrast between formal and functional regions and the presence of both natural elements, those given by nature, and elements or artefacts, created by human technology, cultural landscapes.

On the other hand, regional definition can draw upon subtleties such as life-styles and involve the perceptions of both inhabitants and/or neighbours. E Estyn Evans touched a vital point when in 1973 he noted that Sauer's use of the term 'geographical personality' embraces 'the whole dynamic relation of life and land' (1992, 68). In fact the roots of this holistic idea, often defined by using the term 'personality', are deeply rooted and are best exemplified by the French term *pays*, implying an area with its own innate identity (Braudel 1988, 37, 41-57; Everitt 1986, 5-6, 43-68).

Pragmatically defined regions embracing the whole of England were identified and/or constructed by Sir Dudley Stamp as a part of the Land Utilisation Survey conducted between 1930 and 1947 (Stamp 1962), and by Darby (1986) and his co-workers in the magisterial reconstruction of the geography of England as revealed by Domesday Book – although the individual county- based interpretations do not synthesize into a broader picture. Joan Thirsk in *The Cambridge Agrarian History of England*, volumes IV and V (see Thirsk 1987), has included substantial analyses of regional contrasts in farming in both the seventeenth and eighteenth centuries. Analysis of all these must await a more lengthy presentation, but in association with Figures 15.1 and 15.2 short regional descriptions have been created which incorporate two components: definitive features, comprising specific characteristics touching settlement, and associated features, other characteristic or wholly commonplace features (Roberts and Wrathmell 2000a). This flexible system – based upon procedures used in terrain analysis (Mitchell 1973, 64-99) – allows definitions to vary according to the objective of the task, for the definitive features of one circumstance can become associated features in another, which might, for instance, emphasize the characteristics of an area's field systems rather than its settlement. This is merely to reiterate that the definition of regions is a tool of analysis rather than an end-product, one way of bringing order to what exists, or appears to exist, in the real world.

Preliminary results – the two settlement maps and a map of regional divisions

Figure 15.1 is fundamentally simple: it has been created using the Ordnance Survey Old Series one inch to one mile maps reprinted by Harry Margary (1975-81): using a five-point scale, a plain size-graded dot represents each nucleation.

The largest are indisputably urban, but the gradation from large, through medium to small and very small, suggests the presence of towns, large villages, sometimes market villages, ordinary villages, down to small readily discernible hamlets. Inevitably, there is no absolutely objective way of allocating a settlement to each category: experience and judgment were needed. However, were the map to be redone, the same overall distribution would emerge, although the texture of the pattern would alter slightly because of variations in judgment. This distribution allows key provincial boundaries to be plotted. Perhaps the most fundamental difficulty derives from the chronological range of the source maps: these fall between 1809 and 1869. If a line is drawn from Holderness to the Ribble, then the maps to the south all date before 1844. In effect those to the north embrace some local landscapes in which the effects of a drive to a mature industrial economy were already being felt, and this distortion must taken into account when interpreting both maps (Figs 15.1 and 15.2).

Mapping dispersion poses many more problems: the two parallel bands of shading in the scale for Figure 15.2 are organized in such a way that extremely low densities carry the lightest shading, with extremely high densities being the darkest. In fact, there is a continuous gradation between the two bars, zig-zagging up and down, a device to allow single value and mixed value scores to be mapped at the same time. This mapping is based upon readings of the intensity of dispersion within sample 2 x 2 kilometre squares, taken at some 4500 points, in areas where nucleations were absent. Of course, these avoid readings at locations where an obvious contrast in dispersion occurs, spanning a headdyke for instance. Within each sample square the number of dispersed entities were counted – farmsteads, houses and other isolated buildings – according to a set of operating rules. This figure was then compared with an hypothesized intensity scale, 0, 1, 2, 3, 5, 8, 13, 21, and 34, based on the Fibonacci ratio or Golden Mean (Laithwaite 1994, 199-211). These measurements have been converted to simple descriptive terms such as 'extremely low densities', 'high densities' and the like. The upper bar indicates areas – local regions – where mixtures of two sample scores are usual, e.g. low and medium densities, high and very high densities etc.

There are additional complexities not to be pursued further here, but the resulting map

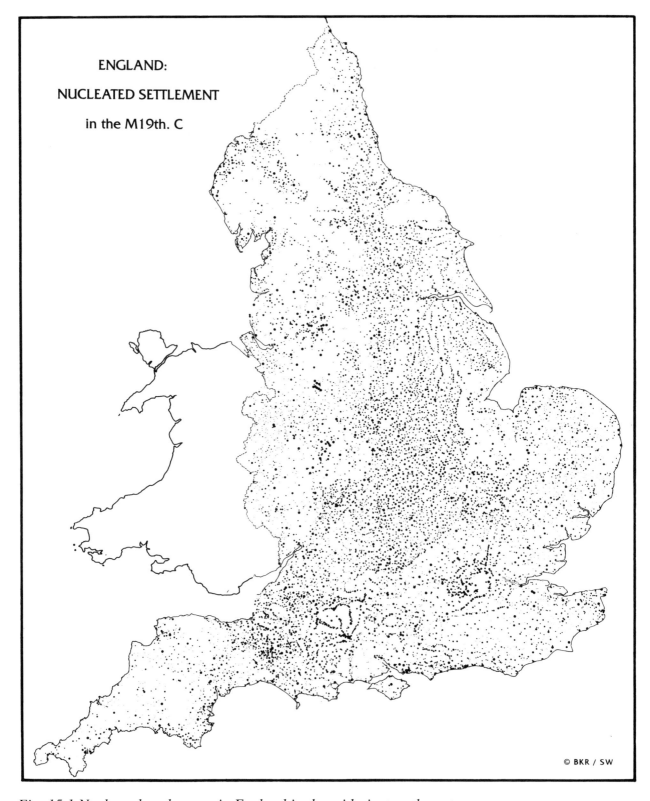

Fig. 15.1 Nucleated settlements in England in the mid-nineteenth century

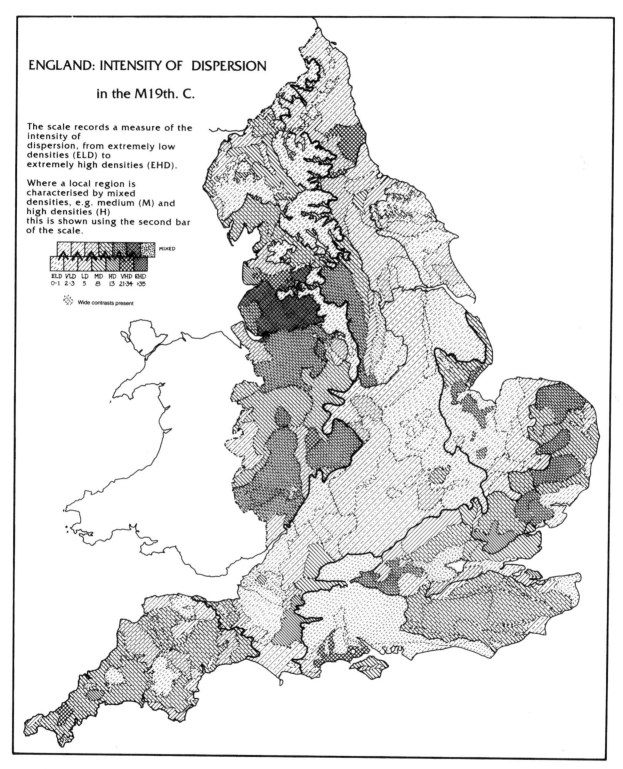

ENGLAND: INTENSITY OF DISPERSION

in the M19th. C.

The scale records a measure of the intensity of dispersion, from extremely low densities (ELD) to extremely high densities (EHD).

Where a local region is characterised by mixed densities, e.g. medium (M) and high densities (H) this is shown using the second bar of the scale.

MIXED

| ELD | VLD | LD | MD | HD | VHD | EHD |
| 0·1 | 2·3 | 5 | 8 | 13 | 21·34 | >35 |

Wide contrasts present

Fig. 15.2 The density of dispersed settlements in England in the mid-nineteenth century

creates a visual impression of the broad regional variations of dispersion. These assessments confirm the presence of the three provinces, and, when studied in combination with the map of nucleations, the variations allow the identification of sub-provinces and local regions on the basis of the presence, absence and varied combinations of both nucleation and dispersion. While the maps shown here are provisional, Figure 15.3 records and names a complete national network of provinces, sub-provinces and local regions. One fact is indisputably clear: not only are the provincial boundaries seen in Figures 15.1, 15.2 and 15.3 to be seen in national maps of enclosure (Gonner 1912, maps; Slater 1907, 73; Darby 1973, 323), of deserted medieval villages (Beresford and Hurst 1979, 66), moated sites (Aberg 1978, fig 1), woodland in 1086 (Darby 1977, 193), they are even detectable in distributions of Scandinavian and Anglo-Saxon place-names (Rackham 1986, 83; Dodgson and Butlin 1978, 47, 59). We conclude that these major boundaries represent substructural elements buried deeply within the development trajectories of English cultural landscapes. Of course, there is no certainty that sub-provincial and local regional boundaries are as old: some undoubtedly very ancient, but others are no older than the nineteenth century. Some may be mere fictions, created by the mapping techniques.

One point must be emphasized: all of the boundaries seen in Figure 15.3 are derived from the evidence of nineteenth century settlement contrasts. Where one of these clearly follow a physical boundary this was accepted, but no 'neo-determinism' is involved: the boundaries are based upon settlement data not physical data. Further, it is important to appreciate that the identification of the same provincial boundaries on other maps, created by different scholars at different times from different sources, demonstrates a convergence of evidence. Figures 15.1 and 15.2, based upon the earliest tolerably uniform map cover, admit not only a retrospective examination of earlier evidence, but may also permit a degree of retrogressive analysis, sifting away some of the later layers, such as industrial accretion, to use the more fragmentary earlier sources to reconstruct conditions in former centuries (Baker 1972, 16-17; Prince 1971).

Interpreting the maps – a discussion

The interpretation of these maps is undoubtedly an intricate process. Nevertheless, one fact is fundamental – each map can be perceived as resulting from a series of separate temporal layers which are in effect concealed because of the crudity of the mapping. Each is the product of a particular temporal phase of development. These temporal and spatial dimensions are enormously complex, and can be considered further in discussion of Figure 15.4. While Maitland's term 'palimpsest' is vivid, suggesting an over-written document, it is a normal condition of reality that the 'document' is over-written not once, but again, and again, and again.... The end-product is an intricate pastiche of fragments – points and pieces, lines and areas – inherited from all possible antecedent phases of landscape development, both early and recent, blended into an essentially coherent functional whole, the living landscape. In this sense, landscapes support a four-dimensional quality.

But this is only part of the story, because each generic layer, representing a former lived-in, used, valued landscape, acts as a temporal filter, affecting what elements from all preceding cultural landscapes are preserved, adapted, altered, transmuted or wholly destroyed as they are passed onwards through a particular trajectory to succeeding generations. The land usages imposed by each generation, developments in settlement, agriculture and industry, are powerful forces, paradoxically at one and the same time invoking both preservation and destruction. The regional impact of these processes is important. On one hand, some developments initiate *divergence*, for example, developments on or near coalfields, or beneath a growing town, in which former landscapes are metamorphosed into wholly different forms, while in rural contexts the changes brought about by the presence of a great rural estate can generate marked local differentiation. A clear example in the north is seen in the distinctive white buildings associated with the Raby estate.

On the other hand, it is probable that the pre-enclosure champion, open field countrysides of the Central Province result from a process of *convergence*, with landscapes which were initially inherently rather different, being drawn towards a normative pattern. Farming based upon communally organized townfields and meadowlands, was integrated into a functioning system together with varied amounts of common grazing land and woodland in such a way that the countrysides of the lower Tees Valley share many cultural characteristics with those of the inner Midlands. Both of these, we postulate, and must seek to prove, developed *over*

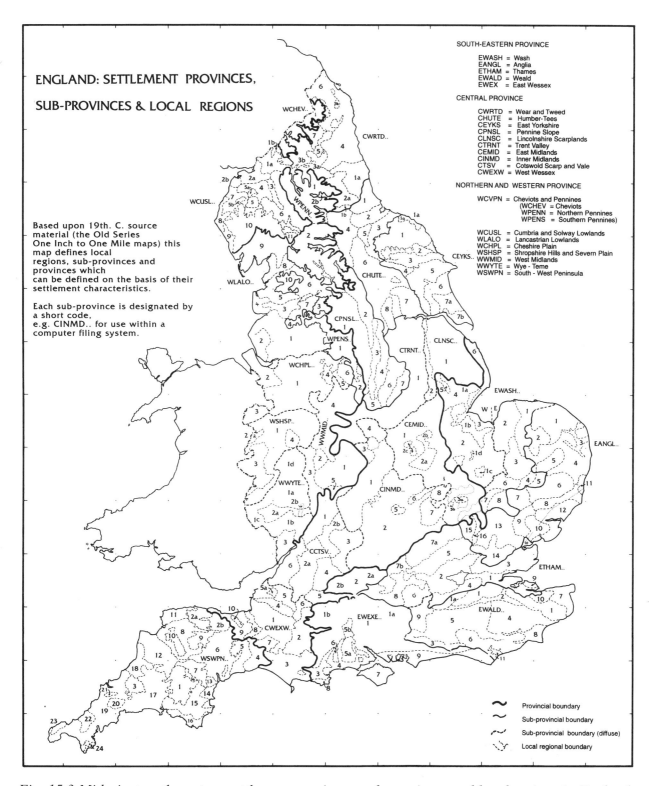

ENGLAND: SETTLEMENT PROVINCES,

SUB-PROVINCES & LOCAL REGIONS

SOUTH-EASTERN PROVINCE

EWASH = Wash
EANGL = Anglia
ETHAM = Thames
EWALD = Weald
EWEX = East Wessex

CENTRAL PROVINCE

CWRTD = Wear and Tweed
CHUTE = Humber-Tees
CEYKS = East Yorkshire
CPNSL = Pennine Slope
CLNSC = Lincolnshire Scarplands
CTRNT = Trent Valley
CEMID = East Midlands
CINMD = Inner Midlands
CTSV = Cotswold Scarp and Vale
CWEXW = West Wessex

NORTHERN AND WESTERN PROVINCE

WCVPN = Cheviots and Pennines
(WCHEV = Cheviots
WPENN = Northern Pennines
WPENS = Southern Pennines)

WCUSL = Cumbria and Solway Lowlands
WLALO = Lancastrian Lowlands
WCHPL = Cheshire Plain
WSHSP = Shropshire Hills and Severn Plain
WWMID = West Midlands
WWYTE = Wye - Teme
WSWPN = South - West Peninsula

Based upon 19th. C. source
material (the Old Series
One Inch to One Mile maps) this
map defines local
regions, sub-provinces and
provinces which
can be defined on the basis of their
settlement characteristics.

Each sub-province is designated by
a short code,
e.g. CINMD.. for use within a
computer filing system.

~ Provincial boundary

~ Sub-provincial boundary

~ Sub-provincial boundary (diffuse)

~ Local regional boundary

Fig. 15.3 Mid-nineteenth century settlement provinces, sub-provinces and local regions in England

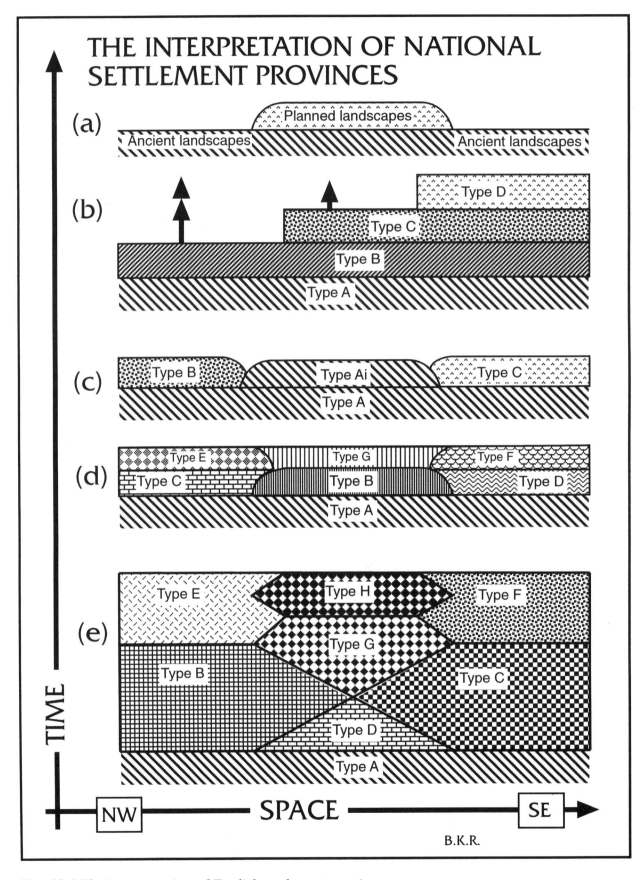

Fig. 15.4 The interpretation of English settlement provinces

landscapes whose characteristics once resembled the 'ancient landscapes' of the two remaining provinces (Roberts and Wrathmell forthcoming). Ultimately, from these speculations one fundamental question emerges: what accounts for the presence of the three provinces seen within many maps which depict landscape elements which are known to have been present in the medieval period?

Interpreting provinces: a model
The model seen in Figure 15.4 is designed to frame further questions which have a direct bearing upon the interpretation of Figures 15.1 and 15.2, and ultimately the development of the landscapes of north-eastern England.

Figure 15.4(a) shows a simple version formulated from Rackham's observations. The diagram represents a slice across England, from the NW to the SE, from the Lake District to Kent. If Rackham is correct, and the open field countrysides which before enclosure dominated the Central Province landscapes are indeed 'planned' while those to the north and west and south-east are 'ancient', then the planned countrysides must be superimposed over ancient countrysides. This apparently simple observation raises many questions. If the enclosure of the planned champion landscapes took at least 400 years from the first late medieval village desertions to the General Enclosure Act of 1845 – as is clearly the case – then the events which brought these same landscapes into being could well be as protracted and diverse.

Figures 15.4(b), (c) (d) and (e) raise even more complex issues. The first three may be quickly dismissed. It is conceivable that the three great provinces represent successive layers, with Type C and Type D being successively superimposed over Type B, which represents an older landscape whose coherent development was arrested by the incursion of the changes – perhaps the arrival of new peoples. In this matter, are echoes of the arguments presented by Sir Cyril Fox (1952, 86-89) a model no longer accepted, but which, nevertheless, contains some elements of truth. Figure 15.4 (c) suggests that the Central Province could represent the basic landscape type, from which Type B and Type C developed, while (d) shows a more complex situation in which the three provinces result from a succession of developmental phases. There may be elements of truth in both of these generalisations. Figure 15.4(c) may be true insofar that there was likely to have been a diffusion

of organised two and three course rotations in open field systems outwards from the Central Province.

Figure 15.4 (d) shows a more complex layering, and the transition from Type B to Type G can be taken as representing the 400 years of the documented enclosure movements, i.e. those associated with Tudor Village depopulation, with enclosures by agreement in the sixteenth and seventeenth centuries, and finally Parliamentary enclosure, which brought radical changes to the countrysides of open arable and commons present at earlier times (Beresford and Hurst 1979, fig. 13; Slater 1907, 73: Gonner 1912, maps A-D). Types E and F represent the landscapes of the north-west and the south-east respectively, here shown with different shading to emphasize their differences as much as their similarities, although this should not disguise the fact that deep structural similarities are also present (Aberg 1978, fig. 1). We seek to test this model (Roberts and Wrathmell forthcoming).

Several further points must be made: first, it is conceivable that the Central Province became as it is because of the presence of deeply bedded but long-defunct landscape characteristics. In the case of Figure 15.4(e) the variety of shading is used to present schematically a series of local regions: the transition from Type B to Type A again symbolises the four hundred years of enclosing activity. The zig-zags of the lateral boundaries of each local region are reminders that the boundaries between the Central and the two outer provinces, while in measure stable, were never absolutely fixed, and at the level of the local region adjustments can be expected. This is particularly true in a temporal context which must in fact extend over not just four hundred years, but at least six thousand if we accept the arrival of ecologically potent farming communities as a 'beginning'. It can be seen that 'at depth', in the remoter past, below the Time 2 line, the local differentiation is modelled as being more diverse than above the line, where the more uniform shading represents the presence of only subtle contrasts.

Second, the sinuous line, winding upwards through time is a reminder of deeply seated thread of continuity which may have been present and which for many periods of time represented a powerful factor structuring the countysides within the whole Central Province. We believe this thread to be remarkably simple, namely the presence of large tracts of cleared and ploughed land in contrast to those found within the two outer provinces (Roberts and Wrathmell 2000b, 85-95). It is this quality which helped meld the diverse local regions forming the province into the distinctive tract of countryside visible in Figures 15.1, 15.2 and 15.3.

The map as a research tool: rural settlement in northern England

This national review may seem to have no place in a volume focused on the north of England: however, our emphasis upon the importance of the map as a research tool, instead of a mere spatial catalogue, was already to be seen in *Archaeology in the North* (Clack and Gosling 1976). Nevertheless, this study was inevitably a part of its time. If the rich haul of data collected – and how easy it is to forget the companion gazetteer – had been lodged within a computer system, then a more powerful and lasting tool of analysis could have been established, one which could by now have been upgraded and expanded. Nevertheless, the 'white space' problem would have eventually loomed large. In fact, throughout *Archaeology in the North* the only complete map with no 'white space' is a generalized map of land utilization embracing urban areas, land suitable for cultivation, marginal and permanent grassland, and finally moorland. While there is no doubt that the authors and compilers saw the importance of superimposing the varied distributions upon this and other base maps, the publishing format of the time made this impossible.

We have mapped *The North* of 1976 as part of our current work; this leads to several conclusions, pointers to further lines of enquiry.

First, we recognize that the nucleations and dispersed settlements continue north of the Scottish/English border: settlement types and place-names do not simply stop, neither do they wholly change character. In short, to understand The North, the limited and English view provided in this paper must be extended to the whole of Great Britain (Nicholaison 1976, figs 2 and 3).

Secondly, if *The North* of 1976 is seen as a small segment of the total distribution presented here, then certain points emerge:

(1) the Central Province extends northwards from the Tees lowlands, to the Tyne valley and through the Northumbrian coastal plain to the Tweed valley. The similarities and differences between this area and the remainder of the province will need rigorous delineation and

exploration in the light of the questions deriving from Figure 15.4 (e); nevertheless, there are slight signs that the line of villages occupying the preferred settlement zone along the based of the Magnesian limestone escarpment, providing a boundary between the Humber-Tees lowland sub-province (Fig. 15.3, CHUTE) and the Wear-Tweed lowland sub-province (Fig. 15.3, CWRTD), represents an important cultural boundary. To the south and east lie townships and parishes once largely dominated by open townfields divided into forms of strip holdings while to the north and west lie townships and parishes in which such fields were a significantly smaller portion of the total land surface and the cultural scene was formerly dominated by vast tracts of common pasture. Village depopulation and the development of the coalfield masks this contrast but close examination of the former distribution of woodland emphasises its importance (Watts 1976, fig. 20.5; Roberts and Wrathmell 2000b, fig. 7.1)

(2) the Eden valley and Solway Plain form a clear outlier of the Central Province and possess particular qualities, notably separation by mountain masses and narrow passes, combined with internal and peripheral diversity, compact, yet open to diverse cultural influences from all points of the compass. Although it lacks the vital tie-beam of Domesday Book, this *pays* has been much-studied, yet retains vast potential as a cultural laboratory.

(3) *The North's* mountainous core, divided by imposed political and administrative boundaries, forms a zone with broadly homogeneous settlement characteristics, although of course detailed work reveals local subtleties. In terms of settlement it is to be seen as part of the Northern and Western Province. There could be no better illustration of one fundamental limitation of Figures 15.1 and 15.2: they are based upon generic characteristics. Settlement must also – a small word needing emphasis – be studied within its functional contexts, township and parish, manor and great estate, parts of twin interlocking hierarchies, one secular, the other ecclesiastical, frameworks of organized space. Thus the Raby estate, formerly part of the lands of St. Cuthbert, extended from the lowlands of the Tees to the uplands, integrating terrains with contrasting physical potential into a single unit. Only in this way can genetic characteristics be safely defined.

Finally, were the generalized detail of land use noted above to be extended retrogressively to a regional reconstruction of unimproved land in the later eighteenth century, then – as they stand – the maps of *Archaeology in the North* (Clack and Gosling 1976) could be used, particularly if they were scanned into a graphics computer. To give but one example: the system of settlement in the Central Province is based upon nucleated rural settlements and associated town-field systems, intermixed with some areas of dispersion, and framed by the essential resources of woodland and rough grazing. The regional relationship between these local land use patterns and the northern distribution of, for example, non-defended settlements of putative Iron Age or Romano-British date (Clack and Gosling 1976, 29) is worthy of broad-brush attention. Where will the earthwork record of such settlements have been wholly overwritten by medieval townfield furlongs? Where will it have survived on the upland pastures or within pasture crofts close to village cores which developed in the medieval centuries (Roberts 1993)?

To conclude, we believe that this national work is important because it is designed to place any site from any part of the country into a generalized but broadly accurate context. Scarcity or prolixity can be assessed with reference to the known numbers of sites within any local region, sub-province or province, which then become frameworks for reference and comparison. Local regional characteristics provide a specific context, and at this level local reality emerges, place, which forms, and always has formed, a setting for the lives of its inhabitants. One detailed northern picture, within County Durham, is currently being explored by a research project focussing upon the vast tracts of medieval waste is being undertaken by one of us (BKR) in collaboration with Richard Britnell of the History Department at Durham. In this matter the logical working framework of the ancient county with its rich store of documents is nevertheless seen as no more than sample selected for study, to test the hypothesis that it is effectively superimposed across the even more ancient contrast between the Tees-Humber sub-province to the south and the Wear-Tweed sub-province to the north.

Acknowledgements
Our thanks are due to English Heritage for funding the work which forms the basis of this collateral study, and particularly to David Stocker whose contribution to a paper to be published as an outcome of the RURALIA conference in Prague, September 1995, has been used as a basis for the opening section of this article.

Chapter 16: The Development of Towns in the North

C Pamela Graves*

Introduction

This paper will consider future possible research topics for urban archaeology in the North of England. Although entitled 'the development of towns', *development*, in the sense of a chronological evolution features as only one theme of interest in this paper. Whilst it is still necessary to discover the topographical spread and contraction of towns, I would suggest that we can understand this concept of development better if social issues are integral to our investigations. I suggest that fruitful research aims can be achieved if we analyse the town as a social environment, and ask questions of what the medieval town-dweller experienced in their occupation of this urban space. The point is not to try to reconstruct 'ideas inside people's heads' (Barrett 1987, 471 *contra* Hodder 1986, see 1991 edition), for this insight would be available only through unique documents, and even then questionable as an objective. Rather, the point is to analyse the town as a material environment, comprised of buildings, public, private or differently defined spaces, in which material objects were produced, used, discarded or exchanged, and in which specific social identities were created. We may ask *how* these social identities were created, and whose interests they served? By taking a material approach to the experience of urban social life we can ask who created the environments; who had authority and the resources to create them? We can ask how some aspects or functions of the material environment might change through time or be deployed in different ways by different groups? Consequently, we can identify sources of potential conflict in the control and use of the urban environment: instances of subversion of norms; and change in the construction of social knowledge through time.

Martin Carver has suggested that the townscape, as an archaeological phenomenon, is a palimpsest of political choices through time: 'the preferred corporate investment of the day, expressed as streets broad and narrow, monuments, refuse disposal services,' amongst other things (Carver 1993, 4). To these might be added the control of waste property and gardens, even perhaps particular imports. Carver continues with the opinion that, 'The investment in turn reflects the political mood of the community,' (Carver 1993, 4). I suggest that much of the work which is carried out in future in towns in the North of England can be related to major themes of political and corporate investment, for example, of lordship; how institutions like the Church penetrate the everyday lives of townspeople and are reproduced by them; how urban communities enfranchise themselves and achieve and express this in material terms.

In 1993 the CBA Urban Research Committee published the recommendations of a colloquium held at the University of Durham on urban themes AD 1000-1600. In 1994, a synthetic paper on medieval and later towns by John Schofield was included in the RAI special volume *Building on the Past* (Schofield 1994b). Most of that paper forms the final chapter of the Schofield and Vince volume on *Medieval Towns* (1994). Olivier 1996 and Williams 1997 both have implications for the study of urban archaeology. In the course of this paper I will make reference to these documents.

Research on medieval urban origins

I have not structured this paper in terms of the chronological development of towns in the North, but origins are a good point at which to start. Since the location of archaeological excavation has been defined largely by threat, the picture it has provided of origins remains partial, and it is unclear in some cases whether we are seeing settlement continuity or disjuncture. It is not that I think the definition of a town is important, but I do think one of the exciting possibilities which towns in the North hold for us is the exploration of the diversity of borough foundation, in particular, the subject of lordship in its effects and challenges.

In Newcastle, the discovery of an extensive cemetery dating from *circa* AD 700 and continuing in use up to the eleventh and twelfth centuries, after the foundation of the castle presents us with the problem of where the dead who filled this cemetery originally worked and lived. Although there are slight remains of sub-Roman activity and pottery within the area of the later medieval Castle, no post-Roman, pre-AD 1080 finds have been located beyond the Castle spur. All considerations of the name 'Monkchester',

*Address: Department of Archaeology, University of Durham, South Road, Durham DH1 3LE

the identification of Pandon with Bede's *Ad Murum* and the tradition of a royal Saxon palace there (cf Brand 1789, 383), or the possibility of early settlement around St Andrew's church, remain speculation. Four sherds of residual Saxon pottery dating to between the 7th and 9th centuries were found in later contexts in Oakwellgate, Gateshead, across the River Tyne (Nolan 2000, 23). Of as much importance, however, would be the wider social and political context of the region in which we could place it. Following Eric Cambridge's study of the early ecclesiastical organisation of County Durham (1984), may the curious circumstance of Newcastle's four churches be explained in a pre-Conquest minster and dependent chapels? In this respect, the archaeological patterning of Carlisle's pre-Norman settlement which seems to have been focused around the churches of St Mary and St Cuthbert is well served by the advent of Summerson's excellent two volume *Medieval Carlisle* (1993) produced by the Cumberland and Westmoreland Antiquarian and Archaeological Society, and Angus Winchester's *Landscape and Society* (1987). McCarthy (1999b) has reviewed the evidence for early medieval Carlisle and posed a number of remaining research questions. By the late eleventh century there seems to have been more than one settlement, with a complex pattern of tenure which may be related to the splitting of a single lordship into several estates. The twelfth century borough developed from the threefold allocations to the castle, the priory and the townspeople.

The results of excavations carried out in Hexham, Northumberland (Cambridge and Williams 1995), would seem to set the future investigation of the town's development in terms of the competing jurisdictions of the Priory of St Andrew, and the Archbishops of York. This would accord with Tom Corfe's suggestion that the burgesses of Hexham had little control over the creation of their town, perhaps in contrast to neighbouring Corbridge (Corfe 1995).

In Darlington Market Place, County Durham, excavations in 1994 located successive ditches which have been interpreted as boundary ditches to a churchyard that lay to the west (Adams, Carne and Bosveld unpub). As the churchyard expanded to the east, the boundary ditches were recut further eastward each time. Carne and Adams have concluded that the graveyard must belong to a church that pre-dated the late twelfth century foundation to the east, and they suggest

that this may have been a Saxon church (Adams, Carne and Bosveld unpub, 16). This raises, once more, an older question as to the existence of a late Saxon burh or at least the connection between Saxon churches and market places. It has been suggested that the feasts of the Church year created 'urban moments' by attracting crowds and commerce (Morris 1987, 190) in places whose settled population was otherwise sparse, and in which trade occurred only intermittently (Wood 1986; Sawyer 1981, 160-1). Was this a deliberate, and therefore politically symbolic, juxtaposition or replacement of churches by the Norman Bishop le Puiset, of the sort now familiar to us elsewhere? A well known example was Bishop Flambard's clearance of the houses on the peninsula in Durham to create the *placea*, as recorded by Symeon of Durham (Bonney 1990, 26 and 36; Arnold 1882 vol. 1, 140). Excavations at 61-3 Saddler Street, Durham, revealed a reorganisation of early tenements which was probably contemporary with these events (Carver 1979). Whether the context was Darlington or Durham, we might suppose that an alteration of the familiar topography of home, commerce and spiritual investment would have a profound effect on the consciousness of the townspeople and their recognition of themselves as subjects of their new overlord.

It remains a basic problem in many of the small towns of Northumberland that we do not understand either the origins or the development of the town. Whilst historical town plan and documentary analysis has proved useful as applied to, for example, Alnwick (Conzen 1960) and Cockermouth on the Cumbrian coast (Winchester 1986), much of the evidence which might inform an understanding of development in smaller towns in the North may only be retrievable through excavation. In his review of the archaeology of medieval towns in Lancashire, White (1996, 125) noted that 'we have not yet defined archaeologically a single burgage plot or a single medieval house site in any Lancashire town.' Here, again, some of the interesting questions which may be asked relate to the differences between seigniorial and monastic boroughs; occupation prior to the granting of charters; and the effects of different authorities on the layout and use of the towns through time.

A methodology for future urban research

In pragmatic terms, due to the great amount of work which has been done there is a definite need, at this point in time, to produce overviews or syntheses of our state of knowledge of towns in the different counties, identifying the value of archaeological deposits, where assessable. This is best achievable through the urban archaeological strategy projects instigated by English Heritage (1992) as piloted in Durham City (Lowther, Ebbatson, Ellison and Millett 1993); currently embarked upon in Newcastle upon Tyne (Graves and Heslop in prep); and being considered in Carlisle. In the first stage of such projects, all relevant data will be collated and related to a computerised mapping system for the modern town. This will allow archaeologists to map the nature and extent of known deposits; and by extrapolation, the collated data should alert archaeologists to the potential value of deposits which have not been investigated. The second stage will be to write a synthesis of what is known about the development, archaeology and history of the urban centre, but this should also allow archaeologists to ask questions about what we should like to know. The third stage will be the formulation of a strategy for the curation of the archaeological resource. This is surely a tool with which archaeologists can balance conservation with targeted research aims for excavation.

Assessments of small towns (Extensive Urban Surveys), where archaeological interventions have been few in number and often extremely restricted in area, have been undertaken in Northumberland and Tyne and Wear, again funded by English Heritage and the local authorities. Further urban surveys may follow. The quality of information which might survive in small towns in the North has been demonstrated in Hartlepool (Daniels 1990 and 1991).

The amount of archaeological work which has been carried out in Northern towns since 1976 ranges enormously: from The Lanes in Carlisle city, perhaps unparalleled in extent anywhere in Britain (McCarthy 1993; McCarthy 1999a; McCarthy forthcoming; Zant in prep.); to, for example, Alnwick, Northumberland, where there has been very little archaeological intervention. There would be little value in reproducing a comprehensive gazetteer of archaeological interventions in the North since 1976; instead, the remainder of this paper will return to the themes suggested at the beginning. Examples will be drawn from the work of the last 20 years to pose questions about the creation of social identity in urban contexts, control, the enfranchisement of urban communities, the townscape as an arena in which different authoritative claims compete and coalesce.

Questions and directions for future urban research

There has been very little archaeological research into the walled town of Berwick, with regard to its evolution, or its archaeological potential. What little is known of the early origins of Berwick were stated by Margaret Ellison in her 1976 survey, supplemented by Hunter in 1982 and repeated by Lancaster University Archaeological Unit in January 1996. More detailed research into the area of Marygate has been carried out by the Lancaster Unit in that assessment, including consideration of all the historic cartographic evidence. Since 1996 we have had growing evidence of the depth or quality of deposits underlying a number of parts of Berwick. Hunter carried out some trial trenches at the Ness end, revealing that the waterfront deposits were several metres deep. Given the potential for preservation of organic materials, environmental evidence and the structure of the historic waterfront, the archaeological value of this area is obviously great. Archaeological work carried out at the New Quay in 1996 revealed medieval dumping of domestic rubbish beneath eighteenth century ballast make-up (Griffiths 1999). This potential has been underscored by work carried out between 1998-99, including the location of a possibly maintained communal waste dump (Young 2001). A surface of cobbles was noted c.1m below the present ground surface in the south-east corner of Palace Green.

Further questions may be posed concerning Berwick: what is the relationship of Spades Mire to the town? What date are the defences? According to White (1963) the earthwork antedates the plough rigs and may be thirteenth century in date, possibly before AD 1296. Schofield and Vince (1994, 30, Fig 2.3, after Bond 1987) date these defences to the early thirteenth century, but cite no evidence and give no explanation for this. What did these earthworks enclose? Do they represent an example of shrinkage in the area enclosed?

There is a complex sequence in the foundation of religious houses, their destruction and relocation at Berwick. It may pay to examine the original sites of the religious institutions, where known, prior to the Scots wars, with relation to the early growth of the town; and then to compare this pattern with the development after the wars. There is some dispute as to the identification of the Love Lane/Bridge Terrace discoveries (Bishop 1997, 2; Young 2001, 15). Who continues to support these religious houses and hospitals? Those which are mentioned in Dunbar's fifteenth century poem 'The Freiris of Berwik', e.g. the 'Masone Dew', 'Jacobene freiris of the quhyt hew, The Carmeleitis, and the Minouris,' (Mackay Mackenzie 1932, 183); the Domus Dei, and the Dominican Friary – do these all represent renewed interest and patronage on the part of the townspeople after a relative period of stability, and is this distinct from royal patronage of the earlier period? What is the relevance of the positions of the Domus Dei, Domis Pontis and Chapel of Ravensdale on the waterfront, close to the bridge (cf the location of the Domus Dei in Newcastle upon Tyne)? Hospitals, like the Maison Dieu and Domus Dei, were often placed at marginal points of the medieval town, such as bridges and waterfronts; and ports of entry, as a whole, were particularly appropriate locations for the socially and spiritually liminal symbolism of such institutions (Gilchrist 1995, 8-61). The twin foci of the early town of Berwick appear to have been the riverfront and the tollbooth. The important Red Hall – the base for the colony of Flemish merchants in Berwick, remains unlocated; and the White Hall, also probably a merchant hall, was possibly situated in Segate. The social geographies and functions of medieval towns were at once both spiritual and economic. We are surely mistaken in creating a false dichotomy between these considerations in framing both our archaeological research designs and interpretations.

It has been argued that Berwick, in common with other Scottish burghs, had been granted a marketing monopoly over an extended rural hinterland, which had effectively created 'a theoretical economic *contado*' 'unknown in such territorial breadth in the rest of Europe,' (Dennison 1998, 104). Consequently, many questions can be raised as to the relationship between the town and the countryside; and the changes effected by the town's political absorption into England in 1482. How do the various suggestions for the processing of grain either inside (Cotton, Hale and Rutherford 2001, 73), or outside the town (Huntley 1999, 105) fill in this picture, and is there a chronological distinction? Equally valid for consideration is Gidney's conclusion that 'the fisheries of Berwick do not seem to have been as important to the meat supply of the city as the pastoral farmers of the hinterland' (1999, 102).

By contrast, and on a smaller scale, Hartlepool was laid out from the late eleventh century as an enlargement of the two-row green plan seen in the villages of North-East England. The earliest property could 'more readily be equated with rural settlement practice than with urban and is in marked contrast with the contemporary situation in Durham' as suggested by Carver in 1979 (Daniels 1990, 401). Are there other manifestations of rural or hybrid settlement practices in the early occupation of the town? What implications are there for the development of 'urban' practices and identity in this context?

Land reclamation and urban identity

The medieval waterfront at Newcastle upon Tyne has been examined through excavation at ten sites between the Close Gate in the west (Fraser, Maxwell and Vaughan 1994) and the Swirle in the east (Ellison *et al* 1993). The process of reclamation and development follows a pattern previously recognized at other medieval coastal and riverside towns in Europe, e.g. London; Hull; King's Lynn; Bergen, Norway; Lubeck, northern Germany (Fraser, Jamfrey and Vaughan 1995, 207; O'Brien *et al* 1988, 156; Myrvoll 1991; Fehring 1989). The historical development of trading in Newcastle may be understood in terms of a struggle engaged in by the burgesses of Newcastle to achieve a monopoly on the Tyne in competition with the Priory of Tynemouth and the Bishop of Durham (O'Brien 1991). We need now to try to relate the detail recovered from excavation to those political and economic groups within the town, and the processes by which they asserted their power and identity. The reclamation appears to have progressed piecemeal by a series of revetment walls retaining huge tips of ballast derived from shipping engaged in trade along the eastern and southern English coasts. The earliest date for the beginning of this process has been provisionally identified as the twelfth century, on the Stockbridge Magistrates Court site excavated in 1995 by Lawrence Truman (Truman 1995, 25). O'Brien excavated the area formerly occupied by Fenwick's Entry and Broad Garth. The site of twelfth century pottery manufacture was located at Dog Bank, on a cliff which would have dropped down to the river (O'Brien *et al* 1988). Below this, O'Brien located part of a revetment wall dating to the first half of the thirteenth century, from which quays were built out at right angles, into the river (1988). A massive episode of dumping occurred which filled the spaces between the quays and created what is presumed to be a continuous platform of raised ground. Streets were laid out over what had been the piers by the end of the thirteenth century. It is unclear whether each of the streets had its own watergate and landing stage before the continuous quayside was created, possibly in the latter half of the fourteenth century.

The waterfront above Tyne Bridge developed as a series of stages with individual properties being enlarged at different rates (Fraser et al 1994 and 1995). 'At any one time a common alignment appears to have been rapidly established on adjacent properties, although the only evidence for a cohesive strategy for the waterfront in the medieval period occurs with the construction of the section of the town wall between the Riverside Tower and property 2,' (Fraser et al 1995, 207). This occurred in the fifteenth century.

As O'Brien (1991) has pointed out, the town's investment in its riverside infrastructure was considerable, and the quantity and value of maritime trading as far as the Baltic, the Low Countries and France grew enormously from the second half of the thirteenth century. Yet what do we mean by 'the town'? We do not know who was laying out the plots, who was controlling the process of reclamation. The Customs of Newcastle were formulated before the mid-twelfth century and gave the burgesses certain privileges and monopolies (Johnson 1925, 169-79). We might suppose that, in the early years, the borough court, as a focus for communal activity towards the accumulation of capital in excess of the farm they owed to the king was not a sufficient basis on which to embark on a single phase, unified project of reclamation. We do not understand fully the role of the religious institutions in the process either, for the Hospital of the Blessed Virgin Mary certainly leased out land on the Close (Oliver 1924 passim). Land transactions gave rights of all land up to the groundebb of the tide, thereby allowing reclamation on the part of the individual tenant (e.g. a demise of 1288; Oliver 1924, 85-6). The rich would acquire the land, and there would follow subinfeudation, but perhaps the initial piecemeal development reflects the efforts of individuals. The remarkable thing is that there were periodic attempts to create a unified frontage, and that in these we may be seeing the beginnings of communal action and the pooling of capital. It is

surely no coincidence that this begins to happen after the foundation of the merchant guild in 1216 (Howell 1967, 35), and the greater opportunity the guild afforded those burgesses who had specifically mercantile interests to pursue goals of mutual interest with a greater coherence and collective resources. It is from their ranks that bailiffs and the officers of civic government were to arise. I think we must surely see the chronology and form of the waterfront development in terms of the political maturity of these groups. Between 1305 and 1342, there are clear indications that they had formed an elite class within the town (Brand 1789 2, 166; Howell 1967, 38-9). Is it a coincidence, then, that the building of the town wall along the river front, where it would be a visible symbol of the town elite's prestige and unity of purpose to the busy river traffic, occurs after the town has achieved the ultimate recognition of independence and corporate identity, of county status, c.1400? Further, there are a number of issues involving the spiritual aspect of the merchant guild which helped to create at once both the sense of belonging to one group and the distinction of rank amongst the merchants.

This example introduces one of the most exciting possibilities available to archaeologists in the North of England: that is the opportunity to exploit the contrasts that different conditions of lordship in the boroughs afford, and that the different conditions under which urban communities might act and create their own identity afford. For example, how does the process of waterfront reclamation at Hartlepool uncovered by Robin Daniels and his colleagues (Daniels 1991) compare with that described at Newcastle upon Tyne? At Hartlepool, the lordship was held by the Brus family until the fourteenth century wars with Scotland. The pre-dock construction, dock, and sea-defences were constructed between the twelfth and thirteenth centuries. In the twelfth and thirteenth centuries the Brus family encouraged the development of the town, and at the same time built a fabulous church, then encouraged the Franciscans to settle in an impressive friary (Daniels 1986). From the end of the thirteenth century, the Anglo-Scottish wars afforded the merchants of Hartlepool a massive increase in trade as they supplied the English armies. Daniels has said that by the end of the Anglo-Scottish wars the economic impetus within Hartlepool had died out (1991, 50). By the sixteenth century there were large areas of waste within the town's boundaries.

Victualling and consumption patterns

Two of the themes put forward by the CBA Urban Research Committee (1993) were victualling and the role of the town in stimulating agricultural innovation for a centralised market. In some of the seventeenth-century landfill deposits from the Mansion House site in Newcastle, the animal bone showed signs of selective animal husbandry. This has been taken to be indicative of the agricultural revolution about a hundred years before it is assumed normally (Davis and Bullock 1995, 191, 194-5). What other evidence is there for this, and how might we begin to understand it in terms of the necessity to feed an urban population, and its concomitants in the countryside? Amongst the earliest faunal evidence for selective breeding of this sort are remains from early sixteenth-century deposits in Lincoln (Dobney et al 1997). The Newcastle deposits, however, may tie in with documented evidence for early agricultural improvement in large demesne estates in the South-East of Northumberland and North-East of County Durham (Wrathmell 1975, 169-73). Land here was being depopulated and enclosed for the creation of intensive grazing units for both sheep and cattle in the late sixteenth and early seventeenth centuries. As the population of Tyneside expanded, towns and mining communities could no longer sustain self-sufficiency in food supply. This would have provided a powerful incentive for agrarian change which should be explored in more detail by drawing the documentary, landscape and faunal evidence together.

From here we might explore the idea of market towns dominating their hinterlands, in the distribution of foodstuffs and other items. The potentially significant circumstances of Berwick have been referred to above. The supply of food from the hinterland may be contrasted with the limited evidence for exotic plant taxa which might otherwise be expected from a port (Cotton, Hale and Rutherford 2001, 81; Huntley and Stallibrass 1995). The plenteous salmon fisheries seem to have furnished export rather than local consumption (Gidney and Stokes 2001). In many ways simplistic models of dependency are outmoded. Chris Dyer has suggested that we should be looking, instead, at consumption (1989a and b). Consumption patterns are embedded in the social concerns and practices of different social groups or classes, and not simply reducible to relative wealth. Thus, for example, the aristocracy bought specially imported foodstuffs from the major ports, and often London, to furnish their lavish feasts. Both unusual food and, for example, costly fabrics, were given as gifts which reinforced relations amongst a broadly conceived group of kin and allies, as well as feudal superiors and patrons. Evidence of this is found plentifully in the Paston and Lisle letters (Davis 1971-6; St Clare Byrne 1981). Following the pattern Dyer has identified elsewhere in England (1989a), the nobility might use basic foodstuffs, and animal fodder or bedding, sent from their own estates as feudal renders whilst staying in the houses they owned in Carlisle or Newcastle upon Tyne. The gentry had different patterns of consumption, and were far more likely to use the provincial capitals and major towns for their supplies. The lower classes, whose mobility was curtailed, tended to rely on local provender.

The process by which so-called trade goods end up in archaeological deposits is therefore complex, and embedded not only in the feudal structure, but will reflect the habits and aspirations of a range of social groups. Changes in the patterning may not simply reflect different trading connections, but the emergence of new dominant classes within different preoccupations. In the North of England, examination of archaeologically retrieved data in conjunction with documentary sources for local areas might be possible in a place like Carlisle where the archaeology has paid careful attention to environmental data, and where there is documentation as well.

Allied to the theme of consumption, Dr Chris Cumberpatch (pers comm) has drawn attention to the need to create a review of ceramic material from Cleveland and County Durham, and to establish a type series. Similarly, the ceramics from Berwick need to be put in a context of both Scottish as well as Northern English types (cf. Jenner 1999, 83). Within Newcastle, the advent of imported redware vessels begins as a slow trickle in the fourteenth century but steadily increases through the fifteenth and sixteenth centuries, in inverse proportion to the use of locally-produced reduced greenwares (Ellison 1981, particularly 96, Fig 6). This phenomenon needs to be examined in conjunction with the advent of other imported domestic items and forms of building material, for example Low Countries brick and tile. I would suggest that the chronology and quantity of such imports runs concurrently with the growth in export of coal to the Low Countries from the late fourteenth century (cf O'Brien 1991). As Newcastle merchants created these contacts, is there enough evidence to suggest that the consumption choices of the merchant elite here indicate that they were developing a similar lifestyle, sharing the same material preferences, to their counterparts in other ports around the North Sea rim? Gaimster and Nenk (1997, 172) have argued for a 'Hanseatic' material culture and lifestyle as applicable to London, Norwich and Southampton. Newcastle was a major North Sea port but the same questions have not been asked of the archaeology and social history here. Moreover, I would warn against the kind of analysis that seeks either direct parallels for the patterns found in the South of England, or assigns a 'poor cousin' interpretation to the evidence should it prove that assemblages from Newcastle do not match the full range and quality of imports found in the South. Rather, if the Hanseatic culture is viewed (or theorized) as a range of choices, then the consumption and lifestyle preferences of a North country urban elite may reflect particular assimilations, selections and innovations through which they created their own distinct regional identity, or variation on the general theme.

Towns and innovation

The Council for British Archaeology recommends the analysis of the town as the centre or conduit of innovation, of, for example, technological innovation. The role that Tyneside was to play in the industrialization of the North should alert us to early manifestations of technological change, or manufacturing specialization. What role did late medieval religious institutions play in developing the industrial processes, particularly mineral exploitation, of the North? How did this affect urban markets and the creation of wage-labour dependency?

I would also suggest that we need to think about the role of towns as centres for the production and dissemination of texts in the course of the later middle ages, and of particular kinds of knowledge. We might consider this in respect of the painted wooden Augustine screens in Carlisle Cathedral. These screens carry images and texts of the legends of Saints Augustine, Cuthbert and Anthony written in contemporary Cumbrian dialect English, dating to the last quarter of the fifteenth century. Both the range of images and textual quotations were carefully selected by the Bishop of Carlisle, formerly a monk of Durham Cathedral Priory. They are fixtures in a public place of worship, and surely a significant contrast and counter to the proliferation of individual aids to contemplation which

we understand to have circulated amongst an increasingly literate urban population, and those members of the urban elite who left the town to live on rural estates. These were the same people, often, who used private chapels on their estates and sat in screened family chapels or pews in their parish churches. These people developed a more individualistic spirituality than the majority of their humbler contemporaries: the kind of privatized religion which accompanied the privatization of domestic space (Graves 1996, and 2000; Richmond 1984). Of what date, and what nature, are the earliest printed products from Northern towns; who controlled their content and dissemination; and what audience did they address?

Urban space and social reproduction

This brings me back to the theme of the way in which urban space was inhabited and how social groups were reproduced. We can ask questions of the spatial distribution of crafts and trades, of different types of building. Daniels' work on the use of space in medieval Hartlepool burgage plots is one of the best examples of more than just a theoretical application of this approach (Daniels 1990). This is one area where we can make a virtue of the restrictions of PPG16 and make more of standing buildings, of cartographic, pictorial and documentary sources. Issues such as privacy, household, gender and age relations may be explored through existing structures and excavation archive (cf. Johnson 1993; Johnson 1996 *passim*; Grenville 1997). We can move on from here in townscape terms to think about who occupied waste and derelict properties, for example. In Carlisle, as in Newcastle upon Tyne, we find felons, foreigners, 'Scots and Unfreemen', established in the tails of much-divided burgage plots, squatting or camping out on commons (for antipathies to such people see, e.g. Bourne 1736, 50; Howell 1967, 97-8 and *passim*). Newcastle has produced fascinating evidence for the spatial patterning of non-regulated crafts and occupations in the sixteenth century (Vaughan 1981, 189; Nolan 1990), and such themes should be explored further.

Work of outstanding quality has, of course, been carried out on the church of the North of England, and needs no repetition here. However, we might think about using this information in terms of the creation of Christian identities: would the way in which ecclesiastical spaces could be used differ substantially between the two dioceses of Durham and Carlisle, or from parish to parish? There may certainly be a difference between Berwick, prior to 1482, and Newcastle: 'Scottish towns, unlike their English and most continental counterparts, did not house multiple parishes,' (Dennison 1998, 112-3). Newcastle, as noted above, had four churches which were regarded, through popular practice, as parish churches. What effects did this have on patterns of patronage, burial, the idea of an urban 'community' and social differentiation?

We might think about the way in which urban communities formed themselves. In the emergence of the craft guilds we find a plethora of powerful groups. They built not only public buildings like guildhalls as expressions of their wealth and taste, but individual company halls. The dynamics of the guilds in a town like Newcastle are fascinating as, for example, the hostmen gained a monopoly of the coal trade, and then political ascendancy. The reuse of the claustral ranges of the Dominican Friary by trade companies after the Dissolution of the Monasteries has been researched by Harbottle and Fraser (1987). The situation can be contrasted with that in Durham where, unusually, it was the bishop who indirectly controlled craft membership, and upheld standards of manufacture, and where it was the bishop's temporal chancellor who was responsible for craft and trade company discipline (Bonney 1990). There were no craft halls in Durham, and no recognizably distinct forms of housing created by a wealthy merchant group.

What can we learn from the role of the craft guilds in the Corpus Christi procession and plays in Northern English towns? In Newcastle, the numerous craft guilds and the Merchant Adventurers company were extremely influential and were responsible for the organization of both the Corpus Christi procession and plays, and other frequent public entertainments and ceremonies (Anderson 1982). By contrast, in Durham, the Corpus Christi procession seems to have been much more of a merger of craft and clerical interests (Rubin 1991, 260; 268; Fowler 1902, 107). M R James (1983) and Charles Phythian-Adams (1972) have written of the way in which the commercial success of each craft determined its role in the hierarchy of the procession, and that, consequently, processional order could change from year to year, determined not by an unchanging conception of the world, but by success in a competitive commercial market. These processions were believed to present an image of the *community* of the town,

but this was a partial and exclusive image. We can ask, similarly, who controlled the cycle of religious drama in Northern towns: clerics or guildsmen? How did this affect perceptions of public and commercial space, or perceptions of commercial practice itself? Matters of jurisdiction and economics were often played out in the public ritual occupation of space and lay at the heart of both spiritual and civic identities (Fleming 2000; Graves 2000). These themes are brought together in a current project that explores the role of civic ceremonial and the form and distribution of seventeenth-century timber-framed buildings in Newcastle (Graves, Heslop and Taylor in prep). This demonstrates that the form of such buildings is not merely a reflection of architectural fashion as diffused to the provinces, but, rather, a factor in the creation of particular social and political relationships in the town at that date.

Finally, at the launch of the Society for Church Archaeology in 1996, Richard Morris suggested that the Reformation marked one of the most defining moments in the history of England, Scotland and Wales, effecting the change from a medieval, organic concept of society, to an atomized, early modern society dominated by the concept of individualism. In the context of the launch, Morris suggested that we should, perhaps, be looking at churches as the locus of this change. I would contend that in urban studies we have tended to underplay the manifestations of religion and spiritual concerns in, for example, commercial practice in the later middle ages. I would suggest that we do not benefit by either this separation of religion from economics and trade, or the medieval : post-medieval period division. Rather, there is much to be gained by taking account of a broad period of transition. This is the view taken by the Societies for Medieval and Post-Medieval Archaeology in both their *Age of Transition* (November 1996; Gaimster and Stamper 1997) and *Archaeology of Reformation* (February 2001) conferences. I would end this consideration of the directions in which we might take the archaeological analysis of Northern towns with an appeal that we should apply modern theoretical rigour to the themes developed by Weber in *The Protestant Ethic and the Spirit of Capitalism* (1930 translation; 1985 edition) and R H Tawney in *Religion and the Rise of Capitalism* (1922; 1984 edition).

Chapter 17: Medieval Boroughs of Northern England

*Robin Daniels**

Editors Note
This paper was not given at the conference in 1996, but is included as being relevant to the volume.

Introduction

This survey of the medieval boroughs of northern England was undertaken from a very specific viewpoint; it is not intended as a synthesis of the archaeological and other information from these settlements but rather as an investigation into their rural origins.

This interest in the rural aspects stems from excavations in Hartlepool – probably the most extensively explored small town in the region. Excavations at Church Close in 1984 – 85 revealed a substantial agricultural phase in the earliest history of the 12th century planted town (Daniels 1990). This led to queries about the real economic status of newly established, or developing towns within the fragile economy of the north of England in the late 11th and 12th centuries. An extension of this was the comparison of the 'urban' plan forms to those of the newly created planned villages of the North of England. Given the quite distinct two-row green form of the planned village was an equally distinct form used for the towns?

The pre-occupation with the rural aspects of the towns means that the major urban centres of the region such as York, Durham and Carlisle which had substantive settlements prior to the Norman Conquest will have little place in this paper, which will focus instead on the smaller urban centres. Newcastle as a post-conquest foundation, although clearly the site of an important earlier settlement as evidenced by the cemetery sealed beneath the castle, might be expected to figure here, but the archaeological evidence from Newcastle so far throws through little light on the 12th century town.

Before proceeding further there are two areas to clarify. The first is the geographical spread of the survey; which covers the current county of North Yorkshire and the historic counties of Durham, Northumberland, Westmoreland and Cumberland. While there is a bias towards the north-east this does to a large extent reflect the greater number of towns in the north-east as well as the greater amount of archaeological work carried out on them.

The second area of clarification is much less easy and comprises those settlements chosen as the subject of the study. The definition of a town is a complex problem and in seeking a straightforward solution I have decided to look only at those settlements which have evidence of official borough status, while acknowledging that there are unchartered settlements which had all the characteristics of an urban settlement; the settlements studied for this paper are set out in Table 1. Indeed there is a clear hierarchy of settlement in which chartered and unchartered towns may occur side by side. The hierarchy which emerges is one dominated by regional centres such as York, Durham, Newcastle and Carlisle followed by fully developed urban centres such as Hartlepool, Scarborough, Kendal and Morpeth. Beneath this tier there is a category of undeveloped centres which has two components, 'estate centres' and 'undeveloped' boroughs.

The 'estate centres' are major rural administrative centres, often the head of shires. These centres are often clearly of pre-Conquest origin and might acquire markets. It may even be possible that the initial attempts to establish urban centres after the Norman Conquest were based on these settlements. The majority of these settlements were not, however, located with the best access to the major riverine and coastal communication routes, and this hindered their development.

The 'undeveloped' boroughs may have been granted charters but they were never destined to prove an economic success and in some cases they vanished completely. While placed on communication routes these boroughs and their hinterland could not generate enough economic activity to ensure their success.

At the bottom of this particular hierarchy is the large planned village which is so much a phenomenon of northern England. These were substantive nucleated settlements designed to be the powerhouses of the economic development of the region, and in order to establish the context for the boroughs these need to be examined in a little more detail.

*Address: Tees Archaeology, Sir William Gray House, Clarence Road, Hartlepool TS24 8BT

Nucleated Rural Settlements of Northern England

The classic planned village of northern England comprises two rows of farmsteads laid out either side of a village green or broad street, as can be seen at Elwick, Hartlepool (Fig 17.3). To the rear of the two rows there might be a lane or path providing access to the fields. This settlement type has been extensively explored by Brian Roberts (e.g. Roberts 1990). The archaeological evidence suggests that this plan form post-dates the Norman Conquest; there is no archaeological evidence in the north of England to suggest that it significantly pre-dates the 12th century. Indeed there is little evidence for nucleated settlement in the north prior to the conquest. Perhaps only the estate centres would have constituted such nucleations, accounting for their consistent complexity of form.

There is therefore a clear possibility that the pattern of planned settlements was a product of the Norman Conquest as the politics and economy of the area were brought under Norman control and developed. This pattern of nucleated rural settlement seems to be in place by the mid-12th century and is clearly set out in the Boldon Book of 1183. It is against this measure of plan-form and settlement chronology that the urban settlements will be compared.

Borough Foundation: Chronology

If one accepts that the majority of planned rural settlements were in place by the mid 12th century, how does this compare to the process of borough foundation (where only a date range for borough status is known then the latest date has been used). Table 2 demonstrates that just under 20% of the boroughs of north-east England and just over 8% of those of the north-west had been created by 1150. Given that the new seigneurial powers were faced with the task of re-establishing the economy of the area after two centuries of internecine warfare, it is clear that they saw the creation of a sound rural infrastructure as being more important than the development of urban centres.

By the end of the 12th century greater advances had been made in borough creation as the rural infrastructure settled down and the economy began to develop. In the north-east 47.8% of all boroughs had now been established and in the north-west 24.9%. These figures compare very favourably with the national figure of 19.85% (Beresford and Finberg 1973). Indeed the much higher than average figure for the

north-east suggests a greater impetus to the process of borough foundation than seen elsewhere. This may reflect a rapid recovery and expansion of the economy from a low point a century earlier, and this recovery was continued into the first half of the 13th century when the north-west in particular seems to have seen the development of its economy on the back of the wool trade. There is a tailing off of the process in the latter half of the 13th century, but a slight renewal in the 14th. Given that this was the period of the Anglo-Scottish Wars which saw intense economic disruption in the north of England, these are brave moves, although in the case of Skinburness, Cumberland the wars provided a spate of activity as it functioned as a supply port for the English campaigns in Ireland and the North Sea (McNamee 1997). Indeed the Scottish Wars had a positive impact on a number of centres, stimulating economic activity in those towns used as supply bases. It is particularly interesting to note that the period of most intense Scottish activity (1300-25) saw three boroughs created within the region, although none was to prove the most successful of ventures.

Borough Foundation: Topographical Location

The topographical location of the boroughs was examined in respect to their position on communication routes, that is the coast, navigable reaches of a river, or on land based routes. Fig 17.1 and Table 1 demonstrate that 48 out of 58 are positioned to make best use of water routes; out of these, 36 are on rivers and 12 on the coast. Those positioned on rivers are often sited at bridging points giving access to markets on both sides of the river, generating tolls for use of the bridge and providing a defensive location against raiders using the rivers.

Of the 10 boroughs which rely on land-based routes, seven are in the south-eastern part of the region, indeed south of the River Tees. This must suggest that the local economy in this area had developed to such an extent that it was possible for these boroughs to develop as local centres of exchange rather than as foci of longer distance trade. The three inland boroughs in the north-west comprise Market Brough, sited on the Stainmore Pass, the major E-W route across the Pennines; Penrith, also sited on a major communication route; and Greystoke, whose existence was probably solely an unsuccessful product of the castle there.

Table 1: Medieval Boroughs of Northern England

Name & County	First Evidence of Borough	Relationship of Seigneurial centre to Borough	Seigneurial Centre	Plan Form	Topographic Location	Agrarian Character
1. Barnard Castle, Durham	1175[1]	Integrated	Barnard Castle[2]	Complex	River[2]	Back Lane
2. Bishop Auckland, Durham	c1243[1]	Axial	Bishop's Palace[2]	2-row[2]	River[2]	Long Tofts
3. Darlington, Durham	1183[1]	Adjacent	Bishop's Palace	Complex[2]	River[2]	
4. Durham	1130[1]	Integrated	Castle[2]	Complex[2]	River[2]	
5. Durham (Old Borough / Crossgate)	1229[1]		Suburb[2]	2-row[2]	River[2]	
6. Elvet, Durham	1188[1]		Suburb[2]	2-row[2]	River[2]	
7. Gateshead, Durham	1153[1]		–	2-row[2]	River[2]	
8. Hartlepool, Durham	c1162-85[1]		–	Grid[2]	Coast[2]	Excavated
9. St Giles, Durham	c1180[1]		Suburb[2]	2-row[2]	River[2]	
10. Stockton, Durham	1283[1]	Axial	Bishop's Manor	2-row[2]	River[2]	Village + Borough
11. Wearmouth, Durham	1180-86[1]		–	2-row?[2]	Coast[2]	
12. Alnmouth, Nberland	1147[1]		–	2-row[2]	Coast[2]	
13. Alnwick, Nberland	1157-85[1]	Adjacent	Castle[2]	Complex[2]	River[2]	Back Lane[2]
14. Bamburgh, Nberland	1169-70[1]	Remote	Castle[2]	2-row[2]	Inland[2]	
15. Berwick, Nberland	1119-24[1]	Remote	Castle[2]	Complex[2]	River[2]	
16. Corbridge, Nberland	1201[1]		–	Complex[2]	River[2]	
17. Felton, Nberland	1323[1]		–	2-row[?]	River[?]	Long Tofts
18. Harbottle, Nberland	1245[1]	Adjacent	Castle[2]	2-row[2]	River[2]	Long Tofts
19. Haydon Bridge, Nberland	1365[1]		–	2-row[2]	River[2]	Back Lane and Long Tofts
20. Hexham, Nberland	1547[1]		–	Complex[2]	River[2]	Back Lane[2]
21. Holy Island, Nberland	1396[1]	Remote	Castle[2]	Complex[2]	Coast[2]	
22. Mitford, Nberland	pre-1326[1]	Remote	Castle[2]	Unknown[2]	River[2]	
23. Morpeth, Nberland	1188-1239[1]	Remote	Castle[2]	Complex[2]	River[2]	Back Lane and Long Tofts[2]

Name & County	First Evidence of Borough	Relationship of Seigneurial centre to Borough	Seigneurial Centre	Plan Form	Topographic Location	Agrarian Character
24. Newbiggin on Sea, Nberland	1307[1]		–	2-row[2]	Coast[2]	
25. Newbrough, Nberland	c1320[1]		–	2-row[2]	Inland[2]	
26. Newburn, Nberland	1201[1]		–	2-row[2]	River[2]	
27. Newcastle upon Tyne, Nberland	1100-35[1]	Adjacent	Castle[2]	Complex[2]	River[2]	
28. Newton in Warkworth, Nberland	1249[1]		Suburb[2]	Unknown[2]	Coast[2]	
29. Norham, Nberland	1160-80[1]	Remote (Axial)	Castle[2]	2-row[2]	River[2]	Back Lane[2]
30. Rothbury, Nberland	1201[1]		–	2-row[2]	River[2]	Back Lane and Long Tofts[2]
31. Warenmouth, Nberland	1247[1]		–	Unknown[2]	Coast[2]	
32. Warkworth, Nberland	1249[1]	Axial	Castle[2]	2-row[2]	River[2]	Long Tofts
33. Bootham, YNR	1275[1]		Suburb[2]	Complex[2]	River[2]	
34. Helmsley, YNR	1186 - 1227[1]	Adjacent	Castle[2]	Complex[2]	Inland[2]	Back Lane[2]
35. Kirkby Moorside, YNR	1154-79[1]	Remote	Manorial Centre[2]	2-row[2] (complex)	Inland[2]	Back Lane[2]
36. New Malton, YNR	1154-79[1]	Adjacent	Castle[2]	Complex[2]	River[2]	Back Lane[2]
37.Northallerton, YNR	1298[1]	Remote	Manorial Centre[2]	2-row + 2-row[2]	Inland[2]	Back Lane[2]
38. Pickering, YNR	1100-34[1]	Adjacent	Castle[2]	Complex[2]	Inland[2]	Back Lane[2]
39. Richmond, YNR	1093-1136[1]	Integrated	Castle[2]	Complex[2]	River[2]	Open Fields
40. St Olave's Borough (York), YNR	1088-93[1]		Suburb[2]	Complex[2]	River[2]	
41. Scarborough, YNR	1155[1]	Axial	Castle[2]	Grid[2]	Coast[2]	
42. Skelton, YNR	1240[1]	Axial	Castle[2]	2-row[2] (complex)	Inland[2]	Excavated Evidence
43. Stokesley, YNR	1347[1]	Axial	Manorial[2]	2-row[2] (complex)	River[2]	Back Lane and Long Tofts[2]
44. Thirsk, YNR	1145[1]	Adjacent	Castle[2]	2-row[2] (complex)	River[2]	Back Lane[2]
45. Whitby, YNR	1128[1]		–	Unknown[2]	Coast[2]	
46. Yarm, YNR	1273[1]		–	2-row + 2-row[2]	River[2]	Property sizes on West St

Name & County	First Evidence of Borough	Relationship of Seigneurial centre to Borough	Seigneurial Centre	Plan Form	Topographic Location	Agrarian Character
47. Carlisle, Cm	1130[1]	Adjacent	Castle[2]	complex[2]	River[2]	
48. Cockermouth, Cm	1209 - 15[3]	Adjacent	Castle[2]	2-row[2] (complex)	River[2]	Back Lane, Long Tofts and Barns (Village + Borough)
49. Egremont, Cm	1202[1]	Axial	Castle[2]	2-row[2] (complex)	River[2]	Charter
50. Greystoke, Cm	1366[1]	?	Castle[2]	Unknown[2]	Inland[2]	
51. Keswick, Cm	1373[1]		?	2-row[2] (complex)	River[2] (lake))	Back Lane
52. Newton Arlosh (Kirkby Johannis), Cm	1305[1]		?	?	Coast[2]	Back Lane
53. Penrith, Cm	1222[3]	Axial	Manorial[3]	Complex[2]	Inland[2]	Back Lane
54. Skinburness, Cm	1301[1]		?	?	Coast[2]	
55. Wavermouth, Cm	1300[1]		?	Unknown[2]	Coast?[2]	
56. Appleby, Wm	1179[1]	Axial	Castle[2]	2-row[2] (complex)	River[2]	Back Lane
57. Kendal, Wm	1246[1]	Remote	Castle[2]	2-row[2] (complex)	River[2]	Barns
58. Market Brough, Wm	1196[1]		–	2-row[2]	Inland[2]	Back Lane

Footnote

1. Indicates derived from Beresford and Finberg 1973
2. Indicates derived from 1st Edition Ordnance Survey
3. Indicated derived from Winchester unpub

Table 2: Dates of Borough Foundation

Date	North East England		North West England		All of Northern England		England	
By 1150	9	19.6%	1	8.3%	10	17.2%	Upto 1200 96	19.8%
1150-1200	13	28.2%	2	16.7%	15	25.9%		
1201-1250	11	23.9%	4	33.4%	15	25.9%	135	27.8%
1251-1300	5	10.9%	1	8.3%	6	10.3%	126	25.9%
1301-1400	7	15.2%	4	33.4%	11	19%	95	19.5%
1401-1500	0		0		0		17	3.5%
1500-	1	2.2%	0		1	1.7%	17	3.5%
Total	46	100%	12	100%	58	100%	486	100%

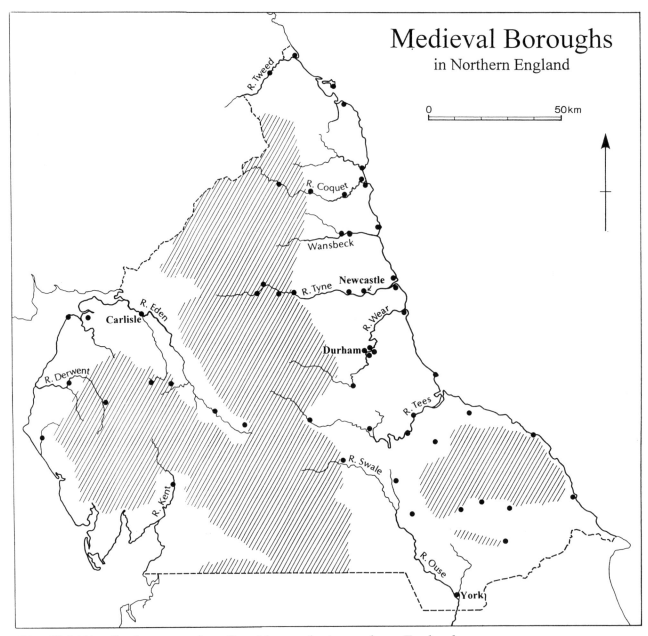

Fig. 17.1 Distribution map of medieval boroughs in northern England

Borough Foundation: Relationship to Castles and other Seigneurial Centres

The presence of a castle is often seen as being closely related to the development of boroughs (Lomas 1992, 163) and there is no doubt that where a castle and borough are juxtaposed there is an intimate and mutually beneficial relationship. It would, however, be wrong to associate these two settlement types too closely; even in the north of England with its troubled history, only 25 of 58 boroughs were located in the vicinity of pre-existing castles (Table 1). While this figure may at first appear surprising, closer

examination reveals that it echoes the national trend. Beresford (1988) has shown that on a national level 80% of towns founded between 1066-1100 were associated with castles and that this trend continued in the first quarter of the 12th century. Much the same trend is visible in the north with the relationship peaking in the first quarter of the 12th century and significantly a second peak occurring in the second quarter of the 13th century (Fig. 17.2).

These two peaks coincide with the aftermath of major political upheavals, the first the consolidation of Norman control of the region and the

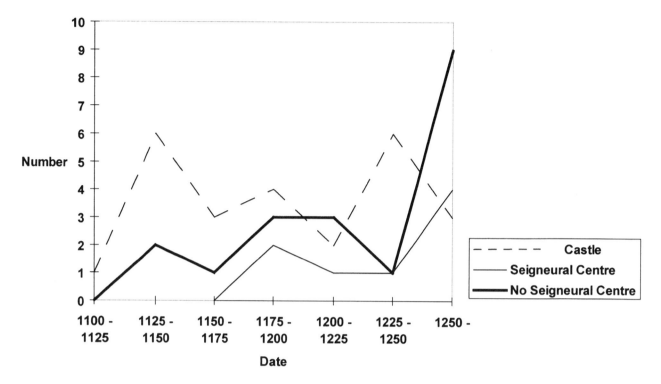

Fig. 17.2 Graph of chronological relationship between seigneurial centres and boroughs

major period of village establishment and the second coming hard on the heels of one of the most destructive periods of Anglo-Scottish relations.

Morphology of Boroughs

The following section will examine the plan form of the boroughs in more detail (Figs 17.3 and 17.4). The principal source for this exercise has been the 1st edition 6" Ordnance Survey maps dating from the mid 19th century. This raises obvious questions in treating these as the medieval plan of a settlement, but it is felt that useful conclusions can be drawn.

The following section of the paper would most obviously benefit from archaeological information and for this reason the Sites and Monuments Records of North Yorkshire, Cleveland, Durham, Northumberland and Tyne and Wear were consulted. The basic question was the same: has there been an archaeological excavation of a significant size which has thrown any light on the early development of a small town? In this case the exercise was not restricted to the chartered boroughs but was extended to all those settle-

ments which the relevant archaeologist regarded as an urban settlement.

The results of this survey were not unexpected but are none the less devastating. Apart from Hartlepool, no small town in the north-east of England has had work carried out in it which can begin to address problems of their early development. The ongoing work in Scarborough, North Yorks, is beginning to throw light on these questions, but has always been on a relatively small scale; there may be some help from possible future work in Berwick, but the only significant programme of work in addition to Hartlepool has been a single excavation in Yarm, Stockton-on-Tees (see below) and recent work in Darlington, Co Durham (Adams, Bosveld & Carne unpub), where excavations in the market place have identified a cemetery of a church preceding the present one and in a different location, and there is a promise of further development-led work adjacent to the market place.

Morphology of Boroughs: Plan Forms

We have already seen that the characteristic plan

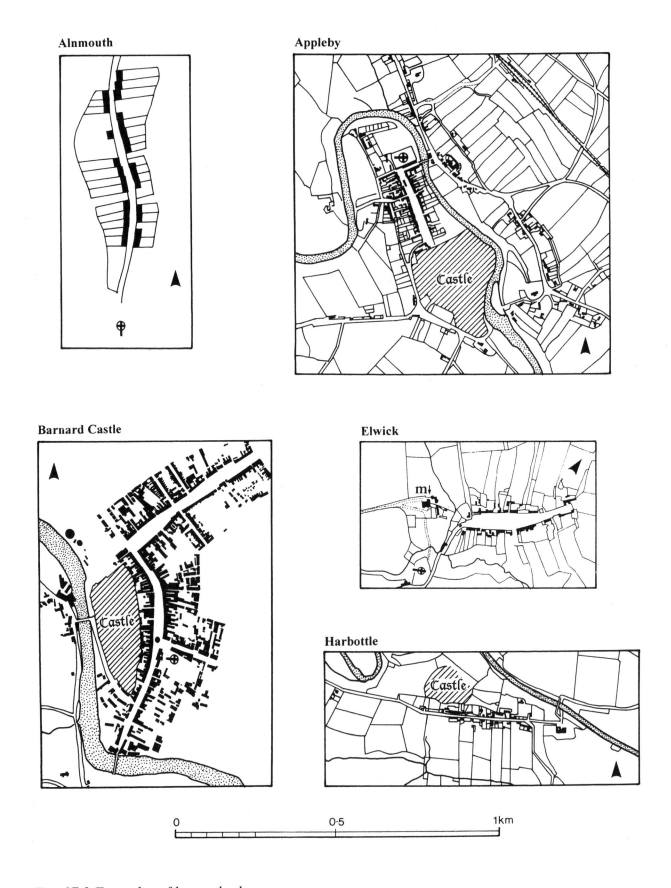

Fig. 17.3 Examples of borough plans

Hartlepool

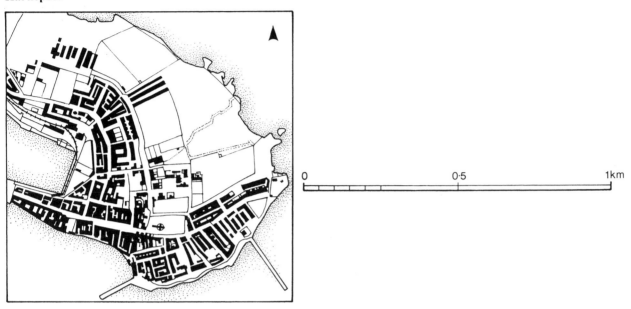

Helmsley

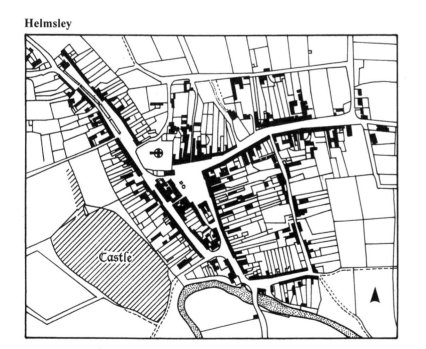

Yarm

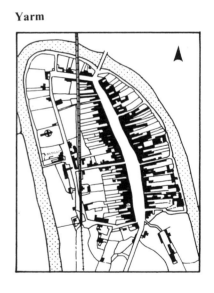

Fig. 17.4 Examples of borough plans

form of the rural settlement in the area comprised two rows of properties either side of a broad street or green. Do the towns echo this arrangement or is a completely different approach employed? Twenty of the 58 boroughs (35.1%) have a simple two-row plan, typified by Alnmouth, Northumberland (Fig 17.3), while a further ten use a more complex version of the two-row form, for example Yarm, Stockton-on-Tees (Fig 17.4), where there are essentially two settlements side by side. The two-row form is therefore the basis for over 50% of the boroughs of the area. There are four instances where the plan form is not known while in eighteen cases a complex pattern such as that seen at Helmsley, North Yorks (Fig 17.4) does not lend itself to easy classification. Nevertheless there are a number of instances in which a two-row element is a clear component of a more complex form. In only two cases, Hartlepool (Fig 17.4) and Scarborough, North Yorks., both major ports, is there a suggestion of the use of a grid system. The conclusion to be drawn from this information must surely be that there was no different concept for the form of a town and that, the two-row concept was not perceived as a purely rural solution, but rather as the base of any settlement planning exercise whether in town or country. It is also instructive to note that complexity of form is not a phenomenon restricted to urban settlements and it is quite clearly present in estate centres which have no ostensible urban function.

Morphology of Boroughs: Seigneurial Centres

In 32 of the boroughs a seigneurial centre is closely associated with the settlement. However a closer examination of the physical inter-relationship can reveal a clearer picture of the extent of the physical interaction between the two. In order to classify this relationship four categories have been used:

Axial – where the settlement is laid out with a clear axial relationship to the seigneurial centre, Warkworth, Northumberland and Appleby, Cumberland (Fig 17.3) are classic examples of this.

Integrated – the seigneurial centre is clearly an integral part of the settlement plan and may have had a direct influence on it, Barnard Castle, Durham (Fig 17.3) and Richmond, North Yorkshire are clear examples of this.

Adjacent – in this situation the seigneurial centre has a close physical relationship to the settlement but is not an integral component of the plan and the plan does not seem to have been influenced in any way by the seigneurial site. Helmsley (Fig 17.4) falls into this category.

Remote – the settlement and seigneurial site are some distance apart and clearly have no significant physical interaction except through a communication link.

Eight boroughs have an axial relationship with a seigneurial centre, while in three instances there is an integrated relationship. In eleven case, the two are adjacent to each other and in nine boroughs the seigneurial centre is at some distance.

The axial relationship is the most interesting of these and probably indicates a clear concept, perhaps implemented as a whole. This is in stark contrast to the most frequent relationship which is where the two settlement types are adjacent and where there appears to be no conceptual underpinning to the physical relationship of castle and settlement.

It is therefore interesting to reflect that while the castle and settlement might always have had a close political, social and economic relationship there are relatively few instances in which that relationship is clearly expressed in a physical sense.

Morphology of Boroughs: Relationship to Rural Settlements

In the last section of this paper the morphological relationship between boroughs and rural settlements will be examined more closely, particularly with a view to defining any rural elements within the borough.

Back Lanes

Roberts has discussed the role of the back lane (Roberts 1990, 111) and this element of the rural settlement plan, comprising the boundary and communication route between the private space of the toft and the public space of the fields, is significant. The presence of a back lane along a block of tofts may reasonably imply that the fields immediately beyond are being farmed at least partially from those tofts. The presence of a Back Lane within a borough plan may therefore suggest that a farming function has been incorporated into the setting up of the borough.

Twenty of the 58 boroughs have clear evidence of back lanes; therefore over 34% of the 'urban' settlements of the area were established with a clear provision being made for part of the settlement to sustain itself from agriculture.

The importance of a farming economy to the boroughs can also be demonstrated when one examines the juxtaposition of boroughs with pre-existing farming settlements. Lomas (1992, 164) has drawn particular attention to this and cites the occurrence of 'Bondgates' as at Darlington, Co. Durham and Helmsley, North Yorks as one indicator of this. Stockton is a further example: in this case a farming settlement, recorded in the Boldon Book of 1183, has a borough attached to it shortly afterwards. In the north-west Winchester (nd) has identified the rural settlement of Ureby as the precursor to Cockermouth and demonstrated the survival of the long tofts of this settlement in the eastern part of the town.

Property Sizes

In his 1990 article Brian Roberts described the toft structure seen in medieval villages and went on to suggest '…when such compartments are packed into tight spaces and the 'tofts' are more completely infilled with buildings they form the basis of urban layouts'. The intention of this section is almost the opposite of this statement, to look at properties within boroughs and to seek direct rural parallels in terms of size and function of the property. That is, to identify not differences but similarities.

The most obvious starting point is the size of the property/toft. The size of such properties varies from settlement to settlement, but recurring dimensions are a width of 4 perches and a length of 9-12 (Roberts 1990). If a perch is taken as 18 feet, (although in practice there were a number of different lengths for a perch), then this gives a metric width of c. 21m and a length of up to 64m. This would create a reasonable size of farmstead, allowing for dwelling and agricultural buildings as well as intense cultivation of the rear of the toft. Logically a commercial economy would not require properties of such a size even if industrial activity was being carried out in the property. However, should a farming element be required within the economy, then larger properties would be required.

In the case of Yarm one can see a clear application of this dichotomy. The western and earlier part of the settlement, containing the mid-12th century church, possesses properties which are much larger than those on the High Street. Excavation on Westgate in Yarm (Evans &

Heslop 1985) confirmed the 12th century date of these properties and demonstrated the existence of an earthfast timber building built parallel to the frontage. The High Street was certainly in existence by the 13th century and may date from the latter part of the 12th century, but the differentiation between the two components is clear and must reflect different economic circumstances at the time of the laying out of each.

The residual survival of two similarly large properties can be seen on the 19th century map of Helmsley. These lie at the eastern end of the north row of the significantly named 'Bondgate', confirming the agricultural association of that name in the boroughs. The deserted borough of Skelton, which had ceased to exist by the end of 14th century, has the earthwork remains of properties c25m wide, and small-scale excavation revealed a medieval longhouse, (Tees Archaeology SMR 1017).

Confirmation of an agricultural component to a late 11th/12th century borough has also come from Hartlepool, where excavations demonstrated a property with a frontage of 23.8m (just over 4 perches) and a length of c. 45m. This property was occupied by an earthfast timber building which was placed parallel to the frontage and may have been a long-house. To the rear of the property there was extensive evidence of cultivation. These factors all point to the occupants of this plot being more reliant on farming than commercial or industrial activity for their survival. Subsequently the property saw a level of industrial activity developing and finally the timber building was burnt down and the property was laid out anew, being occupied by three buildings gable end on to the street from the mid 13th century and throughout the rest of the medieval period (Daniels 1990).

Long Tofts

The relationship between property sizes and a farming economy can also be demonstrated through the length of the properties. There are a number of instances of rural settlements exhibiting exceptionally long tofts. These may be interpreted as a form of 'infield' agriculture, and they tend to occur in upland and more marginal areas where farming conditions are more difficult. It is therefore of particular interest to note the presence of long tofts at nine of the boroughs, six of these being in Northumberland. Again this must be a clear indication of a degree of reliance on agriculture to sustain the settlement.

Agricultural Buildings

In two instances in the north-west, Cockermouth and Kendal, Angus Winchester (nd) has drawn attention to the presence of barns at the rear of urban properties. These are a clear indication of a rural component to the urban economy, and it would be worthwhile examining other settlements for this phenomena.

Conclusion

This paper has attempted to throw a little more light on the small towns of the north of England and in particular to explore the nature of their economies. The evidence would seem to suggest that while these settlements have been placed in the optimum locations to take advantage of communication routes the reality of the economic situation was such that their originators saw the need for a substantial agricultural component to be incorporated into the settlements to provide any chance of survival. There is no clearer example of this than Richard de Lucy's charter to Egremont, Cumberland, dated 1197 –1202. It sets out a purely agricultural range of dues and customs, granting the burgesses free pannage and common pasture and requiring them to reap and plough for one day and one morning as service for their burgage. A second charter from Richard de Lucy also granted the burgesses rights to assart and till the land, as well as place their shielings on it. These are not the traditional expectations of an urban community! (Winchester nd)

The hypothesis set out above is clearly capable of further testing archaeologically, and the economic development of these boroughs is surely a clearer barometer of the regional and sub-regional economies than the picture given by the major regional centres. The point at which a transition to a more fully urban economy took place across the region is of particular interest, as indeed is the question of how many of the boroughs ever truly achieved this transition.

A recent publication came to the conclusion that 'small towns should be dealt with as rural landscapes rather than as dense urban settlements' (Schofield & Vince 1994). This paper confirms that conclusion, and must end with a plea for a co-ordinated programme of excavation and research into the small towns of the region.

Acknowledgements

I would like to thank Linda Smith (North Yorks SMR), Niall Hammond (Durham), Liz Williams (Northumberland), Dave Heslop (Tyne & Wear) and Mike McCarthy (Carlisle) for their assistance in producing this paper. The Northumberland, Cumbria and North Yorkshire Record Offices also provided valuable assistance in obtaining copies of the maps of the settlements. The illustrations were prepared by Peter Hart–Allison and Margaret Finch of Tees Archaeology.

Section 6: Post-Medieval

Chapter 18: An Archaeology of Medieval to Early Modern in Northern England

*Matthew H. Johnson**

Introduction

The aim of this paper is to provide an overview of some themes within late and post-medieval archaeology in northern England. It is purely personal in nature: it reflects the biases, prejudices, and current concerns of the author. Other views are possible and I hope that the comments in this paper will encourage debate, not shut it down or claim that alternatives are not legitimate. In this respect the most important word in the title is the indefinite article – *An* archaeology...

I am going to talk about the late medieval and early modern periods, ie *c.*1350-1750, and want to divide my observations into past, present and future. For the past, I want to make some comments on the development of historical archaeology over the last few decades and years; for the present, I want to comment on why the North is important, interesting, worthy of study; and for the future, where we go from here. The one key point running through the discussion of all these areas is that late and post-medieval archaeology has the ability to address wide-ranging and controversial research questions that are important enough to preoccupy scholars not just within archaeology, but in a range of disciplines dealing with the period – and that this *ability* is also a *responsibility*. We have a responsibility to explain why the minutiae of, for example, clay pipe forms and timber frame construction are relevant to a wider audience if we want to be taken seriously as a research discipline. It is often easy to forget, in the day-to-day hassles of professional life or the push and pull of conservation management and heritage interests, that the only ultimate justification of archaeological enquiry is to find out about human beings in the past.

Past

In recent decades, historical archaeology has moved beyond mere chronology and description of narrowly defined artefact classes. We now have more contact with history, and more assertiveness in the archaeology/history relationship. Archaeology is no longer the handmaiden of history. At the same time as historical archaeology has grown up, the discipline of history has changed; many (not all) historians have moved away from a narrow obsession with names, dates and places, towards social and economic life and a more sophisticated approach to the *longue durée*. In the last decade, many historians have explored still more exciting areas: culture, text, gender, mentality, power, discourse are the new buzzwords in the so-called 'New Cultural History' (Hunt 1989).

I want to pick out one development in historical thought that particularly affects us as archaeologists: a renewed interest in the small scale, the everyday, the unspoken (eg Isaac 1983; Underdown 1985). Historians have stressed that many of the great changes embedded in the transition between medieval and modern were played out, renegotiated, at the level of day-to-day household, family and parish life. Such everyday changes were often implicit, unspoken, but real and tangible for all that. To take one very small example, we can see the so-called 'rise of the individual' in changes in everyday cooking and eating habits: in the increased use of individual rather than communal plates and dishes, the provision of individualized place settings, and the provision of individual chairs rather than benches (Deetz 1977).

This means that if we want to understand the context of the houses we survey and the rubbish we dig up from the fifteenth to eighteenth centuries, we cannot simply talk about exclusively 'economic' history, but we also need to look in a much deeper and more complex way at habits, manners, everyday attitudes and mentalities. Indeed, the whole concept of an 'economic' realm, divorced from the religious, social, cultural and political, is not an idea that late medieval people would have recognized; spheres of life we often consider separate were embedded one in another.

Let me take a very simple artefact to illustrate the point: the humble clay pipe. Up till now, most studies of clay pipes have focused on production, and have concentrated on the definition of types, production centres and dates (Crossley 1990, 274-83). But I suggest the clay pipe is

*Address: Department of Archaeology, University of Durham, South Road, Durham DH1 3LE

much more than this. As an artefact of tobacco consumption, it is also positioned within a very complicated network of different social practices and relations. Such consumption of tobacco went along with alcohol consumption within taverns, alehouses and other public arenas at a variety of social and cultural levels. It was thus part of a set of culturally subversive relations (alehouses were notorious haunts of the masses, centres of illicit activity and social ferment: Clark 1983). At the same time, the clay pipe is an artefact of colonial contact; the tobacco trade with Virginia and elsewhere rose on the back of an emergent imperial structure. Finally, tobacco consumption was gendered; Queen Elizabeth enjoyed a pipe, it is said, but other mentions of female consumption are rare. Such a discussion of the meanings of clay pipes could be extended (Johnson 1996, 183-6), but enough has been said here to indicate that the humble clay pipe can be 'read' in a whole series of different ways, placed into a series of different contexts, and can be found to be as complex in its meanings as any historical document or literary text. (The complex iconography we find on pipes – coats of arms, scenes depicted in vernacular style – has, as far as I am aware, never been related to these different contexts; there is scope for a fascinating research project here.)

We need to rethink in a very fundamental way our attitudes not just to clay pipes, but to all aspects of the transition between the medieval and modern worlds.

Present

What role did the North play in this transition? In many traditional historical accounts, the North is portrayed as a backward part of the country, one of the 'dark corners of the land' in modern historical thought as much as it was in seventeenth-century Puritan thinking. Such a conception of 'the North-as-backward' can only be coherent if one believes in a national narrative of linear development in which each region of England undergoes the same changes sooner or later. In such narratives, the North is seen as 'lagging behind' the south in agricultural, industrial and cultural 'progress'. Such beliefs are all the more contagious when they are not overtly stated. It is a simple exercise to show that this assumption is implicit within many, if not most, archaeological studies of areas of northern England, although citation of specific examples would be misconstrued as personal attacks.

There seem to me to be four problems here.

The first is that this is very much a London or Southern centred view in which change originates in the south-east and diffuses outwards, like ripples from a pebble dropped in a pond. A good example of this kind of thinking, dubbed by Binford many years ago the 'aquatic theory of culture' (Binford 1962), is the so-called Vernacular Threshold. The Vernacular Threshold, apparently, started in the Home Counties and moved north and west, resulting, in Peter Smith's memorable phrase, in the dating of the Threshold in terms of the train time from London (Smith 1985, 686-9). The problem is even if such a model works it is not only an oversimplification, as the work of Stuart Wrathmell (1984) and others has shown, but also that it *describes* a process; it does not *explain* it. The 'growing influence of London' does not explain why that influence was growing, why a region or community was choosing to respond in the way it did, and so on.

The second problem is that the entire area of the North is lumped together as one region. It is difficult to see how an area which includes the Vale of York, Wensleydale, the Cumbrian mountains, the Solway plain, the western Cheviots and a host of other very different areas can be characterized as one region. Recent historical scholarship has suggested it might be better to see the North in the sixteenth and seventeenth centuries not as a distinctive area in its own right, but as just another series of cultural provinces, each with its own changing relationship with the capital. I make no judgements about which view is right; merely that the question should be asked rather than pre-judged.

The third problem is that the nation of 'England' is taken as an unproblematic unit. We should be cautious of assuming the self-evident nature of England at a time in the late twentieth century when ideas of English identity and nationalism are in a state of flux. There are many features of Border castles, for example, that are more readily explicable in terms of southern Scottish influence. It is difficult to argue that a Cumbrian or Northumbrian farmer had more in common, in terms of lifestyle and self-perception, with a Kentish yeoman than with his lowland Scots counterpart. If nothing else, the period 1400-1750 was the period during which the idea of the modern nation state was being actively created. We cannot take its modern form or existence for granted.

The fourth problem is that it is taken for granted that there is one direction in which things are changing. Some take 'economic progress', the inexorable rise of industry on the back of the profit motive, as inevitable; others take 'the feudal/capitalist transition' as given. This is not the place for a lengthy theoretical excursus on these ideas. In the view of many, however, including this writer, such grand narratives are well past their sell-by date.

Future

What does the archaeological record of the North have to offer that can attack these questions? There is not the space here to give a complete checklist – indeed such a list is potentially infinite, and by omission might imply that other lines of enquiry were not as potentially fruitful.

One thing the North has is an outstanding set of archaeological sites where profound and intimate studies of late medieval elite culture can be examined. I am referring to castles. As Philip Dixon has noted, we think that the standing fabrics of castles have been studied to death; as he has shown himself at Norham, Knaresborough and elsewhere (Dixon 1988; Dixon and Marshall 1994), this is far from the case. Detailed analysis of standing fabrics can throw up new and important reassessments of structures that have previously been thought of as 'well-known'. I would extend Dixon's observation to the landscape context of castles. We think we know everything there is to know about a Warkworth or a Bamburgh; however, I have yet to find a reference in the published literature to the ridge and furrow that can be seen clearly across the river to the west of Warkworth, or the ha-ha that faces the level ground to the south of the bailey.

If we do not understand the fabric and landscape context of castles as well as we might, I suggest the same is true of the people who inhabited these structures – the late medieval elites themselves. It is at best intellectually sloppy, and at worst highly ethnocentric, to write of Northern lords who were 'touchy about honour', 'excessively ambitious' or even 'the Gazza of the fifteenth century' (the last one admittedly from a recent English Heritage magazine). Such comments would be instantly condemned if applied to someone from another culture today; and the Middle Ages were certainly another culture. The changing behaviour of fifteenth- and sixteenth-century aristocracy and gentry is an interesting problem, explored most notably by Mervyn James (1986), and one way into the problem is to look at their view of themselves,

not just through what they wrote down on paper, but through their architecture, domestic and religious, and the tombs they fashioned for themselves. The castles of Alnwick and Raby, and the fittings listed in documents such as the Lumley Inventory (Hervey 1918), tell us far more about their view of their world than most dry historical narratives. Castles acted as stage settings at a variety of levels, from meals in the Great Hall, through the courtyard to their setting within the landscape. Within them, also, arose some of the patterns of behaviour that were critical to modernity: changing table manners, patterns of deference and patronage, privacy and access to the lord, and patterns of élite consumption (a theme I shall return to briefly below).

What we need are more intimate studies of the standing fabric of castles, combined with excavation and documentary research where necessary, but most importantly addressing the landscape context of castles and the way they fitted into the values and mentalities of their time. Such studies must necessarily be interdisciplinary rather than archaeological in the narrow sense of the term, drawing from sources we often regard as the domain of different specialisms – church architecture, tomb furnishings, documents. Dave Austin has discussed these themes in relation to Barnard Castle, and the publication of this site will provide an excellent case study.

What is true of castles applies equally to other classes of standing monument, particularly country houses and churches. The landscape context of country houses needs theoretical liberation. If architecture is a complex statement about the values and self-image of the owner, so is the garden and the estate landscape around it, as I have discussed elsewhere (Johnson 1996, 145-51). We need to rescue garden history from the dead hands of the traditional garden historians; as Tom Williamson has noted (1995), gardens are about power, not just about plants.

The second thing the North has is some wonderful vernacular architecture. As with castles, we risk the obvious aesthetic pleasures of these buildings blinding us to the question that strictly concerns us as archaeologists: what do these buildings tell us about the people who built them and lived in them? I want to question two assumptions here. First, much of the existing literature is dominated by endless discussions of tenure and agricultural prices. These are important factors in the building and rebuilding of houses, but it is important to remember that both prices and tenure were experienced subjectively. To clarify, the degree of security afforded by a particular tenurial arrangement, for example, was not purely objective; it depended on the tenants' view of their world.

Secondly, I would like to make a comment against the idea of 'innate conservatism' in relation to vernacular architecture. What goes for lords who were supposedly 'touchy about honour' goes for 'conservative and backward' peasants also. When ordinary people chose to build a house in traditional style, I suggest this was a conscious if implicit decision on their part. The yeomen of County Durham were consciously improving their farming practices in the seventeenth century (Hodgson 1979), and they would have been familiar with a number of examples of Classical architecture (Durham market place being surrounded with a wonderful loggia, based on Italian Renaissance models, that has now disappeared). Nevertheless they chose to build their own houses in a regional idiom. If we want to explain why they chose to do so, and move beyond platitudes of rural Northern conservatism, we need to refer to values of regionalism and local affiliation that I suggest were expressed by, and embedded in, forms of vernacular material culture – values that, again, are the subject of much recent debate among historians (eg Underdown 1985; Phythian-Adams 1993).

Values of regionalism underwent a profound transformation in the eighteenth century that similarly needs exploration. Georgian principles of architecture were not simply passively accepted: they were actively manipulated in smaller towns and villages across the North. Many Northern villages present an array of stone houses of different social levels with elements of Georgian design that have not been applied wholesale: the front door slightly off-centre, the room on one side of the central hall slightly larger than the other, and so on.

One way into the problem of vernacular style is to reassess the changing distinction between vernacular and polite architecture in the North. We possess a number of classes of building that sit astride this boundary, from small castles like Edlingham, to tower-houses, through to the vernacular tradition of bastles. How far were gentry houses simply imitative of those above them in the social order, and how far were they genuine renegotiations of a distinctive social class?

Not only does the North have some wonderful architecture, it also has some wonderful

agrarian landscapes. Again, the interpretation of these landscapes needs to be theorized. Brian Roberts's work on settlement morphology (Roberts and Wrathmell, this volume) has allowed him to develop a very complex and profound view of the different paths by which rural settlement evolved. I suggest that this is a necessary first step. There is a danger that the subtlety of Roberts's analysis may blind us to its nature and function as a descriptive classification. We need to move beyond description to explanation; to suggest why different areas developed in different ways, and to specify the cultural, social and economic forces behind these developments.

Archaeologists are in a uniquely suitable position to insist that change in the countryside was cultural and social as well as economic, and that the realms of the domestic, agrarian, political, social and economic were embedded one in another; we see similarities in physical form that run across areas covered by different historical specialisms. I have argued elsewhere that there is a very close link between domestic and agrarian reforms, and in particular between the socially middling ethic of improvement seen in vernacular houses and that seen in agrarian practices as a whole (Brooks and Barry 1994; Johnson 1996). Enclosure is the most well-known artefact of rural 'improvements'; just as we need to theorize vernacular style, so we need to rescue enclosure from the economic historians.

The last theme I want to pick out is that of artefact studies and so-called 'environmental archaeology', although there is nothing specifically 'Northern' about these comments. Hitherto, studies have concentrated on productive and marketing aspects of artefacts, most obviously in the fields of pottery, clay pipe and tile manufacture, but also in the interpretive stress on questions of subsistence and management practices in faunal and plant assemblages (eg Huntley and Stallibrass 1995). These are valuable areas to explore, but there are other exciting avenues. In particular, recent controversy over the nature of consumption and the domestic environment (Weatherill 1988; McKendrick et al 1982) offers archaeologists working in these areas a wonderful opportunity to address current historical debates. I suggest we need to see more studies along the lines of the London medieval volumes (eg Egan and Pritchard 1991) that put different classes of artefacts back on the table together. My earlier example of cooking was not entirely random; it should be evident how integrated archaeological studies of food consumption can proceed from an integrated study of all classes of artefact, faunal and plant remains, studies that, again, can address directly some of the very exciting issues raised by writers on consumption such as Norbert Elias, Mary Douglas and more recent writers.

Epilogue

All the way through this paper I have stressed that, in future, archaeology should address wide-ranging research questions. One area that has a reputation for not doing this is industrial archaeology. Industrial archaeologists have repeatedly stated that this reputation is undeserved, although it is striking that the relevance and importance of industrial archaeology both as a branch of archaeology as a whole, and in terms of its importance in understanding the historical periods it is concerned with, tends to be assumed rather than argued through. This is particularly true in the North, whose identity as a distinct region of England has traditionally been based on its industrial past; there is not space here to explore the validity or continuing usefulness of this tradition.

There is clearly an opportunity here; as with our lovely ruined castles and vernacular houses, we have some wonderful industrial landscapes in the North. Clearly, also, there is a perception that industrial archaeology is almost coterminous with the past, present and future of post-medieval concerns, to the extent that at the conference upon which this volume is based all three of the papers given after the 'medieval' section explicitly addressed themselves to 'industrial' questions to the exclusion of almost all others. Now Alfrey and Clark (1993) are beginning to address significant questions at Ironbridge Gorge, and I have read excellent unpublished papers by Garry Campion and Shane Gould, but I know of no parallel work in the North.

There are three issues here. First, industry was not the only or even the primary mode of life in the North before 1750, even if it was growing. It is unclear to me on *a priori* grounds why it should be so predominant in post-medieval studies. Secondly, the category 'industry' is one of those derived from modern economic life; can it really be applied to practices of extraction and manufacture within a pre-industrial society? My limited understanding of

economic thought before c1750 would suggest not (eg Tribe 1979; Webster 1975). Thirdly, in most archaeological discussions industrial processes are rarely placed even in their immediate cultural and social context, despite the growing volume of published scholarship that can provide that context. Studies by architectural and social historians are rarely referenced: for example Charles Webster's study of the links between technical advance and political reform (1975), Michel Foucault's studies of panoptic society (1979), and Thomas Markus's wonderful book on architecture and power (1993).

I am looking forward to being proved wrong in this assessment over the next few years; of being comprehensively refuted by the appearance of wide-ranging, exciting syntheses of industrial archaeology in the North that challenge existing historical arguments over the period, and link the development of industrial processes to their cultural and social context. Such studies will reveal how, exactly, our industrial archaeological colleagues are moving their area of the discipline forward in terms of new concepts and ideas; how they are addressing wide-ranging questions of critical importance to historical understanding; and why, precisely, industrial archaeology is so important to an understanding of the post-medieval period.

Chapter 19: Overview of the Industrial Period

S. M. Linsley*

Introduction

The conference out of which this volume arises was based on the premise that in the twenty years since the publication of *Archaeology in the North: Report of the Northern Archaeological Survey* (Clack and Gosling 1976), 'our knowledge of practically every aspect of northern archaeology' has been revolutionized. However, *Archaeology in the North* had exceedingly little to say about the post-medieval periods. Its chronological survey ended in the sixteenth century, and while it contained sections on 'Service Industries', 'Extractive Industries' and 'Agriculture', these sections were not devoted to the archaeology of those industries, but rather they were within the context of potential threats to the archaeological resource. Only in the article on 'Upper Redesdale' was there any reference to remains from the Industrial Revolution period. *Archaeology in the North*, therefore, offers no baseline against which to measure advances in the field of industrial archaeology, but it is certain that our understanding of the period of concern has not been revolutionized in the past twenty years. Indeed, we would not expect archaeological work to effect such a transformation in our understanding of the industrial revolution period, for the evidence deducible from the written information available for that period is unlikely to be completely overturned by archaeological investigation. Nonetheless there are numerous areas of potential understanding for the post-medieval periods where archaeological analysis alone can be, and has been, fruitful. That so few of these areas have been satisfactorily examined can be attributed to the widespread, but not universal, neglect or under-resourcing of studies in the archaeology of the post-medieval periods, particularly within academic circles; in this respect academia lags behind the more popular but still scholarly concerns with the post-medieval periods as witnessed, for example, by the revised editions of the Pevsner series of books on *The Buildings of England* (eg Pevsner 1985; Pevsner and Richmond 1992).

The importance in our history, and therefore in our archaeology, of the Industrial Revolution period with its emergence of an industrialized society should not need to be emphasized.

Understanding the variety of human behaviour and experience during so complex a period requires the fullest utilization of all forms of available material evidence, and presents analytical and intellectual challenges which have their parallels in all other fields of archaeology. Yet, given the low levels of academic interest and financial resources for the archaeological study of the industrial period, it does seem necessary, yet again, to make the case for its more serious consideration.

Twice in its history, the North of England has held a pivotal position in the affairs of Britain, and to a certain extent of Western Europe. The first period was in the seventh century AD, the so-called 'Golden Age of Northumbria', when the northern monastic institutions had a primary influence on the spiritual and cultural development of Western Europe. The second was during the Industrial Revolution. Faujas Saint Fond (1799), writing of Tyneside, noted:

> This beautiful river, the Tyne, is rendered highly interesting by the number and variety of the manufactures carried on upon its banks. On one hand are seen brick-fields, potteries, glasshouses, and chemical works... on the other, manufactories in iron, tin and every kind of metal: machines for making brass-wire, plate-metal, etc. This multitude of establishments, rising opposite to one another, diffuses everywhere so much activity and life... that the eye is agreeably astonished, and the soul feels a lively satisfaction in contemplating such a magnificent picture. Humanity rejoices to see so many useful men finding ease and happiness in a labour which contributes, at the same time, to the comforts and enjoyments of others: and, in the last resort, to the prosperity of the government, which watches over the safety of all.

Many of the activities noted by Saint Fond had much earlier beginnings in the north: iron manufacture at least from the twelfth century, lead-working at least from the thirteenth century, capitalistic glass manufacture from the early seventeenth century, and brick-making probably from the same century, although not all were centred on Tyneside. The industrial power of the north was to become greater still. As W E Gladstone, then Chancellor of the Exchequer and soon to be Prime Minister, remarked in Newcastle upon Tyne (1862):

*Address: Centre for Lifelong Learning, University of Newcastle upon Tyne, Newcastle upon Tyne NE1 7RU

I know not where to seek even in this busy country, a spot or a district in which we perceive so extraordinary and multifarious a combination of the various great branches of mining, manufacturing, trading and ship building industry, and I greatly doubt whether the like can be shown, not only within the limits of this land, but upon the whole surface of the globe.

As a politician it is just conceivable that Gladstone might have said the same thing in Glasgow or, with slight variations, in Birmingham. But certainly North England, and not just the Newcastle district, was alive with diverse but often interrelated industrial activities; indeed its influence in the economy of Great Britain may then have been at its high-water mark. By the middle of the nineteenth century, the North had more or less given railways to the world, it had the most important coal industry in Great Britain, it had been regarded as the seat of the nation's chemical and glass industries, its shipyards were breaking records with monotonous regularity, its lead and lead products industry was the greatest in the country, and Teesside was emerging as the most important iron-producing area in the United Kingdom. Whether Gladstone's remarks were justified or not, it cannot be doubted that the North exhibited an advanced industrial base by the beginning of the second half of the nineteenth century.

Although by the end of the nineteenth century the North was producing 40 million tons of coal per year, 40% of Britain's iron and almost 40% of the world's ships, some of its other industries, such as the lead industry, had entered terminal decline. In more recent years basic industries such as coal-mining and ship-building have also been greatly diminished in their importance. There has been, therefore, within the northern region, a daunting wealth of field evidence for industrialization, but the pace of de-industrialization, if that is indeed what we are witnessing, has presented archaeologists of that period with recording challenges which simply could not be met. The pace of technological, economic and social change has been bewildering, and shows no sign of slowing down.

Recording and analysis for the industrial period

It is neither desirable nor possible in this short paper to detail all the work of recording and analysis in the field of industrial archaeology in the north over recent years, but some successful work will be identified and, in outlining some gaps in our knowledge, some pointers to future work priorities may emerge.

The history of the railways of the north has probably received more attention than any other aspect of the post-medieval and industrial periods. Much of this has concentrated on the period after 1825, and has been mainly document-based. Of the earliest period of railway development, that of the horse-drawn wooden waggonways post-1605, two pieces of published work stand out. The first, by Lewis (1970), considers the development of the wooden waggonway with particular reference to north-east England; the second, by Bennett et al (1990), considers the waggonways within a smaller geographical area, essentially south of the Tyne, but emphasizing the economic, social and land-owning framework within which their development occurred. Although both pieces of work are extremely valuable, field evidence played little role in the analysis, except for the meticulous tracing of routes on the ground in the latter work. Consequently there are gaps in our knowledge which remain to be filled by fieldwork. We still know little, for example, about the extent of deployment of cuttings and embankments on the waggonways, or their forms of construction; likewise we know little of the acceptable gradients, with or against the load. Yet it is abundantly clear from the documentary record that these could be matters of acute concern to waggonway builders. Until this year we have had to rely solely on documentary evidence for details of waggonway track, but the chance discovery of a substantial section of wooden waggonway at Lambton, County Durham, excavated by John Nolan and others in March 1996 (Ayris 1998), has shown how deficient the documentary record has been. Since a similar find may not occur again in the north, the importance of this field evidence cannot be overstated.

Of the second form of mineral railway which appeared in the north, and preceded the locomotive-hauled public railway of the nineteenth century, little detailed work has been published, an exception being Mountford's work on the Bowes Railway (1976). A variety of prime movers were used in combination on these essentially rope-worked railways, including gravity, stationary engines, horses and locomotives. Such lines were common on the colliery railways of the north, particularly in County Durham, but they have not yet been adequately studied. Candidates for a thorough archival and archaeological study include the Hetton Colliery railway, the Rainton and Seaham (Londonderry) railway, the Stanhope and Tyne railway, and the Earl of Durham's railway. Archaeological studies on these lines could again elucidate railbed engineering, the limiting alignments and gradients for particular forms of inclined plane, and location determinants for stationary haulage engines.

The locomotive-hauled railway of the nineteenth and twentieth centuries, the third phase of railway development in the north, has received much attention, building on Tomlinson's definitive work on the North Eastern Railway (1914). Many published works have concentrated on particular lines or railway companies (Gard and Hartley 1969; Dean and Gard 1975; Hoole 1965; Sewell 1992), but there remains scope for a more comprehensive treatment of the railways of the region. Existing publications have rarely utilized fieldwork and archaeological evidence, and whilst the design of railway stations has received some attention, the development of lime depots, coal depots, signal and level crossing boxes, linesman's cabins, bridges and viaducts, remain little studied. Likewise the engineering involved in the conversion from rope-worked railway to locomotive-hauled railway, as on the Stanhope and Tyne railway, is as yet unstudied. Additionally, the topographic, social and economic factors determining the precise routes taken, and the influence of railways on collateral developments, merit greater attention than has so far been given. In the latter context, Rennison's unpublished PhD thesis (1987) demonstrates the influence of the railways in catalysing port and harbour development on the north-east coast, while two articles have described how the need to build up passenger traffic led railway companies to develop the seaside resorts of Saltburn on the east coast, and Silloth on the west (Harrison and Harrison 1980; Smith 1978). It has been argued that the development of the railway system in Britain was a factor in the dilution of regional identities, marking, for example, the beginning of the end of vernacular traditions in building, a suggestion which would surely merit fieldwork investigations into the geographic sphere of influence of the railways in this respect.

The railways of the north were born of the coal trade, and there has been no more important industry in the north's history than the coal industry. Consequently there are several good document-based histories of the industry, and of its labour relations. A recent study of Whickham from 1560 to 1765 (Levine and Wrightson 1990) has greatly enlarged our understanding of the industry in the post-medieval period; the west Cumbrian industry from 1600 to the 1980s has been usefully covered by Wood (1988); and the five-volume *History of the British Coal Industry* (Flynn 1984; Ashworth 1986; Church 1986; Supple 1987; Hatcher 1993) has provided much-needed context for the post-medieval and industrial periods.

It is curious, however, that the field evidence for this industry has been so under-studied that it is not yet possible to assess the quantity or quality of that evidence. For example, numerous sites throughout the region exhibit evidence of bell-pit mining, and although none, to my knowledge, have been properly surveyed and analysed, a superficial examination of some of these sites suggests considerable variation in the precise patterns of working. Bell-pit chronology and technology are poorly understood, and whilst evidence suggests that it was a form of mining practised in the earliest days of the coal industry, say in the twelfth century, it was also practised in the nineteenth and twentieth centuries, and probably every century in between. Although generally and understandably characterized as a 'primitive' form of extraction, the longevity of the technique suggests the possibility of more complex factors at work. It may be, for example, that bell-pit working for coal represented the most cost-effective and safe means of seasonal working in rural areas where demand was low, for the very technique implies no maintenance during a shut-down period, and no problems in restarting, neither of which factors would be true for single-shaft working. Only one bell pit, for ironstone, has been excavated in the north, and it failed to produce dating evidence. A planned programme of survey and selected excavation could yield much evidence on the parameters of bell-pit mining, evidence which simply does not exist in the documentary record. There are numerous other areas where only archaeological investigation can provide answers to many of the questions concerning coal mining in the post-medieval periods, and although ruthlessly efficient site clearance has followed the closure of most collieries on the main coalfields of the north, there is considerable scope for further work of the kind carried out by the Royal Commission at Cockfield in County Durham (unpublished), on the Scremerston and Stublick coal measures of

Northumberland, in the Lumley and Pontop areas of Durham, and on the coalfields of east and west Cumbria, particularly to illuminate phases of the industry before 1800. Of the social archaeology of the industry, some excellent work on the colliery cottage in the north-east has been carried out by Brown (1988; 1995).

Other extractive industries which have received considerable attention from historians, but less from archaeologists, are the non-ferrous metal mining and processing industries of the north, particularly the lead industry (Postlethwaite 1913; Raistrick and Jennings 1965; Raistrick 1977; Hunt 1970; Raistrick and Roberts 1984; Holland 1986; Donald 1989). Lead mining and processing has a long, probably continuous history in the region, at least from the thirteenth to the twentieth century, but our understanding of the earlier periods is weak. We are particularly ignorant about the precise modes of smelting in the medieval and early post-medieval periods, and whilst some bole-smelting sites have been tentatively identified, only excavation of such sites offers the potential of furthering that understanding. Although the documentary evidence for the industrial period is extensive, very considerable gaps in our knowledge remain. Cranstone (1992) has provided a useful introduction to a typology of hushes, and one hush has been surveyed by Fairbairn (nd), but some fundamental aspects of hushing, such as the frequency of the hushing cycle, remain a mystery. Progress is being made in surveying underground mine workings (eg Critchley 1984); the Killhope dressing floor has been excavated (Cranstone 1989a); smelt mills in North Yorkshire were surveyed, not always with satisfactory precision, by Clough (1980); and some work on carriers' ways and on the orefield turnpikes is under way (Blackburn 1992; Linsley 1992; Elliott nd, but *c* 1994; Fennell 1996). But archaeological work is needed on more dressing floors and smelt mills, on the chronology and the extent of chronological overlapping, on various technologies of washing and dressing, on the detailed variations and individual chronologies of smelt-mill flues, on the networks of carriers' ways, on the impact of the industry on land improvement to altitudes not seen since the first millennium BC, and so on.

The iron and steel industries of the north also have a long pedigree, with widespread and varied activities from medieval times to the present. The Cumbrian industry in the post-medieval period was well described by Fell (1908), and its

eighteenth-century industry has received considerable attention since then. However, the medieval and post-medieval history of the north-eastern industry has not been sufficiently researched to allow its significance to be assessed. Only the Wheelbirks blast furnace is known to have been worked in the north in the sixteenth century, and the Allensford blast furnace for part of the seventeenth century. Both of these Northumberland sites have been investigated (Linsley and Heatherington 1978; Linsley 1981-2), and since neither appears to have been very long-lived, the possibility of hitherto unidentified furnace sites of the same periods must be admitted. With the exception of Cumbrian sites such as Duddon and Newlands, known and promising blast furnace sites of the eighteenth century, such as Chester-le-Street, Bedlington (Evans 1992), and possibly Lee Hall near Bellingham, have received little archaeological investigation. The important wrought-iron and cementation-steel industries of the north-east's Derwent valley have fared somewhat better, with documentary and archaeological investigations at Derwentcote and Winlaton mill; regrettably these archaeological investigations were not able to be pursued to their logical conclusions (Cranstone 1989b; 1997; nd). The large-scale, sometimes integrated iron and steel works of the nineteenth century have received little archaeological investigation, and since site clearance has usually followed the demise of those works, opportunities to carry out such investigation are now extremely limited. However, the Ridsdale works in Northumberland, a scheduled ancient monument, should be available for such study at some time in the future. The Brinkburn ironworks site, also in Northumberland, would almost certainly repay close study, while the remains of the Tyne Iron Works at Lemington on Tyne are in ever more urgent need of survey and analysis.

To detail the work completed, in progress, or un-commenced, in all the other areas of concern in the industrial period is well beyond the scope of this paper, but it may be useful to note some of them briefly. The varied agricultural regimes of the region have been largely unstudied, only a little work having been done on farm buildings (Linsley 1985), and hardly any on field systems, except from documents (Butlin 1973; 1975; Brassley 1985). Water-powered industries such as milling and textiles have received scant attention. The clay products industries are in need of much further research; Davison (1986) has compiled an inventory of north-eastern brickworks, and Linsley (1977) reported on one such works. Most port and harbour developments have yet to be analysed from their field evidence; and so on. In contrast, two excavations have been carried out on lime-burning sites in recent years, and these have demonstrated a much greater longevity for the running-kiln type than was previously assumed. The first of these excavations was on a tidewater site near the Newcastle quayside, where quite unexpectedly a large bank of limekilns, dated to the fourteenth century, was exposed (Ellison *et al* 1993). The second excavation was of a single kiln at Beadnell on the Northumberland coast, where the surviving structures have been dated to *c* 1500 (Williams and Williams 1996). (In both cases, the similarities in construction to kilns of the eighteenth and nineteenth centuries were marked.) It seems unlikely that these were unique structures of their period, and an investigation of other tidewater and coastal sites might prove rewarding; no such early site has yet been located inland, a fact which begs many questions.

The above examples are probably sufficient to indicate that scope for future archaeological work in the industrial period is considerable, but the relatively low level of active involvement by archaeologists in this period makes an assessment of over-arching archaeological priorities somewhat superfluous. As appears to be the case in other fields of archaeology, the pressures of rescue recording, and of PPG 16, slant industrial archaeologists towards reactive rather than pro-active work.

Preservation of industrial monuments

With notable exceptions, public attitudes towards industrial preservation have not been enlightened, although the situation has undoubtedly improved over the past quarter-century. English Heritage has taken the eighteenth-century Derwentcote Forge in County Durham and the Stott Park Bobbin Mill in Cumbria into guardianship, and continues to grant-aid several other industrial monuments in the region. Some important ironworks sites in Cumbria have been preserved, although doubts remain over the fate of others. Durham County Council, with grant aid from other bodies, restored the 1727 waggonway bridge at Causey Arch, and has developed the Killhope lead mining, washing and dressing site as a museum of the lead industry. Northumberland County Council is responsible for the important West

Wylam railway bridge and the track alignments to it. In Northumberland the National Trust has, over the past few years, taken a keen interest in preserving industrial monuments within its care, particularly at Cragside, once the home of Sir W G Armstrong, the Tyneside inventor, engineer and industrialist; it has also assessed the historical significance of the nineteenth-century farmsteads under its ownership. In North Yorkshire, the National Trust has encouraged the excavation and recording of alum manufacturing sites within its ownership (see for example Marshall 1995). Several water-powered corn mills have been preserved throughout the region, particularly in Cumbria; a coal-mining museum has been established at Woodhorn in Northumberland; a number of railway preservation societies appear to be making steady progress; several limekilns are being actively preserved. Perhaps in no other field of archaeology is so much left to the admirable activities of voluntary preservation groups, as for example the care and maintenance of industrial monuments such as the water-pumping station at Ryhope, Tyne and Wear, or the Bowes Railway in the same county, both scheduled ancient monuments. Many other similarly encouraging examples could be cited, but until recently there has been no concerted attempt to secure a truly representative and coherent range of industrial monuments.

There have, of course, been many significant archaeological losses, often where failures of imagination, will or finance have seen opportunities for preservation lost. The town of Sunderland developed to serve the coal trade, of which ship-building was an obvious corollary. It is therefore regrettable that the Lambton and Hetton coal drops were unnecessarily replaced by landscaped areas. Similarly the towns of Hodbarrow and Consett and the Middlesbrough area of Teesside, all essentially products of the iron and steel industries, now show little of their former *raison d'être*. Many industrial monuments which presently survive by mere good fortune, or by benign neglect, steadily decay with the passage of time.

Some attitudes to the archaeology of the industrial periods

Although this 'Overview' is ostensibly about Northern England, it is appropriate, for proper context, to consider some national developments and some apparently widespread attitudes concerning industrial archaeology. In September

1995, English Heritage produced a most welcome policy statement (English Heritage 1995); it now sees industrial archaeology as an integral part of its conservation work. Thus the possibility of an unrepresentative surviving field archive of the industrial period, which seemed inevitable under the haphazard and often idiosyncratic enthusiasms which formerly informed the decisions of English Heritage on listing and scheduling, has at last been confronted. The 'Monuments Protection Programme' presently being undertaken by English Heritage, which is systematically treating the various industries of the country with a view to achieving statutory protection for sites of national interest, is a long overdue but welcome step in the right direction. However, the fate of sites of regional, but less than national, importance remains uncertain. On education, policy 7 notes: 'our commitment to education and training in industrial archaeology and conservation of the industrial heritage will be maintained through relevant publications and lectures by English Heritage staff' (*ibid*).

One might have wished for a stronger statement on education, but it is accepted that English Heritage's primary responsibility is the conservation of the built heritage; its involvement in education has to be relevant but subservient to that main task. But, in declaring the need for education in industrial archaeology, it is to be hoped that other agencies, notably the archaeology departments of the universities, will take up the gauntlet; of such a development, I have little reason to be sanguine. A brief and non-exhaustive survey of attitudes to the teaching of industrial archaeology in archaeology departments was carried out in 1995 (Green 1995). Responses to a simple questionnaire were received from 11 university departments in England, Wales and Scotland.

To the question *Does the department offer any modules on Industrial Archaeology?*, ten respondents answered in the negative. To the question *Are there any plans to offer Industrial Archaeology as an option at undergraduate or postgraduate level?*, ten respondents again answered in the negative. The reasons given for negative answers included some which were sympathetic but not particularly hopeful while present financial constraints persist:

> Industrial Archaeology is something we should offer... we have considered it... but we do not have the finance for the extra member of staff who would be necessary.
>
> Industrial Archaeology, along with post-

medieval archaeology, remain long-term goals for this department, but are not realizable at present – for purely financial, not academic reasons.

Were the financial situation in universities to ease up so that the prospect of offering additional areas of expertise became possible, I imagine we would very seriously look at this area of study. It has to be remembered, of course, that Industrial Archaeology is a *relatively* new phenomenon and undoubtedly this accounts for its sparse appearance in University Syllabuses.

Other respondents simply cited staffing problems:

> We have no plans to offer a separate course on this... because it is not a research field of an internal member of staff.
>
> No staff available I am afraid.

One respondent clearly indicated that his department gave Industrial Archaeology a low priority in the future planning of its courses:

> The reason... is probably that the Department does not rank Industrial Archaeology as highly as some other specialisations which are *either* taught in the department *or* may be the subject of future posts, if and when such posts become available.

Some respondents referred to the teaching of Industrial Archaeology within extra-mural departments, and it seems clear that, as far as British universities are concerned, this is where it will maintain its toehold for the foreseeable future. This is not a consoling situation.

I do not seek to criticize specifically the general tenor of the responses, but merely to observe the circular argument which emerges – we have no-one to teach Industrial Archaeology, therefore it cannot be taught, therefore there will be no-one to teach it in the future. This situation is exacerbated by the understandable wish of universities to appoint lecturers who will complement existing departmental strengths and interests.

There is, it would seem, a general prejudice against the teaching of Industrial Archaeology within many university archaeology departments. Some have suggested that such attitudes stem from a belief that the essence of archaeology lies in information gathered from fieldwork, mainly relating to buried remains, and perhaps particularly from excavation, although these techniques also play a part in Industrial Archaeology. In this context it is notable that the phrase 'not strictly archaeological' is used to describe certain features of the course in 'Landscape archaeology' at the University of Newcastle upon Tyne, presumably to denote the use of documents, maps, etc – an entirely laudable withering away of distinctions between 'history' – from documents, and 'archaeology' – from field evidence. Indeed, as Landscape Archaeology becomes more embedded in university courses, and should Industrial Archaeology ever be allowed in, the day may come when I will no longer see good archaeology graduates, in their first jobs after graduation, obliged to work in county record offices without having studied palaeography or the various forms of OS maps as part of their undergraduate studies, or out in the field unable to distinguish between sandstone, ironstone, limestone, concrete and breeze-block. The day might come when they will recognize that blocks of masonry with plug and feather holes *might* indicate Roman construction, but *could* indicate twentieth-century construction, and even that day when they can confidently describe and record more complete structures like the machinery of a watermill, or of a water-pumping engine with its cranks, con-rods, camshafts, and compound double-acting cylinders.

There is little evidence to suggest that this is happening, or is about to happen, and the consequent ongoing loss to the whole subject of archaeology therefore continues. If indeed there really is a prejudice against the academic subject of industrial archaeology, it may be so inbred as to pass unrecognized by its perpetrators. I offer by way of evidence a caption to a photograph of a limekiln, in a book by an eminent archaeologist (one who is broadly sympathetic to Industrial Archaeology), which simply reads 'Derelict industrial landscape'. Forbid that I should ever upset a colleague by describing Lindisfarne Priory as a 'Derelict medieval religious landscape'.

Acknowledgement
Much of this chapter first appeared as Linsley, S M, 2000, Industrial Archaeology in the North East of England, 1852-2000, in Cossons, N, (ed), *Perspectives on Industrial Archaeology*, Science Museum, London, 115-138. Permission to re-use that material here has been kindly granted by the Board of Trustees of the Science Museum

Conclusion

Robin Daniels[*]

The title of the 1996 conference, *Past, Present and Future: The Archaeology of the North of England* was intended to convey two impressions, the dynamic of archaeological research and a sense of identity of the north of England. Anthony Harding's *Introduction* to this volume has looked in some detail at the identity of the region and we are all working at a time when the importance of regional identity has been clearly realised as being relevant for the past as well as the future. It may therefore be hoped that one of the results of the conference will be the publication of further works which treat the archaeology of the north in its own right rather than as an area subordinate to and lagging behind our more southerly brethren.

It is of course unfortunate that the publication of this volume has been a little delayed and there have of course been many new developments over the intervening years. Nevertheless the importance of this volume lies in the way in which it brings together significant contributions from leading archaeologists, contributions which in their totality allow a view to be formed of the archaeology of northern England. As such it is hoped that the volume and its bibliography will act as a quarry for those examining various periods in the north and allow those specialising in particular areas to place their work in the context of other periods and trends. In the present climate of increasing period and thematic specialisation such a volume provides a valuable reference point.

As this volume was going to press tentative steps were being taken to move forward the development of 'research frameworks' for the north of England and it is hoped that this volume will provide a useful background to this process. In organising the conference and seeking to publish the papers a number of us had in mind the possibility of a programme of period and theme based conferences as a means of further exploring themes and ideas thrown up by Past, Present and Future. Such a process might well help in bringing together the increasingly diverse community of archaeologists in the north and provide a focus for identifying a shared way forward. It can only be hoped that in some way the 1996 conference and these papers have been a step in this direction.

*Address: Tees Archaeology, Sir William Gray House, Clarence Road, Hartlepool TS24 8BT

Bibilography

Aberg, F A (ed), 1978 *Medieval Moated Sites*, CBA Res Rep 17, London

Abramson, P, 1995 A late Iron Age settlement at Scotch Corner, North Yorkshire, *Durham Archaeol J* 11, 7-18

Abramson, P, 1996 Excavations along the Caythorpe gas pipeline, north Humberside in 1992, *Yorkshire Archaeol J* 152, 1-87

Adams, M, 1995a *Ingram and Upper Breamish Valley Landscape Porject: Interim Report 1995*, University of Durham, Unpublished Report

Adams, M, 1995b The Ingram and Upper Breamish Valley landscape project, *Univ Durham Newcastle Archaeol Rep* 18, 30-42

Adams, M, 1999 Beyond the Pale: some thoughts on the later prehistory of the Breamish valley, in Bevan 1999, 111-22

Adams, M, Carne, P and Bosveld, L, Unpublished *Darlington Market Place: Archaeological Excavations 1994*. Durham County Council SMR No 4000

Akerman, J Y, 1860 Report on researches in an Anglo-Saxon cemetery at Long Wittenham, Berkshire, in 1859, *Archaeologia* 38, 327-52

Alfrey, J and Clark, K, 1993 *Landscapes of Industry*, London

Allason-Jones, L, 1988 Small finds from turrets on Hadrian's Wall, in J C Coulston (ed) *Military Equipment and the Identity of Roman Soldiers*, Brit Archaeol Rep Int Ser 394, 197-233, Oxford

Allason-Jones, L, 1989 *Women in Roman Britain*, London

Allason-Jones, L, 1991 Roman and native interaction in Northumberland, in V A Maxfield and M J Dobson (eds), *Roman Frontier Studies 1989*, Exeter

Allason-Jones, L, 1995 'Sexing' small finds, in P Rush (ed), *Theoretical Roman Archaeology: Second Conference Proceedings*, 22-32, Aldershot

Allason-Jones, L, 1996 *Roman Jet in the Yorkshire Museum*, York

Allason-Jones, L and Bishop, M C, 1988 *Excavations at Roman Corbridge: The Hoard*, HMBC Monograph 7, London

Allason-Jones, L and Dungworth, D B, 1995 Metalworking on Hadrian's Wall, *Proceedings of the 16th Roman Frontier Studies Congress*

Allason-Jones, L and Jones, J M, 1994 Jet and other materials in Roman artefact studies, *Archaeol Aeliana*, 5 ser, 22, 265-72

Allason-Jones, L and Miket, R F, 1984 *Catalogue of Small Finds from South Shields Roman Fort*, Society of Antiquaries of Newcastle upon Tyne Monograph 2, Newcastle upon Tyne

Allison, E, 1988 *The Bird Bones from Hardendale Quarry, Shap, Cumbria*, Ancient Monuments Lab Rep 51/88, London

Anderson, J J, 1982 *Records of Early English Drama: Newcastle upon Tyne*, Toronto

Annable, R, 1987 *The Later Prehistory of Northern England*, Brit Archaeol Rep Brit Ser 160, Oxford

Armit, I, 1991 The Atlantic Scottish Iron Age: five levels of chronology, *Proc Soc Antiq Scot* 121, 181-214

Armit, I, 1999 Life after Hownam: the Iron Age in south-east Scotland, in Bevan 1999, 65-79

Armstrong, P, Tomlinson, D and Evans, D H, 1991 *Excavations at Lurk Lane Beverley, 1979-82*, Sheffield Excavation Rep 1, Sheffield

Arnold, C J, 1982 Stress as a stimulus for socio-economic change: Anglo-Saxon England in the seventh century, in C Renfrew and S Shennan (eds), *Ranking, Resource and Exchange – Aspects of the Archaeology of Early European Society*, 124-31, Cambridge

Arnold, T (ed), 1882 Historia Ecclesiae Dunhelmensis in *Symeonis Monachi Opera Omnia*, Rolls Series 75, vol 1

Ashmead, P and Wood, R H, 1974 Second report on the archaeological excavations at Kirkhead Cavern, *North-West Speleology* 2, 24-33

Ashworth, W, 1986 *The History of the British Coal Industry, Vol 5: 1946-1982*, Oxford

ASUD 2000 *Quarry Farm, Ingleby Barwick, Stockton-on-Tees: archaeological recording and evaluation*, Archaeological Services, University of Durham Report 660

Austen, P S, 1991 *Bewcastle and Old Penrith: A Roman Outpost Fort and a Frontier Vicus*, Cumberland Westmorland Antiq Archaeol Soc Res Ser 6, Kendal

Austin D, 1989 *The deserted medieval village of Thrislington, County Durham: excavations 1973-74*. Soc for Medieval Archaeol Monograph 12, Lincoln

Ayris, I M, Nolan, J and Durkin, A, 1998 The Archaeological Excavation of Wooden Waggonway Remains at Lambton D Pit, Sunderland, *Industrial Archaeol Rev* XX, 2-22

Bailey, R N, 1977 A cup-mount from Brougham, Cumbria, *Medieval Archaeol* 21, 176-80

Bailey, R N, 1980 *Viking Age Sculpture in Northern England*, London

Bailey, R N, 1991 Gold Plaque, Bamburgh, Northumberland, in L Webster and J Backhouse (eds), *The Making of England – Anglo-Saxon Art and Culture AD 600-900*, 58-59, London

Bailey, R N and Cramp, R J, 1988 *Corpus of Anglo-Saxon Stone Sculpture in England. Vol II: Cumberland, Westmorland and Lancashire North-of-the-Sands*, Oxford

Baillie, M, 1999 *Exodus To Arthur – Catastrophic Encounters with Comets*, London

Baldwin Brown, G, 1915 *The Arts in Early England: Saxon Art and Industry in the Pagan Period, Vols III and IV*, London

Barber, K E, 1981 *Peat Stratigraphy and Climatic Change: A Palaeoecological Test of the Theory of Cyclic Peat Bog Regeneration*, Rotterdam

Barber, K E, Chambers, F M, Maddy, D, Stoneman, R and Brew, J S, 1994 A sensitive high resolution record of late holocene climatic change from a raised bog in northern England, *The Holocene* 4, 198-205

Barclay, G, 1995 What's new in Scottish prehistory?, *Scottish Archaeol Rev* 9/10, 3-14

Barkle, R, 1998 Botcherby Nurseries, Carlisle, *Past* 29, 5

Barnatt, J, 1989 *Stone Circles of Britain*, Brit Archaeol Rep Brit Ser 215, Oxford

Barnett, S M, 2000 Luminescence dating of pottery from later prehistoric Britain, *Archaeometry* 42, 431-457

Barrett, J C, 1987 Contextual archaeology, *Antiquity* 61:233, 468-73

Barrett J, Bradley, R and Green, M, 1991 *Landscape, Monuments and Society: the Prehistory of Cranborne Chase*, Cambridge

Bartley, D D, Chambers, C and Harte-Jones, B, 1976 The vegetational history of parts of south and east Durham, *New Phytologist* 77, 437-68

Beckensall, S, 1988-9 The rock motifs, in Smith 1988-9, 39-44

Bennett, G, Clavering, E and Rounding, A, 1990 *A Fighting Trade – Rail Transport in Tyne Coal, 1600-1800*, Gateshead

Beresford, M W, 1988 *New Towns of the Middle Ages*, Bristol

Beresford, M W and Finberg, HPR, 1973 *English Medieval Boroughs: A Handlist*, Devon

Beresford, M W and Hurst, J G, 1971 *Deserted Medieval Villages*, London

Beresford, M W and St Joseph, J K S, 1979 *Medieval England: an Aerial Survey*, 2 ed, Cambridge

Bevan, B (ed), 1999 *Northern Exposure: interpretative devolution and the Iron Ages in Britain*, Leicester Archaeology Monograph 4, Leicester

Bewley, R H, 1986 Survey and excavation in the Solway Plain, Cumbria (1982-4), *Trans Cumberland Westmorland Antiq Archaeol Soc*, 2 ser, 86, 19-40

Bewley, R H, 1992 Excavations on two crop-mark sites in the Solway Plain, Cumbria. Ewanrigg settlement and Swarthy Hill 1986-1988, *Trans Cumberland Westmorland Antiq Archaeol Soc*, 2 ser, 92, 23-47

Bewley, R H, 1993 Survey and excavation at a cropmark enclosure, Plasketlands, Cumbria, *Trans Cumberland Westmorland Antiq Archaeol Soc* 93, 1-18

Bewley, R H, 1994 *Prehistoric and Romano-British Settlement in the Solway Plain, Cumbria*, Oxbow Monograph 36, Oxford

Bewley, R H, Longworth, I H, Browne, S, Huntley, J P and Varndell, G, 1992 Excavation of a Bronze Age Cemetery at Ewanrigg, Maryport, Cumbria, *Proc Prehist Soc* 58, 325-54

Bidwell, P T, 1991 Later Roman barracks in Britain, in *Roman Frontier Studies 1989, Proc 15th Int Congress of Roman Frontier Studies*, eds V A Maxfield and M J Dobson, 9-15, Exeter

Bidwell, P T, 1996 The exterior decoration of Roman buildings in Britain, in P Johnson (ed), *Architecture in Roman Britain*, CBA Res Rep 94, 19-29, York

Bidwell, P, (ed) 1999 *Hadrian's Wall 1989-1999.A summary of recent excavations and research*, Kendal

Bidwell, P T and Holbrook, N, 1989 *Hadrian's Wall Bridges*, English Heritage Archaeol Rep 9, London

Bidwell, P T and Snape, M E, 1996 *Evaluation of Archaeological Sites Threatened by River*

Erosion at Corbridge, Northumberland: Post-Excavation Assessment, Tyne and Wear Museums

Bidwell, P T and Speak, S, 1994 *Excavations at South Shields Roman Fort, Vol I*, Soc of Antiquaries of Newcastle upon Tyne Monograph 4, Newcastle upon Tyne

Biggins, J A, Biggins, J, Coxon, R and Watson, M 1997 Survey of the prehistoric settlement at Gardener's Houses Farm, Dinnington, *Durham Archaeol. J.* 13, 43-54

Biggins, J A and Taylor, D J A, 1999 A survey of the Roman fort and settlement at Birdoswald, Cumbria, *Britannia* 30, 91-110

Binford, L R, 1962 Archaeology as anthropology, *American Antiquity*, 28:2, 217-215

Birley, E and Charlton, J, 1934 Third report on excavations at Housesteads, *Archaeol Aeliana*, 4 ser, 11, 185-205

Birley, E, Charlton, J and Hedley, W P, 1932 Excavations at Housesteads 1931, *Archaeol Aeliana*, 4 ser, 9, 222-37

Birley, R, 1977 *Vindolanda: a Roman Frontier Post on Hadrian's Wall*, London

Bishop, M, 1997 *Land next to Tintagel House, Berwick-upon-Tweed*, unpublished

Bishop, M C and Dore, J N, 1989 *Corbridge: Excavations of the Roman Fort and Town 1947-80*, English Heritage Archaeol Rep 8, London

Blackburn, A, 1992 Life on the lead ways, in B Chambers (ed), *Men, Mines and Minerals of the North Pennines*, 58-70, Killhope

Blake, B, 1960 Excavations of native (Iron Age) sites in Cumberland, 1956-58, *Trans Cumberland Westmorland Antiq Archaeol Soc*, 2 ser, 59, 1-14

Bond, C J, 1987 Anglo-Saxon and Medieval defences, in J Schofield and R Leech (eds), *Urban Archaeology in Britain*, CBA Res Rep 61, 92-116

Bone, P, 1989 The development of Anglo-Saxon swords from the fifth to the eleventh century, in S C Hawkes (ed), *Weapons and Warfare in Anglo-Saxon England*, 63-70, Oxford

Bonney, M, 1990 *Lordship and the Urban community: Durham and its overlords 1250-1540*, Cambridge

Bonsall, C, 1981 The coastal factor in the Mesolithic settlement of north-west England, in B Gramsch (ed), *Mesolithikum in Europa*, 451-72, Potsdam

Bonsall, C (ed), 1989 *The Mesolithic in Europe*, Edinburgh

Bonsall, C, Sutherland, D, Tipping, R and Cherry, J, 1987 The Eskmeals Project 1981-1985: an interim report, *Northern Archaeol* 7, pt 1, 3-30

Bonsall, C, Sutherland, D, Tipping, R and Cherry, J, 1989 The Eskmeals Project: late Mesolithic settlement and environment in north-west England, in C Bonsall (ed), *The Mesolithic in Europe*, 17-25, Edinburgh

Bourne, H, 1736 *The History of Newcastle upon Tyne*, Newcastle upon Tyne

Bowden, M, 1996 Recent archaeological field-work in the Howgill Fells by the Royal Commission on the Historical Monuments of England, *Trans Cumberland Westmorland Antiq Archaeol Soc*, 2 ser, 96, 1-11

Bowden, M and Blood, K, forthcoming Reassessment of two late prehistoric sites: Maiden Castle and Greenber Edge

Bowden, M, Mackay, D A and Blood, N K, 1989 A new survey of Ingleborough hillfort, North Yorkshire, *Proc Prehist Soc* 55, 267-71

Bowden, M and McOmish, D, 1987 The required barrier, *Scottish Archaeol Rev* 4, 76-84

Bowman, A K, 1994 *Life and Letters on the Roman Frontier: Vindolanda and its People*, London

Bowman, A K and Thomas, J D, 1983 *Vindolanda: the Latin Writing Tablets*, Britannia Monograph 4, London

Bowman, A K and Thomas, J D, 1994 *The Vindolanda Writing-Tablets (Tabulae Vindolandensis II)*, London

Bradley, R, 1978 *The Prehistoric Settlement of Britain*, London

Bradley, R, 1990 *The Passage of Arms*, Cambridge

Bradley, R, 2000 *The Good Stones. A New Investigation of the Clava Cairns*, Edinburgh

Bradley, R and Edmonds, M, 1993 *Interpreting the Axe Trade*, Cambridge

Brand, J, 1789 *The History and Antiquities of the Town and County of the Town of Newcastle upon Tyne*, 2 vols, London

Branigan, K (ed), 1980 *Rome and the Brigantes*, Sheffield

Brassley, P, 1985 *The Agricultural Economy of Northumberland and Durham, 1640-1750*, New York and London

Braudel, F, 1988 *The Identity of France. Vol I: History and Environment*, London

Breeze, D J, 1984 Demand and supply on the northern frontier, in R Miket and C Burgess (eds), *Between and Beyond the Walls: Essays in the Prehistory and History of Northern*

Britain in Honour of George Jobey, 264-86, Edinburgh

Breeze, D J, 1986 The frontier in Britain 1977-83, in C Unz (ed), *Studien zu den Militargrenzen Roms III*, 21-34, Stuttgart

Breeze, D J, 1990 The impact of the Roman army on the native peoples of Northern Britain, in H Vetters and M Kandler, *Akten des 14. Internationalen Limeskongresses 1986 in Carnuntum*, 85-98, Vienna

Breeze, D J, 1991 The frontier in Britain 1984-89, in B Dobson and V A Maxfield, *Roman Frontier Studies 1989*, 35-43, Exeter

Breeze, D J, and Dobson, B, 1987 *Hadrian's Wall*, 3rd edition, London

Brooks, C and Barry, J (eds), 1994 *The Middling Sort of People: Culture, Society and Politics in England, 1550-1800*, Basingstoke

Brophy, K, 1999 The cursus monuments of Scotland, in A Barclay and J Harding (eds), *Pathways and Ceremonies. The Cursus Monuments of Britain and Ireland*, Oxford

Brown, H D, 1988 *The Colliery Cottage 1830-1915: The Great Northern Coalfield*, unpublished PhD thesis, Univ of Newcastle upon Tyne

Brown, H D, 1995 Colliery cottages 1830-1915: the Great Northern Coalfield, *Archaeol Aeliana*, 5 ser, 23, 291-305

Brown, L, 1991 Quernstones, in Cunliffe and Poole 1991, 390-7

Bryant, C and Jary, D (eds), 1996 *Anthony Giddens: Critical Assessments*, London, Routledge

Bullion, S, forthcoming The human bone, in R M Newman and R H Leech *Excavations at Dacre, Cumbria*

Burgess, C, 1968 *Bronze Age Metalwork in Northern England c. 1000-700 BC*, Newcastle

Burgess, C, 1984 The prehistoric settlement of Northumberland: a speculative survey, in R Miket and C Burgess (eds), *Between and Beyond the Walls*, 126-75, Edinburgh

Burgess, C, 1985 Population, climate and upland settlement, in Spratt and Burgess 1985, 195-230

Burgess, C, 1992 Discontinuity and dislocation in later prehistoric settlements: some evidence from Atlantic Europe, in C Mordant and A Richard (eds) *L'habitat et l'occupation du sol à l'Age du Bronze*, Paris

Burgess, C, 1995 Bronze Age settlements and domestic pottery in northern Britain: some suggestions, in I Kinnes and G Varndell (eds),

'Unbaked Urns of Rudely Shape': Essays on British and Irish Pottery for Ian Longworth, Oxbow Monograph 55, 145-58, Oxford

Burl, A, 1988 "Without sharp north". Alexander Thom and the great stone circles of Cumbria, in C Ruggles (ed), *Records in Stone*, Cambridge

Burnham, B, 2000 Roman Britain in 1999: I. Sites explored, 4. Northern counties, *Britannia* 31, 393

Butler, L A S and Morris, R K (eds), 1986 *The Anglo-Saxon church: essays on architecture, archaeology and history in honour of Dr H M Taylor*, CBA Res Rep 60, London

Butlin, R A, 1973 Field Systems of Northumberland and Durham, in Baker, A R H, and Butlin, R A (eds), *Studies of Field Systems in the British Isles*, 93-144, Cambridge

Butlin, R A, 1975 Rural change in Northumberland, 1600-1880, in A D M Philips and R J Turton (eds), *Environment, Man, and Economic Change*, 218-237, London

Buxton, K M and Howard-Davies, C L E, 2000 *Brigantia to Britannia: Excavations at Ribchester 1980 and 1989/90*

Cambridge, E, 1984 The early church in County Durham: a reassessment, *J Brit Archaeol Assoc* 137, 65-85

Cambridge, E and Williams, A, 1995 Hexham Abbey: A review of recent work and its implications, *Archaeol Aeliana*, 5 ser, 23, 51-138

Campbell, E, 1997 The Early Medieval vessel glass and The Dark Age ceramics, in P Hill (ed), *Whithorn & St Ninian – The Excavation of a Monastic Town 1984-91*, 297-322, Stroud

Cantor, L, 1982 *The English Medieval Landscape*, London

Carruthers, W, 1993 *Charred and Mineralised Plant Macrofossils from Paddock Hill, Octon, Thwing, Yorkshire*, Ancient Monuments Lab Rep 14/93, London

Caruana, I D, 1992 Carlisle: excavation of a section of the annexe ditch of the first Flavian fort, 1990, *Britannia* 23, 45-109

Caruana, I D, forthcoming *The Roman Forts at Carlisle: Excavations at Annetwell Street 1973-84*

Carver, M O H, 1979 Three Saxo-Norman Tenements in Durham City, *Meieval Archaeol* XXIII, 1-80

Carver, M O H, 1980 Early Medieval Durham: the Archaeological Evidence, in *Medieval Art and Architecture at Durham Cathedral*

Carver, M O H, 1993 *Arguments in Stone: Archaeological Research and the European Town in the First Millennium*, Oxbow Monograph 29, Oxford

Casey, P J, 1994 The end of fort garrisons on Hadrian's Wall: a hypothetical model, in F Vallet and M Kazanski (eds), *L'armie romaine et les barbares du IIIe au VIIe siècle*, 259-68, Paris

Casey, P J, Howard, P and Wright, J, 1995 *The Scotch Corner (Violet Grange Farm) geophysical research project*, Unpublished report, North Yorkshire County Council, Northallerton

Casey, P, Noel, M and Wright, J, 1992 The Roman Fort at Lanchester, Co Durham: a Geophyical Survey and Discussion of Garrisons, *Archaeol J* 149, 69-81

Cessford, C, 1998 Exogamous Marriages between Anglo-Saxons and Britons in Seventh Century Northern Britain, in D Griffiths (ed), *Anglo-Saxon Studies in Archaeology and History 9 (for 1996)*, 49-52, Oxford

Challis, A J and Harding, D, 1975 *Later Prehistory from the Trent to the Tyne*, Brit Archaeol Rep Brit Ser 20, Oxford

Chambers, B (ed), 1992 *Men, Mines and Minerals of the North Pennines*, Killhope

Chapman, J C and Mytum, H C (eds), 1983 *Settlement in North Britain 1000 BC-AD 1000: Papers Presented to George Jobey*, Brit Archaeol Rep Brit Ser 118, Oxford

Charles-Edwards, T, 1989 Early medieval kingships in the British Isles, in S Bassett (ed), *The Origins of Anglo-Saxon Kingdoms*, 28-39, Leicester

Charlesworth, D, 1978 Roman Carlisle, *Archaeol J* 135, 115-37

Charlton, D B and Day, J C, 1978 Excavation and field survey in Upper Redesdale, *Archaeol Aeliana*, 5 ser, 6, 61-86

Charlton, D B and Mitcheson, M, 1984 The Roman cemetery at Petty Knowes, Rochester, Northumberland, *Archaeol Aeliana*, 5 ser, 12, 1-31

Cherry, J and Cherry, P J, 1983 Prehistoric habitation sites in west Cumbria: Part I, the St Bees area and north to the Solway, *Trans Cumberland Westmorland Antiq Archaeol Soc*, 2 ser, 83, 1-14

Cherry, J and Cherry, P J, 1984 Prehistoric habitation sites in west Cumbria: Part II, the Nethertown and Seascale areas, *Trans Cumberland Westmorland Antiq Archaeol Soc*, 2 ser, 84, 1-17

Cherry, J and Cherry, P J, 1985 Prehistoric habitation sites in west Cumbria: Part III, the Drigg and Ravenglass areas, *Trans Cumberland Westmorland Antiq Archaeol Soc*, 2 ser, 85, 1-10

Cherry, J and Cherry P J, 1986 Prehistoric habitation sites in west Cumbria: Part IV, the Eskmeals area, *Trans Cumberland Westmorland Antiq Archaeol Soc*, 2 ser, 86, 1-17

Cherry, J and Cherry, P J, 1987a Prehistoric habitation sites in west Cumbria: Part V, Eskmeals to Haverigg, *Trans Cumberland Westmorland Antiq Archaeol Soc*, 2 ser, 87, 1-10

Cherry, J and Cherry, P J, 1987b *Prehistoric Habitation Sites on the Limestone Uplands of Eastern Cumbria*, Cumberland Westmorland Antiq Archaeol Soc Res Ser 2, Kendal

Cherry, J and Cherry, P J, 2000 A late Mesolithic assemblage from |Levens Park, *Trans Cumberland Westmorland Antiq Archaeol Soc*, 2 ser, 100, 25-32

Cherry, P, 1998 Prehistoric habitation sites at Grassington, North Yorkshire, *Yorkshire Archaeol J* 70, 1-23

Cherry, P and Cherry, J, 1996 Coastline and upland in the Cumbrian Neolithic, *Northern Archaeol* 13/14, 17-33

Church, R, 1986 *The History of the British Coal Industry. Vol 3: 1830-1913*, Oxford

Clack, P A G and Gosling, P F, 1976 *Archaeology in the North: Report of the Northern Archaeological Survey*, Durham

Claris, P and Quartermaine, J, 1989 The Neolithic quarries and axe factory sites of Great Langdale and Scafell Pike: A new field survey, *Proc Prehist Soc* 55, 1-25

Clark, J G D, 1972 *Star Carr: A Case Study in Bio-Archaeology*, London

Clark, P, 1983 *The English Alehouse: A Social History, 1200-1830*, Harlow

Clark, P and Slack, P (eds), 1972 *Crisis and order in English towns, 1500-1700*, London

Clarke, D L, 1976 Mesolithic Europe: the economic basis, in G d G Sieveking, I H Longworth and K E Wilson (eds), *Problems in Economic and Social Anthropology*, 449-82, London

Cleary, A S E, 1989 *The Ending of Roman Britain*, London

Cleary, A S E, 1993 Roman Britain in 1992: I. Sites explored, England, *Britannia* 24, 284-309

Clogg, P and Ferrell, G, 1990-1 Geochemical survey in Northumberland, *Northern Archaeol* 11, 43-50

Clough, R T, 1980 *The Lead Smelting Mills of the Yorkshire Dales and Northern Pennines*, Keighley

Coggins, D, 1986 *Upper Teesdale – The Archaeology of a North Pennine Valley*, Brit Archaeol Rep Brit Ser 150, Oxford

Coggins, D and Fairless, K J, 1997 Ritual succession? Excavations at the multi-period site of Middle Hurth, Upper Teesdale, Co Durham, *Durham Archaeol J* 13, 1-19

Coggins, D and Fairless, K J, 1983 Bracken Rigg: a Bronze Age settlement site in Upper Teesdale, *Durham Archaeol J* 1, 5-22

Coggins, D and Fairless, K J, 1995 An early settlement site at Bleabeck Washfold, Upper Teesdale, *Durham Archaeol J* 11, 1-5

Coggins, D, Fairless, K and Batey, C, 1983 Simy Folds: an early medieval settlement site in Upper Teesdale, *Medieval Archaeol.* 27, 1-26

Coggins, D and Gidney, L J, 1988 A late prehistoric site at Dubby Sike, Upper Teesdale, Co Durham, *Durham Archaeol J* 4, 1-12

Coggins, D, Laurie, T and Young, R, 1989 The late Upper Palaeolithic and Mesolithic of the north Pennine dales in the light of recent fieldwork, in Bonsall 1989, 164-74

Colgrave, B and Mynors, R A B (eds), 1969 *Bede's Ecclesiastical History of the English People*, Oxford

Collingwood, R, 1938 The hill fort on Carrock Fell, *Trans Cumberland Westmorland Antiq Archaeol Soc* 2 ser 38, 32-41

Collingwood, W G, 1908 Report on an exploration of the Romano-British settlement at Ewe Close, Crosby Ravensworth, *Trans Cumberland Westmorland Antiq Archaeol Soc*, 2 ser, 8, 355-68

Conzen, M R G, 1960 *Alnwick, Northumberland: A Study in Town-Plan Analysis*, Institute of British Geographers Publication 27, London

Cook, A M, 1981 *The Anglo-Saxon Cemetery at Fonaby, Lincolnshire*, Occ Papers in Lincolnshire History and Archaeology 6, Sleaford

Corder, P, 1928 *The Roman Pottery at Crambeck, Castle Howard*, Roman Malton and District Report No 1, York

Corfe, T, 1995 The Medieval Topography of Hexham, *Hexham Historian* 5 (September), 22-32

Cotton, J, Hale, D and Rutherford, M, 2001 Plant Microfossil and Pollen Assessment and Analysis, in R E Young *Excavations within Berwick-upon-Tweed, 1998-1999*, Tyne and Wear Museums/Northumbrian Water Limited, 73-87

Coulston, J C, 1985 Roman archery equipment, in M C Bishop (ed), *The Production and Distribution of Roman Military Equipment. Proceedings of the Second Roman Military Equipment Research Seminar*, Brit Archaeol Rep Int Ser 275, 220-366, Oxford

Coulston, J C (ed), 1988 *Military Equipment and the Identity of Roman Soldiers*, Brit Archaeol Rep Int Ser 394, Oxford

Council for British Archaeology, 1993 *Urban Themes: AD 1000-1600*, Report of a CBA Working Party, York

Cowell, R, 2000 The Neolithic and Bronze Age in the lowlands of north west England, in *Northern Pasts. Interpretations of the Later Prehistory of Northern England and Southern Scotland*, Brit Archaeol Rep Brit Ser 302, Oxford

Cowell R and Innes, J, 1994 *The Wetlands of Merseyside*, Lancaster

Cramp, R J, 1974 Anglo-Saxon Monasteries of the North, *Scot Archaeol Forum* 5, 104-24

Cramp, R J, 1976 Monastic sites, in D M Wilson (ed), *The Archaeology of Anglo-Saxon England*, 201-52, London

Cramp, R J, 1983 Anglo-Saxon settlement, in J C Chapman and H C Mytum (eds), *Settlement in North Britain 1000 BC-AD 1000*, Brit Archaeol Rep Brit Ser 118, 263-97, Oxford

Cramp, R J, 1984 *Corpus of Anglo-Saxon Stone Sculpture in England. Vol I: County Durham and Northumberland*, Oxford

Cramp, R J, 1988a Northumbria: the archaeological evidence, in S T Driscoll and M R Nieke (eds), *Power and Politics in Early Medieval Britain and Ireland*, 69-78, Edinburgh

Cramp, R J, 1988b Decorated moulds, in R Daniels The Anglo-Saxon monastery at Church Close, Hartlepool, Cleveland, *Archaeol J* 145, 187-90

Cramp, R J, 1994 Monkwearmouth and Jarrow in their continental context, in K Painter (ed) *'Churches built in Ancient Times': Recent Studies in Early Christian Archaeology*, 279-94. Soc Antiq London Occas Paper 16

Cramp, R J, 1995a The making of Oswald's Northumbria, in C Stancliffe and E Cambridge (eds), *Oswald: Northumbrian King to European Saint*, 17-32, Stamford

Cramp, R J, 1995b *Whithorn and the Northumbrian Expansion Westwards*, Third Whithorn Lecture, 17th September 1994, Stranraer

Cramp, R J, in prep a *Excavations at Jarrow*

Cramp, R J, in prep b *Excavations at Monkwearmouth*

Cramp, R J, in prep c *Excavations at the Hirsel, Coldstream*

Cranstone, D, 1989a The archaeology of washing floors: problems, potentials, and priorities, *Industrial Archaeol Rev* 12 (1), 40-9

Cranstone, D, 1989b *Derwentcote Forge and Furnace: The History*, unpublished dissertation, Dept of Continuing Education, Univ of Newcastle upon Tyne

Cranstone, D, 1992 To hush or not to hush: where, when, and how, in B Chambers (ed), *Men, Mines and Minerals of the North Pennines*, 41-8, Killhope

Cranstone, D, 1997 *Derwentcote Steel Furnace: An Industrial Monument in County Durham*, Lancaster

Cranstone, D, nd *Report on Excavations at Winlaton Mill*, unpublished

Critchley, M F, 1984 The Nenthead mines, *Bull Peak District Mines Hist Soc*, Matlock Bath

Crone, B A, 1993 Crannogs and chronologies, *Proc Soc Antiq Scot* 123, 245-54

Crossley, D, 1990 *Post-Medieval Archaeology in Britain*, Leicester

Crow, J G, 1989 *Housesteads Roman Fort*, London

Crow, J G, 1991a A review of current research on the turrets and curtain of Hadrian's Wall, *Britannia* 22, 51-63

Crow, J G, 1991b Construction and reconstruction of Hadrian's Wall, in B Dobson and V A Maxfield (eds), *Roman Frontier Studies 1989*, 44-7, Exeter

Crow, J G, 1994 High Rochester, survey and excavation 1993, *Archaeol Rep 1993, Universities of Durham and Newcastle upon Tyne* 17, 31-7

Crow, J G, 1995 *Housesteads*, London

Crow, J G, 2000 Harbottle Castle, *Archaeology in Northumberland 1999-2000*, Morpeth

Crow, J G, forthcoming *Excavations on Hadrian's Wall from Steel Rigg to Housesteads*

Crow, J G and Jackson, M, 1997 The excavation of Hadrian's Wall at Sewingshields and the discovery of a long cist burial, *Archaeol Aeliana*, 5 ser, 25, 61-69

Cunliffe, B W, 1974 *Iron Age Communities in Britain*, London

Cunliffe, B W and Poole, C, 1991 *Danebury: an Iron Age Hillfort in Hampshire. The Excavations 1979-88*, CBA Res Rep 73, York

Curle, A O, 1923 *The Treasure of Traprain: A Scottish Hoard of Roman Silver Plate*, Glasgow

Daniels, C M, 1979 Fact and theory on Hadrian's Wall, *Britannia* 10, 357-64

Daniels, C M, 1980 Excavations at Wallsend and the fourth century barracks on Hadrian's Wall, in W S Hanson and L Keppie (eds), *Roman Frontier Studies 1979*, Brit Archaeol Rep 71, 173-93, Oxford

Daniels, C M, 1989 *The Eleventh Pilgrimage of Hadrian's Wall*, Newcastle upon Tyne

Daniels, C M and Rushworth, A, forthcoming *Excavation and Survey at Housesteads Roman Fort*

Daniels, R, 1986 The excavation of the church of the Franciscans, Hartlepool, Cleveland, *Archaeol J* 143, 260-304

Daniels, R, 1988 The Anglo-Saxon monastery at Church Close, Hartlepool, Cleveland, *Archaeol J* 145, 158-210

Daniels, R, 1990 The development of medieval Hartlepool: excavations at Church Close, 1984-85, *Archaeol J* 147, 337-410

Daniels, R, 1991 Medieval Hartlepool: Evidence of and from the Waterfront, in G L Good, R H Jones and M W Ponsford (eds), *Waterfront Archaeology: Proceedings of the third International conference, Bristol*, CBA Research Report 74, 43-50, Oxford

Darbishire, R D, 1873 Note on discoveries in Ehenside Tarn, *Archaeologia* 44, 273-92

Darby, H C (ed), 1973 *A New Historical Geography of England*, Cambridge

Darby, H C, 1986 *Domesday England*, Cambridge

Dark, K R, 2000 The Late Roman Transition in the North: a discussion, in T Wilmott and P Wilson (eds), *The Late Roman Transition in the North*, Brit Archaeol Rep Brit Ser 299, 81-88, Oxford

Dark, S P, 1996 Palaeoecological evidence for landscape continuity and change in Britain ca AD 400-800, in K R Dark (ed), *External Contacts and the Economy of Late Roman and Post-Roman Britain*, 23-51, Woodbridge

Davies, J, 1983 The Mesolithic sites of Northumberland, *Northern Archaeol* 4, pt 11, 18-24

Davis, N (ed), 1971-6 *Paston Letters and Papers of the Fifteenth Century*, Oxford

Davis, S J M and Bullock, A, 1995 The Animal and Fish Bones in R Fraser, C Jamfrey, and J Vaughan, Excavation on the Site of the Mansion House, Newcastle, 1990, *Archaeol Aeliana*, 5 ser, 23, 191-97

Davison, P J, 1986 *Brickworks of the North East*, Gateshead

Day, S P, 1993 Preliminary results of high resolution palaeoecological analyses at Star Carr, Yorkshire, *Cambridge Archaeol J* 3, 129-40

Day, S P and Mellars, P A, 1994 'Absolute' dating of Mesolithic human activity at Star Carr, Yorkshire: new palaeoecological studies and identification of the 9600 BP radiocarbon 'plateau', *Proc Prehist Soc* 60, 417-22

Dean, S C and Gard, R M, 1975 *The Stockton and Darlington Railway*, Newcastle upon Tyne

Deetz, J, 1977 *In Small Things Forgotten*, New York

Dennison, E P, 1998 Power to the people? The myth of the medieval burgh community, in S Foster, A Macinnes and R MacInnes, *Scottish Power Centres from the Early Middle Ages to the Twentieth Century*, 79-99, Glasgow

Dickinson, S, forthcoming The early medieval farmstead at Bryant's Gill, Kentmere

Dickinson, T M, 1982 Fowler's Type G penannular brooches reconsidered, *Medieval Archaeol* 26, 41-68

Dixon, P, 1988 The donjon of Knaresborough; the castle as theatre, *Chateau Gaillard* 14, 121-40

Dixon, P and Marshall, P, 1994 The great tower in the 12th century: the keep at Norham, *Archaeol J* 150, 410-22

Dobney, K M, Jaques, S D and Irving, B G, 1997 *Of Butchers and Breeds: Report on vertebrate remains from various sites in the City of Lincoln*, Lincoln Archaeological Studies 5

Dobson, B and Maxfield, V A, (eds) 1991 *Roman Frontier Studies 1989*, Exeter

Dobson, R B (ed), 1984 *The Church, Politics and Patronage In the Fifteenth Century*, Gloucester and New York

Dodgson, R A and Butlin, R A (eds), 1978 *An Historical Geography of England and Wales*, London

Donald, M B, 1989 *Elizabethan Copper: The History of the Company of Miners Royal, 1568-1605*, Whitehaven

Dore, J N and Allason-Jones, L, forthcoming Excavation report on Halton Chesters, *Archaeol Aeliana*

Doyle, A C, 1902 *The Professor Challenger Stories*, London

Driel Murray, C van (ed), 1989 *Roman Military Equipment: The Sources of Evidence. Proceedings of the 5th Roman Military Equipment Conference*, Brit Archaeol Rep Int Ser 476, 255-79, Oxford

Driel Murray, C van, 1990 New light on old tents, *J Roman Milit Equip Stud* 1, 109-37

Driscoll, S T and Yeoman, P A, 1997 *Excavations within Edinburgh Castle in 1988-91*, Soc Antiqs Scot Monograph 12, Edinburgh

Dumayne, L, 1995 Human impact on vegetation in northern Cumbria since the Bronze Age: relating palynological and archaeological evidence, *Trans Cumberland Westmorland Antiq Archaeol Soc*, 2 ser, 95, 23-33

Dumayne, L and Barber, K E, 1994 The impact of the Romans on the environment of northern England: pollen data from three sites close to Hadrian's Wall, *The Holocene* 4, 165-73

Dumayne, L, Stoneman, R, Barber, K and Harkness, D, 1995 Problems associated with correlating calibrated radiocarbon-dated pollen diagrams with historical events, *The Holocene* 5, 18-23

Dungworth, D B, 1995 *Iron Age and Roman Copper Alloys from Northern Britain*, unpublished PhD thesis, Univ of Durham

Dungworth, D B, 1996 The Production of Copper Alloys in Iron Age Britain, *Proc Prehist Soc* 62, 399-421

Dungworth, D B, 1999 EDXRF analysis of horse harness from the hoard, in Fitts et al 1999, 37-40

Dunwell, A, 1999 Edin's Hall fort, broch, and settlement, Berwickshire (Scottish Borders): recent fieldwork and new perceptions, *Proc Soc Antiq Scot* 129, 303-57

Durden, T, 1995 The production of specialised flintwork in the later Neolithic: a case study from the Yorkshire Wolds, *Proc Prehist Soc* 61, 409-32

Dyer, C C, 1989a *Standards of Living in the Later Middle Ages: Social Change in England, c1200-1520*, Cambridge

Dyer, C C, 1989b The consumer and the market in the later middle ages, *Economic History Review*, 2 ser, 42, 305-27

Edwards, G and Bradley, R, 1999 Rock carvings and Neolithic artefacts on Ilkley Moor, West Yorkshire, in R Cleal and A MacSween (eds) *Grooved Wrae in Britain and Ireland,* Oxford

Edwards, K, 1998 Detection of human impact on the natural environment: palynological views, in J Bayley (ed), *Science in Archaeology. An Agenda for the Future*, London

Egan, G and Pritchard, F, 1991 *Dress Accessories c 1150 – c 1450*, Medieval Finds from Excavations in London 3, London

Elliott, C nd *The North Pennine Orefield Turnpikes and their Improvements in the 1820s under John Loudon McAdam*, unpublished dissertation, Dept of Archaeology, Univ of Newcastle upon Tyne

Ellison, M, 1976 An Archaeological Survey of Berwick-upon-Tweed, in P A G Clack, and P F Gosling, *Archaeology in the North, Report of the Northern Archaeological Survey*, 147-64, London

Ellison, M, 1981 The Pottery, in B Harbottle, and M Ellison, An excavation in the Castle Ditch, Newcastle upon Tyne, 1974-6, *Archaeol Aeliana*, 5 ser, 9, 95-164

Ellison, M, McCombie, G M, MacElvaney, M, Newman, A, O'Brien, C, Taverner, N and Williams, A, 1993 Excavations at Newcastle Quayside: waterfront development at the Swirle, *Archaeol Aeliana*, 5 ser, 21, 151-234

Elliston-Allen, D, 1968 *British Tastes – An Enquiry into the Likes and Dislikes of the Regional Consumer*, London

English Heritage, 1991 *Exploring Our Past: Strategies for the Archaeology of England*, London

English Heritage, 1992 *Managing the Urban Archaeological Resource*, London

English Heritage, 1995 *Industrial Archaeology: A Policy Statement by English Heritage*, London

English Heritage, 1996 *Hadrian's Wall World Heritage Site Management Plan, July 1996*, London

Evans, C, 1992 Manufacturing iron in the North East during the eighteenth century: the case of Bedlington, *Northern Hist* 28, 178-96

Evans, D H & Heslop, D H, 1985 Two Medieval Sites in Yarm, *Yorks Archaeol J* 57, 43-77

Evans, E E, 1973 *The Personality of Ireland*, reprinted by the Lilliput Press 1992

Evans, J, 1995 Later Iron Age and 'native' pottery in the north-east, in Vyner 1995, 46-68

Evans, J, 2000 The End of Roman Pottery in the North, in T Wilmott and P Wilson (eds), *The Late Roman Transition in the North*, Brit Archaeol Rep Brit Ser 299, 39-46, Oxford

Everitt, A, 1986 *Continuity and Colonization: the Evolution of Kentish Settlement*, Leicester

Fairbairn, R, nd *Hushes on Middle Fell, in Alston Moor*, unpublished

Fairless, K J F and Coggins, D C, 1980 Excavations at the early settlement site of Forcegarth Pasture North 1972-4, *Trans Architect Archaeol Soc Durham Northumberland* 5, 31-8

Fairless, K J F and Coggins, D C, 1986 Excavations at the early settlement site of Forcegarth Pasture South 1974-75, *Durham Archaeol J* 2, 25-40

Fairweather, A D and Ralston, I B M, 1993 The Neolithic timber hall at Balbridie, Grampian Region, Scotland: the building, the date, the plant macrofossils, *Antiquity* 67, 313-323

Farmer, D H, 1983a Bede: Lives of the Abbots of Wearmouth and Jarrow, trans, in D H Farmer

Farmer, D H (ed), 1983b *The Age of Bede*, London

Faujas Saint Fond, B, 1799 *Travels in England, Scotland and the Hebrides*, London

Faull, M L, 1977 British survival in Anglo-Saxon Northumbria, in L Laing (ed), *Celtic Survival*, Brit Archaeol Rep Brit Ser 37, 1-56, Oxford

Faull, M L (ed), 1984 *Studies in Late Anglo-Saxon Settlement*, Oxford

Fehring, G P, 1989 Archaeological Evidence from Lubeck for Changing Material Culture and Socio-economic Conditions from the 13th to the 16th Century, *Medieval Archaeol* XXIII, 60-81

Fell, A, 1908 *The Early Iron Industry of Furness and District*, Ulverston

Fell, C and Davis, R V, 1988 The petrological identification of stone implements from Cumbria, in T Clough and W Cummins (eds) *Stone Axe Studies, Volume 2*, London

Fennell, J, 1996 *The Allendale Turnpike and its Significance in the History of Turnpike Building in the North Pennines*, unpublished dissertation, Dept of Archaeology, Univ of Newcastle upon Tyne

Fenton-Thomas, C, 1990 *Pollen Analysis in the Landscape: The Dynamics of Rural Settlement and Land-use in the Tyne-Tees*

Region from the First Millennia B.C. and A.D., unpublished BA dissertation, Univ of Durham

Fenton-Thomas, C, 1992 Pollen analysis as an aid to the reconstruction of patterns of land-use and settlement in the Tyne-Tees region during the first millennia BC and AD, *Durham Archaeol J* 8, 51-62

Ferrell, G, 1992 *Settlement and Society in the Later Prehistory of North-east England*, unpublished PhD thesis, Univ of Durham

Ferrell, G, 1995 Space and society: new perspectives on the Iron Age of North-east England', in J D Hill and C G Cumberpatch (eds), *Different Iron Ages: Studies of the Iron Age in Temperate Europe*, Brit Archaeol Rep Int Ser 602, 129-48, Oxford

Ferrell, G, 1997 Space and society in the Iron Age of north-east England, in Gwilt and Haselgrove 1997, 228-238

Ferris, I and Jones, R, 2000 Transforming an Elite: Reinterpreting Late Roman Binchester, in T Wilmott and P Wilson (eds), *The Late Roman Transition in the North*, Brit Archaeol Rep Brit Ser 299, 1-11, Oxford

Fink, R O, 1971 *Roman Records on Papyrus*, Cleveland

Fitts, R L, Haselgrove, C C, Lowther, P C and Turnbull, P, 1994 An Iron Age farmstead at Rock Castle, Gilling West, North Yorkshire, *Durham Archaeol J* 10, 13-42

Fitts, R L, Haselgrove, C C, Lowther, P C and Willis, S H 1999 Melsonby revisited: survey and excavation 1992-95 at the site of the discovery of the "Stanwick", North Yorkshire, hoard of 1843, *Durham Archaeol J* 14, 1-52

Fleming, A, 1986 *Swaledale Ancient Land Boundaries Project, Third Interim Report (1986 season)*, Unversity of Sheffield Unpublished Report

Fleming, A, 1989 *Swaledale Ancient Land Boundaries Project, Sixth Interim Report (1989 season)*, Unversity of Sheffield Unpublished Report

Fleming, A, 1993 *Swaledale Ancient Land Boundaries Project, Tenth Interim Report,* Unversity of Sheffield Unpublished Report

Fleming, P, 2000 Conflict and urban government in later medieval England: St Augustine's Abbey and Bristol, *Urban History* 27:3 (December), 325-43

Flynn, M W, 1984 *The History of the British Coal Industry. Vol 2: 1700-1830*, Oxford

Foster, S, Macinnes, A and MacInnes, R, 1998 *Scottish Power Centres from the Early Middle Ages to the Twentieth Century*, Glasgow

Foucault, M, 1979 *Discipline and Punish: The Birth of the Prison*, Harmondsworth

Fowler, E, 1963 Celtic metalwork of the fifth and sixth centuries AD – a re-appraisal, *Archaeol J* 120, 98-160

Fowler, J T (ed), 1902 *The Rites of Durham*, Surtees Society 107

Fox, C, 1932 *The Personality of Britain*, Cardiff

Frank, R, 1982 A Holocene peat and sand dune sequence on the coast of northeast England – a preliminary report, *Quaternary Newsletter* 36, 24-32

Fraser, R, Jamfrey, C and Vaughan, J, 1995 Excavation on the Site of the Mansion House, Newcastle, 1990, *Archaeol Aeliana*, 5 ser, 23, 145-214

Fraser, R, Maxwell, R and Vaughan, J E, 1994 Excavation Adjacent to Close Gate, Newcastle, 1988-9, *Archaeol Aeliana*, 5 ser, 22, 85-151

Frere, S S, 1986 The use of Iron Age hill forts by the Roman army in Britain, in C Unz (ed), *Studien zu den Militargrenzen Roms III*, 42-46, Stuttgart

Frere, S S, 1988 Roman Britain in 1987: I. Sites explored, *Britannia* 19, 416-484

Frere, S S, 1991 Roman Britain in 1990: I. Sites explored, *Britannia* 22, 222-292

Frere, S S, 1992 Roman Britain in 1991: I. Sites explored, *Britannia* 23, 256-308

Frodsham, P (ed), 1996 *Neolithic Studies in No-man's-land, Northern Archaeol* 13/14

Frodsham, P, Topping, P and Cowley, D (eds), 1999 *'We Were Always Chasing Time.' Papers presented to Keith Blood (Northern Archaeol,* 17/18), Newcastle

Funari, P P A, 1991 Dressel 20 amphora inscriptions from Vindolanda: the reading of the unpublished evidence, in B Dobson and V A Maxfield, *Roman Frontier Studies 1989*, 65-72, Exeter

Gaimster, D, 1994 The archaeology of post-medieval society, *c* 1450-1750: material culture studies in Britain since the war, in B Vyner (ed), *Building on the Past: Papers Celebrating 150 Years of the Royal Archaeological Institute*, 293-312, London

Gaimster, D R M and Nenk, B, 1997 English Households in Transition c.1450-1550: the ceramic evidence, in D R M Gaimster and P Stamper *The Age of Transition: The Archaeology of English Culture 1400-1600,*

The Society for Medieval Archaeology Monograph 15, Oxbow Monograph 98, 171-95, Oxford

Gaimster, D R M and Stamper, P (eds), *1997 The Age of Transition: The Archaeology of English Culture 1400-1600*, The Society for Medieval Archaeology Monograph 15, Oxbow Monograph 98, Oxford

Gale, S J and Hunt, C O, 1985 The stratigraphy of Kirkhead Cave, an Upper Palaeolithic site in northern England, *Proc Prehist Soc* 51, 283-304

Gale, S J and Hunt, C O, 1990 The stratigraphy of Kirkhead Cave, an Upper Palaeolithic site in northern England: discussion, *Proc Prehist Soc* 56, 51-6

Gannon, A R, 1999 Challenging the past: the resurvey of Braidwood hillfort, in Frodsham *et al* 1999, 105-11

Gard, R M and Hartley, J R, 1969 *Railways in the Making*, Newcastle upon Tyne

Gardiner, J, 1993 The flint assemblage, in J A Davis, Excavation of an Iron Age pit group at London Road, Thetford, *Norfolk Archaeol* 41, 456-8

Gates, T, 1983 Unenclosed settlements in Northumberland, in J C Chapman and H C Mytum (eds), *Settlement in North Britain 1000 BC – AD 1000: Papers Presented to George Jobey*, Brit Archaeol Rep Brit Ser 118, 103-48, Oxford

Gates, T, 1995 *Air Photography and the archaeology of the Otterburn Training Area*, Unpublished, Northumberland National Park, Hexham

Gates, T, 1999 *The Hadrian's Wall landscape from Chesters to Greenhead: an air photographic study. Final Project Report*, Unpublished, Northumberland National Park, Hexham

Gates, T and O'Brien, C F, 1988 Cropmarks at Milfield and New Bewick and the recognition of 'Grubenhäuser' in Northumberland, *Archaeol Aeliana*, 5 ser, 16, 1-12

Geake, H, 1992 Burial practice in seventh- and eighth-century England, in M O H Carver (ed), *The Age of Sutton Hoo: The Seventh Century in North-western Europe*, 83-94, Woodbridge

Gidney, L J, 1999 The Animal Bones, in W B Griffiths, Excavations at the New Quay, Berwick-upon-Tweed, 1996, *Archaeol Aeliana*, 5 ser, 27, 100-102

Gidney, L J and Stokes, P, 2001 The Animal Bones, in R E Young *Excavations within Berwick-upon-Tweed, 1998-1999*, Tyne and Wear Museums/Northumbrian Water Limited, 43-48

Gilchrist, R, 1995 *Contemplation and Action: The Other Monasticism*, Leicester University Press

Gilks, J A, 1987 Later Bronze Age pottery from Kirkhead Cave, Cumbria, *Trans Cumberland Westmorland Antiq Archaeol Soc*, 2 ser, 87, 37-41

Gladstone, W E, 1862 As reported in the *Newcastle Chronicle*, 11 November 1862

Gobalet, K W, 2001 A critique of faunal analysis: inconsistencies among experts in blind tests, *Journal of Archaeological Science* 28, 377-386

Gonner, E C K, 1912 *Common Land and Enclosure*, reprinted 1966, London

Good, G L, Jones, R H and Ponsford, M W (eds), 1991 *Waterfront Archaeology: Proceedings of the third International conference*, Bristol, 1988, CBA Research Report 74, Oxford

Goodwin, K and Huntley, J P, 1988 *Analysis of Waterlogged Plant Remains from Castle Street, Carlisle, Cumbria*, Ancient Monuments Lab Rep 77/88, London

Grant, A, 1991 Animal husbandry, in Cunliffe and Poole 1991, 447-85

Grattan, J and Gilbertson, D, 1994 Acid loading from Icelandic tephra falling on acidified ecosystems as a key to understanding archaeological and environmental stress in northern and western Britain, *J Archaeol Sci* 21, 851-9

Graves, C P, 1996 Social space in the English medieval parish church, in C Bryant and D Jary *Anthony Giddens: Critical Assessments*, 262-88, London, Routledge

Graves, C P, 2000 *The Form and Fabric of Belief: an archaeology in pursuit of the lay experience of Christianity in later medieval Norfolk and Devon*, Brit Archaeol Rep Brit Ser 311, Oxford

Graves, C P and Heslop, D, in prep *The Archaeology of Newcastle upon Tyne*, London

Graves, C P, Heslop, D and Taylor, G, in prep *The Newcastle upon Tyne Virtual Environment Project*

Green, M J, 1998 Vessels of death: sacred cauldrons in archaeology and myth, *Antiq J* 78, 63-84

Green, R M, 1995 *Industrial Archaeology: A Discussion of a Developing Discipline and the Reactions to It*, unpublished dissertation,

Dept of Archaeology, Univ of Newcastle upon Tyne

Grenville, J, 1997 *Medieval Housing*, Leicester

Griffen, T D, 1994 *Names from the Dawn of British Legend – Taliesin, Aneirin, Myrddin, Arthur*, Llanerch, Lampeter

Griffiths, D W, 1992 The coastal trading ports of the Irish Sea, in J Graham-Campbell (ed), *Viking Treasure from the North West: The Cuerdale Hoard in its Context*, National Museums and Galleries on Merseyside Occasional Papers, Liverpool Museum No 5, 63-72, Liverpool

Griffiths, D W, 1994 Trade and production centres in the post-Roman North: the Irish Sea perspective, in P O Nielsen, K Randsborg and H Thrane (eds), *The Archaeology of Gudme and Lundeborg*, Arkeologiske Studien 10, 184-7, Copenhagen

Griffiths, W B, 1989 The sling and its place in the Roman imperial army, in C van Driel Murray (ed), *Roman Military Equipment: The Sources of Evidence. Proceedings of the 5th Roman Military Equipment Conference*, Brit Archaeol Rep Int Ser 476, 255-79, Oxford

Griffiths, W B, 1999 Excavations at the New Quay, Berwick-upon-Tweed, 1996, *Archaeol Aeliana*, 5 ser, 27, 75-108

Grimes, W F and Close-Brooks, J, 1993 The excavations of Caesar's Camp, Heathrow, Harmondsworth, Middlesex, *Proc Prehist Soc* 59, 303-60

Gwilt, A and Haselgrove, C C (eds), 1997 *Reconstructing Iron Age Societies: New Approaches to the British Iron Age*, Oxbow monograph 71, Oxford

Gwilt, A and Heslop, D, 1995 Iron Age and Roman querns from the Tees Valley, in Vyner 1995, 38-45

Haigh, D and Savage, M, 1984 Sewingshields, *Archaeol Aeliana*, 5 ser, 12, 33-147

Halliday, S P, 1982 Later prehistoric farming in south-eastern Scotland, in Harding 1982, 74-87

Halliday, S P, 1999 Hut circle settlements in the Scottish landscape, in Frodsham *et al* 1999, 49-65

Hambleton, E, 1999 *Animal husbandry regimes in Iron AgeBritain: a comparative analysis of faunal assemblages from British Iron Age sites,* Brit Archaeol Rep British Series 282, Oxford

Hamerow, H and Picken, J, 1995 An early Anglo-Saxon cemetery at Andrew's Hill, Easington, County Durham, *Durham Archaeol J* 11, 35-66

Harbottle, B and Ellison, M, 1981 An Excavation in the Castle Ditch, Newcastle upon Tyne, 1974-6, *Archaeol Aeliana*, 5 ser, 9, 75-250

Harbottle, B and Fraser, R, 1987 Black Friars, Newcastle upon Tyne, after the dissolution of the monasteries, *Archaeol Aeliana*, 5 ser, 15, 23-149

Hardie, C, 1994 *Research Suggestions for the Tyne-Solway Ancient and Historic Landscapes Programme*, Northumberland County Council

Harding, A 1981 Excavation in the prehistoric ritual complex near Milfield Northumberland, *Proc Prehist Soc* 47, 87-135

Harding, A, and Lee, G, 1987 *Henge Monuments and Related Sites of Great Britain*, Brit Archaeol Rep Brit Ser 175, Oxford

Harding, D W, 1979 Air survey in the Tyne-Tees region 1969-79, in N J Higham (ed), *The Changing Past*, 21-30, Manchester

Harding, D W (ed), 1982 *Later Prehistoric Settlement in South-East Scotland*, Univ of Edinburgh, Dept of Archaeol Occ Paper 8, Edinburgh

Harding, D W, 1984 *Holme House, Piercebridge: Excavations 1969-70. A Summary Report*, Univ Edinburgh Dept Archaeol Project Paper 2

Harding, J, 2000 Later Neolithic ceremonial centres, ritual and pilgrimage: the monument complex of Thornborough, North Yorkshire, in A Ritchie (ed), *Neolithic Orkney in its European Context*, Cambridge

Harding, J, Frodsham, P and Durden, T, 1996 Towards an agenda for Neolithic studies in Northern England, *Northern Archaeol* 13/14, 189-201

Harding, J and Johnston, R (eds), 2000 *Northern Pasts. Interpretations of the Later Prehistory of Northern England and Southern Scotland*, Brit Archaeol Rep Brit Ser 302, Oxford

Harrison, J H and Harrison, A, 1980 Saltburn by the Sea: the early years of the Stockton & Darlington Railway Company's venture, *Industrial Archaeol Rev* 4 (2), 135-159

Haselgrove, C C, 1980 A cropmark site on Strawberry Hill, Shadforth, County Durham, *Trans Archit Archaeol Soc Durham Northumberland*, new ser, 5, 39-43

Haselgrove, C C, 1982 Indigenous settlement patterns in the Tyne-Tees lowlands, in P A G Clack and S Haselgrove (eds), *Rural*

Settlement in the Roman North, 57-104, Durham

Haselgrove, C C, 1984 The later pre-Roman Iron Age between the Humber and the Tyne, in P R Wilson, R F J Jones and D M Evans (eds), *Settlement and Society in the Roman North*, 9-25, Bradford

Haselgrove, C C, 1999 Iron Age societies in central Britain: retrospect and prospect, in Bevan 1999, 253-278

Haselgrove, C C, 2000 Iron Age agriculture in north-east England and south-east Scotland, in R Buxó and E Pons (eds), *Els Productes Alimentaris d'origen vegetal a l'Edat del Ferro de l'Europa Occidental: de la Producció al Consum*, Sèrie Monogràfica 18, Museu d'Arqueologia de Catalunya, 97-105, Girona

Haselgrove, C C (ed), forthcoming *Cartimandua's Capital? Excavations and fieldwork at the Iron Age and early Roman site at Stanwick, North Yorkshire 1984-89*, Yorkshire Archaeol Monograph series, Leeds

Haselgrove, C C and Allon, V, 1982 An Iron Age settlement at West House, Coxhoe, County Durham, *Archaeol Aeliana*, 5 ser, 10, 25-51

Haselgrove, C C, Armit, I, Champion, T, Creighton, J, Gwilt, A, Hill, J D, Hunter, F and Woodward, A, 2001 *Understanding the British Iron Age: an agenda for action*, Salisbury, Trust for Wessex Archaeology / The Prehistoric Society

Haselgrove, C C, Ferrell, G and Turnbull, P, 1988 *The Durham Archaeological Survey*, Dept of Archaeology Occ Paper 2, Durham

Haselgrove, C C and Healey, E, 1992 The prehistory of the Tyne-Tees lowlands: some recent finds, *Durham Archaeol J* 8, 1-24

Haselgrove, C C, Lowther, P C and Turnbull, P, 1990 Stanwick, North Yorkshire III: excavations on earthworks sites 1981-6, *Archaeol J* 147, 37-90

Hatcher, J, 1993 *The History of the British Coal Industry. Vol 1: Before 1700*, Oxford

Haughton C and Powlesland D, 1999 *West Heslerton, The Anglian Cemetery*, Nottingham

Hayes, R H, Hemingway, J E and Spratt, D A, 1980 The distribution and lithology of beehive querns in north-east Yorkshire, *J Archaeol Sci* 7, 297-324

Hedges, R E M, Housley, R A, Bronk Ramsey, C, and Van Klinken G J, 1994 Radiocarbon dates from the Oxford AMS system: Archaeometry datelist 18, *Archaeometry* 36/2, 337-74

Hervey, M, 1918 A Lumley inventory of 1609, *Walpole Society* 6, 36-50

Heslop, D H, 1984 Initial excavations at Ingleby Barwick, Cleveland, *Durham Archaeol J* 1, 23-34

Heslop, D H, 1987 *The Excavation of an Iron Age Settlement at Thorpe Thewles, Cleveland, 1980-2*, CBA Res Rep 65, London

Heslop, D H, forthcoming The querns, in Haselgrove forthcoming

Higham, N J, 1980 Native settlements west of the Pennines, in Branigan 1980, 41-7

Higham, N J, 1981 Two enclosures at Dobcross Hall, Dobston, *Trans Cumberland Westmorland Antiq Archaeol Soc*, 2 ser, 81, 1-6

Higham, N J, 1982 'Native' settlements on the north slopes of the Lake District, *Trans Cumberland Westmorland Antiq Archaeol Soc*, 2 ser, 82, 29-33

Higham, N J, 1983 A Romano-British farm site and field system at Yanwath Wood near Penrith, *Trans Cumberland Westmorland Antiq Archaeol Soc*, 2 ser, 83, 49-58

Higham, N J, 1986 *The Northern Counties to AD 1000*, London

Higham, N J, 1987 Landscape and land use in northern England: a survey of agricultural potential *c* 500 BC-AD 500, *Landscape History* 9, 35-44

Higham, N J, 1993 *The Kingdom of Northumbria AD 350-1100*, Stroud

Higham, N J and Jones, G D B, 1975 Frontiers, forts and farmers; Cumbrian aerial survey 1974-5, *Archaeol J* 132, 16-53

Higham, N J and Jones, G D B, 1983 The excavation of two Romano-British farm sites in north Cumbria, *Britannia* 14, 45-72

Hill, J D, 1995 *Ritual and Rubbish in the Iron Age of Wessex*, Brit Archaeol Rep British Series 242, Oxford

Hill, P, 1982a Towards a new classification of prehistoric houses, *Scottish Archaeol Rev* 1, 24-31

Hill, P, 1982b Settlement and chronology, in Harding 1982, 4-43

Hill, P, 1982c Broxmouth hillfort excavations, 1977-1978: an interim report (2nd edn), in Harding 1982, 141-88

Hill, P, 1987 Traprain Law: the Votadini and the Romans, *Scottish Archaeol Rev* 7, 96-103

Hill, P, 1992 Excavations 1990-1991: interim report, *Whithorn* 4, Whithorn

Hill, P, 1997 *Whithorn & St Ninian – The Excavation of a Monastic Town 1984-91*, Stroud

Hingley, R, 1990 Boundaries surrounding Iron Age and Romano-British settlements, *Scottish Archaeol Rev* 7, 96-103

Hingley, R, 1992 Society in Scotland from 700 BC to AD 200, *Proc Soc Antiq Scot* 122, 7-53

Hird, M L, forthcoming *Fascicule 3. The Roman Pottery from the Southern End of The Lanes, Carlisle: Excavations 1981-2*

Hirst, K, 1998 Scotby Road, Durranhill, Carlisle, *Past* 29, 4-5

Hirst, S M, 1985 *An Anglo-Saxon Inhumation Cemetery at Sewerby, East Yorkshire*, York University Archaeological Publications 4, York

Hodder, I, 1991 *Reading the Past: current approaches to interpretation in archaeology*, (2nd edn), Cambridge

Hodgson, N, 1991 The *Notitia Dignitatum* and the late Roman garrison of Britain, in B Dobson and V A Maxfield (eds), *Roman Frontier Studies 1989*, 84-92, Exeter

Hodgson, N, 1994 Excavations at South Shields 1993-4: the prehistoric occupation of the site, *Archaeology North* 8, 30-4

Hodgson, N, Stobbs, G and Veen, M van der, forthcoming An Iron Age settlement and remains of earlier prehistoric date beneath South Shields Roman fort, *Archaeol J* 158

Hodgson, R I, 1979 The progress of enclosure in County Durham, 1550-1870, in H S A Fox and R A Butlin (eds), *Change in the Countryside: Essays on Rural England, 1500-1900*, London

Holbrook, N, 1988 The settlement at Chester House, Northumberland, *Archaeol Aeliana*, 5 ser, 16, 47-59

Holdsworth, P, 1991 Dunbar, *Current Archaeol* 127, 315-7

Holland, E G, 1986 *Coniston Copper: A History*, Milnthorpe

Homans, G C, 1960 *English Villagers of the Thirteenth Century*, New York

Homans, G C, 1969 The explanation of England's regional differences, *Past and Present* 42, 18-34

Honey, J, 1991 *Does Accent Matter?*, London

Hooke, D. 2001 (ed) *Landscape – the richest historical record* (Society for Landscape Studies, supplementary series 1), Amesbury

Hoole, K, 1965 *A Regional History of the Railways of Great Britain. Vol 4: North East England*, Newton Abbot

Hope-Taylor, B, 1977 *Yeavering: An Anglo-British Centre of Early Northumbria*, Dept of Environment Archaeol Rep 7, London

Hoskins, W G, 1988 *The Making of the English Landscape*, with Introduction by C Taylor, London

Howell, R, 1967 *Newcastle upon Tyne and the Puritan Revolution: A Study of the Civil War in North England*, Oxford

Huckerby, E and Wells, C, 1993 Recent work at Solway Moss, Cumbria, in R Middleton (ed), *North West Wetlands Survey Annual Report*, 24-32, Lancaster

Hunt, C J, 1970 *The Lead Miners of the Northern Pennines in the Eighteenth and Nineteenth Centuries*, Manchester

Hunt, L (ed), 1989 *The New Cultural History*, Berkeley

Hunter, F, 1997 Iron Age hoarding in Scotland and northern England, in A Gwilt and C Haselgrove (ed) *Reconstructing Iron Age Societies: New Approaches to the British Iron Age* (Oxbow monogr 71), Oxford, 108-33

Hunter, F, 1999 Artefacts, in Dunwell 1999, 332-42

Hunter, J R, 1982 Medieval Berwick-upon-Tweed, *Archaeol Aeliana*, 5 ser, 10, 67-124

Huntley, J P, 1988 *Plant Remains from Ewanrigg, Cumbria*, Ancient Monuments Lab Rep 85/88, London

Huntley, J P, 1989a *Plant Remains from Annetwell Street, Carlisle: A Synthesis*, Ancient Monuments Lab Rep 107/89, London

Huntley, J P, 1989b *Plant Remains from Catcote, Cleveland*, Ancient Monuments Lab Rep 16/89, London

Huntley, J P, 1993 *Caythorpe Gas Pipeline – CGP92. The Plant Remains*, archive report for Northern Archaeological Associates, Barnard Castle

Huntley, J P, 1994a *A1 Walshford-Dishforth (WD93). The Plant Remains. Part II: Fields 88 – 105*, archive report for Northern Archaeological Associates, Barnard Castle

Huntley, J P, 1994b *Bayram Hill, North Yorkshire: BH93. The Environmental Samples*, Durham Environmental Archaeol Rep 01/94, Durham

Huntley, J P, 1994c *Allerton Grange, North Yorkshire: AG94. The environmental samples*, Durham Environmental Archaeol Rep 15/94, Durham

Huntley, J P, 1994d *Chester-le-Street: Park View. The plant remains*, Durham Environmental Archaeol Rep 20/94, Durham

Huntley, J P, 1994e *Catterick (A1) North Yorkshire: CAS sites 506 & 511. An assessment of the palaeoenvironmental samples*, Durham Environmental Archaeol Rep 03/94, Durham

Huntley, J P, 1994f *A1 Walshford-Dishforth (WD93). The Plant Remains. Part I: Fields 73, 76 and 79*, archive report for Northern Archaeological Associates, Barnard Castle

Huntley, J P, 1994g *The Heugh, Lindisfarne. The carbonised plant remains*, Durham Environmental Archaeology Report, 38/94, 5

Huntley, J P, 1995 The carbonised plant remains, in Abramson 1995, 16-18

Huntley, J P, 1996a The carbonised plant remains, in Abramson 1996, 80-81

Huntley, J P, 1996b *Plant Remains from Ribchester, Lancashire: RB89*, Ancient Monuments Lab Rep 36/96, Durham

Huntley, J P, 1999a Environmental samples, in W B Griffiths Excavations at the New Quay, Berwick-upon-Tweed, 1996, *Archaeol Aeliana*, 5 ser, 27, 103-5

Huntley, J P, 1999b Saxon-Norse economy in northern Britain: food for thought, *Durham Archaeol. J.* 14-15, 77 – 81

Huntley, J P, 1999c Environmental evidence from Hadrian's Wall, in Bidwell, P, (ed), *Hadrian's Wall 1989-1999*, Carlisle, 49-64

Huntley, J P, 2000 Late Roman Transition in the North: the Palynological Evidence, in T Wilmott and P Wilson (eds), *The Late Roman Transition in the North*, Brit Archaeol Rep Brit Ser 299, 67-71, Oxford

Huntley, J P, forthcoming The carbonised plant remains, in M Bishop, Excavations at the Roman fort of Roecliffe, near Boroughbridge, North Yorkshire

Huntley, J P and Stallibrass, S M, 1995 *Plant and Vertebrate Remains from Archaeological Sites in Northern England: Data Reviews and Future Directions*, Archit Archaeol Soc Durham Northumberland Res Rep 4, Durham

Ingle, C J, 1987 The production and distribution of beehive querns in Cumbria: some initial considerations, *Trans Cumberland Westmorland Antiq Archaeol Soc*, 2 ser, 87, 11-17

Inman, R, 1988 Romano-British settlement in the south Tees basin, in J Price and P R Wilson (eds), *Recent Research in Roman Yorkshire*, Brit Archaeol Rep British Series 193, 219-34, Oxford

Inman, R, Brown, D R, Goddard, R E and Spratt, D, 1985 Roxby Iron Age settlement and the Iron Age in north-east Yorkshire, *Proc Prehist Soc* 51, 181-213

Isaac, P C and Allan, R E A (eds), 1949 *Scientific Survey of North-East England*, Newcastle upon Tyne

Isaac, R, 1983 *The Transformation of Virginia, 1760-1820*, Chapel Hill, North Carolina

Jacobi, R, 1976   Britain inside and outside Mesolithic Europe, *Proc Prehist Soc* 42, 67-84

James, M R, 1983 Ritual, drama and social body in the late medieval town, *Past and Present* 98, 3-29

James, M R, 1986 *Society, Politics, Culture: Studies in Early Modern England*, Cambridge

James, S, Marshall, A and Millett, M, 1984 An early medieval building tradition, *Archaeol J* 141, 182-215

Jenkins, R, 1997 *Rethinking Ethnicity – Arguments and Explorations*, London, Thousand Oaks and New Delhi

Jenner, A, 1999 The Pottery, in W B Griffiths, Excavations at the New Quay, Berwick-upon-Tweed, 1996, *Archaeol Aeliana*, 5 ser, 27, 83-91

Jobey, G, 1959 Excavations at the native settlement at Huckhoe, Northumberland, 1955-7, *Archaeol Aeliana*, 4 ser, 37, 217-78

Jobey, G, 1960 Some rectilinear settlements of the Roman period in Northumberland: Part 1, *Archaeol Aeliana*, 4 ser, 38, 1-38

Jobey, G, 1962 A Iron Age homestead at West Brandon, Durham, *Archaeol Aeliana*, 4 ser, 40, 1-34

Jobey, G, 1963 Excavation of a native settlement at Marden, Tynemouth, *Archaeol Aeliana*, 4 ser, 41, 19-35

Jobey, G, 1964 Enclosed stone-built settlements in Northumberland, *Archaeol Aeliana*, 4 ser, 42, 41-62

Jobey, G, 1965 Hill-forts and settlements in Northumberland, *Archaeol Aeliana*, 4 ser, 43, 21-64

Jobey, G, 1967 Excavation at Tynemouth Priory and Castle, *Archaeol Aeliana*, 4 ser, 45, 33-104

Jobey, G, 1968 A radiocarbon date for the palisaded settlement at Huckhoe, *Archaeol Aeliana*, 4 ser, 46, 293-5

Jobey, G, 1970 An Iron Age settlement and homestead at Burradon, Northumberland, *Archaeol Aeliana*, 4 ser, 48, 51-95

Jobey, G, 1971 Excavations at Brough Law and Ingram Hill, *Archaeol Aeliana*, 4 ser, 49, 71-93

Jobey, G, 1973 A native site at Hartburn and the Devil's Causeway, Northumberland, *Archaeol Aeliana*, 5 ser, 1, 11-53

Jobey, G, 1975 A souterrain at Millfieldhill, Northumberland, *Archaeol Aeliana*, 5 ser, 3, 215-17

Jobey, G, 1978 Iron Age and Romano-British settlements on Kennel Hall Knowe, North Tynedale, Northumberland, *Archaeol Aeliana*, 5 ser, 6, 1-28

Jobey, G, 1980 Green Knowe unenclosed platform settlement and Harehope cairn, Peeblesshire, *Proc Soc Antiq Scot* 110, 72-113

Jobey, G, 1982 The settlement at Doubstead and Romano-British settlement on the coastal plain between Tyne and Forth, *Archaeol Aeliana*, 5 ser, 10, 1-23

Jobey, G, 1983 Excavation of an unenclosed settlement on Standrop Rigg, Northumberland, and some problems related to similar settlements between Tyne and Forth, *Archaeol Aeliana*, 5 ser, 11, 1-21

Jobey, G, 1985 The unenclosed settlements of Tyne-Forth: a summary, in D A Spratt and C Burgess (eds), *Upland Settlement in Britain – The Second Millennium BC and After*, Brit Archaeol Rep Brit Ser 143, 177-94, Oxford

Jobey, G and Tait, J, 1966 Excavations on palisaded settlements and cairnfields at Alnham, Northumberland, *Archaeol Aeliana*, 4 ser, 44, 5-48

Jobey, I and Jobey, G, 1987 Prehistoric, Romano-British and later remains on Murton High Crags, Northumberland, *Archaeol Aeliana*, 5 ser, 15, 151-97

Johnson, C, 1925 The Oldest version of the Customs of Newcastle upon Tyne, *Archaeol Aeliana*, 4 ser, 1, 169-79

Johnson, M H, 1993 *Housing Culture: Traditional Architecture in an English Landscape*, London

Johnson, M H, 1996 *An Archaeology of Capitalism*, Oxford

Johnston, R, 2000 Dying, becoming, and being the field: prehistoric cairnfields in Northumberland, in J Harding and R Johnston (eds), *Northern Pasts. Interpretations of the Later Prehistory of Northern England and*

Southern Scotland, Brit Archaeol Rep Brit Ser 302, Oxford

Jones, G D B and Walker, J, 1983 Either side of Solway: towards a minimalist view of Romano-British agricultural settlement in the north-west, in J C Chapman and H C Mytum (eds), *Settlement in North Britain 1000 BC-AD 1000*, Brit Archaeol Rep Brit Ser 118, 185-204, Oxford

Jones, G J R, 1961 Settlement patterns in Anglo-Saxon England, *Antiquity* 35, 221-32

Jones, G J R, 1976 Multiple estates and early settlement, in P H Sawyer (ed), *Medieval Settlement*, 15-40, London

Jones, R T, Sly, J and Hocking, L, 1987 The vertebrate remains, in A C M Olivier, Excavation of a Bronze Age funerary cairn at Manor Farm, near Borwick, north Lancashire, *Proc Prehist Soc* 53, 163-70

Keeley, H C M (ed), 1984 *Environmental Archaeology: a Regional Review*, DoE Inspectorate of Ancient Monuments, London

Keevill, G, in prep Excavations to the west of Carlisle Cathedral

Kendrick, T D, 1937 St. Cuthbert's Pectoral Cross and the Wilton and Ixworth Crosses, *Antiq J* 17, 283-93

Kenward, H and Allison, E, 1994 Rural origins of the urban insect fauna, in A R Hall and H K Kenward (eds), *Urban-Rural Connexions: Perspectives from Environmental Archaeology*, Oxbow Monograph 47, 55-77, Oxford

Kilbride-Jones, H E, 1980 *Celtic Craftsmanship in Bronze*, London

King A, 1978 'Gauber High Pasture, Ribblehead – an interim report', in R. A. Hall (ed), *Viking Age York and the North*, 31-36, C.B.A. Res. Rep. 27, London

Koch, J T, 1997 *The Gododdin of Aneirin – Text and Context from Dark-Age North Britain*, Cardiff

Laing, L, 1975 *The Archaeology of Late Celtic Britain and Ireland c. 400-1200 AD*, London

Laithwaite, E, 1994 *An Inventor in the Garden of Eden*, Cambridge

Lamb, H H, 1981 Climate from 1000 BC-AD 100, in M K Jones and G W Dimbleby (eds), *The Environment of Man: The Iron Age to Anglo-Saxon Period*, Brit Archaeol Rep British Series 87, 53-65, Oxford

Lambert, J (ed), 1996 *Transect through time; the archaeological landscape of the Shell North Western Ethylene Pipeline*, Lancaster Imprints 1

Lancaster University Archaeological Unit (LUAU), 1995 *Field Survey Cumbria 1980-94*, Unpublished report

Lancaster University Archaeological Unit (LUAU), 1996a *Haweswater Estate, Cumbria Second Season of Archaeological Survey (1995/6) Interim Report*, Unpublished report

Lancashire University Archaeological Unit, 1996b *Marygate, Berwick-upon-Tweed, Northumberland, Archaeological assessment* (January 1996)

Lane, A and Campbell, E, forthcoming *Dunadd: An Early Dalriadic Capital*, Cardiff Studies in Archaeology, Oxford

Laurie, T C, 1984 First evidence for the early Postglacial and Mesolithic occupation of the Tees valley and the uplands between the Tees and the Swale rivers, *Yorks Archaeol Soc Res Bull* 21, 1-3, figs 1-5

Leech, R H, 1983 Settlements and groups of small cairns on Birkby and Birker Fells, Eskdale, Cumbria, Survey undertaken in 1982, *Trans Cumberland Westmorland Antiq Archaeol Soc n ser* 83, 15-26

Leeds, E T, 1949 *A Corpus of Early Anglo-Saxon Great Square-Headed Brooches*, Oxford

Legge, A J and Rowley-Conwy, P A, 1988 *Star Carr Re-Visited*, London, Birkbeck College

Leighley, J, 1963 *Land and Life: a Selection from the Writings of Carl Ortwin Sauer*, Berkeley and Los Angeles

Lethbridge, T C, 1931 *Recent Excavations in Anglo-Saxon Cemeteries in Cambridgeshire and Suffolk*, Cambridge

Levine, D and Wrightson, K, 1990 *The Making of an Industrial Society: Whickham 1560-1765*, Oxford

Lewis, M J T, 1970 *Early Wooden Railways*, London

Linsley, S M, 1977 Capheaton Tilery, *Intrust* 5, special issue, Newcastle upon Tyne

Linsley, S M, 1981-2 Furnace rediscovered – a provisional note, *Industrial Archaeol Rev* 6 (1), 69-72

Linsley, S M, 1985 The fixed barn threshing machine and its influence on farmstead layout in Northumberland, in *Making Sense of Building*, CBA Group 3 Publication, 117-135

Linsley, S M, 1992 The road past Killhope and some other orefield turnpikes, in B Chambers *Men, Mines and Minerals of the North Pennines*, 71-80, Killhope

Linsley, S M and Heatherington, R, 1978 A seventeenth century blast furnace at Allensford, Northumberland, *J Hist Met Soc* 12 (1), 1-11

Lomas, R, 1992 *North-East England in the Middle Ages,* Edinburgh

Long, C D, 1988 The Iron Age and Romano-British settlement at Catcote, Hartlepool, *Durham Archaeol J* 4, 13-36

Loveluck, C P, 1990 *A Re-interpretation of the Sprouston Cropmark Palimpsest in Relation to the Yeavering and Milfield Types of Site*, unpublished BA dissertation, Univ of Durham

Loveluck, C P, 1994 *Exchange and Society in Early Medieval England, 400-700 AD*, unpublished PhD thesis, Univ of Durham

Loveluck, C P, 1995 Acculturation, migration and exchange: the formation of an Anglo-Saxon society in the English Peak District, in J Bintliff and H F Hamerow (eds), *Europe Between Late Antiquity and the Middle Ages: Recent Archaeological and Historical Research in Western and Southern Europe*, Brit Archaeol Rep Int Ser 617, 84-98, Oxford

Loveluck, C P, 1998 The Development of the Anglo-Saxon Landscape, Economy and Society on Driffield, East Yorkshire, 400-750 AD, in D Griffiths (ed), *Anglo-Saxon Studies in Archaeology and History 9 (for 1996)*, 25-48, Oxford

Loveluck, C P, 1999 Archaeological expressions of the transition from the late Roman to early Anglo-Saxon period, in lowland East Yorkshire, in P Halkon and M Millett (eds), *Rural Settlement and Industry: Studies in the Iron Age and Roman Archaeology of Lowland East Yorkshire*, Yorks Archaeol Rep 4, 228-236, Leeds

Loveluck, C P, in press The Archaeology of post-Roman Yorkshire, AD 400 to 700 – Overview and Future Directions for Research, in P J Ottaway, T Manby and S Moorhouse (eds), *The Archaeology of Yorkshire – A Resource Assessment*, Yorks Archaeol Rep and Univ of York Archaeol Rep, York

Lowe, C E, 1991 New light on the Anglian 'minster' at Hoddom, *Trans Dumfries Galloway Nat Hist Antiq Soc*, 3 ser, 66, 11-35

Lowndes, R A C, 1963 'Celtic' fields, farmsteads and burial mounds in the Lune Valley, *Trans Cumberland Westmorland Antiq Archaeol Soc*, 2 ser, 63, 77-95

Lowndes, R A C, 1964 Excavation of a Romano-British farmstead at Eller Beck,

Trans Cumberland Westmorland Antiq Archaeol Soc, 2 ser, 64, 6-13

Lowther, P, Ebbatson, L, Ellison, M and Millett, M, 1993 The City of Durham: an archaeological survey, *Durham Archaeol J* 9, 27-119

Lucy, S, 1998 *The Early Anglo-Saxon Cemeteries of East Yorkshire – An analysis and reinterpretation*, Brit Archaeol Rep Brit Ser 272, Oxford

Lucy, S, 2000 *The Anglo-Saxon Way of Death – Burial Rites in Early England*, Stroud

MacGregor, M, 1976 *Early Celtic Art in North Britain*, Leicester

Macinnes, L, 1982 Pattern and Purpose: the settlement evidence, in D Harding, *Later Prehistoric Settlement in South-East Scotland*, 57-74, Edinburgh

Mackay Mackenzie, W (ed), 1932 *The Poems of William Dunbar*, London

Macklin, M G and Passmore, D G, 1992 Climate and cultural signals in Holocene alluvial sequences: the Tyne basin, northern England, in S Needham and M G Macklin (eds), *Alluvial Archaeology in Britain*, Oxbow Monograph 27, 123-38, Oxford

Macklin, M G, Rumsby, B T, Heap, T and Passmore, D G, 1994 Thinhope Burn, Northumberland, in J Boardman and J Walden (eds), *The Quaternary of Cumbria: Field Guide*, Quaternary Res Assoc, 50-7, Oxford

Maitland, F W, 1897 *Domesday Book and Beyond*, reprinted in 1960, London

Manby, T G, 1980 Bronze Age settlement in eastern Yorkshire, in J C Barrett and R Bradley (eds), *Settlement and Society in the British Later Bronze Age*, Brit Archaeol Rep 83, 307-70, Oxford

Manby, T G, 1988 The Neolithic period in Eastern Yorkshire, in T G Manby (ed), *Archaeology in Eastern Yorkshire*, 35-88, Sheffield

Manning, W H, 1975 Economic influences on land use in the military areas of the Highland Zone during the Roman period, in J Evans, S Limbury and H Cleere, *The Effects of Man on the Landscape: The Highland Zone*, CBA Res Rep 11, 112-16

Margary, H, 1975-1981 *The Old Series Ordnance Survey Maps of England and Wales*, Lympne

Markus, T, 1993 *Buildings and Power: Freedom and Control in the Origin of Modern Building Types*, London

Marriott, A D, 1991 *Settlement in the Lune Valley*, unpublished BA dissertation, Univ of Durham

Marshall, G, 1995 Redressing the balance – an archaeological evaluation of North Yorkshires coastal alum industry, *Industrial Archaeol Rev* 18 (1), 39-62

Martin, M, 1997 Wealth and treasure in the West, 4th-7th century, in L Webster and M Brown (eds), *The Transformation of the Roman World, AD 400-900*, 48-66, London

Masters, L, 1984 The neolithic long cairns of Cumbria and Northumberland, in *Between and Beyond the walls* (eds R Miket, and C Burgess), 52-73

McCarthy, M R, 1990 *A Roman, Anglian and Medieval Site at Blackfriars Street, Carlisle: Excavations 1977-9*, Cumberland Westmorland Antiq Archaeol Soc Res Ser 4, Kendal

McCarthy, M R, 1991 *The Roman Waterlogged Remains and Later Features at Castle Street, Carlisle: Excavations 1981-2*, Cumberland Westmorland Antiq Archaeol Soc Res Ser 5, Kendal

McCarthy, M R, 1993 *Carlisle: History and Guide*, Stroud

McCarthy, M R, 1995a Review of Prehistoric and Romano-British Settlement in the Solway Plain, Cumbria, by Robert Howard Bewley, *Antiquaries Journal Book Supplement*, 75, 26

McCarthy, M R, 1995b Archaeological and environmental evidence for the Roman impact on vegetation near Carlisle, Cumbria, *The Holocene* 5, 491-5

McCarthy, M R, 1999a, Carlisle (*Luguvalium*), in P Bidwell (ed). *Hadrian's Wall 1989-1999. A summary of recent excavations and research*, 168-77, Kendal

McCarthy, M R, 1999b Carlisle and St Cuthbert, *Durham Archaeol J*, 14-15, 59-67

McCarthy, M R, 2000 *Roman and Medieval Carlisle, The Southern Lanes: Excavations 1981-2*, Dept of Archaeological Sciences, University of Bradford, Res Rep 1, Carlisle

McCarthy, M R, forthcoming *Excavations in The Lanes, Carlisle*: Volume 1 the Southern Lanes

McCord, N, 1991 *North-east History from the Air*, Chichester

McCord, N and Jobey, G, 1968 Notes on air reconnaissance in Northumberland and Durham, *Archaeol Aeliana*, 4 ser, 46, 51-67

McKendrick, N, Brewer, J and Plumb, J H, 1982 *The Birth of a Consumer Society*, London

McNamee, C, 1997 *The Wars of the Bruces: Scotland, England and Ireland, 1306 – 28,* East Linton

McOmish, D, 1999 Wether Hill and Cheviots hillforts, in Frodsham *et al* 1999, 113-21

Mercer, R, 1981 Excavation at Carn Brea, Illogan, Cornwall, *Cornish Archaeol* 20, 1-294

Mercer, R and Tipping, R, 1994 The prehistory of soil erosion in the northern and eastern Cheviot Hills, Anglo-Scottish Borders, in S Foster and T C Smout (ed), *The History of Soils and Field Systems,* 1-25, Aberdeen

Miket, R, 1980 A re-statement of evidence for Bernician Anglo-Saxon burials, in P Rahtz, T M Dickinson and L Watts (eds), *Anglo-Saxon Cemeteries, 1979,* Brit Archaeol Rep Brit Ser 82, 289-305, Oxford

Miket, R and Burgess, C (eds), 1984 *Between and Beyond the Walls: Essays in the Prehistory and History of Northern Britain in Honour of George Jobey,* Edinburgh

Miket, R and Pocock, M, 1976 An Anglo-Saxon Cemetery at Greenbank, Darlington, *Medieval Archaeol* 20, 62-74

Miles, D, 1984 *Archaeology at Barton Court Farm, Abingdon, Oxon,* CBA Res Rep 50, London

Milner, N and Waddington, C, 2001 Evidence for early occupation at Howick, *Archaeology in Northumberland* 2000-2001, 6, Morpeth

Mitchell, C, 1973 *Terrain Evaluation,* London

Mitcheson, M M, 1984 A bibliography of the published works of George Jobey, in Miket and Burgess 1984, 411-14

Mithen, S J, 1990 *Thoughtful Foragers,* Cambridge

Moffett, L, Robinson, M A and Straker, V, 1989 Cereals, fruit and nuts: charred plant remains from Neolithic sites in England and Wales and the Neolithic economy, in A Milles, D Williams and N Gardner (eds), *The Beginnings of Agriculture. AEA Conference Symposium Number 8,* Brit Archaeol Rep Int Ser 496, 243-261, Oxford

Moloney, C, Holbrey, R, Wheelhouse, P and Roberts, I, forthcoming Catterick Racecourse, North Yorkshire: re-use and adaptation in the landscape from prehistoric to Anglian times, *Archaeol J* 159

Morris, R, 1987 Parish churches, in J Schofield and R Leech (eds), *Urban Archaeology in Britain,* CBA Res Rep 61, 177-91, London

Morris, R, 1989 *Churches in the Landscape,* London

Mortimer, J R, 1905 *Forty Years' Researches in British and Saxon Burial Mounds of East Yorkshire,* London

Mountford, C, 1976 *The Bowes Railway,* Newcastle upon Tyne

Musty, J, 1995 Science diary, *Current Archaeology* 142, 393-5

Myrvoll, S, 1991 Vagen and Bergen: the changing waterfront and the structure of the medieval town, in G L Good, R H Jones and M W Ponsford (eds), *Waterfront Archaeology: Proceedings of the third International conference, Bristol,* CBA Research Report 74, 150-61, Oxford

Newman, R M, 1984 The problems of rural settlement in Northern Cumbria in the pre-Conquest period, in M L Faull (ed), *Studies in Late Anglo-Saxon Settlement,* 155-76, Oxford

Newman, R M (ed), 1996 *The Archaeology of Lancashire: Present State and Future Priorities,* Lancaster University Archaeological Unit

Newman, R M and Leech, R H, forthcoming *Excavations at Dacre, Cumbria*

Nicholaisen, W.F.H. 1976 *Scottish Place-Names,* London

Nieke, M R and Duncan, H B, 1988 Dalriada: the establishment and maintenance of an Early Historic kingdom in northern Britain, in S T Driscoll and M R Nieke (eds), *Power & Politics in Early Medieval Britain and Ireland,* 6-21, Edinburgh

Nolan, J, 1990 The Castle of Newcastle upon Tyne after c.1600, *Archaeol Aeliana,* 5 ser, 18, 79-126

Nolan, J, 2000 Excavations at Oakwellgate, Gateshead, *Archaeology North* 17, Winter 2000, 23-4

Northover, P, 1988 The analysis and metallurgy of British Bronze Age swords, in I Colquhoun and C Burgess, *The Swords of Britain (Prähistorische Bronzefunde IV,5),* 130-46, Munich

O'Brien E, 1999 *Post-Roman Britain to Anglo-Saxon England: Burial Practices Reviewed,* BAR Brit. Ser. 289, Oxford

O'Brien, C, 1991 Newcastle upon Tyne and its North Sea trade, in G L Good, R H Jones and M W Ponsford (eds), *Waterfront Archaeology: Proceedings of the third International conference, Bristol,* CBA Research Report 74, 36-42, Oxford

O'Brien, C, Bown, L, Dixon, S, Donel, L, Gidney, L J, Huntley, J P, Nicholson, R and Walton, P, 1989 Excavations at Newcastle

Quayside: the Crown Court site, *Archaeol Aeliana*, 5 ser, 17, 141-205

O'Brien, C, Bown, L., Dixon, S and Nicholson, R, 1988 *The Origins of Newcastle Quayside, Excavations at Queen Street and Dog Bank*, The Society of Antiquaries of Newcastle upon Tyne Monograph Series 3

O'Brien, C and Miket, R, 1991 The early medieval settlement of Thirlings, Northumberland, *Durham Archaeol J* 7, 57-91

O'Floinn, R, 1989 Secular metalwork in the eighth and ninth centuries, in S Youngs, *The Work of Angels: Masterpieces of Celtic Metalwork, 6th-9th Centuries AD*, London

O'Sullivan, D M, 1984 Pre-Conquest settlement patterns in Cumbria, in M L Faull (ed), *Studies in Late Anglo-Saxon Settlement*, 143-54, Oxford

O'Sullivan, D M, 1993 Sub-Roman and Anglo-Saxon finds from Cumbria, *Trans Cumberland Westmorland Antiq Archaeol Soc*, 2 ser, 93, 25-42

O'Sullivan, D M, 1998 A Group of Pagan Burials from Cumbria?, in D Griffiths (ed), *Anglo-Saxon Studies in Archaeology and History 9 (for 1996)*, 15-23, Oxford

O'Sullivan, D M, in prep Excavations on Lindisfarne

O'Sullivan, D M and Young, R, 1995 *Book of Lindisfarne Holy Island*, English Heritage, London

Oliver, A M, 1924 *Early Deeds Relating to Newcastle upon Tyne*, Surtees Society 137

Oliver, T, 1993 *Excavations of a post-Roman settlement at Fremington, near Brougham, North Western Ethyline Pipeline: Archaeological Studies*, 23-4

Oliver, T, Howard-Davis, C and Newman, R, 1996 A post-Roman settlement at Fremington, near Brougham, in J Lambert (ed), *Transect Through Time*, Lancaster Imprints 1, 127-69, Lancaster

Olivier, A, 1996 *Frameworks for Our Past: A review of research frameworks, strategies and perceptions*, London

Oswald, A, 1997 A doorway on the past: practical and mystic concerns in the orientations of roundhouse doorways, in Gwilt and Haselgrove 1997, 87-95

Oswald, A, Dyer, C, and Barber, M, 2001 *The Creation of Monuments: Neolithic Causewayed Enclosures in the British Isles*, Swindon

Owen, O A, 1992 Eildon Hill North, in J S Rideout, O A Owen and E Halpin (eds), *Hillforts of Southern Scotland*, AOC Monograph 1, 21-72, Edinburgh

Padley, T G, 1991a *Fascicule 2. The Metalwork, Glass and Stone Objects from Castle Street, Carlisle: Excavations 1981-2*, Cumberland Westmorland Antiq Archaeol Soc Res Ser 5, Kendal

Padley, T G, 1991b *Fascicule 3. The Wooden, Leather and Bone Objects from Castle Street, Carlisle: Excavations 1981-2*, Cumberland Westmorland Antiq Archaeol Soc Res Ser 5, Kendal

Pearson, T, 1987 *An Archaeological Survey of Scarborough*, Scarborough

Pearson, T, 1998 Yeavering Bell, Berwick-upon Tweed [District], Northumberland, unpublished report, RCHME

Peers, C and Radford, C A R, 1943 The Saxon monastery of Whitby, *Archaeologia*, 89, 27-88

Pennington, W, 1970 Vegetation history in the North-West of England: a regional synthesis, In D, Walker and R,G,West (eds,), *Studies in the vegetational history of the British Isles*, 41-79, London: Cambridge University Press

Pennington, W, 1975 The effect of Neolithic man on the environment of north-west England – the use of absolute pollen diagrams, in J Evans, S Limbrey and H Cleere (eds), *The Effect of Man on the Landscape: The Highland Zone*, London

Pevsner, N, 1985 *The Buildings of England: County Durham*, 2nd edn revised by E Williamson, London

Pevsner, N and Richmond, I, 1992 *The Buildings of England: Northumberland*, 2nd edn revised by J Grundy, G McCombie, P Ryder and H Welfare, London

Philpott, R, 1991 *Burial Practices in Roman Britain*, Brit Archaeol Rep Brit Ser 219, Oxford

Phythian-Adams, C, 1972 Ceremony and the citizen: the communal year at Coventry 1450-1550, in P Clark and P Slack (eds) *Crisis and order in English towns, 1500-1700*, 57-85, London

Phythian-Adams, C (ed), 1993 *Societies, Cultures and Kinship, 1580-1850: Cultural Provinces and English Local History*, Leicester

Piggott, C M, 1948 The excavations at Hownam Rings, Roxburghshire, *Proc Soc Antiq Scot* 82, 193-225

Piggott, C M, 1949 The Iron Age settlement at Hayhope Knowe, Roxburghshire: excavations 1949, *Proc Soc Antiq Scot* 83, 45-67

Piggott, S, 1949 A wheel of Iron Age type from County Durham, *Proc Prehist Soc* 15, 191

Piggott, S, 1950 Swords and scabbards of the British Early Iron Age, *Proc Prehist Soc* 16, 1-28

Piggott, S, 1958 Native economies and the Roman occupation of north Britain, in I A Richmond (ed), *Roman and Native in North Britain*, 1-27, Edinburgh

Platell, A, 1999 A late Roman and sub-Roman site at Newton Bewley, Hartlepool, *Teeside Archaeol Soc Bull* 4, 17-27

Pocock, M, 1971 A note on two Early Anglo-Saxon brooches, *Yorks Archaeol J* 42, 407-9

Postlethwaite, J, 1913 *Mines and Mining in the English Lake District*, Whitehaven

Potter, T W and Andrews, R D, 1994 Excavation and survey at St Patrick's Chapel and St Peter's Church, Heysham, Lancashire, 1977-8, *Antiq J,* 74, 55-134

Powell, T G E, 1963 Excavations at Skelmore Heads, near Ulverston, 1957 and 1959, *Trans Cumberland Westmorland Antiq Archaeol Soc*, 2 ser, 63, 1-27

Powlesland, D, 1997 Early Anglo-Saxon Settlements, Structures, Form and Layout, in J Hines (ed), *The Anglo-Saxons From The Migration Period To The Eighth Century – an ethnographic perspective*, 101-117, Woodbridge

Powlesland, D, Haughton, C and Hanson, J, 1986 Excavations at Heslerton, North Yorkshire 1978-82, *Archaeol J* 143, 53-173

Pratt, K E, 1996 Development of methods for investigating settlement and land-use using pollen data. A case-study from north-east England circa 8000cal BC – cal.AD 500, Unpublished Ph.D thesis, *Departments of Archaeology and Biological Sciences*, Durham, University of Durham

Price, J, 1988 Romano-British glass bangles from East Yorkshire, in J Price and P R Wilson (eds), *Recent Research in Roman Yorkshire*, Brit Archaeol Rep Brit Ser 193, 339-66, Oxford

Price J and Wilson P R (eds), 1988 *Recent Research in Roman Yorkshire*, Brit Archaeol Rep Brit Ser 193, 339-66, Oxford

Proudfoot, E and Aliaga-Kelly, C, 1998 Towards an Interpretation of Anomalous Finds and Place-names of Anglo-Saxon Origin in Scotland, in D Griffiths (ed), *Anglo-Saxon Studies in Archaeology and History 9 (for 1996)*, 1-13, Oxford

Quartermaine, H, forthcoming a The lead, in R M Newman and R H Leech, *Excavations at Dacre, Cumbria*

Quartermaine, H, forthcoming b The glass, in R M Newman and R H Leech, *Excavations at Dacre, Cumbria*

Quartermaine, J, 1989 Interim results of survey work on Stockdale Moor and Town Bank, West Cumbria, *Trans Cumberland Westmorland Antiq Archaeol Soc new ser* 89, 25-31

Quartermaine, J and Leech, R (forthcoming), *Upland Settlement of the Lake District; the results of recent surveys*

Rackham, D J, 1977 *Kennel Hall Knowe, 1976, Northumberland: Bone*, Ancient Monuments Lab Rep 2976, London

Rackham, D J, 1985 *An Analysis and Interpretation of the Sample of Animal Bones from Thorpe Thewles, Cleveland*, Ancient Monuments Lab Rep 4567, London

Rackham, D J, 1987 The animal bone, in Heslop 1987, 99-109 and Fiche 5/F1-G14, Fiche 6/A1-F8, London

Rackham, O, 1986 *The History of the Countryside*, London

Raftery, B, 1994 *Pagan Celtic Ireland*, London

Raistrick, A, 1977 *Two Centuries of Industrial Welfare*, Hartington, Buxton

Raistrick, A and Jennings, B, 1965 *A History of Lead Mining in the Pennines*, London

Raistrick, A and Roberts, A, 1984 *Life and Work of the Northern Lead Miner*, Beamish

Ramm, H, 1980 Native settlements east of the Pennines, in Branigan 1980, 28-40

RCAHMS, 1956 *An Inventory of the Ancient and Historical Monuments of Roxburghshire*, Edinburgh

RCAHMS, 1957 *An Inventory of the Ancient and Historical Monuments of Selkirkshire*, Edinburgh

RCAHMS, 1967 *Inventory of the County of Peeblesshire*, Edinburgh

RCAHMS, 1997 *Eastern Dumfriesshire: an archaeological landscape*, Edinburgh

Reece, R, 1980 Town and country: the end of Roman Britain, *World Archaeol* 12 (1), 77-92

Rennison, R W, 1987 *The Development of the North-East Coal Ports, 1815-1914: The Contribution of Engineering*, unpublished PhD thesis, Univ of Newcastle upon Tyne

Reynolds, D M, 1982 Aspects of later timber construction in south-east Scotland, in Harding 1982, 44-56

Richards, M, 1996 'First farmers' with no taste for grain, *British Archaeol* 12, 6

Richmond, C, 1984 Religion and the Fifteenth-Century English Gentleman in R B Dobson (ed) *The Church, Politics and Patronage In the Fifteenth Century*, 193-208, Gloucester and New York

Roberts, B K, 1975 Cockfield Fell, *Antiquity* 49, 48-50

Roberts, B K, 1990 Back Lanes and Tofts, Distribution Maps and Time, Medieval Nucleated Settlement in the North of England, in B E Vyner (ed) *Medieval Rural Settlement in North East England*, 107-125, Durham

Roberts, B K, 1993 Some relict landscapes in Westmorland: a reconsideration, *Archaeol J* 150, 433-55

Roberts, B K and Wrathmell, S, 2000 *Atlas of Rural Settlement in England,*English Heritage, London

Roberts, B K and Wrathmell, S, 2001 Peoples of Wood and Plain: an exploration of national and local regional contrasts, in D Hooke (ed) *Landscape: the richest historical record*, Society for Landscape Studies, supplementary series 1, 85-95, Amesbury

Roberts, B K and Wrathmell, S forthcoming *Region and Place*

Robinson, M, 2000 Further considerations of Neolithic charred cereals, fruit and nuts, in A.S. Fairbairn (ed), *Plants in Neolithic Britain and beyond*, 85-90, Oxford

Rubin, M, 1991 *Corpus Christi: The Eucharist in Late Medieval Culture*, Cambridge

Salisbury, C, 1986 Comments on Kirkhead Cave, an Upper Palaeolithic site in northern England, *Proc Prehist Soc* 52, 321-3

Salisbury, C, 1988 Late Upper Palaeolithic artefacts from Lindale Low cave, Cumbria, *Antiquity* 62, 510-13

Salisbury, C, 1992 The Pleistocene exploitation of Cumbria: a review of the evidence, *Trans Cumberland Westmorland Antiq Archaeol Soc*, 2 ser, 92, 1-7

Salisbury, C, 1997 The prehistoric occupation of Blenkett Wood near Allithwaite, *Trans Cumberland Westmorland Antiq Archaeol Soc*, 2 ser, 97, 1-10

Salway, P, 1965 *The Frontier People of Roman Britain*, Cambridge

Sawyer, P H, (ed), 1976 *Medieval Settlement: Continuity and Change*, London

Sawyer, P H, 1981 Fairs and markets in early medieval England, in N Skyum-Nielsen and N Lund (eds), *Danish medieval history; new currents*, 153-68, Copenhagen

Schofield, J, 1994a Looking back with regret; looking forward with optimism: making more of surface lithic scatter sites, in N Ashton and A David (eds), *Stories in Stone*, 90-8, Oxford

Schofield, J, 1994b Medieval and later towns, in B E Vyner (ed), *Building on the Past: Papers Celebrating 150 Years of the Royal Archaeological Institute* 195-214, London

Schofield, J and Leech, R (eds), 1987 *Urban Archaeology in Britain*, CBA Res Rep 61, London

Schofield, J and Vince, A, 1994 *Medieval Towns*, Leicester

Scull, C J, 1991 Post-Roman phase I at Yeavering: a re-consideration, *Medieval Archaeol* 35, 51-63

Scull, C J and Harding, A F, 1990 Two early medieval cemeteries at Milfield, Northumberland, *Durham Archaeol J* 6, 1-29

Selkirk, R, 1983 *The Piercebridge Formula*, Cambridge

Sewell, G W M, 1992 *The North British Railway in Northumberland*, Braunton, Devon

Sheehan, G, 1998 *Medieval Yorkshire Towns,* Edinburgh

Sheppard, T, 1913 *An Anglo-Saxon Cemetery at Hornsea*, Hull Museum Publ No 97, Hull

Sheppard, T, 1938 *Anglo-Saxon Cemeteries in East Yorkshire,* Hull Museum Publ No 195, Hull

Sherlock, S J and Welch, M G, 1992 *An Anglo-Saxon Cemetery at Norton, Cleveland*, CBA Res Rep 82, York

Shirley, R, 1994 *Village Greens of England*, unpublished PhD thesis, University of Durham

Simmons, I G, 1996 *The Environmental Impact of Later Mesolithic Cultures*, Edinburgh

Simmons, I G and Innes, J B, 1996a Disturbance phases in the Mid-Holocene vegetation at North Gill, North York Moors: form and process, *J Archaeol Sci* 23, 183-91

Simmons, I G and Innes, J B, 1996b Prehistoric charcoal in peat profiles at North Gill, North Yorkshire Moors, England, *J Archaeol Sci* 23, 193-97

Skyum-Nielsen, N and Lund, N (eds), 1981 *Danish medieval history; new currents*, Copenhagen

Slater, G, 1907 *The English Peasantry and the Enclosure of Common Fields*, London

Smith, C, 1988-9 Excavations at Dod Law West hillfort, Northumberland, *Northern Archaeol* 9, 1-55

Smith, I M, 1984 Patterns of settlement and land use of the late Anglian period in the Tweed Basin, in M L Faull (ed), *Studies in Late Anglo-Saxon Settlement*, 177-96, Oxford

Smith, K, 1984 Field survey in north Cleveland, in *Fieldwalking for Archaeology: Techniques and Results*, 23-30, Cleveland County Archaeology

Smith, P, 1985 Rural building in Wales, in J Thirsk (ed), *Agrarian History of England and Wales Vol Five: 1640-1750. Vol Two: Agrarian Change*, 686-813, Cambridge

Smith, R A, 1923 *British Museum Guide to Anglo-Saxon Antiquities 1923*, Anglia edition, 1993, Ipswich

Smith, W R, 1978 Silloth: a product of yesterday, *Industrial Archaeol Rev* 3 (1), 75-85

Snape, M E, 1992 Wallsend fort ditches, *The Arbeia J* 1, 62

Snape, M E, 1993 Morton Walk, South Shields, *The Arbeia J* 2, 55-9

Snape, M E, 1994 An excavation in the Roman cemetery at South Shields, *Archaeol Aeliana*, 5 ser, 22, 43-66

Spikins, P J, 1999 *Mesolithic Northern England. Environment, Population and Settlement,* Brit Archaeol Rep Brit Ser 283

Spikins, P J, 2000 Ethno-facts or ethnofiction? Searching for the structure of settlement patterns, in R Young (ed) *Mesolithic Lifeways: Current Research from Britain and Ireland,* Leicester Archaeology Monograph, 7, 105-108

Spratt, D and Burgess, C, 1985 *Upland Settlement in Britain: The Second Millennium BC and After,* Brit Archaeol Rep Brit Ser 143, Oxford

Spratt, D, Goddard, K E and Brown, D R, 1976 Mesolithic settlement sites at Upleatham, Cleveland, *Yorkshire Archaeol J* 48, 19-26

Spratt, D and Simmons, I, 1976 Prehistoric activity and environment on the North York Moors, *J Archaeol Sci* 3, 193-210

St Clare Byrne, M (ed), 1981 *The Lisle Letters*, 6 vols, Chicago

Stallibrass, S M, 1991a *The Animal Bones from a Bronze Age Cairn at Hardendale Nab, Cumbria, 1986,* Ancient Monuments Lab Rep 89/91, London

Stallibrass, S M, 1991b *Hardendale Nab Bronze Age Cairn, Cumbria: A Synthesis of the Biological Reports from the 1986 Excavation,* Ancient Monuments Lab Rep 55/91, London

Stallibrass, S M, 1991c *Animal Bones from Excavations at Annetwell Street, Carlisle, 1982-4. Period 3: The Earlier Timber Fort,* Ancient Monuments Lab Rep 132/91, London

Stallibrass, S, 1995 Review of the vertebrate remains, in J P Huntley and S Stallibrass, *Plant and Vertebrate remains from archaeological sites in northern England: data reviews and future directions,* Architect Archaeol Soc Durham Northumberland Res Rep 4, 84-198, Newcastle

Stallibrass, S, 2000 How little we know, and how much there is to learn: what can animal and human bones tell us about the late Roman transition in northern England?, in T Wilmott and P Wilson (eds), *The Late Roman Transition in the North*, Brit Archaeol Rep Brit Ser 299, 73-79, Oxford

Stallibrass, S M, 1996 The animal bone, pp. 72-80 in P Abramson, 1996

Stamp, L D, 1962 *The Land of Britain: its Use and Misuse*, London

Stead, I M, 1979 *The Arras Culture*, London

Stead, I M, Bourke, J B, and Brothwell, D, 1986 *Lindow Man: the Body in the Bog*, London

Stevens, C E, 1966 The social and economic aspects of rural settlement, in C Thomas (ed), *Rural Settlement in Roman Britain*, CBA Res Rep 7, 108-28, London

Still, L and Vyner, B E, 1986 Air photographic evidence for later prehistoric settlement in the Tees Valley, *Durham Archaeol J* 2, 11-24

Still, L, Vyner, B and Bewley, R, 1989 A decade of air survey in Cleveland and the Tees Valley hinterland and a strategy for air survey in County Durham, *Durham Archaeol J* 5, 1-10

Stokes, P R G, 1996 *Animal Bones from South Shields Roman Fort: Spatial Patterning and Butchery Practices*, unpublished MA thesis, Univ of Durham

Summerson, H, 1993 *Medieval Carlisle: The City and the Borders from the Late Eleventh to the Mid-Sixteenth Centuries*, Cumberland and Westmoreland Antiquarian and Archaeological Society Extra Ser 25, HBMCE, 2 vols

Supple, B, 1987 *The History of the British Coal Industry. Vol 4: 1913-1946*, Oxford

Swain, H, 1988 Pottery survival in the field, *Scottish Archaeol Review* 5, 87-9

Swanton, M, 1964 An Anglian cemetery at Londesborough, in East Yorkshire, *Yorks Archaeol J* 41, 262-86

Tawney, R H, 1984 *Religion and the Rise of Capitalism*, Harmondsworth

Taylor, D J A, Robinson, J, and Biggins, J A, nd *A Report on a Geophysical Survey of the Fort and Vicus at Halton Chesters for The Roman Research Trust*, Timescape Archaeol Surveys

Taylor, G, 1993 Detection and identification of dyes on pre-Hadrianic textiles from Vindolanda, *Textile History* 14(2), 115-24

Taylor, R J, 1993 *Hoards of the Bronze Age in Southern Britain: Analysis and Interpretation*, Brit Archaeol Rep 228, Oxford

Terry, J, 1995 Excavations at Lintshie Gutter Unenclosed Platform Settlement, Crawford, Strathclyde, 1991, *Proc Soc Antiq Scot* 125, 369-427

Thirsk, J, 1987 *England's Agricultural Regions and Agrarian History, 1500-1750, Studies in Economic and Social History*, London

Thomas, A C, 1959 Wheel-made post-Roman sherds, in G Jobey Excavations at the native settlement at Huckhoe, Northumberland, 1955-7, *Archaeol Aeliana*, 4 ser, 37, 258-261

Thomas, A C, 1971 *Britain and Ireland in Early Christian Times AD 400-800*, London

Tinniswood, A and Harding, A, 1991 Anglo-Saxon occupation and industrial features in the henge monument at Yeavering, Northumberland, *Durham Archaeol J* 7, 93-108

Tipping, R, 1986 The stratigraphy of Kirkhead Cave, an Upper Palaeolithic site in northern England: a comment, *Proc Prehist Soc* 52, 323-6

Tipping, R, 1994 The form and fate of Scotland's woodlands, *Proc Soc Antiq Scot*, 124, 1-54

Tipping, R, 1996 The Neolithic landscape of the Cheviot Hills and hinterland, *Northern Archaeol* 13/14, 17-33

Tipping, R, 1997 Pollen analysis and the impact of Rome on native agriculture around Hadrian's Wall, in Gwilt and Haselgrove 1997, 239-253

Tolan-Smith, C, 1996 'And then came farmers to the North', *British Archaeol* 11, 7

Tolan-Smith, C, 1997 *Landscape Archaeology in Tynedale*, Newcastle-upon-Tyne

Tomlinson, P and Hall, A R, 1996 User guide to the Environmental Archaeology Bibliography (EAB), *Ancient Monuments Laboratory Reports* 96

Tomlinson, W W, 1914 The North Eastern Railway, London

Topping, P, 1989a Early cultivation in Northumberland and the Borders, *Proc Prehist Soc* 55, 161-79

Topping, P, 1989b The context of cord rig cultivation in later prehistoric Northumberland, in M Bowden, D MacKay and P Topping (ed), *From Cornwall to Caithness: Some Aspects of British Field Archaeology*, Brit Archaeol Rep Brit Ser 209, 145-58, Oxford

Topping, P, 1992 The RCHME Southern Cheviot Landscape Project, *Past* 13, 13-15

Topping, P, 1993 Lordenshaws hillfort and its environs, *Archaeol Aeliana*, 5 ser, 21, 15-27

Topping, P and McOmish, D, 2000 Excavations at Wether Hill, Northumberland, 1999: final interim report, *NAG News* (Northumberland Archaeol Group), May 2000

Trechmann, C T, 1936 Mesolithic flints from the submerged forest at West Hartlepool, *Proc Prehist Soc* 2, 161-8

Tribe, K, 1979 *Land, Labour and Economic Discourse*, London

Trueman, M, 1985 *Lead fittings from Monkwearmouth and Jarrow*, unpublished MA dissertation, Univ of Durham

Truman, L, 1995 Stockbridge Excavation, Newcastle upon Tyne, *Archaeology North* 10 (Winter), 22-5

Turnbull, P, 1995 A lost bronze bucket from Westmorland, *Trans Cumberland Westmorland Antiq Archaeol Soc*, 2 ser, 95, 55-9

Turner, J, 1981 The Iron Age, in I G Simmons and M J Tooley (eds), *The Environment in British Prehistory*, 250-81, London

Turner, R C, 1988 A Cumbrian bog body from Scaleby, *Trans Cumberland Westmorland Antiq Archaeol Soc*, 2 ser, 88, 1-7

Turner, R C, 1989 Another Cumbrian bog body, found in Seascale Moss in 1834, *Trans Cumberland Westmorland Antiq Archaeol Soc*, 2 ser, 89, 21-3

Turner, R C, 1990 A Romano-British cemetery at Lanchester, Durham, *Archaeol Aeliana*, 5 ser, 18, 63-77

Turner, V E, 1987 Results of survey work carried out in the Caldbeck Fells, Cumbria, *Trans Cumberland Westmorland Antiq Archaeol Soc new ser*, 87, 19-26

Turner, V E, 1991 Results of survey work carried out between the Shap and Askham Fells,

Cumbria, *Trans Cumberland Westmorland Antiq Archaeol Soc new ser*, 91, 1-11

Tweddle, D, forthcoming Pre-Conquest, medieval, and post-medieval fine metalwork, in R M Newman and R H Leech, *Excavations at Dacre, Cumbria*

Tylecote, R F, 1968 Metallographic examination of Bronze Age artefacts from the north of England, in Burgess 1968, 48-56

Tyler, A, 1978 *Richmond: An Archaeological Study,* Richmond

Underdown, D, 1985 *Revel, Riot and Rebellion: Popular Politics and Culture in England 1603-1660,* Oxford

Unz, C (ed), 1986 *Studien zu den Militargrenzen Roms III,* Stuttgart

van der Veen, M, 1982 *Carbonised Plant Remains from Neolithic Thirlings (Northumberland),* Ancient Monuments Lab Rep 3831, London

van der Veen, M, 1984 *The Plant Remains from Whitton Hill, Northumberland,* Ancient Monuments Lab Rep 4399, London

van der Veen, M, 1988 Carbonised grain from a Roman granary at South Shields, north-east England, *Der Prähistorische Mensch und seine Umwelt* 31, 353-65

van der Veen, M, 1992 *Crop Husbandry Regimes: an Archaeobotanical Study of Farming in Northern England 1000 BC-AD 500,* Sheffield Archaeol Monograph 3, Sheffield

Vaughan, J E, 1981 The Leather, in B Harbottle and M Ellison, An Excavation in the Castle Ditch, Newcastle upon Tyne, 1974-6, *Archaeol Aeliana,* 5 ser, 9, 184-190

Vyner, B E, 1984 The excavation of a Neolithic cairn at Street House, Loftus, Cleveland, *Proc Prehist Soc* 50, 151-95

Vyner, B E, 1988 The hillfort on Eston Nab, *Archaeol J* 145, 60-98

Vyner, B E (ed), 1994 *Building on the Past: Papers celebrating 150 years of the Royal Archaeological Institute,* London

Vyner, B E (ed), 1995 *Moorland Monuments: Studies in the Archaeology of North-east Yorkshire in Honour of Raymond Hayes and Don Spratt,* CBA Res Rep 101, York

Vyner, B E and Daniels, R, 1989 Further investigation of the Iron Age and Romano-British settlement site at Catcote, Hartlepool, Cleveland, 1987, *Durham Archaeol J* 5, 11-34

Waddington, C, 1999 *A Landscape Archaeological Study of the Mesolithic – Neolithic in the Milfield Basin, Northumberland,* Brit Archaeol Rep Brit Ser 291, Oxford

Waddington, C, 2000a Recent research on the Mesolithic of the Milfield Basin, Northumberland, in R Young (ed) *Mesolithic Lifeways: Current Research from Britain and Ireland,* Leicester Archaeology Monograph, 7, 165-178

Waddington, C, 2000b The Neolithic that never happened? in J Harding and R Johnston (eds), *Northern Pasts. Interpretations of the Later Prehistory of Northern England and Southern Scotland,* Brit Archaeol Rep Brit Ser 302, Oxford

Walker, D, 1965a Excavations at Barnscar, 1957-8, *Trans Cumberland Westmorland Antiq Archaeol Soc n ser*, 65, 53-65

Walker, D, 1965b The post-glacial period in the Langdale Fells, English Lake District, *New Phytol,* 64, 488-510

Watts, V E 1976 The Evidence of Place-Names II, in P Sawyer (ed), *Medieval Settlement: Continuity and Change,* 122-132, London

Weatherill, L, 1988 *Consumer Behaviour and Material Culture in Britain, 1660-1760,* London

Webb, J, 1983 Eddius Stephanus: Life of Wilfrid, trans, in Farmer D H Farmer, *The Age of Bede,* 103-182

Weber, M, 1985 *The Protestant Ethic and the Spirit of Capitalism* (trans T Parsons), London

Webster, C, 1975 *The Great Instauration: Science, Medicine and Reform 1626-1660,* London

Welfare, A, 1986 The Greenlee Lough (Northumberland) palimpsest: an interim report of the 1985 season, *Northern Archaeol* 7, pt 2, 35-7

Welfare, H, 1980 Jigsaw puzzle and dustbin: air photography and the Iron Age in southern Scotland, in L M Thoms (ed), *Settlements in Scotland 1000 BC-AD 1000 (Scottish Archaeol Forum 10),* 1-11, Edinburgh

Welfare, H, 1983 Review of R Whimster, *Burial Practices in Iron Age Britain, Scottish Archaeol Rev* 2, 75-9

Welfare, H, 1984 The southern souterrains, in Miket and Burgess 1984, 305-23

Welfare, H and Everson, P, 1984 Surveys of industrial landscapes, *Royal Commission on the Historical Monuments of England Ann Rev* 1983-4, 18-21

Welfare, H, Bowden, M and Blood, K, 1999 Fieldwork and the castles of the Anglo-

Scottish Borders, in P Pattison, D Field and S Ainsworth (ed), *Patterns of the Past: Essays in Landscape Archaeology for Christopher Taylor*, Oxford, 53-60

Welfare, H and Swan, V, 1995 *Roman Camps in England: The Field Archaeology*, London

Wells, C, 1991 The environmental history of part of south Cumbria (High Furness, Duddon and Lyth valleys) from the Early Bronze Age to historic times, *North West Wetlands Survey Annual Report 1991*, 38-9, Lancaster

Weyman, J, 1984 The Mesolithic in north-east England, in R Miket and C Burgess (eds), *Between and Beyond the Walls: Essays in the Prehistory and History of Northern Britain in Honour of George Jobey*, 38-51, Edinburgh

Wheeler, R E M, 1954 *The Stanwick Fortifications*, Soc Antiq London Res Rep 17, Oxford

White, A, 1996 Medieval towns, in R Newman (ed), *The Archaeology of Lancashire: Present State and Future Priorities*, 125-38, Lancaster University Archaeological Unit

White, K G, 1963 The Spades Mire, Berwick-upon-Tweed, *Proc Soc Antiq Scot* 96, 355-60

Whitford, B, 1968 Two prehistoric dugout canoes from the River Wear at Hylton, near Sunderland, County Durham, *Archaeol Aeliana*, 4 ser, 46, 297-301

Whitworth, A, 1994 Recording the Roman Wall, *Archaeol Aeliana*, 5 ser, 22, 66-75

Williams A, and Williams, E, 1996 Excavation of a Medieval Lime Kiln on Beadnell Point, Northumberland, *Archaeol Aeliana*, 5 ser, 24, 109-117

Williams, C T, 1985 *Mesolithic Exploitation Patterns in the Central Pennines*, Brit Archaeol Rep Brit Ser 139, Oxford

Williams, T, 1997 *Archaeology and English Heritage: Agenda for the Future*, Draft document, London

Williamson, T, 1987 Early co-axial field systems on the East Anglian boulder clays, *Proc Prehist Soc* 53, 419-431

Williamson, T, 1995 *Polite Landscapes: gardens and society in eighteenth-century England*, Stroud

Willis, S H, 1996 The Romanization of pottery assemblages in the East and North-East of England during the first century AD: a comparative analysis, *Britannia* 27, 179-222

Willis, S H, 1998 Samian pottery in Britain, *Archaeol J* 155, 82-133

Willis, S H, 1999 Without and within: aspects of culture and community in the Iron Age of north-eastern England, in Bevan 1999, 81-110

Willis, S H, forthcoming a The pottery, in Haselgrove forthcoming

Willis, S H, forthcoming b The briquetage, in Haselgrove forthcoming

Wilmott, T, 1997 *Birdoswald: Excavations on a Roman Fort on Hadrian's Wall and its successor settlements, 1987-92*, English Heritage Archaeol Rep 14, London

Wilmott, T, 2000 The late Roman transition at Birdoswald and on Hadrian's Wall, in T Wilmott and P Wilson (eds), *The Late Roman Transition in the North*, Brit Archaeol Rep Brit Ser 299, 13-23, Oxford

Wilson, D, 1983 Pollen analysis and settlement archaeology of the first millennium bc from north-east England, in Chapman and Mytum 1983, 29-54

Wilson, P R, Jones, R F J and Evans, D M (eds), 1983 *Settlement and Society in the Roman North*, Bradford

Winchester, A J L, 1986 Medieval Cockermouth, *Trans Cumberland and Westmoreland Antiquarian and Archaeol Soc* 86, 109-128

Winchester, A J L, 1987 *Landscape and Society in Medieval Cumbria*, Edinburgh

Winchester, A J L, nd *Small towns of Cumbria*, unpub MS

Wood, I N, 1986 The audience of architecture in post-Roman Gaul, in L A S Butler and R K Morris (eds), *The Anglo-Saxon church: essays on architecture, archaeology and history in honour of Dr H M Taylor*, CBA Res Rep 60, 74-79, London

Wood, O, 1988 *West Cumberland Coal, 1600-1982/3*, Cumberland and Westmorland Antiquarian and Archaeological Society, Extra Ser 24, Kendal

Wood, R H, Ashmead, P and Mellars, P A, 1969 First report on the archaeological excavations at Kirkhead Cavern, *North-West Speleology* 1, 19-24

Wooliscroft, D J, 1989 Signalling and the design of Hadrian's Wall, *Archaeol Aeliana*, 5 ser, 17, 5-20

Wrathmell, S, 1975 *Deserted and Shrunken Villages in Southern Northumberland from the Twelfth to the Twentieth Centuries*, unpublished PhD thesis, Department of Archaeology, University College, Cardiff

Wrathmell, S, 1984 The vernacular threshold of Northern peasant houses, *Vernacular Archit* 15, 29-33

Yeoman, P A, 1990 Edinburgh Castle: Iron Age fort to garrison fortress, *Fortress* 4, 22-26

Young, R E, 2001 *Excavations within Berwick-upon-Tweed, 1998-1999*, Tyne and Wear Museums/Northumbrian Water Limited

Young, R, 1984 *Aspects of the Prehistoric Archaeology of the Wear Valley, Co. Durham*, unpublished PhD thesis, Univ of Durham

Young, R, 1985 Potential sources of flint and chert in the north-east of England, *Lithics* 5, 3-9

Young, R, 1986 Destruction, preservation and recovery: Weardale, a case study, in T G Manby and P Turnbull (eds), *Archaeology in the Pennines. Studies in Honour of Arthur Raistrick*, Brit Archaeol Rep Brit Ser 158, 213-27, Oxford

Young, R, 1987 *Lithics and Subsistence in North-East England*, Brit Archaeol Rep Brit Ser 161, Oxford

Young, R, 1989 Mixed lithic scatters and the Mesolithic-Neolithic transition in north-east England: a speculation, in I Brooks and P Phillips (eds), *Breaking the Stony Silence*, Brit Archaeol Rep Brit Ser 213, 161-85, Oxford

Young, R, 1994a 'Destruction is only one facet'... A study in the formation processes and the generation of distribution patterns for later prehistory in Northern England, *Landscape Hist* 16, 5-16

Young, R, 1994b Polished stone axes between the Tyne and the Tees, *Durham Archaeol J* 10, 1-12

Young, R, 1997 The flint, in Coggins, D, and Fairless, K, 1997 Ritual succession? Excavations at the multi-period site of Middle Hurth, Upper teesdale, Co. Durham, 1978-79, Durham Archaeol J, 13, 1-20 (8-15)

Young, R, 2000 Aspects of the 'coastal Mesolithic' of the north-east of England, in R Young (ed) *Mesolithic Lifeways: Current Research from Britain and Ireland*, Leicester Archaeology Monograph, 7, 179-190

Young, R, forthcoming The flint, in Cramp in prep b [*Excavations at Monkwearmouth*]

Young, R and Humphrey, J 1999 Flint use in England after the Bronze Age: time for a re-evaluation? *Proc Prehist Soc* 65, 231-242

Young, R and O'Sullivan, D M, 1993 Nessend, Lindisfarne, and the 'coastal' Mesolithic of northern England, *Archaeology North,* 6, 9-15

Young, R and Simmonds, T, 1995 Marginality and the nature of later prehistoric upland settlement in the north of England, *Landscape Hist* 17, 5-16

Zant, J, forthcoming *Roman Carlisle, The Northern Lanes: Excavations 1978-82*

Zant, J, in prep *Excavations in The Lanes, Carlisle: Volume 2, the Northern Lanes*

Zant, J and Giecco, F, 1999 Recent work in Carlisle, *Current Archaeology*, 164, 306-9